An introduction to
anthropology
VOLUME TWO
Ethnology

The Dorsey Series in Anthropology

An introduction to anthropology

volume two

Ethnology

VICTOR BARNOUW

Professor of Anthropology
University of Wisconsin–Milwaukee

1978

DP

Third edition
THE DORSEY PRESS Homewood, Illinois 60430
Irwin-Dorsey Limited Georgetown, Ontario L7G 4B3

This book is dedicated to my wife
SACHIKO

Cover: Nepalese children.

Photo: Marc Riboud, Magnum Photos

Third Edition
First Printing, January 1978

ISBN 0-256-02001-9
Library of Congress Catalog Card No. 77–089798
Printed in the United States of America

LEARNING SYSTEMS COMPANY —
a division of Richard D. Irwin, Inc. — has developed a
PROGRAMMED LEARNING AID
to accompany texts in this subject area.
Copies can be purchased through your bookstore
or by writing PLAIDS,
1818 Ridge Road, Homewood, Illinois 60430.

Preface

This two-volume work is designed as a general introduction to the field of anthropology. Both volumes may be used together in a one-semester introductory course on that subject. Courses in Introduction to Anthropology are also often presented in two semesters, the first usually dealing with physical anthropology and archaeology, the second with ethnology. With this division in mind, Volume One of the present work was prepared to cover the first semester, Volume Two the second. A brief section on linguistics is included in Volume Two.

Anthropology today has to do with humans at all times and places; it is not limited to the study of early people and "primitive" non-Western cultures, as it was sometimes held to be. This two-volume work ranges from the distant past, before *Homo Sapiens* actually appeared on the scene, down to our troubled present and deals with both the physical and cultural evolution of human beings.

This edition of Volume Two follows the organization of the previous edition except that some material, formerly contained in Chapter 3, "Some Modern Ethnological Schools," has now been moved to Chapter 24, "Anthropological Theory: A Historical Review." It was felt that anthropological theory is better presented after the student has been introduced to the general subject-matter of sociocultural anthropology. This also allows for a more expanded treatment of the topic. Chapter 10, "Male-Female Relations" is new, added in response to a recent surge of interest in sex roles in our own society and in other societies. Some chapters have been reduced or collapsed into one. There is now only one chapter on anthropological linguistics and one on culture and personality, whereas there were formerly two for each subject. The latter chapter has been considerably re-written. Four chapters on marriage and family organization have been reduced to three.

I am indebted to two readers who reviewed and criticized the previous edition of Volume Two: Judith Brown of Oakland University and Jamil Hanifi of Northern Illinois University. Those who commented on earlier editions include Bert Gerow of Stanford University, James Clifton of the University of Wisconsin–Green Bay, Iwao Ishino of Michigan State University, David H. Spain of the University of Washington, Thomas Wayne Johnson of California State University at Chico, Hal Nelson of the ARIES corporation in Minneapolis, Michael J. Lowy of the University of Pittsburgh, Richard A. Thompson of the University of Arizona, Alta Jablow of CUNY Brooklyn College, and William Madsen of the University of California at Santa Barbara.

Finally, I am especially grateful to my wife Sachiko, to whom this book is dedicated, for all her patience, encouragement, and help while the manuscript was in progress.

December 1977   VICTOR BARNOUW

Contents

ix

part one

Introduction

1

An introduction

Anthropology is the study of human beings (from Greek *anthropos,* man, and *logia,* study). It is concerned mainly with a single species, *Homo sapiens,* rather than with many diverse organisms, as in the cases of botany and zoology, although physical anthropologists also study the various primate species related to humans. Our objective is to learn all we can about our species—how we have become what we are, what we have accomplished, and what our potentialities may be.

Of course, anthropology is not the only field that focuses on human beings. There are many others, including sociology, psychology, history, law, economics, and political science. We do not need to draw clear-cut boundary lines between these various disciplines. There are many areas of overlap among them, each field having its own distinctive characteristics and emphases.

Anthropology may be broadly divided into physical anthropology and cultural anthropology. Physical anthropology studies *Homo sapiens* as a physical organism, while cultural anthropology is concerned with human cultures or ways of life, both in the present and in the past. Cultural anthropology may be subdivided into three main branches: archaeology, linguistics, and ethnology. Before discussing these subdivisions, let us first consider the concept of culture.

Culture

Culture refers to learned behavior, acquired by experience, as opposed to inborn, genetically determined behavior. This use of the term must be distinguished from older colloquial meanings ex-

3

pressed in phrases like "a man of culture." In the anthropological sense, all human beings have culture.

Although anthropologists sometimes use the word *culture* in a broad generic sense, they also speak about *a* culture, like Eskimo culture or Hopi culture. Here is a definition of culture in this sense. *A culture is the way of life of a group of people, the configuration of all of the more or less stereotyped patterns of learned behavior that are handed down from one generation to the next through the means of language and imitation.* The nub of this definition is the first clause: "the way of life of a group of people." This way of life has some integration and cohesion to it—hence the term *configuration*. It consists of patterns of learned behavior that are transmitted through language and imitation, not through instinct or any direct action of the genes, although the *capacity* for culture is determined by heredity. These patterns are only relatively fixed and are amenable to change; hence they are said to be "more or less" stereotyped. A person is destined to learn the patterns of behavior prevalent in the society in which he grows up. He does not necessarily learn them all, for there may be cultural differences appropriate to persons of different age, sex, status, and occupation, and there may also be genetically determined differences in learning ability. Moreover, the culture patterns of a society may change with the appearance of new inventions or through contact with other ways of life. We cannot understand human behavior very well without the concept of *culture*, which will be the main subject of this volume.

The use of the term in this anthropological sense is relatively recent. In 1871 Edward B. Tylor, an English writer, published a two-volume work, *Primitive Culture*, in which he defined culture as "that complex whole which includes knowledge, belief, art, law, morals, custom, and any other capabilities and habits acquired by man as a member of society." (Tylor 1877:I, 1). A weakness in this definition is that it omits the element of integration, although that is hinted at in the phrase "complex whole." Tylor's definition and the title of his book established culture as a separate field for investigation that could be studied apart from psychology or biology, since cultural phenomena were believed to have their own laws.

Another definition of culture, given many years later by Ralph Linton, stressed the factor of integration: "A culture is the configuration of learned behavior and results of behavior whose component elements are shared and transmitted by the members of a particular society" (Linton 1945:32.) Some anthropologists object to the inclusion of "results of behavior"—which refers to material culture—in this definition. Should we include artifacts, tools, buildings, and boats in our definition?

For Ward H. Goodenough, culture is essentially a set of ideas, including ideas about objects; it does not include the objects themselves. Goodenough (1957:167–68) writes: "A society's culture consists of whatever it is one has to know or believe in order to operate in a manner acceptable to its members. . . . It is the theory, not the phenomena alone, which ethnographic description aims to present." Culture in this sense can be distinguished from actual behavior; culture consists of the rules that determine behavior rather than the behavior itself. Anthropologists, then, have different ways of defining and conceiving of culture, but, in general, there is agreement that culture consists of learned patterns of behavior common to members of a given society. A *society* is a more or less organized group of people of both sexes who share a common culture. Society and culture are not interchangeable terms, for society refers to a group of people, while culture refers to their way of life or the sets of learned ideas they share.

Let us return now to a review of the subdivisions of anthropology.

One unique aspect of anthropology that distinguishes it from the other social sciences is that it contains a branch, *physical anthropology*, that is concerned with *Homo sapiens* as a physical organism and with our evolution from simpler forms of life.

Physical anthropology

Whatever else he may be, *Homo sapiens* is an animal (not a mineral or a plant); he is a vertebrate, a mammal, and a Primate, the order of mammals that also includes, among others, the apes and monkeys. Physical anthropologists are concerned with tracing our relationships to related species and with reconstructing the evolutionary branching and differentiation of the Primate order, particularly with respect to *Homo sapiens* and our closest relatives.

Physical anthropologists have pursued at least four kinds of research in this connection: (1) the analysis of primate fossils, with an attempt to place them in a geological, temporal sequence; (2) comparative anatomical study of living primates, including such features as blood chemistry, tooth-cusp patterns, and many other features; (3) observation of living primates in the field; and (4) laboratory experimentation with apes, monkeys, and other animals. One focus of physical anthropology, then, is primate and human evolution.

A second focus is human variation. All human beings on earth today belong to a single species, *Homo sapiens*. All human groups, in other words, are capable of breeding with others and of producing fertile offspring. Within this single species, however, there is a good deal of variation with respect to such features as skin color, hair form, and other attributes.

Archaeology

Archaeology is the study of extinct cultures, while *ethnology* is the study of living ones. Anthropological archaeologists are usually concerned with what are called *prehistoric* cultures, those that existed before the development of written records. Archaeologists willingly make use of written records if they are available, as in Mesopotamia, Egypt, and Guatemala, but often they have nothing to work with but the relics and remains of bygone peoples—potsherds, arrowheads, clay figurines, and tools of bone, stone, or other durable materials. Since systems of writing developed only about 5,000 years ago, while there were ancestors of ours who were able to make tools about 2.6 million years ago, it is evident that the period of prehistory is immensely long. We depend upon the archaeologist, working with the paleontologist, geologist, physical anthropologist, and other specialists to reconstruct what happened during these hundreds of thousands of years. In many parts of the world—Australia, Melanesia, Polynesia, most of the New World, and Africa—writing was only recently introduced. Here, again, the archaeologist works to uncover the past.

Archaeologists seek to reconstruct culture history and the lifeways of people of the past. They also try to understand cultural processes insofar as they may be inferred from the archaeological remains and

Excavation at
Cahokia, Illinois.

other evidence. Because much of human life is intangible and perishable, leaving no permanent imprint behind, the reconstruction of prehistory, past lifeways, and cultural processes will never be complete. Even so, archaeologists have been able to learn a great deal about the distribution and ways of life of the hunters of the Old Stone Age. They have also learned where some of the first horticultural settlements appeared in the Old World and the New, where metal tools were first employed, and where writing and city life first developed. Through a combination of archaeology and ethnology we can determine much about the evolution and spread of human cultures. Archaeology is not limited to the distant past, for *historic site* archaeologists work in settlements where their excavation work can be combined with information from written records, as in the case of American colonial sites.

Linguistics is the study of languages. Although other animals besides humans have communication systems, and although the cries of apes and monkeys seem to have communicative functions, no other organism is known to have as elaborate a system of symbolic communication as *Homo sapiens*. The transmission of culture from generation to generation is made possible by language, which enables us to preserve the traditions of the past and to make provisions for the future. **Linguistics**

Not all linguists are anthropologists, but some anthropologists specialize in the study of languages. Ethnologists—anthropologists who study contemporary cultures—often learn the language of the people whom they are studying in the field. It is possible to do ethnological fieldwork with bilingual interpreters, but it is much better if the anthropologist understands the local speech. All kinds of subtleties may be lost in translation, for example, in a discussion of religious concepts.

Descriptive, or structural, linguistics deals with the characteristic sound units employed in a language and its grammatical system.

Historical linguistics deals with changes in language over time, including sound shifts and the influence of one language on another. Sometimes efforts have been made to reconstruct culture patterns of past times from a study of items of vocabulary, as has been done in the case of the Indo-European languages of the Old World.

Cognitive anthropology is a branch of ethnology but may also be seen as a branch of anthropological linguistics. It is concerned with the ways in which the speakers of a particular language classify and conceptualize phenomena. Some anthropologists have tried to assess the ways in which the language of a particular society structures the perceptions or world view of its speakers.

Linguistics, then, has a bearing on many other fields of research, not only on ethnology but also on fields outside of anthropology, such as psychology and philosophy.

Ethnology

Ethnology is the study of contemporary cultures. Ethnologists go to a particular society, let us say an Eskimo group; they get to know the people, learn something of their language, and keep a record of observations and interviews. Ethnologists have varied interests and objectives, but all of them try to delineate some of the characteristic culture patterns of the groups they study. Ethnologists may be particularly interested in how kinship is reckoned in the Eskimo community, what religious beliefs the people have, or how the religion is related to other aspects of the culture. They may study techniques of food getting and seal hunting, the material equipment used in the process, and the methods of making dogsleds, harpoons, and warm clothing. They may be interested in how children are brought up and what personality traits are fostered in the society, how people get along with one another, how men acquire their wives, and how many they may have.

A detailed written description of a particular culture is known as an *ethnography,* or ethnographic account.

An ethnologist usually studies a particular society, or at least one at a time. But it should be pointed out that ethnological works are not limited to descriptions of particular cultures or to comparisons of two or three of them. There are also efforts to generalize on a broad scale about cultures in general, for example about societies with a hunting-gathering basis of subsistence, peasant societies, matrilineal societies, and so on.

Some of the first American anthropologists tried to get as complete an inventory of the culture they were studying as possible, including material culture (tools and equipment used), kinship organization, religious beliefs, marriage customs, subsistence techniques, folklore, games, food recipes, and so forth. More recently there has been a tendency to focus on particular problems and to narrow the scope of investigation. We now have some specialized subfields within the general branch of ethnology, such as social anthropology and culture-and-personality.

Social anthropology is concerned with the social structure of a society, its patterns of social interaction. This field is really no different from sociology, except, perhaps, that social anthropologists generally study non-Western societies. Social anthropology is not the same thing as cultural anthropology. It may be seen as a branch of cultural anthropology, which covers a larger field. For their purposes social anthropologists ignore many aspects of culture, such as material culture, how traps and snares are made, food recipes, and so on, and focus on such matters as kinship organization, class stratification, and social relations in general.

Culture-and-personality is a field that overlaps with psychology, particularly the psychology of personality; it is concerned with the mutual interplay of culture and personality, but especially with the ways in which the culture of a society influences the individuals who grow up within its milieu. Economic anthropology, political anthropology, and the cross-cultural study of religion, folklore, art, and music (ethnomusicology) are other specialized fields of study within ethnology.

Before going on to discuss the subject of culture further, let us review some information about the physical characteristics of our species. Within the grouping of eutherian, or placental, mammals, *Homo sapiens* belongs to the order of Primates, which also includes the lemurs, tarsiers, monkeys, and apes. An outstanding characteristic of the primates is their prehensile (grasping), five-digited hands and feet, generally equipped with flat or slightly curved nails. Grasping hands and feet are well suited to life in the trees, where most primates spend their time, although some, such as the baboon, gorilla, and humans, move about on the ground. Life in the trees demands good eyesight. Most of the primates, whose eyes are set close together on the frontal plane, have overlapping stereoscopic vision and color vision. Monkeys pick up objects with their hands and examine them, and they can feed themselves with their hands. Their forelimbs and hind limbs have become differentiated, with the forelimbs used for exploration and the lower limbs for support, a differentiation most developed in human beings.

The Primate order is divided into two suborders: the Prosimii, or lower primates, including the lemurs and tarsiers, and the Anthropoidea, or higher primates, including the New World and Old World monkeys, the apes, and humans.

The superfamily within the Anthropoidea to which we belong is that of the Hominoidea. Its other members are the apes, who differ from the monkeys in lacking external tails, cheek pouches, and some other features. The apes have long arms, rather short legs, a semierect posture, and a broader, more basin-shaped pelvis than those of monkeys. The gibbon and orangutan are Southeast Asiatic apes; the chimpanzee and gorilla are African ones.

Unlike many lower vertebrates, most of the primates are social animals that live the year round in groups consisting of males, fe-

The physical nature of *Homo sapiens*

males, and offspring. The young are relatively helpless at birth and depend upon maternal care more than most mammals do. The period of dependency increases from the lower to the higher primates.

Terrestrial primates, such as baboons, move about in larger bands than arboreal ones and cover a wider range. They show more differentiation of dominant-submissive behavior than arboreal species and more sexual dimorphism, showing striking differences in size and strength between males and females.

There are not only differences in social organization between primate species, but differences may also occur within a species among groups that have adjusted to different environments. This suggests that such organization is determined not only by genetic factors but also by learning, which is facilitated by the long period of infant dependence. The development and spread of new patterns of behavior have been noted in some groups of primates: for example, the practice among some groups of macaques in Japan of washing sweet potatoes before eating them. A refinement was later added to this pattern: carrying sweet potatoes to wash in the sea rather than in the nearby brook, perhaps because of the salty taste.

Macaque standing upright in water.

While walking into the sea the macaques assumed an erect posture, which they continued to carry on land more frequently than before. Here is a complex of learned patterns of behavior that is shared by a particular group of macaques but not found among macaques elsewhere. We might call this *protocultural* behavior. It differs from our learned behavior in lacking the use of language.

Primates, represented by small prosimians, appear in the fossil record about 60 million years ago; they had become abundant by about 57 million years ago. In the Old World, fossil finds that consist mainly of teeth and jaw fragments, and perhaps represent ancestral types of Old World monkeys and apes, have been found in the Egyptian Fayum dating from around 35 million years ago. Possible ancestors of ours are represented by the tooth and jaw fragments of the hominoid genus *Ramapithecus* found in East Africa, northwestern India, and parts of Europe, dating from about 14 million years ago.

This brings us to the characteristics of *Homo Sapiens* and how we differ from other primates. The two most important differences are our upright posture and very large brain and more complex central nervous system, in comparison with those of other primates. Several distinctive features of the human skeleton represent adaptations to upright posture and bipedalism: a curve in the lumbar region of the spine; a broad, basin-shaped pelvis; longer legs than arms; and some characteristics of the feet, including arches from front to back and from side to side, a well-developed heel, and a nonopposable big toe in line with the other toes. *Homo sapiens* also has a chin, a bony nose bridge and cartilaginous tip, a median groove in the upper lip, outrolled lips showing a membranous red portion, and V-shaped, or parabolic, jaws in contrast to the long, U-shaped jaws of apes.

Early hominids

Between 1 million and 4 million years ago, there were apelike but upright bipedal hominids living in parts of Africa. The first fossil evidence of this was an immature juvenile skull found in South Africa in 1924 and named *Australopithecus africanus* (South African ape) by Raymond Dart. In the following decades, more such finds were made in South and East Africa, so that by now over 1,400 fossil remains have been recovered. Despite the "ape" label originally given by Dart, it is now recognized that the australopithecines, as they have been called, were not apes but hominids, having more in common with ourselves than with the apes. They lacked chins and had brains that were not much larger than those of present-day apes, although their brains were relatively large in proportion to body size.

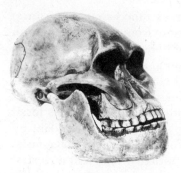
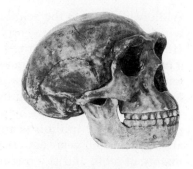

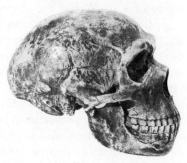

Reconstructed
plaster casts of
skulls of (*top,
from left*)
*Australopithecus
africanus* and
Peking man, (*right*)
"Classic"
Neanderthal man.

The discovery of these remains has shown that our ancestors must have assumed upright posture before they developed large brains.

The archaeological evidence suggests that these hominids used stone tools; they probably used tools of wood, bone, and horn as well.

A later stage of hominid evolution was that of *Homo erectus,* represented by such finds as Java man and Peking man, living between 1 million and 300,000 years ago. These people were of about the same height as modern humans. The brains were much larger than those of the australopithecines but smaller than those of modern *Homo sapiens,* although the larger skulls fall within the modern human range. They had low skulls with heavy brow ridges and large, chinless jaws with big teeth.

Homo erectus must have spread over much of the Old World, for the fossilized remains have been unearthed in Africa, China, and Indonesia. Since stone tools have often been found in the same geological levels, there is no doubt that *Homo erectus* had a culture, including the use of choppers or pebble tools and sometimes hand axes. Moreover, the use of fire was known at this time, as attested in cave sites in both Europe and China. Armed with tools and the knowledge of fire, hominids were able to move into cool northerly regions in Europe and China, as well as occupying warmer zones in Africa, southern Asia, and Indonesia. By that time humans must have acquired a language, and there must have been some division of labor, with men specializing as hunters and women as collectors and perhaps preparers of food. Home bases, to which members of a band returned, were a feature of this stage, although they probably originated earlier in the australopithecine stage.

The Neanderthals are generally considered to represent a stage intermediate between *Homo erectus* and modern humans. Although not formerly so classified, Neanderthals are now regarded as having been a form of *Homo sapiens,* designated *Homo sapiens neanderthalensis.* The Neanderthals lived in Europe and parts of Asia from around 100,000 to around 35,000 years ago. From the *Homo erectus* stage, the Neanderthals inherited such traits as thick skull walls and brow ridges, low elevation of the skull, and large jaws, but they differed from *Homo erectus* in having a much larger brain, as large as modern humans. The skull was not high domed, however, but long and flattish, broadening out behind the ears.

People of modern physical type, *Homo sapiens sapiens,* with chins and more high-domed skulls, lived in Europe during the Upper Paleolithic period between around 30,000 and 11,000 years ago, and the earlier Neanderthal type then seems to have disappeared.

To conclude, we have seen that *Homo sapiens sapiens* is a vertebrate, a eutherian mammal, and a primate. In the order of Primates we belong to the suborder Anthropoidea and the superfamily of Hominoidea. In the latter category, which also includes the Pongidae, or apes, *Homo sapiens sapiens* is classified in the family of Hominidae. *Homo sapiens sapiens,* or man of the present day, is the only living hominid, and all contemporary human beings are of the same species.

2

The historical background
of ethnological research

Reasonably good ethnographic accounts are much older than any comparable works in the fields of archaeology or physical anthropology. Moreover, they come from diverse sources. We have, for example, descriptive accounts of India made by some Chinese Buddhist pilgrims, dating from the 5th century A.D., and also accounts by Islamic scholars who visited India from the Near East around the 10th century A.D. This independent development of ethnographic description in different parts of the world is understandable; it seems natural that a traveler encountering strangers with different features, clothing, language, and customs should keep a record of his experiences for the benefit of his countrymen.

Greek and Roman accounts

Some of the ancient Greeks, who sailed their ships up and down the Mediterranean in the 8th century B.C., found that knowledge about different ports and peoples was helpful to merchants who went to sea to trade. Early records, known as pilot books, gave information and instructions to the traveler.

Herodotus

More advanced than these beginnings was the work of the historian Herodotus (484–25 B.C.). He was a great traveler who visited Macedonia, Thrace, Babylon, Palestine, and Egypt. Herodotus' long account of Egypt is particularly interesting. He remarked that the Egyptians did things quite differently from the Greeks: women traded in the market, while men sat at home at the loom. Women

14

carried burdens on their shoulders; men carried them on their heads. Sons did not have to support their parents, but daughters had to. In noting contrasts such as these, Herodotus seemed to have a rather dispassionate, relativistic point of view. He did not try to demonstrate the superiority of the Greeks, although that is sometimes implied. He knew that Egyptian civilization was much older than that of Greece. He had a historical interest in tracing some Greek customs back to Egypt. Most of the names of Greek gods originated in Egypt, he tells us. "The Egyptians were also the first to introduce solemn assemblies, processions, and litanies to the gods; of all which the Greeks were taught the use by them" (Blakeney 1936:143).

Archaeologists can reconstruct much of the ancient Egyptian culture from their findings, but Herodotus' account of Egypt in the 5th century B.C. contains much information that would have been lost forever if he had not recorded it. The section on Egypt, of course, is only part of Herodotus' *History*, which ranges over a wide field.

Tacitus

The Roman historian Tacitus (circa A.D. 55–after A.D. 117) wrote a lengthy account of the barbarians of northern Europe. His work, *Germania,* is well organized, beginning with a discussion of the environment and giving details of the Germans' physical appearance, their house types, and customs. Unlike Herodotus, Tacitus did not visit the country he described but got his information secondhand from soldiers and other persons who had traveled in the north. In writing this book, Tacitus seems to have been partly motivated by a desire to shock the decadent Romans of his day by picturing the rude vigor and virtue of the primitive Germans. At any rate, his work is a convincing picture of how the northern tribes were living at that time.

In Europe, after the fall of the Roman Empire, there was an apparent decline of curiosity, or at least of ethnographic descriptions, about other cultures. But, in the 13th century, Europeans had to recognize the existence of the Mongols, who pressed on their eastern borders. Two Franciscan friars were sent to the Mongol courts in Asia: Giovanni da Pian del Carpini between 1245 and 1247 and Willem van Rubroek in 1253–54. Along with intelligence reports, these men included some information about Mongol customs. In the latter part of the 13th century, Marco Polo spent 17 years in the service of Kublai Khan and added some more to the written literature about eastern Asia. But, otherwise, there was little evidence of interest in ethnological matters in Europe.

Some Islamic scholars outside of Europe maintained this kind of interest, however. Ibn-Khaldun, who was born in Tunis in 1332 and died in Cairo in 1406, was the author of *The Muqaddimah*, a work highly praised by Arnold Toynbee. In *The Muqaddimah*, Ibn-Khaldun contrasted the ways of living of the nomadic Bedouins and sedentary city dwellers, discussed the effects of climate on human character, and made generalizations about the rise and fall of dynasties under headings containing such propositions as the following: "The vanquished always want to imitate the victor in his distinctive characteristics, his dress, his occupation, and all his other conditions and customs." "Bedouins can acquire royal authority only by making use of some religious coloring, such as prophethood, or sainthood, or some great religious event in general" (Ibn-Khaldun 1967).

The age of discovery

The discovery of the New World with its varying cultures, ranging from hunting-gathering bands to the advanced civilizations of Mexico and Peru, shook Europeans out of their provinciality and stimulated the imagination of scholars. These discoveries were accompanied by the new intellectual currents of the Renaissance that had uncovered the past glories of ancient Greece and Rome, John H. Rowe (1965:14) has remarked: "The enthusiasm of the Renaissance for Classical antiquity had the further effect of cracking the shell of ethnocentric prejudice which had traditionally isolated the men of the west." Rowe writes about Pietro Martire d'Anghiera (1457–1526), an Italian scholar and pioneer linguist attached to the court of Ferdinand and Isabella. Pietro Martire was greatly interested in the voyages to the New World, and he interviewed men who returned from there, taking a special interest in ethnographic and linguistic information. Martire acquired a brief vocabulary of Taino words recorded from natives brought back to Spain by Columbus on his first voyage. This was the first European record of an American Indian language. Some Indians from Mexico whom Martire saw wore lip plugs, which he considered to be repulsive, but he noted dispassionately that the Indians themselves thought they were handsome: ". . . an example which teaches us how absurdly the human race is sunk in its own blindness, and how much we are all mistaken. The Ethiopian considers that black is a more beautiful color than white, while the white man thinks otherwise. The hairless man thinks he looks better than the hairy one, and the bearded man better than the beardless" (Rowe 1965:13). This culture-consciousness and sense of cultural relativism were new outlooks for Europeans at that time.

Another scholar whose thinking was similarly stimulated by the voyages of discovery was Michel de Montaigne (1533–92), who wrote about the influence of custom on human perception of reality (1947:4–10):

I do believe, that no so absurd or ridiculous fancy can enter into human imagination, that does not meet with some example of public practice, and that, consequently, our reason does not ground and back up. . . . In one place, men feed upon human flesh; in another 'tis reputed a pious office for a man to kill his father at a certain age. . . . The laws of conscience which we pretend to be derived from nature, proceed from custom; . . . and the common fancies that we find in repute everywhere about us . . . appear to us to be the most universal and genuine. . . .

A Franciscan chronicler of information about Mexican customs, Bernardino de Sahagún (1499–1590), left a valuable ethnographic record, the Florentine Codex. Another early work that resulted from the Spanish conquest of Peru was an account of the Inca civilization by Garcilaso de la Vega, a half-breed Inca whose father was a governor of Cuzco and whose mother came from the Inca ruling class. His major work, *Commentarios Reales Que Tratan del Origen de los Incas* (Part I, 1609 and Part II, 1617) is still an important source of data about Inca culture (de la Vega 1962).

Since the invention of printing coincided with the discoveries in the New World, it was possible for accounts like Garcilaso's to be published, and there was an eager market for them, as well as for the reports of the Jesuits and other missionaries in faraway places.

The voyages of Captain Cook in the 18th century brought large areas of the world, formerly unknown to Europeans, to their attention. Captain James Cook rounded the Cape of Good Hope and sailed to New Zealand; in 1774 he discovered the Sandwich Islands, New Caledonia, and other parts of Polynesia. He made good observations on the customs of natives of New Zealand and Australia, and collected objects of native handiwork, bark cloth, tools, weapons, and so forth.

By the latter part of the 18th century, information was available about non-Western cultures in many parts of the world. Sources include the writings of J. F. Lafitau about American Indians, Martin Dobrizhoffer's description of the Abipones of South America, and many others. Some European writers tried to systematize cross-cultural information about particular topics. For example, an anonymous author published in 1782 *An Accurate Description of the*

The Enlightenment

Early drawing
of Polynesian
outrigger canoe.

Marriage Ceremonies Used by Many Nations. The account included the Jews, the natives of Hudson Bay, Mexicans, Persians, Japanese, Greeks, and Hottentots, among others.

Increasing familiarity with information of this sort made intellectuals of the 18th century aware of the influence of culture upon human behavior, even though they did not use the term *culture.* This culture-consciousness was already advanced in the case of Montaigne in the 16th century, and it is also apparent in the writings of John Locke (1632–1704), who remarked:

Had you or I been born at the Bay of Soldania, possibly our thoughts and notions had not exceeded those brutish ones of the Hottentots that inhabit there. And had the Virginia king Apochancana been educated in England, he had been perhaps as knowing a divine, and as good a mathematician as any in it; the difference between him and a more improved Englishman lying barely in this, that the exercise of his faculties was bounded within the ways, modes, and notions of his own country, and never directed to any other or further inquiries (quoted in Slotkin 1965:173).

Voltaire and Rousseau both made use of ethnological information in their writings. Voltaire was aware of the great age and geographical extent of the civilizations of India and China and argued that the writing of history should not be confined to Europe but should include the other civilizations of the world. Rousseau drew upon descriptions of the Carib Indians of Venezuela to illustrate his conception of man in a "state of nature," the noble savage. In his *Social Contract* (1762), Rousseau wrote: "Man is born free and everywhere he is in chains." He believed that humans are essentially good but have become debased by civilization.

Just the opposite view had earlier been expressed by Thomas Hobbes (1588–1679), who argued that humans are essentially egocentric, aggressive, and out for what they can get. If we have become civilized it is because of the restraints of a firm government. Hobbes cited some American Indian tribes as examples of people without government who live in a brutish manner. Eighteenth-century thinkers tended to support one or the other of these polar views, with liberal reformers like the Earl of Shaftesbury and his followers often attacking the Hobbesian view. Similar conflicting opinions about the nature of humans and society are still in evidence today, with a somewhat Hobbesian conception of humans as aggressive, "carnivorous," territory-defending creatures being expressed by such writers as Konrad Lorenz and Robert Ardrey, while others—for example, Ashley Montagu—hold humans to be essentially harmless animals who fight, not because of the influence of their biological drives, but because they are forced to do so.

An important 18th-century work was Montesquieu's *The Spirit of Laws* (1748), a comparative study of the laws of different societies. Montesquieu adopted from Locke the idea that legislative, executive, and judicial powers should be separated in the state. The views of Montesquieu and Rousseau influenced the writing of the American Declaration of Independence and also the Constitution of the United States, which incorporated the threefold classification of powers.

In an analysis of early societies, Montesquieu pointed to some differences between societies existing at "savage" and "barbarous" levels of cultural development. He noted that the former live in dispersed clans lacking in social cohesion, while the latter are capable of being united to form small nations. Savages are generally hunters, while barbarians are herdsmen and shepherds. Similar cultural evolutionary views were set forth by Turgot, another 18th-century French writer, and by Adam Ferguson and John Millar. These were adumbrations of the cultural evolutionary schemes of the 19th century proposed by Edward B. Tylor, Lewis H. Morgan, and others. Views of this sort did not depend upon the demonstration that biological evolution had taken place; they long antedated Darwin's *Origin of Species*.

**The 19th
century**

In the early 19th century in England and France, there was a conservative, indeed reactionary, school of thought that attacked romantic Rousseauist doctrines and upheld biblical traditions. Its chief representative, Comte Joseph de Maistre (1753–1821), argued that the American Indian savages had degenerated from a formerly higher condition:

Savage races came later than civilized races and represent their disintegration. . . . One thing is sure, the savage is necessarily later in time than civilized man. For example, let us examine America. This country has every characteristic of a new land. But since civilization is of great antiquity in the old countries, it follows that the savages who inhabited America at the time of the discovery descended from civilized man (quoted in Hays 1958: 54).

The English anthropologist Edward B. Tylor (1832–1917) argued that, on the contrary, all the evidence showed that man's earliest tools were simpler than later ones and that there had been a cultural evolution from simple to complex forms running through the three stages of savagery, barbarism, and civilization.

Tylor was mentioned early in Chapter 1 as the man who introduced the term "culture," in its modern anthropological sense, to the English reading public, defining it as "that complex whole which includes knowledge, belief, art, law, morals, custom, and any other capabilities and habits acquired by man as a member of society" (Tylor 1877:I, 1).

Tylor thus provided a new label, a new definition of "culture," and, in defining it, set forth the subject matter of a new science, cultural anthropology.

Another key figure in the development of anthropology in the 19th century was Lewis Henry Morgan (1818–81). A lawyer in upstate New York, Morgan developed an interest in the local Iroquois Indians and became the friend of an educated Seneca Indian, Ely Parker, who later became Commissioner of Indian Affairs during Grant's administration. With Parker, Morgan visited the Tonawanda reservation and became fascinated by the still-living traditions and customs of the Iroquois. After he had defended the Seneca in a land-grant case, Morgan was adopted into the Tonawanda band by the grateful Indians. This gave him a further entrée into the Indian community and a familiarity with it that led to the publication of *League of the Ho-dé-no-sau-nee or Iroquois* in 1851, the first full field study of an American Indian tribe. In the course of learning about Iroquois life, Morgan was surprised to discover that they had different kinship institutions and terminology from those of the Western world.

Mandan chief,
painted by George
Catlin (first half of
the 19th century).

Morgan's subsequent worldwide study of kinship systems will be discussed later in Chapter 24.

Field research: A new emphasis

Three influential figures ushered in the modern phase of anthropology: Franz Boas (1858–1942), Bronislaw Malinowski (1884–1942), and A. R. Radcliffe-Brown (1881–1955). They were professional, academic anthropologists who taught and trained others in their discipline.

Both Boas and Malinowski started out in other fields, in the physical sciences. Boas got a doctoral degree in physics at Kiel, Germany, with a dissertation written on the color of seawater. Malinowski got a Ph.D. in physics and mathematics at the University of Cracow. Although they had grown up and been educated in Germany and Poland, respectively, both of these men wrote most of their anthropological works in English and made their greatest influence felt in the United States and England.

These men also differed from their predecessors in doing more fieldwork. It is true that Morgan visited the Iroquois reservation, but he did not live there as Malinowski lived among the Trobriand Islanders in Melanesia. As a young man, Tylor traveled in Mexico, but that was not the same thing as doing ethnographic research. Most of the 19th-century writers on anthropology were indefatigable readers and compilers of data from books. One thinks of James G. Frazer, who never saw a living "savage" but whose massive work, *The Golden Bough*, ran to 12 volumes. Father Schmidt, who also did no fieldwork, wrote *The Origin of the Idea of God* in 11 volumes. Tylor, Morgan, Frazer, Schmidt, and other 19th-century theorists built up their compilations from reports of early travelers, sea captains, missionaries, and other commentators.

Boas, Malinowski, and Radcliffe-Brown were charismatic teachers who aroused great loyalty and admiration among the students whom they sent out to do fieldwork. Boas warned that primitive cultures all over the world were disappearing under the impact of Western civilization. He pointed out that time was short and that anthropologists should go out to record the facts of native life before these cultures vanished.

Malinowski was a prime exponent of the method of *participant observation*, in which ethnographers immerse themselves in the everyday life of the people whom they study. That is what Malinowski did in the Trobriand Islands where he lived during World War I. Both Boas and Malinowski stressed the value of learning the native language as a way of understanding the culture as experienced by its participants.

The accomplishments and theoretical approaches of Boas, Malinowski, and Radcliffe-Brown are discussed in Chapter 24.

Two surveys of the history of anthropological theory are Marvin Harris, *The Rise of Anthropological Theory: A History of Theories of Culture* (New York: Thomas Y. Crowell Co., 1968), and John J. Honigmann, *The Development of Anthropological Ideas* (Homewood, Ill.: Dorsey Press, 1976). For a collection of essays on the history of anthropology, see George W. Stocking, *Race, Culture, and Evolution: Essays in the History of Anthropology* (New York: Free Press, 1968).

Suggestions for further reading

part two

The study of languages

3

Anthropological linguistics

Linguistics, the study of languages, is one of the four subdivisions of anthropology, along with physical anthropology, archaeology, and ethnology. We deal with it here before continuing with the broader field of ethnology, because it is language that makes possible the universe of shared understanding and behavior patterns that we call culture. It is also *part* of culture, being transmitted from one generation to the next through learning and imitation, as are other aspects of culture.

First, to get some perspective on our own complex system, let us briefly examine some aspects of communication in other animal species.

All animals communicate in some way in various social contexts: in mating, aggressive behavior, relations between parents and offspring, group movements, and other situations. Language is a form of communication that is uniquely human insofar as we can tell. Although the apes share our "organs of speech," as they are called, and although the apes make sounds with those organs, they do not have a language. But, like all the higher primates that live in social groups, they do communicate with one another. A special terminology has been developed for discussing communication processes, whether they be linguistic or nonlinguistic. An *addresser encodes* a *message* in a particular *code* directed through a particular channel to an *addressee* who is able to *decode* the message. The *signal* that is originated by the addresser may be distorted en route by intrusive factors, called *noise*, which the addressee must screen out sufficiently to understand the message.

Animal communication

27

Research in animal communication has been of relatively recent origin, but scientists have already learned how to at least partially break the codes of several such systems. One of the best known is the way in which bees direct other members of their hive to a source of food through a circular dance. In the process, information is conveyed through various channels, not only visual but also olfactory and auditory. The duration of a whirring sound produced by the dancing bee gives information about the distance of the nectar supply, and the odor of the nectar on its wings can be smelled by the worker bees, who thus get an idea of its quality. There seem to be "dialect" differences among bees. Austrian and Italian bees can interbreed and work together if placed in the same colony, but they misinterpret one another's signals and either fly too far or not far enough in search of food.

Primate communica-tion

Primates, even apart from humans, probably communicate more with one another than most animals do because of their year-round social life. Communication is involved in grooming, sexual interaction, play, and other activities carried out together.

Various channels of communication are used by the apes and monkeys. The tactile sense is important in juvenile play, in grooming, and in sexual and affectionate behavior. Sounds are produced not only by the vocal organs but also by other means, as in the chest thumping and ground slapping of the gorilla and in the tree drumming of the chimpanzee. Facial expressions, such as baring of teeth, and special postures also have communicative functions, as they do among ourselves.

The usual primate vocal repertoire of sounds seems to be limited, usually between 10 and 15 sound-signal types. Ground-dwelling primates are often very quiet. Baboons make few vocal sounds, although they give warning barks in time of danger and emit various grunts, roars, and growls on occasion. But they may also remain silent for many hours at a time. Gorillas, when undisturbed, are strong, silent types. The chimpanzees, of course, are noisier.

Since chimpanzees are intelligent, relatively sociable, easy to work with, and vocal, some attempts have been made by human beings to teach young chimpanzees to talk, including chimps raised in a human household from an early age. These efforts have not been successful (see Hayes 1951).

There has been more success in teaching the deaf sign language in the case of a chimpanzee called Washoe to whom a husband-wife team of psychologists, Allen and Beatrice Gardner (1969), have taught more than 100 signs.

Gelada baboons
engaged in
grooming.

The question has been raised whether the capacity to learn a language is a species-specific ability of humans made possible by a unique genetic endowment. Eric H. Lenneberg (1966, 1967) has argued that the basis for language capacity is probably transmitted genetically and that it is not simply due to an increase in intelligence or relative weight of the brain.

The learning of language by a human child follows a very regular sequence of events. In the second six months of life, a child begins learning words. By the age of three and a half to four years, it may be speaking 1,500 words and have an understanding of well over twice that number. But the child does not simply learn words; it also accquires a knowledge of syntax and learns to fit words into an appropriate sequence. When a child repeats its mother's sentences, it often leaves words out but retains the original word order. A care-

**The child's
acquisition
of language**

ful study of the speech of two English-speaking children, aged 27 months and 18 months, showed that nouns and verbs were apt to be retained and, to a lesser degree, adjectives. The elements omitted included inflections, auxiliary verbs, articles, prepositions, and conjunctions (Brown and Bellugi 1966). There is something amazingly intelligent and creative in the child's acquisition of language. Grown-ups do not deliberately teach children rules of grammar and generally do not even have a conscious knowledge of them. But the child somehow figures out what these rules are, so that they soon become part of his or her own unconscious knowledge.

If a child's acquisition of language is a remarkable phenomenon, even more mysterious is the question of how language originated in the first place. It must have developed from the limited repertoire of cries and calls characteristic of the other higher primates. But language is something very different and more complicated than that. Speculation as to how and when this crucial transformation took place has been inconclusive so far.

There are no "primitive" languages that could provide us with earlier stages of linguistic development. All modern languages, whether spoken by the Bushmen of the Kalahari Desert, the Ona of Tierra del Fuego, or the peoples of Europe and the United States, are complex, subtle media of communication. All are capable of expansion and development and can incorporate terms for new things such as "automobile," "airplane," and "television," if such items are introduced to the speakers of the language. All languages are structured and contain phonemes, morphemes, and rules of syntax, to be discussed in the following section.

A language involves a semantic system, a phonological system, and a syntactic system. Perhaps the most mysterious of these is the first, the semantic system, which has to do with the essence of language: communication of meaning. How has meaning come to be associated with particular words? In general, the association between words and things seems to be arbitrary. We use the term *horse;* the French say *cheval* and the Germans *pferd*. It could hardly be argued that one of these terms is better or "closer to the original" than any of the others. It is true that there are onomatopoetic words like "twitter" and "moo" that seem to copy nature, but in most cases the relationship between word and meaning is arbitrary and conventional. Phonological and syntactic systems are dealt with in the field of descriptive linguistics, to which we turn next.

Descriptive linguistics

A basic branch of linguistics is *descriptive*, or *structural*, linguistics, which analyzes the components of language. It deals with a language as a synchronic system, at one period of time. Descriptive linguistics is concerned with both phonology and grammar. *Historical* linguistics deals with changes in languages over time.

In analyzing a language, the linguist breaks it down into its component phonemes and morphemes.

Phonemes

A *phoneme* is a minimal sound unit that serves to distinguish one word or syllable from another for the speakers of a particular language. The English words *pit* and *bit* sound somewhat alike; the initial consonants are both bilabial stops produced with the lips, but we can tell these words apart, as we can with *pin* and *bin, pig* and *big,* and so on. English *p* and *b* are separate phonemes. But we cannot assume that they will be separate phonemes in another language, for different languages may make use of different significant sounds.

The number of phonemes in any language is limited. English contains 24 consonants, 9 vowels, 3 semivowels, and some other features, including pitches and stresses, giving a total of 46 phonemes (Gleason 1955:50). Obviously the 26 standard letters of the English alphabet do not equate with the 46 phonemes of English speech, although some of the letters do reliably signal phonemic sound values. This is true of: *p b t d k g f v s z m n l r w y h.* Linguists have had to prepare phonetic alphabets to replace our traditional one, which is full of inconsistencies. We spell differently words that sound alike (*beat, beet; Beatle, beetle*) and spell alike words that sound differently, as in the verb and noun for *lead.* Some of our letters duplicate the work of others; *x* can be replaced by *ks* and *gz,* while the ambiguous *c* can be replaced by *k* (cat) and *s* (cent).

Linguists have devised new symbols or letters for some of our consonants, such as ð for *th* as in *then,* to be distinguished from θ for *th* as in *thin,* which is a different sound. Other symbols include: č for *ch* as in *chin, ǰ* for the initial sound in *gin;* ŋ for the terminal sound in *sing;* š for the *sh* sound in *shin,* and ž for the terminal sound in *rouge.* A system has also been developed for transcribing vowel sounds more consistently than is done in our alphabetic writing. This facilitates work in the recording, analysis, and comparison of the phonetic systems of different languages. Various schemes of phonetic transcription have been employed by linguists, but a commonly used one is the alphabet adopted by the International Phonetic Association, which makes use of the symbols given above.

There is variation in the pronunciation of the foregoing phonemes, not only on the part of different speakers but often by the same

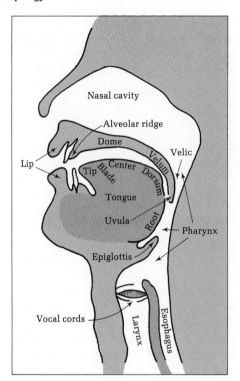

Nasal cavity

Alveolar ridge

Dome

Velic

Lip

Velum

Center Dorsum

Tip

Blade

Tongue

Uvula

Root

Pharynx

Epiglottis

Vocal cords

Larynx

Esophagus

Side view of oral
cavity, showing
palate, tongue,
teeth, and other
organs involved in
producing speech
sounds.

speaker as well. The *t* in *water* may be given slight emphasis in
comparison to the *t* in *tin*. A *t* sound may be produced by application
of the tongue tip to the ridge behind the upper gums, or it may be
made with the tip of the tongue turned back, touching the palate
further away from the front teeth. How the sound is made makes
little difference in English, as long as a recognizable *t* sound results,
and we pay little attention to such variations. But it does make a
difference in Hindi, where a back *t* (which may be represented as t)
has a different phonemic significance from a front *t*. *Roṭi* "bread" is
pronounced in this manner. Hindi also makes distinctions between
front and back *d, k, n,* and *r*.

Different languages, then, may have different phonemes. English
does not employ the German *ch* sound which appears in *Buch*
"book." Yet English, German, and Hindi are all related languages
belonging to the Indo-European language stock. Some African languages make use of suction sounds or clicks which are not found in
English, German, or Hindi. So there is great variation in the phonemic systems of the languages of the world.

Phonemes do not consist of only vowel and consonant sounds but also of different kinds of pitch and stress. The Japanese word *hana* means "nose" if both syllables have the same normal pitch, but it means "beginning" if there is higher pitch on the first syllable and "flower" if there is higher pitch on the second syllable. Differences in stress in English indicate the distinction between noun and verb in such words as *permit, pervert, conduct,* and *convict.*

Morphemes

While phonemes are significant units of sound, *morphemes* are significant units of meaning. A morpheme may be defined as the smallest unit that is grammatically significant. It may be a single syllable or phoneme or it may consist of several syllables.

In the sentence, "The dogs barked at the foolish clown," the words *the, at,* and *clown* are irreducible morphemes; they cannot be meaningfully subdivided. But *dogs* has two morphemes: *dog* and *-s;* the latter indicates plurality. *Barked* consists of *bark* and *-ed;* the suffix indicates past tense. The *-ish* in *foolish* is found in many adjectives like *mulish* and *boyish,* meaning to have the characteristics of a certain category. A morpheme that can stand alone, having meaning by itself, such as *dog* and *fool,* is said to be a *free morpheme,* while affixes like *-ed* and *-ish* that must be combined with a stem are said to be *bound morphemes.*

Languages differ in the extent to which words are inflected. In Chinese most words have one morpheme, while the Eskimo language makes use of many bound affixes, so that words may have ten or more morphemes. To the word *igdlo* "a house," about 80 suffixes can be added. *Igdlorssuaq* means "He builds a large house." There is one word for "When he bade him go to the place where the rather large house was to be built" (Birket-Smith 1959:62–63).

Languages may thus be analyzed with regard to the processes by which words are constructed, the morphology of the grammar.

Syntax

Languages may also be analyzed with regard to the order in which morphemes are arranged and sentences constructed. This is the study of *syntax.* In English, *Dog bites man* is different from *Man bites dog;* here the word order is crucial. It does not matter in Latin, which has different inflected forms for nominative and accusative cases, making possible either *Canis hominem mordet* or *Hominem canis mordet.* Either way, the meaning is clear. Since Chinese lacks inflection, word order is most important in that language. While this is less true of Latin, word order is still of significance in Latin and in all known languages.

As a way of discovering syntactical regularities, linguists break utterances down into *immediate constituents,* or IC's, dividing up sentences and phrases into progressively smaller units, like boxes within boxes. *The dog bit the man* is thus divided into two IC's: *The dog* and *bit the man.* The break is justified by the fact that we could substitute other phrases for *The dog* (for example, *The lion bit the man*) without changing the second segment of the sentence; we could similarly change the second segment without altering the first (*The dog barked*). Each segment may then be subdivided into its own IC's, so that the first has *The* and *dog*, while the second has *bit* and *the man*, with the latter phrase breaking up into *the* and *man*. If we analyze enough sentences in this way, we may find out what the typical constructions are in a particular language. These, of course, vary in different languages. In some, verbs come at the ends of sentences. In French, adjectives usually follow nouns rather than preceding them as in English. Some languages have articles like English *the* and *a,* while others lack them. Some languages have gender distinctions, with which the device of *concord* is associated; that is, words linked with others must have certain requisite forms. Thus, Latin *illa bella puella* "that pretty girl" or *puellarum bonarum* "of the good girls"; here the adjectives agree in gender, number, and case.

Gender categories do not always concern sex. In Cree there is a distinction between animate and inanimate categories, and other sets of distinctions are made in other languages.

Transformational grammar

In 1957, Noam Chomsky, a linguist at M.I.T., published a book called *Syntactic Structures,* which has had a strong impact among linguists and has led to the formation of factions among them, including those for and against Chomsky's views. His work has been mainly in the field of syntax. He does not object to the procedures described above for analyzing syntax but holds that traditional grammars do not set forth all the laws that govern the production of utterances. There is a system in the grammar of any language that a child, simply from hearing people speak, is able to learn. His implicit grasp of the principles underlying the language is known as his *competence,* while his actual speech expression is known as his *performance.* A person is not apt to be consciously aware of his linguistic competence; he speaks correctly without knowing why or how. Working with a small, finite number of phonemes, a much larger but still finite number of morphemes, and some rules of syntax, the speaker of a language is able to produce an endless number of sentences, many of which may never have been spoken before. Because of his (largely unconscious) competence, the speaker is able to creatively generate new and varied statements, which can be understood by others with similar competence. It should be possible to specify all the rules concerning utterances in a particular language that make such communication possible. According to Chomsky, however, traditional grammars do not do this. Analyzing a language by means of the immediate constituent approach may give misleading results. For example, in the sentence "You can always tell a Harvard man, but you can't tell him much," the point of the joke lies in the ambiguity of the phrase "you can tell a Harvard man," which might mean either "You can identify a Harvard man" or "You can inform a Harvard man" (about something). IC analysis does not clarify such ambiguity. "The missionary was eaten" and "The missionary was drunk" have the same word order but carry different connotations. The first sentence is in the passive voice and could be restated in the active voice: "Someone ate the missionary." This is an example of what Chomsky calls a *transformation*. The same idea may be expressed in different ways by different grammatical means. Chomsky uses the terms *surface structure* and *deep structure*. The surface structure may be analyzed by the method of immediate constituents. To get to the deep structure one may have to make transformations, as from the passive to the active voice. The deep structure, which expresses the meaning, is common to all languages. The transformational rules that convert deep to surface structure may differ from one language to another.

Chomsky believes that children are born with a capacity to learn language, although not any particular one. Although languages differ greatly from one another, a normal child can learn any natural language to which it is exposed. Languages, then, despite their differences, share some universal features, and Chomsky believes there is such a thing as universal grammar.

There has been much debate about these ideas. How useful is the concept of deep structure? Can't we get along without it? What does it mean to say that children have a language-learning capacity? It must be so, in some sense, since they do learn to speak, but does this notion tell us anything new?

Chomsky believes his views show up the weakness of empiricist ideas in philosophy and behavioristic concepts in psychology about the acquisition of language. The empiricist and behaviorist traditions hold that the mind of a newborn child is a blank slate that has no knowledge before experience. Knowledge comes from experience, from stimulus-response conditioning, and the association of ideas.

Chomsky believes that the learning of language by children cannot adequately be explained along these lines. What the child hears spoken around him consists of fragmentary bits of language, often incorrect. The child learns to speak before his general intellectual faculties are developed. Besides, all children learn to speak, both the smart and the stupid ones. It cannot be, Chomsky asserts, that the mind is a blank slate at birth; the child's brain must be programmed for language-learning. These, at any rate, are some of the issues concerning transformational grammar, about which there is still a good deal of disagreement.

Historical linguistics

In the late 18th century, it was discovered that Sanskrit, the language brought into India by the Aryans around 1500 B.C., was related to Greek and Latin and to the Romance and Germanic languages of Europe. This was shown by many correspondences in grammar and vocabulary. The term *Indo-European* was applied to this widespread linguistic stock. A school of comparative philology that developed in the 19th century devised some methods of analysis of these Indo-European languages; these could later be applied to linguistic stocks in other parts of the world.

The comparative method

Some examples of *cognate* words, which have both phonemic and semantic correspondences in Sanskrit, Greek, and Latin, are shown in the accompanying table.

	Father sky god	*Sheep*	*Foot*
Sanskrit	Dyaus pitar	avis	pat
Greek	Zeus pater	ouis	pous
Latin	Jupiter	ovis	pes

These correspondences give us more than purely linguistic information; they also tell us something about the culture of early Indo-Europeans, suggesting that they believed in a male sky god and kept sheep. We will come back to such cultural implications later, but first let us consider some purely linguistic features.

Notice that the words for *foot* and *father* begin with *p* in all three languages, while in German and English they start with *f*. Similarly, Latin *piscis* has become English *fish*. In the course of time, the initial Indo-European *p* in these and several other words became *f* in Germanic languages. This sound shift, along with several others, was first discovered by Jakob Grimm in 1822. The shift from *p* to *f* occurred long ago, judging from the earliest available texts in Germanic languages. For example, a 6th-century Gothic manuscript has *fadar* for *father*. An Old English 9th-century text has *feder;* in an Old Saxon 9th-century manuscript we have *fader,* and an Old High German text from the 9th century yields *fater*. From the comparative analysis of these cognate forms, it has been deduced that the primitive Germanic prototype form was *fader* (Bloomfield 1933:303).

Through the same kind of analysis, the probable forms of much earlier Proto-Indo-European words have been ferreted out, giving us some of the vocabulary of the earliest common stock from which later Indo-European languages developed. A knowledge of the direction of sound shifts facilitates such analysis.

Reconstructions from linguistic data

Scholars have tried to figure out, from the vocabularies of Indo-European languages, where the speakers of the early common stock were located. The noun and verb for *snow* are found so often in Indo-European languages that it seems unlikely they came from India. Moreover, there are no Proto-Indo-European words for elephant, tiger, monkey, or fig tree. Nor are they likely to have originated in Iran or the Mediterranean region, since there are no Proto-Indo-European words for camel, donkey, lion, olive, vine, or cypress. There are, however, words for some domesticated animals: dog, cattle, sheep, horse, pig, goat; and for many wild ones: wolf, bear, fox, stag, hare, mouse, snake, hedgehog, turtle, otter, beaver, salmon, eagle, falcon, owl, crane, thrush, goose, duck, fly, hornet, wasp, bee, louse, and flea. The fauna suggest a northerly area, which fits in with the words for plants and trees: barley, birch, beech, aspen, oak, yew, willow, fir, spruce, and alder.

Since turtles are not found in Scandinavia, that area can be ruled out. The homeland seems to have been south of the Baltic Sea. Salmon are found only in rivers that flow into the Baltic and North seas, including the Vistula, Oder, and Elbe. Hence, Paul Thieme (1964) has concluded that the early Indo-European homeland area was in the domain of the salmon rivers and their tributaries, west of the "beech line" outside of Scandinavia, south of the Baltic Sea.

Thieme's reconstruction sounds convincing and may be right, but it should be noted that some other scholars, reasoning along other lines, have located the homeland of the early Indo-Europeans in the steppes of southern Russia and the lands eastward to the Caspian Sea (Piggott 1950:248).

Bloomfield (1933:321) has deduced some residence and social patterns from the linguistic data. Indo-European languages have

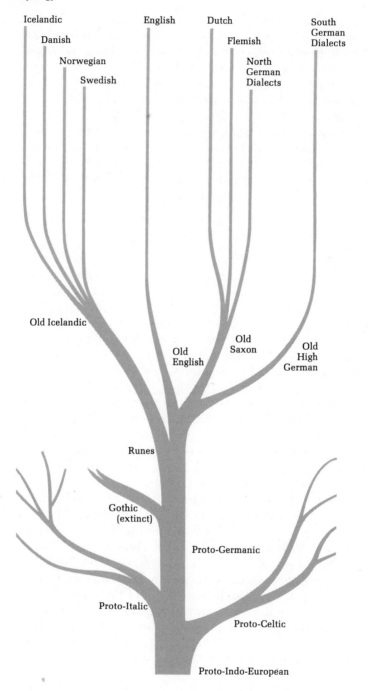

Icelandic

Danish

Norwegian

Swedish

English

Dutch

Flemish

North
German
Dialects

South
German
Dialects

Old Icelandic

Old
English

Old
Saxon

Old
High
German

Runes

Gothic
(extinct)

Proto-Germanic

Proto-Italic

Proto-Celtic

Proto-Indo-European

Family tree of
Germanic
languages, showing
how modern
languages derive
from Proto-
Germanic, which
in turn developed
from the Proto-
Indo-European of
about 5000
B.C.

terms for a woman's relatives by marriage (husband's brother and husband's sister) but not for a man's relatives by marriage. From this he concluded that patrilocal residence was customary. Analyses along similar lines have been carried out for some linguistic stocks in other parts of the world. Thus, Hockett (1964), in a comparative study of Central Algonquian languages, concluded that the Proto Central Algonquians were patrilocal and practiced matrilateral cross-cousin marriage.

Lexicostatistics

Another way in which linguistics has probed into the past is through the method of *lexicostatistics,* sometimes known as *glotto-chronology.* This seeks to assign, through comparison of some terms of their basic vocabulary, an approximate date for the time of splitting of a parent language into two offshoots.

Although the distinction is often vague, the "basic" terms of a language may be distinguished from the "nonbasic" ones. It is assumed that all languages, whatever the associated technological level may be, contain words for some aspects of reality common to human experience, including certain parts of the body, natural objects, and geographical features. Languages also contain numerals, at least up to two or three, and they have words for colors and some categories of plants and animals. "Basic" terms are learned early in childhood and are in common, everyday use. "Nonbasic" terms may be replaced in the process of culture change and contact with other linguistic groups, but the basic vocabulary is more conservative. For example, despite the great amount of borrowing of the Normans from the French and other sources, much of the basic English vocabulary is still Saxon.

Let us say that the comparative method has shown that two languages are related, having diverged from a parent language. We find what words the two daughter languages have for 100 or 200 basic items. If the two languages have many cognate words, like English *man* and German *Mann,* we know that the split between them did not occur very long ago; but if they have very few such cognates, it may be concluded that the division was an ancient one. Calculation of the percentage of cognates provides a rough time index.

Morris Swadesh and some other linguists have argued that the rate of basic vocabulary loss is roughly the same in all languages. Support for this contention has come from more than a dozen studies of languages which have old written records, such as Greek, Latin, Old English, and Old Japanese, whose basic terms may be compared with those of their modern descendants. It has been objected that most of the languages thus studied have been European, and that one cannot assume that American Indian languages, let us say, follow the same pattern. However, similar results have been shown for Japanese, Kannada, and Arabic. More studies of this kind will help to show how consistent is the rate of loss of basic vocabulary in different linguistic stocks.

Meanwhile, on the basis of the comparisons already made, the rate of basic vocabulary retention has been calculated to be about 81 percent per 1,000 years. Two daughter languages will not necessarily retain the same terms; it has been calculated that they will be most likely to have about 66 percent cognate items in the basic vocabulary after 1,000 years. Assuming this to be a constant pattern, the method of lexicostatistics has been applied to pairs of related languages that have no written records in the attempt to find approximate dates for their divergences. This has often, although not always, found some support in nonlinguistic evidence, such as archaeological material.

The method is a promising addition to our techniques for investigating prehistory, but there are many problems in its application. One has been to find a satisfactory word list that could be universally applied. It would have to omit nonuniversal features like ice, snow, palm tree, desert, and sea that are not known to all peoples. Languages do not all categorize the known world in the same way, and paired items from different languages may sometimes not be comparable. Swadesh started with a list of 200 words but could not find words in some languages for all the items listed, so he shortened the list to 100. As Hockett (1958:530) has observed, "The number of meanings for which a human language *must* have words seems amazingly small." The revised 100-word list includes such terms as: *I, thou, we, this, that, many, one, two, big, long, small, woman, man, fish, bird, dog, tree, leaf, root, blood, bone, head, ear, eye, nose, drink, eat, see, hear, sun, moon, star, water, rain, fire, red, green,* and *yellow.*

In a discussion of the validity of the 100-word list, Dell Hymes concludes that it is useful, consistent, and valid in large measure but that the best possible list for the purpose has not yet been drawn up (Hymes 1960:12).

Although the application of lexicostatistics involves many problems, it has often provided results that have seemed convincing. Floyd Lounsbury found a 3,500- to 3,800-year divergence for Iroquois and Cherokee, which was a little shorter than his guess of about 4,000 years. It is known that the Navaho, an Athapaskan-speaking people, must have moved into the Southwest from the North, but the approximate date is uncertain. Most Athapaskan-speaking groups are found in northwestern Canada and Alaska and some on the Pacific Coast and in the Southwest. When the lexicostatistical method was applied to the Navaho of Arizona and the Kutchin of Alaska, the result gave a date of divergence at about 850 years ago. What is needed in such cases is to find other converging lines of evidence.

Comparisons have sometimes been made between language and culture. Both establish "rules" about how things should be done, but these rules are not always followed in practice. One may speak ungrammatically if one wishes, although it sometimes defeats one's own purpose in communicating to do so. Both language and culture are restricting in some ways and liberating in others. Each provides a map, a book of rules, and a shared understanding with others; each provides the individual with a particular set of lenses through which to see reality.

Language and cognition

All languages classify the objects of the surrounding world in some way, but there are many possible ways in which that may be done. Several 19th-century theorists who were intrigued to learn that some "primitive" peoples lack distinguishing terms for green and blue or blue and black concluded from this that such people must be deficient in color vision. But in 1877 an investigation of some Nubians, who used the same word for both blue and black, showed that they were able to sort out blue and black yarn and blue and black pieces of paper. They could clearly tell the difference, although their language did not assign different words to these colors. The color spectrum has continuous gradations, and there are many ways of dividing it up. The Navaho have a word that covers a range from green through blue to purple, while the Zuñi have a term that includes both orange and yellow. Cultures differ in the numbers of colors differentiated. Our own language is rich in color terms, partly through the influence of the fashion business and traditions of the arts. The largest collection of English color terms has over 3,000 entries, although only about eight terms are commonly used. Some languages, on the other hand, have only three color terms, generally corresponding to our black, white, and red.

In all languages there are names for plants, animals, and other aspects of the environment, and different languages may have quite different ways of classifying them.

Folk taxonomies

Cognitive anthropologists use the phrase *semantic domain* to refer to a class of objects that share some characteristic feature or features that differentiate them from other domains. For example, furniture is a domain that includes chairs, sofas, desks, and tables but not sandwiches or parakeets. Items of furniture can be classed in hierarchic fashion to form a *taxonomy,* so that tables, for example, may be subdivided into end tables, dining tables, and so on (Tyler 1969:7–8). Items in lower levels of this classification, such as end tables, are kinds of items in higher levels, such as tables and furniture. There are other kinds of semantic arrangements that do not follow a system of hierarchic ordering. Cognitive anthropologists investigate the principles of organization and classification in the languages they study. If the principles of classification in another language differ from those in our own, we cannot conclude, as some 19th-century writers did, that the language is inferior to ours. It is only recently that we have come to realize how complex some "primitive" classifications are. Claude Lévi-Strauss's work, *The Savage Mind,* documents this very well. With regard to plants, he writes (1966a:5):

A single Seminol informant could identify two hundred and fifty species and varieties of plants (Sturtevant). Three hundred and fifty plants known to the Hopi Indians and more than five hundred to the Navaho have been recorded. The botanical vocabulary of the Subanun of the Southern Philippines greatly exceeds a hundred terms (Frake) and that of the Hanunóo approaches two thousand.

Lévi-Strauss (1966a:5) quotes R. B. Fox to the effect that: "Most Negrito men can with ease enumerate the specific or descriptive names of at least four hundred and fifty plants, seventy-five birds, most of the snakes, fish, insects, and animals, and of even twenty species of ants . . ."

It is understandable that people dependent on plants and animals for food would label and distinguish them, but Lévi-Strauss makes the point that this interest in taxonomy is not only a practical matter. For example, Frank Speck, an authority on the Algonquian-speaking Indians of northeastern North America, states that these Indians have distinct terms for each genus of reptile in their area and some terms for particular species and varieties, although the Indians do not eat these animals or derive any other economic benefits from them. Intellectual curiosity and a need for order, as well as more practical purposes, must have sparked the human urge to classify the multifarious phenomena of nature in the varied languages of the world.

Suggestions for further reading

A classic work is Leonard Bloomfield, *Language* (New York: Henry Holt & Co., 1933). See also Charles F. Hockett, *A Course in Modern Linguistics* (New York: Macmillan Co., 1958); H. A. Gleason, Jr., *An Introduction to Descriptive Linguistics* (New York: Henry Holt & Co., 1955).

Good collections of readings are available in Dell Hymes, ed., *Language in Culture and Society: A Reader in Linguistics and Anthropology* (New York: Harper & Row, 1964); and also in Eric H. Lenneberg, ed., *New Directions in the Study of Language* (Cambridge, Mass.: M.I.T. Press, 1966).

For Chomsky's views, see Noam Chomsky, *Syntactic Structures* (The Hague: Mouton, 1957), and *Chomsky: Selected Readings*, ed. J. P. B. Allen and Paul van Buren (London: Oxford University Press, 1971).

For a thoughtful essay, see John Searle, "Chomsky's Revolution in Linguistics," *The New York Review*, June 29, 1972, pp. 16–24.

part three

Environment, technology, and economy

4

Ecological adaptations

Ecology is the study of the interrelationship of organisms and their environment, including both the physical environment and other living organisms. Human adaptation to the environment involves the sphere of culture, not only with regard to technology but also patterns of social organization that may facilitate or inhibit economic cooperation, community size, and the spacing of social units. Like other animals, human beings must adapt to their environments. Unlike most animals, however, humans also create new environments in which to live, although this is also true of some other creatures, such as bees, ants, termites, and also beavers and other animals that have self-constructed dwellings. The artificial environments humans have constructed have taken many forms, the most extraordinary being the modern megalopolis, the huge termitary of present-day *Homo sapiens*.

Being warm-blooded mammals, equipped with cultural means of coping with nature, human beings have been able to adjust to a great variety of environments, including even polar lands. The food resources available in these different regions show great variation. One aspect of human adaptability has been the accommodation of our intestinal tract to a wide range of foods. We can be either vegetarians or carnivores, or both.

Human communities must cope not only with nature in all its manifestations but also with other human communities that appear within their living space. There are various solutions to such encounters: mutual avoidance, reciprocal exchange, trade, and warfare.

The population size of a community is influenced by the nature of the terrain, level of subsistence, type of technology, and the

47

population policy of its members. The latter may include such features as female infanticide, birth-control practices, and post-partum sex taboos, among others. If a group's adjustment to its environment is successful, population increase is apt to result, although it may be held in check by the population policies just mentioned and by diseases, epidemics, wars, and other disasters.

Human beings spread out across the earth in Upper Paleolithic times, arriving in Australia about 30,000 years ago, in Japan about 24,000 years ago, and moving before that into North America from Siberia through the Bering Straits land bridge. Human beings have lived long enough in different kinds of environments — tropical, temperate, and arctic — to have developed contrasting adaptive racial traits in skin color, hair form, and other characteristics. Contrasting cultural adaptations also took place in these varying environments. Let us now consider some of the kinds of environments in which human beings have lived and the different potentialities these environments may have for the development of human culture.

Geographical environments

Preston E. James (1959) has drawn up a classification of environments based upon vegetation and surface features, which some anthropologists have found useful. In James's scheme there are eight general types: Dry Lands, Tropical Forest Lands, Mediterranean Scrub Forest Lands, Mid-Latitude Mixed Forest Lands, Grasslands, Boreal Forest Lands, Polar Lands, and Mountain Lands.

Dry Lands consist of the arid regions or deserts that occupy similar positions on all the continents, on the west coasts, roughly between 20 degrees and 30 degrees both north and south of the equator. Deserts occupy about 18 percent of the land surface of the earth but, due to shortage of water, hold only about 4 percent of the world's population. Completely waterless sections are unoccupied. Oasis regions in deserts, however, provide very favorable environments, permitting greater densities of population. The Nile Valley has more than 1,700 people per square mile. The Bronze Age civilizations of the Old World developed in such areas, in Egypt, Mesopotamia, and the Indus Valley.

Tropical Forest Lands consist of tropical, semideciduous forests, rainforests and scrub forests found in a belt within 20 degrees latitude on either side of the equator, generally extending toward the poles along the eastern sides of the continents. Tropical Forest Lands vary greatly in population density. The Amazon-Orinoco basin, which is the largest of the Tropical Forest Land areas, is very sparsely settled, but Java and other parts of Southeast Asia have some of the denser populations of the world. Tropical Forest Lands include about 15 percent of the world's land area and about 28 percent of the world's population. The tropical forests do not supply good food resources except for societies that have developed advanced techniques of food production. However, some advanced civilizations developed in Tropical Forest Lands regions, as in Cambodia, Indonesia, and in the lowland Maya area.

Mediterranean Scrub Forest Lands include not only the lands bordering on the Mediterranean Sea but also areas with similar climates elsewhere in mid-latitude regions on the west coasts of continents between about 30 degrees and 40 degrees north and south latitude. Parts of California, Chile, South Africa, and Australia are included.

These regions, which have mild, rainy winters and hot, dry summers, are usually hedged in between mountains and seacoast. They have broadleaf evergreen scrub forests; oaks and chestnuts are common. Only about 1 percent of the earth's land surface falls into this category, but it holds about 4 percent of the world's population.

Mediterranean Scrub Forest Lands are easy to live in for human beings at any level of culture. Many wild fruits and nuts and small game are available, and the weather is mild. California was densely populated by hunting-gathering tribes before the coming of Europeans. Early centers of civilization developed in Israel, Greece, and Italy. Evidently this kind of environment is very favorable for human occupation, although only a small percentage of the world's people inhabits such areas.

In contrast to the foregoing, two fifths of the world's population live in Mid-Latitude Mixed Forest Lands, which make up 7 percent of the world's land area. This is an environment containing mixed broadleaf and coniferous forests, with plenty of rain and seasonal alterations of winter and summer. Areas near the sea may have relatively mild climates; those in the centers of continents have stronger seasonal ups and downs in temperature.

One region embraces eastern North America, including Canada's Saint Lawrence Valley. Another includes most of Europe north of the Mediterranean zone and south of the boreal forests. Here the trees, climate, and other features have much in common with those of eastern North America. Most of China north of the tropical forests and south of the northern and western plains falls into the same category, as does much of Korea and Japan.

This kind of environment, although heavily populated now, was sparsely settled in earlier times. Its occupation depended upon the development of adequate technology for cutting down the forest cover for agriculture and for keeping warm in cold winters.

Grasslands, which occupy zones between forests and deserts, have the advantage of containing much game for hunters, and they also lend themselves to occupation by pastoral nomadic or semi-nomadic herdsmen. Like the Mid-Latitude Mixed Forest Lands, their occupation depends upon the introduction of advanced technology; they have only recently been invaded on a large scale in different parts of the world. Their present percentage of the world's population is still low, perhaps around 6 percent or more, although the Grasslands cover about 19 percent of the earth's surface.

Boreal Forest Lands stretch across the Northern Hemisphere north of the Mixed Forest Lands and Grasslands. This is an area of very cold winters and short, cool summers. Rainfall is sparse, but little evaporation takes place, and there are many lakes, rivers, and swamps. Such environments are found in large parts of Scandinavia, Siberia, Alaska, and Canada. Boreal Forest Lands provide a difficult environment for humans at any level of culture. They cover 10 percent of the earth's land area but have only 1 percent of the world's population.

Polar Lands are those that lie at the northern and southern axes of the earth, including glaciated regions, polar deserts, and tundras. Although flowers bloom during the short summer, the summer is too short to allow the growth of forests. Wood is in short supply. The absence of vegetables forces the Eskimos who inhabit the northern Polar Lands to rely largely on animal food, in contrast to most other hunting-gathering people for whom vegetable foods make up the bulk of the diet. This is obviously a very difficult environment for human beings to cope with. Polar Lands cover 16 percent of the earth's surface but hold only a handful of human beings.

Mountain Lands differ from the preceding categories that are distinguished by types of vegetation; here, the main criterion is surface configuration. Mountains have different types of vegetation and climate at different levels of altitude.

Mountains cover about 12 percent of the earth's land area and hold about 12 percent of its population. The suitability of mountains for occupation depends upon where they are located. Those in low or low-medium latitudes provide good opportunities for exploitation of the environment. Wood and minerals are apt to be available.

Mountains have often served an important role as barriers. For example, the high barrier of the Himalayas has served to wall off India from the cultures of the north and east to a considerable degree. For this reason, mountain passes are important strategic points, trade and fighting units making their way through pass routes. Some of the other types of environments we have examined, such as deserts and tropical forests, may also serve as barriers, as do oceans and other large bodies of water in the absence of adequate means of navigation.

It is evident from the foregoing survey that some environments are more favorable for the development of culture than others. Much

Terraced fields
on mountain
slopes, Nepal.

of the earth's surface is not suitable for human occupation. One of
the astronauts who returned from the third Skylab space mission in
1974 remarked that, when seen from outer space, much of the earth
looks bare and empty and that human beings are crowded into quite
small areas on its surface.

The way in which a human group adapts to a particular environment is not determined by its geographical features alone but is also
influenced by the technology characteristic of the group and by the
way in which the group is organized to exploit the environment. To
illustrate this point with a particular region, the American Southwest
was first occupied by sparse nomadic, hunting-gathering bands.
Later, Pueblo Indians, such as the Hopi and Zuñi, developed an
agricultural way of life living in permanent, closely packed communities. Still later, the Spaniards appeared on the scene with
horses, guns, and metal tools. Each of these groups had its own
particular equipment for coping with the environment and winning
a livelihood from it. And the present-day inhabitants of the same
region, with electricity, air-conditioning, automobiles, and other
modern conveniences, lead a still different way of life.

Western
Arctic

Yukon Subarctic

Mackenzie
Subarctic

Central and
Eastern Arctic

Northwest
Coast

Plateau

Eastern Subarctic

Plains

Great Basin

California

Prairies

East

Oasis

Baja California

Northeast
Mexico

Meso–America

Circum–Caribbean

Culture area map
of North America.

Culture areas

The Preston James classification just reviewed is made up of large general types of environments. Somewhat similar were the ten or so *culture areas* into which anthropologists Clark Wissler (1926) and A. L. Kroeber (1939) divided aboriginal North America. Both noted that different cultural configurations were associated with particular geographical regions and food resources, such as the Northwest Coast salmon area, the California wild-seeds area, and the Plains bison area. Neither Wissler nor Kroeber were geographical or environmental determinists, but they saw environments as setting limits on cultural potentialities. Melville J. Herskovits (1962) also made use of the culture-area concept in describing the cultures of Africa.

In practice, particular human groups often adjust to environmental

Culture areas of Africa, indicated by heavy lines. Broken lines show political frontiers established under European colonial control.

North Africa

Desert

Egypt

Western Sudan

Eastern Sudan

Guinea Coast

East Horn

Congo

East African Cattle Area

Extension of East African Cattle Area

Khoisan

settings that cannot be characterized as broadly as "Grasslands" or "Desert." Fredrik Barth (1956) has shown that three ethnic groups in the small state of Swat in northwestern Pakistan have adjusted to different ecological *niches* within that area. One group consists of sedentary agriculturalists, another of nomadic herders, while a third combines both agriculture and pastoralism. Each group has an economic and political organization that helps it exploit its particular niche; sometimes, there are also symbiotic relations between these groups.

Each human society, then, exploits a particular environment with a particular technological apparatus. Our early ancestors first lived in a tropical forest environment, later moving out into savannas, or tropical grasslands. About 700,000 years ago, humans explored Mediterranean Scrub Forests and the Mid-Latitude Mixed Forests of the Old World, having acquired fire and the use of tools, which helped them withstand the cold weather of the European forests and of northern China.

High centers of civilization developed from a Neolithic base in oasis regions within deserts, along the Nile, the Tigris-Euphrates, and the Indus Rivers. It is only in relatively recent times that humans moved into Polar Lands, unless it be said that the Polar Lands themselves moved down to engulf the Neanderthals in Europe. Polar Lands, Dry Lands, and Boreal Forest Lands are sparsely settled by human beings. But changes in technology permit the invasion of zones formerly unoccupied. The Mid-Latitude Mixed Forest Lands, which now hold two fifths of the world's population, were formerly shunned by humans. New means of transportation serve to conquer barriers. Domestication of the camel helped humans cross deserts. The outrigger canoe enabled them to settle the islands of Polynesia. With airplanes we now cross mountain barriers and Polar Lands.

Suggestions for further reading

On the subject of ecology, see June Helm, "The Ecological Approach in Anthropology," *American Journal of Sociology*, vol. 67 (1962), pp. 630–39. Two collections of readings can be recommended: Jack B. Bresler, ed., *Human Ecology: A Collection of Readings* (Reading, Mass.: Addison-Wesley Publishing Co., 1966); Andrew P. Vayda, ed., *Environment and Cultural Behavior: Ecological Studies in Cultural Anthropology* (Garden City, N.Y.: Natural History Press, 1969).

Two groundbreaking works are: C. Daryll Forde, *Habitat, Economy, and Society* (London: Methuen & Co., 1949); Julian H. Steward, *Theory of Culture Change: The Methodology of Multilinear Evolution* (Urbana: University of Illinois Press, 1955), especially chapters 2, 6, 10, 11, and 12.

For geographical environments, see Preston E. James, with the collaboration of Hibberd V. B. Kline, Jr., *A Geography of Man*, 2d ed. (Boston: Ginn & Co., 1959).

5

Food getting and technological systems

In the course of cultural evolution, human beings have adopted a series of different strategies in getting food. For most of man's career he has been a hunter and gatherer; some societies of this type still exist in marginal areas. About 10,000 years ago, human beings began to domesticate plants and animals in the Old World; at around the same time, plant domestication was also taking place in the New World. The beginning of food production was a turning point in human cultural evolution in both hemispheres.

Food-producing societies can be divided into horticultural and agricultural societies. Horticulture is the earlier form of plant cultivation in which the main tool used is the digging stick. Horticultural societies can be divided into simple and advanced forms, the advanced horticultural societies having metal tools, such as hoes.

Agricultural societies have a still more advanced technology characterized by the use of plow and draft animals in the Old World, terracing and fertilization in pre-Columbian Peru, and irrigation and the use of *chinampas* (artificial islands with topsoil) in pre-Columbian Mexico (Goldschmidt 1959:193–209).

New means of distribution came about with the rise of cities and division of labor; by this system many people neither hunt nor produce food but instead produce some commodity or perform some service that they exchange for food. In our present industrial world, people work for salaries and buy food, which is produced and sold for a profit by farmers and middlemen.

In this chapter we will consider four types of societies that appeared in evolutionary sequence: hunting-gathering, horticultural, agricultural, and industrial.[1] For each of these types of societies we will consider the following questions: How is food obtained and with what sort of technology? How are population size and density affected by this system? What is the composition of social groups engaged in food acquisition and production? How has the system affected the environment? What are the advantages and limitations of this system? In the chapter that follows we will consider the related problem of how goods are distributed in different types of societies.

Hunting-gathering societies

Stone tools were used by hominids in North Africa, and perhaps elsewhere, 2 million years ago. It seems likely that such hominids also used tools of bone, horn, and wood. Early stone tools were choppers and hand axes, not hafted to handles.

The earliest evidence of human use of fire is from a cave in southern France dated at about 750,000 years ago. Charred hearths were also found in the caves of Peking man in China dated at about 500,000 years ago. Early hunters probably used fire not only to cook meat but sometimes to drive animals as well. There is evidence that elephants were trapped in bogs in northern Spain by men who set fire to the surrounding grass, about 300,000 years ago (Howell 1964:85–99).

A great improvement in hunting technology came in the Upper Paleolithic period, from around 30,000 to 11,000 B.C. in Europe. First there was a diversification of tool types, not only in stone tools, such as blades for knives and scrapers and burins for graving tools, but also new implements of bone, horn, and ivory. Most significant of all was the appearance of new *composite* tools consisting of different parts often made of different materials: the throwing-board, or spear-thrower, and the harpoon. The throwing-board adds greater impetus to the thrown spear.

In Mesolithic times in Europe, between approximately 11,000 and 5000 B.C., various inventions connected with fishing were developed: hook, line, and sinker, fishing nets, and dugout canoes. Axes and adzes were hafted to handles. There are remains of Mesolithic sleds with wooden runners. Another important composite tool, the bow and arrow, was used in Europe during the Mesolithic period.

Some Upper Paleolithic and Mesolithic hunting tools were employed in recent times by the Eskimos: harpoon, throwing-board, bow and arrow, and fishing equipment. The Australian aborigines, who were hunting-gathering peoples when first encountered by

---

[1] Other subsistence bases also exist, such as fishing and pastoralism, but these tend to be combined with agricultural food production.

Australian aborigines had a simple hunting-gathering technology, making use of spear, spear-thrower, and boomerang but lacking bow and arrow.

Europeans, were less well equipped technologically. They did not have the bow and arrow but used spears, spear-throwers, and boomerangs.

Hunting-gathering groups usually have a limited inventory of tools. They often move from place to place, and it is inconvenient to be burdened with possessions. Tools can often be made on the spot, when required. Traps are used by many hunting people, although there are some, such as the Vedda of Sri Lanka and the Chenchu of southern India, who did not have any traps or snares at all.

In hunting-gathering societies the main division of labor is between the sexes. The men do the hunting, while the women do most of the gathering, which often means digging for roots and tubers with digging sticks. Such food, rather than meat, tends to make up the bulk of the diet in hunting-gathering societies. To collect seeds, nuts, or fruits, they also need some sort of container. Bags, baskets, and nets are made in many such societies. The Australian aborigines have shallow bark or wooden traylike devices for carrying. The

California baskets made by hunting-gathering Indians, who made watertight baskets in which food could be cooked by dropping in hot stones.

Indians of the Great Basin had skin bags for storing grass seeds. The Bushmen use ostrich eggshells for carrying water. In some such societies good basketry is made, the most impressive being that of the Indians of California, who were able to make watertight baskets in which food could be cooked by dropping in hot stones. Plains Indians used folded leather containers (parfleches) to carry food and other things. Some hunting-gathering peoples, including Eskimos, have used pottery containers, but pottery does not lend itself well to a nomadic way of life.

Since hunting people often deal with skins, leather is often used for clothing and in making tents and boats. The buffalo hunters of the western Plains made great use of the buffalo's products, including their hides.

When collecting wild seeds and grains attains special importance, as it did in the broad-spectrum food exploitation of Mesolithic times, particular implements for reaping wild grains may be developed, such as the Natufian sickles of the Near East, along with grinding stones for crushing seeds and grain.

There is apt to be a relationship between the kinds of animals hunted and the social organization of hunting bands. Herding animals can be hunted communally, while solitary animals, like the moose, are best hunted by a single hunter. In wintertime, Central Eskimos used to sit on the ice beside blowholes waiting for seals to come up for air. Although there were apt to be other hunters nearby, this was a solitary vigil for an Eskimo hunter. "If only a few men go out hunting and famine is impending, he sometimes waits a whole day or even longer, though it be cold and the wind rage over the icy fields" (Boas 1884:475).

Buffaloes were hunted communally by Plains Indians like the Cheyenne, who had rules against individual bison hunting during the summer-camp period.

Communal buffalo hunting was practiced 10,000 years ago in

Colorado, judging from the remains in a ravine where 190 bison skulls were found. These bison belonged to a now extinct species. Some anthropologists believe that many of the animals hunted in the New World at that time became extinct, at least partly because of the efficient hunting techniques of the big-game hunters. Mammoth, mastodon, horse, camel, and ground sloth all disappeared. It has also been suggested that early hunters encouraged the spread of grasslands and drove back forests through brush fires that were either set off accidentally or deliberately started in animal drives like those in northern Spain 300,000 years ago (Stewart 1956).

Although bands that hunt herding animals like buffalo may become sizable, hunting societies usually do not maintain large year-round populations. Often there are seasonal splittings and later recombinations of bands, as occurred in both Plains and Woodland American Indian tribes. Among the Canadian Chippewa or Ojibwa there was a winter dispersal to take maximum advantage of food resources. It was the other way around among the Central Eskimo. Winter, when seals were hunted, was the social time for congregation into groups of 100 to 150 persons. In summer they split up into groups of between 15 and 30 for fishing and hunting caribou.

The dry winter season is a time of congregation for South African Bushman groups, which sometimes number over 100. This coming-together involves more work and energy expenditure for the members. When they split up into smaller units of 20 or 30, less work is demanded. The excitement of social life and initiation ceremonies makes congregation into larger units worthwhile for the members, and yet new stresses are placed upon them at these times, for it is then that quarrels and murders most often take place. The break-up into quieter, smaller units also has its psychological rewards (Lee 1972).

Environmental pressures serve to limit possible population size in hunting-gathering bands. Joseph B. Birdsell (1953) has made a survey of Australian aboriginal population distribution and has calculated the plant and animal resources available in different regions, the distribution of mean annual rainfall, and the population sizes of different tribes. He concluded that statistically the size of an Australian tribe approximates 500 persons, with an effective range of variation between 200 and 800. There is a high degree of correlation between rainfall and population density, which suggests to Birdsell that in this respect the Australian aborigines are subject to rigorous environmental determinism.

It used to be thought that hunting-gathering peoples were generally uncertain and anxious about the food supply, but more recent studies have shown that this is usually not the case. Two or three hours of work may produce enough food for a day, although the quotation from Boas about the Central Eskimo seal hunter cited above shows that there may also be difficult times in some such societies. Marshall Sahlins (1972) has gone so far as to call hunting-gathering groups "the original affluent society," because of their easily satisfied needs and abundant leisure. He claims that starvation is much more common in the world today than it was during the Stone Age. In recent times, at any rate, the hunting-gathering Chenchu of southern India were probably more secure and better fed than many of the agricultural villagers of India: "To wake in the morning with no food in the house does not disturb him in the least. He proceeds leisurely to the jungle to collect roots and fruits, . . . returns to the village in the evening to share with his family all that he has brought home" (von Fürer-Haimendorf 1943:57). No food is stored; all is eaten right away, as is often the case among hunting-gathering peoples. Richard B. Lee, who made a study of subsistence patterns in a Bushman group in South Africa, reports that food is almost always consumed within the local group and within 48 hours of its collection (Lee 1966).

It might seem that a hunting-gathering system is insecure, vulnerable to the disappearance of game and other resources; but human beings lived this way for more than 2 million years, and hunting-gathering is still a viable system in bleak marginal areas like the Kalahari Desert in South Africa. Within a particular region, however, the system may be threatened by population growth, requiring dispersal or adoption of a broad-spectrum exploitation of food resources.

Horticultural societies

An early and still widespread form of food production is *swidden cultivation,* or slash-and-burn horticulture. This process involves clearing a patch of land by burning, planting crops and tending them for a year or more, and then abandoning the plot to lie fallow so that its fertility may be restored and the land used again later. Swidden cultivation is usually done on a small scale, often with plots of an acre or less.

In simple horticultural societies, sowing and planting are done with a digging stick used to punch a hole in the earth through the ashes to plant seeds. In forest conditions, with short periods of cultivation, there are not apt to be many weeds. Hence the main work involved is the initial clearing of the land. Not much time need be spent in preparing the soil, weeding, or manuring, as in more advanced forms of agriculture. Simple horticulturalists, like hunters, can enjoy ample leisure time — another version of the original afflu-

Woman planting
taro in New
Hebrides.

ent society. Labor units need not be large when working the fields.
A husband and wife can work together, or there can be other small
working groups.

Clifford Geertz (1968:25) has written that an Indonesian swidden
plot is not a field at all but a "miniaturized rain forest" having a
heterogeneous variety of food-producing plants protected by a leafy
cover, rather than a single crop in an open field. Roy A. Rappaport
(1971:121) has similarly described the swidden fields of the Tsembaga of New Guinea. There, the plant species are not segregated or
lined up in rows but develop at different layers of the plot: ". . . taro
and sweet potato tubers mature just below the surface; the cassava
root lies deeper, and yams are the deepest of all. A mat of sweet

potato leaves covers the soil at ground level. The taro leaves project above this mat; the hibiscus, sugarcane and pitpit stand higher still. . . ."

In different parts of the world, horticulture has facilitated permanent residence, even though fields have to be periodically abandoned to lie fallow when they become worn out. The population density in horticultural societies tends to be low, with settlements usually having less than 250 people. There is a centrifugal tendency in the need to clear new land and occasionally shift residence. However, chieftainships and kingdoms developed in many advanced horticultural societies, as among the lowland Maya, in Cambodia, Indonesia, and the African kingdoms of Uganda and Dahomey (see p. 198).

It is sometimes alleged that slash-and-burn horticulture is a wasteful form of cultivation, laying bare hillsides and destroying vegetation. While this may often be the case, it is not an inherent evil of the system. Von Fürer-Haimendorf has contrasted two neighboring tribes in India's North-East Frontier from this point of view: the Daflas and the Apa Tani. "Daflas will ruin a whole tract of country by the unregulated felling and burning of forest and then move on, leaving a treeless, desolate wilderness with the fertility of the soil exhausted and the hill slopes covered in useless grass too coarse even for fodder" (von Fürer-Haimendorf 1956:62). The Apa Tani, however, practice a form of conservation, introduce foreign plants into their valley, and have fenced-in groves in which they plant pines, bamboo, and fruit trees. No wasteful plants are allowed to grow. The Apa Tani valley is described as being a carefully tended garden.

A swidden system works well as long as there is plenty of forestland in relation to population; but, as population grows, pressure on the land resources is increased. One solution to this problem is to shorten the fallow period, but this may require more preparation of the soil before sowing. "Thus, the hoe is not introduced just as a technical perfection of the digging stick. It is introduced, typically, when an additional operation becomes necessary, i.e., when forest fallow is replaced by bush fallow" (Boserup 1965:24).

Advanced horticultural societies, then, have more efficient tools than simple horticultural societies, including hoes with separate handle and blade. Horticulture is still widely practiced in many parts of the world, in India, the Congo, the Amazon, Oceania, and among peasants in Mexico and Southeast Asia. It is clearly a viable system of food production; but, following Boserup's view, it is vulnerable to population increase, which leads to reduction of the fallow period and eventual adoption of intensive agriculture.

Women pounding millet into flour in Matourkou, Upper Volta.

Agricultural societies

As the period of fallow is reduced, with the increase of population, the introduction of a plow becomes useful in cutting through weed-infested, grassy soil, which may also require the help of fertilizer, like manure, and the introduction of irrigation to remain productive. In the Old World, the plow and draft animals were introduced in Bronze Age times. The animal that pulled the plow could also provide fertilizer. In the New World, terracing and guano fertilizer were used in Peru, while *chinampas,* artificial islands with topsoil, were used in Mexico.

The agricultural societies having these innovations are associated with the advancement in culture known as civilization. As was discussed in Volume I, the Bronze Age societies of Egypt, Mesopotamia, and the Indus Valley in the Old World, and the civilizations of the Inca of Peru and the Aztecs and Maya of Mexico had a complex of features in common: the development of a state and a ruling elite; urban life; population increase; monumental constructions and mass labor; class stratification; advances in knowledge, such as systems of writing and mathematics; division of labor; trade; and the development of peasantry.

The peasant is the food producer in this system. A peasant differs from a tribesman who raises crops in his dependent relationship to the city and the state. "We see peasants as a peripheral but essential part of civilization, producing the food that makes urban life possible, supporting (and subject to) the specialized classes of political and religious rulers and other members of the educated elite" (Foster 1967:6). The peasant differs from a modern farmer in being less of a businessman concerned with profit, although peasants are often known to be shrewd in their transactions. According to the Russian economist A. V. Chayanov, the fundamental characteristic of a peasant economy is that it is a family economy; peasant food production is a family enterprise concerned with subsistence rather than profit and makes no use of hired labor. When the peasant switches to cash crops, employs hired labor, and seeks to expand through reinvestment, he ceases to be a peasant and becomes a farmer (Chayanov 1966; see also E. R. Wolf 1966).

The peasant's primary concern with his own family does not keep him from involvement with others, although a state of "amoral familism" has been described for some Italian peasant communities in which interfamily cooperation is rare and each family is concerned mainly with its own interests (Banfield 1958).

In societies having irrigation the agriculturalists who draw upon the same water resources are brought into a necessary relationship with one another. In the Bronze Age civilizations, control over the hydraulic system was probably in the hands of a dominant elite group that was able to exact corvée labor (forced, unpaid labor) from the peasants, not only for work in the irrigation channels but for other purposes as well. This, at least, is the thesis advanced by Karl A. Wittfogel (1957). He has also drawn attention to the rowlike arrangements of crops in an irrigation system, which may be contrasted with the description given earlier of the informal and heterogeneous New Guinea swidden plot. "Irrigation agriculture requires a rowlike arrangement of the seeds not only for crops such as corn and potatoes but also for cereals. Plants can be watered by ditches only if proper space for the distributing furrows is provided" (Wittfogel 1956:158). An orderly system of this kind involves more work than the earlier form of horticulture. The soil may be plowed or harrowed several times before being sown. However, the result is a very productive form of food production. Induced by population increase, according to Boserup (1965), intensive agriculture encourages still further increase and greater population density.

Agricultural technology and sources of energy

Besides the plow, an important invention associated with agriculture in the Old World was the wheel, used in the peasant's cart and also the potter's wheel of Bronze Age times. Another early application of this principle, in the first millennium B.C., was the water-raising wheel, a vertical wheel equipped with buckets or pots that lifted water for irrigation purposes. Still another application of this basic invention was the spinning wheel. The useful potentialities of the wheel were not discovered in the New World, although small wheeled objects, evidently used as toys, have been found in Mexico.

Another important feature of advanced agriculture in the Old World was the exploitation of animal energy, which began in Neolithic times. This was not limited to plowing, threshing, and pulling carts. Many peasants and farmers make use of animal energy in drawing water for irrigation, with camels, oxen, or donkeys going round and round or back and forth on an inclined plane. Some time after 200 B.C. oxen were used to provide the power for water-raising wheels by walking round and round a vertical shaft. Donkeys were similarly employed even earlier to keep rotary querns or mills in operation.[2]

Power was also derived from wind and water in the Old World. Windmills and waterwheels were used for irrigation and grinding grain. Windmills proliferated in Holland in the 16th century A.D. and thereafter, since the Low Countries are flat and their streams too sluggish to provide good waterpower. But windmills were also used in France and in Spain, where Don Quixote tilted against them. Their main function was to grind grain, but they were also used for sawing wood and raising water.

In Roman times the waterwheel was used only for grinding grain, but from the 11th century on it was also used for fulling cloth, making pulp for paper, raising water for irrigation, and other purposes.

---

[2] A significant improvement in the exploitation of animal power was the invention of the modern harness which replaced the less efficient form known to the Romans. The improved harness appeared first in China between the 3d and 7th centuries A.D. and in Europe from the 9th century on. At about the same time, the practice of shoeing horses was introduced in Europe. These two improvements together greatly increased the utility of horses and led to their replacing oxen in agricultural work in Europe.

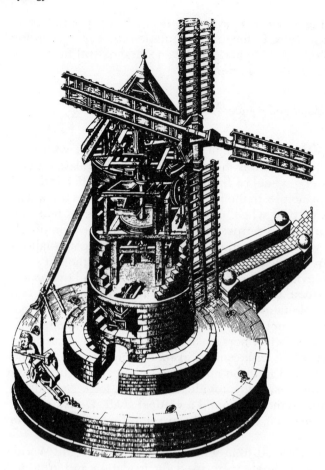

Corn-grinding
tower mill from a
16th century
drawing.

Waterwheels were not used much in Roman times, since the availability of slaves (an alternative source of power) made the laborsaving advantages of inanimate power unnecessary; there was
large-scale unemployment in the Roman Empire, and laborsaving
machinery would only have added to the difficulty. But during the
Middle Ages, when the institution of slavery had declined, the advantages of waterwheels and windmills could be appreciated, and
they came into their own. Thus, under advanced agriculture, much
more energy became available to the food producer than was possible under previous systems.

Types of peasant communities

Peasant communities have assumed many forms in different parts
of the world, and various ways of classifying subtypes have been

The major peasant
regions of the
world.

suggested. Eric Wolf has made a distinction between closed corporate peasant communities and open peasant communities. In a
closed community membership is restricted to people born and
raised within it, and marriages usually take place within the group.
There is corporate control over the land, which may not be sold to
outsiders. Leveling mechanisms often exist to equalize conditions
within the community, such as periodic reallotments of land. Open
peasant communities are more involved in cash crops and marketing
and the national culture. There is no communal jurisdiction over
land in the open communities. In Latin America, closed corporate
communities are found in marginal highland areas, while the open
communities are located in the lowlands. The corporate communities make use of a traditional technology and tend to be poor. Wolf
finds that closed corporate societies with features like those of Latin
America are also found in central Java. While closed corporate communities may be seen as traditional holdovers, they also represent
self-protective reactions on the part of peasants to outside pressure
in colonial regions (E. R. Wolf 1955, 1957, 1966).

Patterns of exchange labor not involving money payments are
common among peasants. Charles J. Erasmus (1956) has described
two types: festive labor and exchange labor. The former type involves feasting a work crew assembled for a task, such as house build-

ing or harvesting, with perhaps more than 10 workers, or even more than 100. Exchange labor is a simple matter of reciprocal exchange. A agrees to work for B, expecting that B will later work a roughly similar amount for him. Exchange labor involves smaller work gangs than festive labor, seldom more than 10 men. These patterns are not so popular as they once were, for the acquisition of farm machinery such as threshing machines obviates some of the need for collective work, while rising food prices tend to make wage labor cheaper than festive labor.

Like horticulture, intensive agriculture has sometimes had deleterious effects on the environment, particularly in the destruction of forests because of population increase, the need for more fields, and also because of demands for timber in house construction, fuel, and other purposes. The heavily populated Indo-Gangetic plain in northern India and Pakistan was once forested but is now relatively bare of trees. The same sort of deforestation occurred in ancient China and was responsible for the annual floods that have plagued northern China ever since. Parts of North Africa that supplied the ancient Romans with grain have become desiccated and semidesert. Central Italy itself lost its forests, which resulted in flooding, as in China.

Industrial societies

Industrial societies with factory production are consequences of the Industrial Revolution, which developed in England during the last third of the 18th century. This was partly the result of tapping a new source of energy.

Waterpower was used in the early stages of the Industrial Revolution in England to provide the energy for cotton mills. This meant that these factories were not located in towns or cities but beside streams near hills in narrow valleys.

The disadvantage of the waterwheel was that it had to be located by a stream. In 18th-century England there was a search for new sources of power, largely to find ways of pumping water out of the deep coal mines that were then being exploited. Several attempts to build a workable steam engine were made before James Watt produced an improved model. This engine was used not only in the mines but later in railways and steamboats as well. Now factories could be built away from streams and near coal mines and also near the cities where a labor force and markets were available. Lewis Mumford (1934:161–62) has discussed some of the sociological consequences of this change:

Wind and water were free; but coal was expensive and the steam engine itself was a costly investment; so, too, were the machines that it turned.

Twenty-four-hour operations, which characterized the mine and the blast furnace, now came into other industries which had hitherto respected the limitations of day and night.

The working day was often lengthened to 16 hours.

Manning Nash (1966:23) has written that in primitive and peasant societies, the

. . . social organization carrying out the making of goods or the tendering of services is dependent on and derived from other sets of social relations. Peasant and primitive societies do not have organizations whose only tasks are those of production, and there are no durable social units based solely on productive activities.

A peasant family household may be a unit of economic production. Among the Tiv of Nigeria a *kraal* is a basic unit of production, representing a local segment of a lineage. Such units do not exist for production alone but have many other functions and purposes.

In the cottage industry of 18th-century Yorkshire, woolen goods were sometimes produced by family units. Paul Mantoux (1961:58) writes: "If the weaver's family was large enough it did everything, its members dividing all the minor operations amongst themselves — the wife and daughters at the spinning wheel, the boys carding the wool, while the man worked the shuttle." Here, the workshop was the home, and the weaver owned both the means of production and the raw material he prepared.

But during the same period in England the factory system was changing the social organization of production. One consequence was a great increase in the size of the work force. This was not a completely new development. There was a shield factory during the period of the Roman Empire that employed 120 slaves. In the early 16th century, the weaving establishment of John Winchcombe, known as Jack of Newbury, was reported to have hired as many as 600 workers, although this may have been an exaggeration. But the first great increase in the size of industrial plants and labor force took place at the time of the Industrial Revolution, when power-driven machinery was applied on a large scale. This machinery was complicated and expensive; since it was worked from one power station, it had to be located in one main building. Such a factory represented a capital of several thousand pounds, and some industrialists owned several of them. In 1802 Peel employed more than 15,000 persons in the cotton industry. All this meant that some men had to be able to amass large sums of capital. In investing so much money they had to be confident of making a profit. Much larger, more distant markets had to be found than the local markets which had absorbed the products of previous means of production. Moreover, continuous supplies of raw materials had to be bought to feed into the machines, which were kept working from 12 to 14 or more hours a day. This involved a commercial as well as an industrial revolution. Karl Polanyi has referred to it as "the great transformation."

For the merchant this means that all factors involved must be on sale, that is, they must be available in the needed quantities to anybody who is prepared to pay for them. Unless this condition is fulfilled, production with the help of specialized machines is too risky to be undertaken both from the point of view of the merchant who stakes his money and of the community as a whole which comes to depend upon continuous production for incomes, employment, and provisions.

Now, in an agricultural society such conditions would not naturally be given; they would have to be created. That they would be created gradually in no way affects the startling nature of the changes involved. The transformation implies a change in the motive of action on the part of the members of society: for the motive of subsistence that of gain must be substituted (Polanyi 1957a:41).

An essential feature of this market system is that it be self-regulating, responsive to laws of supply and demand. Everyone in this system gets a livelihood from selling something; laborers sell their labor, landowners, their land or its produce; and farm and factory owners, their products. A new science, economics, developed as this market system expanded; it was geared to the analysis of this system, concerned with the forces that determine prices in a market economy.

The industrial system, born in the 18th century, grew rapidly in the 19th. It received further impetus from the development of electricity as a source of power.

The principle of the dynamo was discovered by Michael Faraday in 1831; generators were well developed by 1882. The new discoveries were first applied to lighting but soon to other fields as well, such as electric railways and power for factories. Although an electric fan was invented in 1889 and vacuum cleaners were sold in small quantities from around the turn of the century, Samuel Lilley (1966:123) writes that "electric power made no serious impact on the domestic scene till after 1918." The recency of the use of electricity is thus rather astonishing.

Electricity can be developed by energy from many sources, including coal, waterfalls, tides, and windmills. It is easy to transmit and is readily convertible into various forms, in motors, lamps, X-ray tubes, and so forth. Because of the development of electricity, industry is no longer dependent on the coal mine as a source of power; electricity thus facilitates some decentralization of population.

Today, the scale of some industrial organizations is enormous. General Motors, for example, has over 700,000 employees and over 1.3 million stockholders.

Workers coming
out of Rouge Ford
plant.

Not only has the labor force grown vastly in modern corporations, but it has become differentiated into all kinds of subdivisions. A large American corporation today has many stockholders, most of whom have no other connection with its business than owning a few shares. It has a board of directors, a president, an executive committee, and a finance committee. It is apt to have a sales division with an advertising staff, market analysts, and accountants; a manufacturing division with many further subdivisions; and auxiliary departments concerned with research, employee relations, legal advice, and so on. Below all these come the army of employees who operate the machines, supervise others, and turn out the product, whatever it is.

These people have nothing to do with food production but have to buy the food they eat. The farmers who provide it are businesspeople rather than peasants and would not produce such food if there were no profit in it for them.

Agribusiness

Like industry, agriculture has also grown in scale and has benefited from technological development. By 1963 the top 3 percent of America's farms produced more than did the bottom 78 percent and had acquired nearly half the farmland with average-sized holdings of over 4,000 acres, more than 6 square miles apiece. The productivity of such large units is made possible by mechanization. Between 1917 and 1960 the number of tractors increased from 51,000 to nearly 5 million, while the number of horses and mules on American farms dropped from almost 27 million to 3 million (Higbee 1963:3, 10). Big farms hire airplanes to spread fertilizer and pesticides on their fields. Modern agriculture makes abundant use of nitrogen fertilizers, which are an important source of pollution of American lakes and streams.

The machinery and equipment needed to run such big farms are expensive. Hence, *agribusiness*, as it has been called, may have stockholders and management organization (Roy 1967). Canning, refrigeration, and transportation are also involved in food production. There is much regional specialization; lettuce comes from California, wheat from the Dakotas, cheese from Wisconsin. On a family's breakfast table there may be orange juice from California or Florida, bacon and corn products from Iowa, sugar from Louisiana, and coffee from Brazil. So the food costs represent not only payment to the farmer but also costs for food processing, storage, transportation, and marketing. We are a long way from the hunting-gathering system of direct contact with the foods we eat.

The way in which food progresses from producer to consumer in this system is so complicated that it seems vulnerable to dislocation at any of the various steps between farm and supermarket. Another problem is that one needs money or food stamps to buy food, and when unemployment increases and food prices go up, many poor people are in trouble. A striking and hopeful aspect of the system, however, is that so few farmers are able to produce so much food for the predominantly nonfarming population.

Pollution

Much has been written about how modern industry and agriculture have damaged the environment. We have seen that this was true to some degree at each stage of food getting. Hunters probably killed off some species of game in Paleolithic times, horticulturalists denuded hills, and agriculturalists destroyed forests. But industrial societies have had more lethal effects upon the environment than all the earlier systems. With increasingly more people on our planet, there is less free space. In the United States and other advanced industrial nations, more people means more automobiles and more exhaust fumes. More factories belch pollutants into the air. Cities — Los Angeles, for example — are covered with smog, which may become dangerous in the case of temperature inversion, when hot air does not rise and blow pollutants away as it normally does. Because of inversion and air pollution, 12,000 people died in London in 1952; there were similar attacks there in 1956 and 1962. There has been a great increase in emphysema, lung cancer, and bronchitis in our cities. Our atmosphere has also been contaminated by fallout from nuclear explosions, although the number of detonations in the atmosphere has been reduced since the Test Ban Treaty of 1963.

The major rivers of the United States are heavily polluted, as are the Great Lakes, especially Lake Erie. Sewage and factory wastes pour into the rivers; oil slicks are washed ashore on the seacoasts, closing beaches and killing birds.

While demands for fresh water increase, less pure water is available. It has been estimated that an average American throws away 8 pounds of refuse a day, making it increasingly difficult for municipalities to get rid of their mountains of trash and garbage (Chase 1968:64–68). These problems affect not only the United States but the nations of western Europe, the USSR, Japan, and other countries as well.

For a concise discussion of human ecology, see Richard A. Watson and Patty Jo Watson, *Man and Nature: An Anthropological Essay in Human Ecology* (New York: Harcourt, Brace, and World, 1969).

Suggestions for further reading

For the human hunting-gathering stage, see Richard B. Lee and Irven De Vore, eds., *Man the Hunter* (Chicago: Aldine Publishing Co., 1968).

For a detailed discussion of the ecology of a particular horticultural tribe in New Guinea, see Roy A. Rappaport, *Pigs for the Ancestors: Ritual in the Ecology of a New Guinea People* (New Haven, Conn.: Yale University Press, 1967).

An explanation for the shift to intensive agriculture is provided by Ester Boserup, *The Conditions of Agricultural Growth: The Economics of Agrarian Change Under Population Pressure* (Chicago: Aldine Publishing Co., 1965).

For a concise analysis of peasant societies, see Eric R. Wolf, *Peasants* (Englewood Cliffs, N.J.: Prentice-Hall, Inc., 1966). See also Jack M. Potter, May N. Diaz, and George M. Foster, *Peasant Society: A Reader* (Boston: Little, Brown and Co., 1967).

Two books that deal not only with technology but also with some of the sociological aspects are Lewis Mumford, *Technics and Civilization* (New York: Harcourt, Brace & Co., 1934); Samuel Lilley, *Men, Machines, and History: The Story of Tools and Machines in Relation to Social Progress*, rev. ed. (New York: International Publishers, 1966). See also Lynn White, *Medieval Technology and Social Change* (Oxford: Oxford University Press, 1962).

For a more detailed work on technology per se, see Abbott Payson Usher,

A *History of Mechanical Inventions,* rev. ed. (Cambridge, Mass.: Harvard University Press, 1954). For a general text that covers both geographical environments and technology in some detail, see Eliot Dismore Chapple and Carleton Stevens Coon, *Principles of Anthropology* (New York: Henry Holt & Co., 1942).

The consequences of the commercial revolution that accompanied the Industrial Revolution are set forth by Karl Polanyi in *The Great Transformation* (Boston: Beacon Press, 1957). For the consequences of the introduction of the new system into the world's colonial areas, see Eric R. Wolf, *Peasant Wars of the Twentieth Century* (New York: Harper & Row, 1969).

6

Exchange and distribution

Goods are not only produced in every society; they must also be distributed in some way, and there are various ways in which that may be done. Let us take the example of a factory worker in our society. Having cashed a paycheck, he hands some money over to his wife, who goes to the market or grocery store to buy food. But the members of her family do not have to pay her for her labor and skill in preparing meals. Not all transactions, then, are money transactions. We are also familiar with the custom of gift giving, such as occurs at Christmastime. Much of this, again, is within the family, but not exclusively so.

The significance for us here of such nonmonetary exchanges is that factories, money, and markets are relatively recent institutions; before money and markets came into being, goods and services had to be exchanged in some other way. The exchange of gifts may give us a clue to one form of precapitalistic distribution.

Reciprocity

The donation of a gift places the recipient under an obligation. He may not actually want to have the present, but it would be difficult for him to refuse, for in that case the insulted donor might become his enemy. To give and receive gifts is an age-old way of maintaining peace and friendship. The recipient is not only more or less obliged to receive the present, but sooner or later he is obligated to return it with a gift of about equal value. This is known as *reciprocity*. (These generalizations do not apply to gift-giving situations when there are marked disparities of status, i.e., a handout to a beggar or a present from an adult to a child.)

Floating market
scene in
Thailand.

The Japanese are much more involved in giving gifts than Americans are, and they are fully aware of the demands of reciprocity. Here is an example from Tokyo:

Mr. A called at the B's household for a friendly chat and brought a gift of a very special sort of watermelon. He said that he just happened to be passing the fruiterers and thought they would like it. The next day Mrs. B went to the fruiterers to enquire how much such a melon would cost. She was told between 300 and 350 *yen*. She thereupon took to the A's a return gift of two bottles of beer, costing approximately 250 *yen* (Dore 1965:261).

Mrs. B's return gift was worth a little less than his, since she had not asked Mr. A to bring her a melon; but, if she had done so, her present would have had to be a much more generous one.

In many "primitive" societies there is much giving of presents and sharing of goods, and in such societies generosity is always admired. To freely give away a valued present brings prestige. At the same time, the stingy person evokes disapproval. Elizabeth Thomas (1959:22) writes:

A Bushman will go to any lengths to avoid making other Bushmen jealous of him, and for this reason the few possessions that Bushmen have are constantly circling among the members of their groups. No one cares to keep a particularly good knife too long, even though he may want it desperately, because it will become the object of envy . . .

There are powerful sanctions, then, to encourage generosity.

Gifts may be given to members of other societies besides one's own, partly to maintain peace but also to acquire goods not locally obtainable. One kind of exchange, in which the "partners" never see each other, is known as "silent trade." One man leaves some animal skins or other gift in a customary place. The man who collects it replaces it with an exchange gift. In this way, the Pygmies of the Congo trade with their Bantu neighbors without having to confront them.

The institution of the trading partner is found in many societies. Trading partners are men who count on a generally reciprocal pattern of exchange. There may be no immediate equivalent return for a gift, but over the course of time a man expects that his trading partner will even the balance.

Reciprocal exchanges may occur not only between individuals but also between groups, and this may help to strengthen their mutual interdependence. Marriages and gift exchanges establish close ties between neighboring groups.

The kula ring

Most anthropology texts discuss the kula ring, and that custom will be followed here because Malinowski's description of it (1922) is one of the classics of anthropology and because it presents one of the first and most detailed accounts of economic exchanges in a non-Western society.

The area studied by Malinowski between 1914 and 1920 comprised the eastern mainland of New Guinea and the island archipelagoes to the east and northeast, particularly the Trobriand Islands. The inhabitants of these islands are horticulturalists who raise yams and catch fish in a tropical environment well supplied with palms, breadfruit, and mangoes. They have large, seagoing canoes, hollowed from logs and equipped with outriggers, in which they make expeditions to other islands. The expeditions that arouse their greatest interest and enthusiasm are those having to do with the kula.

The kula is a form of ceremonial trade, intertribal in scope, occurring in a wide range of islands. Within this ring two classes of valued objects are exchanged, red shell necklaces and white shell armbands. The necklaces travel in a clockwise direction along the ring, while the armbands move in a counterclockwise direction.

Those who engage in this trade are men, particularly those of higher status, who have learned the magic and etiquette connected with these transactions and who have been able to obtain one or more of the valued objects to trade with. A young man may learn the requisite magic and etiquette from either his father or his mother's brother, one of whom may also give him the trading item he needs to get started. He must then acquire some trading partners, perhaps from among those with whom his father previously exchanged. Chiefs may have hundreds of such partners; commoners, only a few. A partnership is a lifelong relationship, often binding together men of different tribes and different languages.

When a man receives a necklace or armband, he does not keep it long. Like the few possessions of the Bushmen, the armbands and necklaces keep passing from hand to hand, but in this case they pass along regular routes. Most of the armbands are too small to be worn, even by young children; those that can be put on are worn only at important ceremonial dances. The necklaces are also seldom worn, being considered too valuable for everyday use. While such objects are in a man's possession, they are much discussed; some of them are well known and have long histories, like famous diamonds in the Western world. But a man must soon relinquish this prize to a trading partner in the appropriate direction in the circle. Since the geographical expanse covered by this circle is wide, covering hundreds of miles, it may take from two to ten years for an armband or necklace to return to its starting point.

There is no haggling or discussion of price in kula transactions. The partners count on reciprocity, sooner or later. In addition to this ceremonial exchange of precious objects, there is also trade in other goods. When visiting a distant island, the Trobrianders have an opportunity to exchange some of their own special produce for goods that may not be available at home, including coconuts, sago, fish, baskets, mats, clubs, and stones. In this trade, bargaining does take place.

The kula ring illustrates the role of reciprocity in some primitive exchanges. It also shows that economic transactions may be tied up with all sorts of magical and ceremonial activities in a primitive society. Although the kula cycle may seem unusual from our point of view, it is not unique. Exchanges of valued goods following particular routes, similar to the kula, have also been reported for some of the tribes of Australia.

In a discussion of reciprocity, Alvin W. Gouldner has drawn attention to the long lapse of time that occurs before repayment is received in the kula ring and suggests: "This is a time . . . when men are morally constrained to manifest their gratitude toward, or at least to maintain peace with, their benefactors" (Gouldner 1960:174). The state of indebtedness contributes to social stability and integration. Indeed, in some such societies a rough equivalence of payments is preferred to an exact return, which may seem to mark an end to the relationship; a more delayed repayment is often preferred to a prompt one (Bock 1969:211–13).

The Trobriand economy illustrates another principle besides reciprocity: that of *redistribution,* by which goods are funneled to a central place of storage and then redistributed by some central administrative authority.

Redistribution

A Trobriand man assumes the responsibility of providing his married sister and her family with a regular supply of yams, which are kept in a storehouse at her home. Most Trobriand Islanders are monogamous, but a chief may have as many as 60 wives coming from the different constituent communities of his area. Having so many wives, a chief has a correspondingly large number of brothers-in-law, all bringing him yams. One Trobriand chief was reported by Malinowski to receive from 300 to 350 tons of yams a year. This enables a chief to give tremendous feasts to entertain visitors and to be a paragon of generosity.

This system differs from reciprocity in the enhanced status of the chief through whom goods are distributed. The system allows the chief to appropriate some of the goods for his own purposes. As Gerhard E. Lenski has pointed out, in such societies there is usually no clear distinction between the chief's personal wealth and the people's surplus. The chief is a kind of symbol of his tribe; as its representative he is expected to be generous. While this may inhibit his acquisition of private wealth and power to some extent, the chief may be able to accumulate some private stores, particularly when the economy is expanding. The next step might be the creation of a retinue of dependent officials and retainers who will have a vested interest in the chief's power and be able to support him. This is how Lenski has accounted for the development of political power in advanced horticultural societies (Lenski 1966:164–68).

A similar argument has been made by Morton H. Fried, who believes that reciprocity is the mode of exchange associated with simple, egalitarian societies of the hunting-gathering level, while redistribution is found in what he calls "rank societies." These are societies that have reached a Neolithic level of food production and have experienced a growth of population and physical expansion beyond that of the hunting-gathering band. Redistribution may also be found in some favorably situated hunting-gathering societies such as those of the Northwest Coast of North America (Fried 1967: 109–18).

Redistribution need not always work to promote chiefly power. In some Oceanic societies, according to Berndt Lambert (1966), redistribution may have more ritual than economic importance, serving to confirm a chief's authority rather than to establish an economic basis for it.

Polanyi (1957a:51) believes that the principle of redistribution was an important aspect of the large-scale economies of ancient times, including the Babylonian kingdom of Hammurabi and the New Kingdom of Egypt. Modern systems of taxation and the provision of government services may be seen as a form of redistribution.

The Kwakiutl potlatch

The Kwakiutl potlatch was a lavish, carefully staged feast in which much property was given away and sometimes destroyed. The potlatch is another old standby of anthropology texts. It was described at length in an early classic of ethnology, Franz Boas' *The Social Organization and the Secret Societies of the Kwakiutl Indians*, published in 1897. Hundreds of thousands of readers have learned about the potlatch from Ruth Benedict's dramatic account in *Patterns of Culture* (1934).

The Indians who occupied the coastal regions of British Columbia in aboriginal times depended on hunting, fishing, and gathering but were sufficiently well off to live in villages with large, plank-walled, gable-roofed houses. Many other tribes inhabited this area, including the Nootka, Bella Bella, Tsimshian, Haida, and Tlingit, but we will focus on one group, the Kwakiutl.

The Kwakiutl got much of their food from the streams and the sea: salmon, cod, herring, candlefish, halibut, flounder, and many other fishes, and such sea mammals as seals, porpoises, and occasional stranded whales. They also collected many kinds of berries and roots and hunted inland game. Some of their food was stored and preserved for winter, when conditions were less favorable.

In the late 18th century, the coming of whites and the fur trade enriched Northwest Coast culture. When iron knives and other cutting tools were introduced, the Indians produced the splendid totem poles that are the hallmark of their culture. The idea of the totem pole was already present in that culture, but the improved knives greatly facilitated carpentry and wood carving, manifest also in finely made cedar boxes, masks, and other forms of woodwork. Another introduction of the fur trade was the Hudson Bay blanket, which became a form of currency, frequently changing hands, being borrowed and lent at high rates of interest. In Boas' day a cheap, white, woolen blanket was worth 50 cents. Highly valued objects were hammered and decorated sheets of copper, worth hundreds of blankets. Blankets, coppers, and canoes figured prominently in the gift distributions at a potlatch.

Two Kwakiutl women.

Potlatches were held on occasions marking changes of status: a girl's first menstruation, a wedding, a funeral, and various other occasions. A chief would give a potlatch to establish his heir. A potlatch could be given by one tribe to other tribes. The other basic potlatching unit was the *numaym*, a named landholding group, headed by a chief, whose members were related to the chief, usually by patrilineal descent (see p. 113), but sometimes through their mothers or wives.

A potlatch was a channel for redistribution. The male members of a *numaym* gave some of the game and fish they caught to their chief, while the women gave his wife some of their roots and berries. By accumulating such goods the chief was able to prepare for a feast and to pay for the building of canoes, a new house, or the carving of totem poles. He might also borrow blankets in order to have a big supply to give away.

The best potlatcher would be the man who gave away so many

gifts to his guests that they would never be able to repay him. In this way he demonstrated his wealth and splendor. These giveaways were sometimes accompanied by boastful speeches by the host extolling his own greatness and deriding the poverty and inferiority of his guests. There was also destruction of property, the smashing and burning of canoes, and the pouring of buckets of candlefish oil into the flames. The climax might be the breaking of a copper, the pieces being thrown into the fire or into the sea. These extravagant features may have been late developments in the potlatch.

The potlatch served many functions: it announced and validated changes in rank and status, emphasized the solidarity of the *numaym* or tribe, and brought about much redistribution of goods, while providing a lot of drama and excitement in the process.

Leveling mechanisms

The destruction of property, as in the potlatch, may serve as a leveling mechanism, which prevents too much wealth from being amassed by individuals or special groups. The Apa Tani of the Subansiri Valley in northeastern India have a somewhat similar institution called *lisudu*. If a wealthy Apa Tani thinks he has been insulted and wants to humiliate his enemy, he kills one or more *mithan* cows in front of his rival's house. He may also destroy some valuables, such as Tibetan bells, bronze plates, and swords. "If his opponent accepts the challenge he must slaughter at least the same number of mithan and destroy property of equal value in front of the challenger's house. The next move is that the latter kills an even greater number of mithan . . ." (Von Fürer-Haimendorf 1962:111). And so on. This rivalry may lead to the near ruin of both men. Von Fürer-Haimendorf describes a *lisudu* in which the final round resulted in each competitor doing away with 60 *mithan*. In such cases, the rivals borrow cattle from both paternal and maternal relatives. The meat is not wasted since it is eaten by the villagers, who thus profit from this contest of the rich.

The giveaway of horses and other goods on the Great Plains was another, less destructive kind of leveling mechanism. In Mexican villages well-to-do peasants may be required to subsidize fiestas and displays of fireworks, which burn up money while providing pleasure for all. Warfare may also serve, sometimes literally, as a leveling mechanism.

Markets

Many agricultural societies have been able to get along with little or no reliance on money or markets. If the typical family is largely self-sufficient, growing its own grain, raising livestock, spinning its own thread, and making its own clothing, it may not have to depend much on trade and can resort to barter for needed items. Early New England colonial families provide an illustration of such a state of affairs. Even in a society that has long had money and markets, rural people may be able to get along without handling much currency. An example will be given later, in Chapter 12, when we discuss the *jajmani* system by which goods and services are exchanged in rural villages in India, with little use of money involved. But with growing specialization and division of labor, a barter system is apt to become unwieldy. This may explain why market systems using a common medium of exchange have appeared in different parts of the world.

The term *market* is used in two senses: first, as a *place* where buyers and sellers meet to complete transactions and, second, as a *state of affairs,* as when we speak of there being a good market for men's shorts. Market systems have not developed in all horticultural and agricultural societies; they were not found, for example, in Polynesia, but they do have a wide distribution among peasant societies.

Market systems are greatly facilitated by the use of a common medium of exchange, whether it be shell money, as in parts of Micronesia, cacao beans among the Aztecs, or the coinage of advanced Old World civilizations.

Mexican market scene, 1937.

It seems likely that, as a system of exchange, reciprocity preceded redistribution, while the latter antedated the development of market systems. But market systems are fairly old, nevertheless. One of the first known city markets was the *agora* of Athens of the 5th century B.C., which was associated with a coinage system. Markets and coinage may be even earlier in Sardis, the capital of Lydia. The Aztecs and Incas had market systems in the New World.

Market systems vary in the extent to which the market is *open*, that is, the extent to which buyers and sellers are free to enter the market. A market is *free* if the prices are determined by the interactions of buyers and sellers and not by rules and regulations. Manning Nash (1966:30) writes: "At the extreme, when a market is open, competitive, and free it justifies the designation of self-regulating, for the process of price formation will in fact regulate supply and demand and a single price will prevail in that arena of interaction."

Nash further states that in Mesoamerica the market system tends to be open, competitive, and free and thus is largely self-regulating. This is also true of Haiti, although in Haiti special bonds between some buyers and sellers serve as hedges against risk and uncertainty.

In Mexico a market system is encouraged by local specialization. Says Nash (1966:69):

Amatenango del Valle is a pottery-making community where every woman who grows up in the community knows how to make pots, and does. The neighboring community of Aguacatenango does not make a single pot, but keeps pigs as a supplement to its agricultural activities. The Chamulas are active traders and have a roster of handicraft specialties, the Zinacantecos are farmers and sheep herders, and Tenango makes a different sort of pottery than that of Amatenango.

Substantivism versus formalism

Karl Polanyi, whose writings have had much influence in the field of economic anthropology, believed that the modern capitalist price-governed market system differs in kind rather than in degree from primitive exchange systems which utilize such mechanisms as reciprocity and redistribution. A primitive economy is embedded in social relations. In the modern world it is the other way around; social relations are embedded in an economic system that dominates all aspects of modern life. Polanyi believed that, since primitive and modern economic systems are so different, it would be impossible to apply economic theory, which was developed to analyze our own market system, to the understanding of primitive economies. This is the point of view of some workers in the field of economic anthropology who call themselves *substantivists*.

The opposing view, held by the so-called *formalists*, is that economic theory, utilizing such concepts as "maximizing" and "economizing," can be applied to the study of primitive economies. This controversy has been surprisingly heated and drawn out, with highly regarded spokesmen ranged on both sides.

The terms *substantivism* and *formalism* derive from a distinction made by Polanyi between two different meanings of the word *economic:*

The substantive meaning of economic derives from man's dependence for his living upon nature and his fellows. It refers to the interchange with his natural and social environment, in so far as this results in supplying him with the means of material want satisfaction.

The formal meaning of economic derives from the logical character of the means-ends relationship, as apparent in such words as "economical" or "economizing." It refers to a definite situation of choice, namely, that between the different uses of means induced by an insufficiency of those means (Polanyi 1957b:243).

To the uncommitted bystander, the argument appears to be rather unnecessary, especially since no agreement or compromise seems to be in sight. Surely the issue could be settled, one would think, if some formalists simply went ahead and successfully applied economic theory to the data on some primitive society. That is just what some formalists say they have done. R. F. Salisbury's *From Stone to Steel* (1962), a study of the economy of a primitive New Guinea tribe, has been cited by some formalists as an example. But the substantivists remain unimpressed. Their leading spokesman, George Dalton, a disciple of Polanyi's, has commented:

If what anthropologists mean by "applying economic theory" is to count the number of yams produced and the number of labor days needed to build a hut, then most certainly economic theory is applicable to all economies. But this is a rather simplistic notion of what "applying economic theory" means (Dalton 1969:68).

Dalton concedes that economic theory can be applied to peasant economies that have money and market systems but not, he insists, to primitive economies. This debate seems likely to continue. The interested reader will find both sides represented in Dalton's article in *Current Anthropology*, which includes rejoinders by several formalists.

Suggestions for further reading

Two short general works on economic anthropology are recommended: Cyril S. Belshaw, *Traditional Exchange and Modern Markets* (Englewood Cliffs, N.J.: Prentice-Hall, 1965); Manning Nash, *Primitive and Peasant Economic Systems* (San Francisco: Chandler Publishing Co., 1966). There are also two readers: George Dalton, ed., *Tribal and Peasant Economics: Readings in Economic Anthropology* (New York: Natural History Press,

1967); Edward E. LeClair, Jr., and Harold K. Schneider, eds., *Economic Anthropology: Readings in Theory and Analysis* (New York: Holt, Rinehart, & Winston, 1968).

A work that precipitated the controversy between substantivists and formalists is Karl Polanyi, Conrad M. Arensberg, and Harry W. Pearson, eds., *Trade and Market in the Early Empires: Economies in History and Theory* (New York: Free Press, 1957).

For a classic study of reciprocity, see Marcel Mauss, *The Gift: Forms and Functions of Exchange in Archaic Societies* (Glencoe, Ill.: Free Press, 1954).

The classic work on the Kula ring is Bronislaw Malinowski, *Argonauts of the Western Pacific: An Account of Native Enterprise and Adventure in the Archipelagoes of Melanesian New Guinea* (London: George Routledge and Sons, 1922). The reader might also consult a more recent analysis of kula trade made from a different perspective: J. P. Singh Uberoi, *Politics of the Kula Ring: An Analysis of the Findings of Bronislaw Malinowski* (Manchester, England: Manchester University Press, 1962).

Some accounts of the Northwest Coast potlatch may be found in Tom McFeat, ed., *Indians of the North Pacific Coast* (Toronto: McClelland & Stewart, 1966).

For a series of essays on economic anthropology, see Marshall Sahlins, *Stone Age Economics* (Chicago: Aldine-Atherton, Inc., 1972).

part four

Family, kinship,
and
marital residence

7

Marriage and family organization

A general feature of the mammalian order of Primates in which human beings are classified is that its members live in social groups. In some cases, particularly among insectivorous nocturnal forest primates, the groups are small, consisting of only a male, female, and offspring, whereas terrestrial primates that occupy forest fringes and savannas often have large troops with several males, females, and young.

Human societies range greatly in size and scale. Some hunting-gathering bands are small, with about 25 people, but there are also huge nations with populations of many millions, held together by vast networks of roads, railways, and air transport. These nations are by no means independent but have commercial and political ties with other states.

Every human society, whatever its size, has some kind of social structure or organization. The social relations within a human group are much more complex than in the groups of nonhuman primates, since humans have a language that adds new dimensions to their communication with one another. Thus we have terms like "mother," "father," "brother," and "sister," "uncle," "aunt," and "cousin" to designate kin, and in many societies there are also terms corresponding to "chief" and "boss" which reflect political authority. Associated with such terms are concepts of status and role.

A *status* is a person's position in relation to others. An individual occupies many statuses. In our society a man may be a son to his parents, a brother to his sister, a husband to his wife, a father to his children, a foreman in relation to factory workers, a subordinate to higher officials, and maybe also the head of a glee club. A person's

89

overall social status is derived from his composite statuses, giving some general idea of the position he occupies in his society. Status may be ascribed or achieved. An *ascribed status* is one assigned to an individual because of some biological characteristic such as sex or through birth into a particular family. One cannot usually do much about an ascribed status. An *achieved status*, however, is brought about through effort and competition. A *role* is the behavior associated with a status, through which it is maintained.

When analyzing a particular society, an anthropologist or sociologist looks for the social units that comprise it. Very often such units are families. A *family* is a social group whose members usually live together and engage in economic cooperation; it normally includes two or more adults of both sexes responsible for rearing and educating the children who have been born to the female or females of the group or who have been adopted. This chapter deals with the functions of the family and with different types of family and marriage arrangements found in different societies.

Functions of the family

A family is a sexual unit in the sense that husband and wife may have sexual relations that cannot be regarded as illegal or cannot be socially disapproved. But in many societies both premarital and extramarital sexual liaisons are permitted; sexual behavior is not meant to be confined to the family, as in the United States. This shows that satisfaction of the sex drive is not the only reason for establishment and maintenance of a family.

We do not usually think of a family as being engaged in economic cooperation, but families do have economic functions, which are of particular importance in societies where the main division of labor is that between the sexes. In hunting-gathering societies, men do the hunting, while women do most of the collecting, which usually provides most of the caloric intake. Women also prepare meals, make clothing, keep the fire burning, and look after the children, among other things. Such economic partnership, ultimately based on physiological differences between the sexes, continues to be important at more advanced cultural levels, persisting even in our own society, where the division of labor has become so complex.

Marriage also conveys status. Lévi-Strauss (1960:269) speaks of the "true feeling of repulsion which most societies have toward bachelorhood." In most societies a bachelor is felt to be an incomplete person. A similar, though milder, attitude is directed toward childless couples. Marriage and the birth of children are everywhere occasions for congratulations and festivity. A groom or a new father has, in a sense, "arrived."

The family may provide basic security and emotional satisfaction for its members, although it does not always do so. It is within the family that children are socialized and receive at least their earliest education.

The various functions of the family — sexual, reproductive, economic, status enhancing, emotional, and educational — may, of course, all be fulfilled outside the family unit, and sometimes more successfully than within it. It has already been noted that many societies permit premarital and extramarital affairs. Illegitimate children and orphans are often brought up in institutions. Friendships and other emotionally rewarding social ties are formed outside of the family. There are many other sources of status and prestige than being a spouse or parent. Certainly most of the economic cooperation in our society takes place outside the family unit, and children receive most of their education at school. Nevertheless, we still have families.

It is evident that families are quite successful social institutions, despite the fact that they often generate much tension, frustration, and hostility. One reason for the persistence and virtual universality of family groups is that children need the close care, attention, and companionship of adults. Families generally provide for these needs more successfully than larger, more impersonal institutions do. Not only is the adult-to-child ratio usually more satisfactory in the family, allowing for better care, but the parents of a child are more likely to feel some personal involvement with it than a hired nurse is apt to do. Of course, some institutions may be well staffed and well run, while some families may contain neurotic or psychotic parents. For these reasons young children may sometimes be better off in an orphanage than in a home, but, by and large, it seems that they are not. In fact, infants raised in institutions often show apathy and retardation and have a high death rate when adequate mother surrogates are not available.

In view of their virtual universality and the relative success with which family units manage to fulfill their functions, it seems likely that families will continue to exist in the future, although their disappearance has sometimes been predicted by social prophets. In the section on the *kibbutz* at the end of this chapter, we shall consider one alternative to the family unit.

The simplest complete family unit, and a very widespread form, is the nuclear family consisting of husband, wife, and children. Yet there is an even simpler unit, that of mother and child, which is also very common. It is often regarded as a manifestation of breakdown or social disorganization, but in several Latin American countries such units represent one fourth or more of all the households (R. N. Adams 1960).

Exogamy and the incest taboo

In social science parlance it is customary to distinguish between a person's *family of orientation,* into which he has been born, and *the family of procreation,* established when he gets married. Normally one cannot marry into one's family of orientation. A marriage thus brings together people from two different families. In all societies there are rules of exogamy affecting marriage. *Exogamy* is a general term for the requirement to marry outside of a particular group. (For the opposite principle of *endogamy,* see p. 169.) There are different forms of exogamy. In northern India one must marry outside of one's village and sometimes outside of a complex of about 20 villages. One could call this "village exogamy." Unilineal kinship groups such as clans, which will be discussed in the next chapter, are generally exogamous. In this case, we speak of "clan exogamy." We have no clans in the United States. Our exogamous units are small in comparison with those of most societies. A man in our society must at least marry outside of his family of orientation; many would also taboo marriage with a first cousin and various other relatives, such as uncle or aunt. Not only is it forbidden to marry within it but it is also considered very wrong to have sexual relations with a member of one's family of orientation. Incest taboos are present in all societies, particularly with respect to mother-son, father-daughter, and brother-sister relations.

Incest taboos and rules of exogamy are not the same thing. The former concerns sex relations; the latter has to do with marriage. Of course, one cannot marry a person with whom one cannot have sexual relations, but the two concepts should be kept distinct. Understandably, most societies disapprove of sexual relations between persons who are forbidden to marry, although there are some exceptions; in some African tribes a man may have intercourse with women of a lineage into which he may not marry.

The inbreeding theory of incest taboos

Anthropologists have wondered why incest taboos are so important and have offered various explanations to account for their origin. Two theories, which were suggested long ago, are usually rejected as inadequate but have recently found some partial support. One of these is the notion that primitive men somehow discovered that inbreeding has deleterious biological effects. A common response to this suggestion has been that close inbreeding is not necessarily damaging unless there are harmful recessive traits in the genotypes of the persons involved. Cleopatra came of a long line of brother-sister marriages. Brother-sister marriage was also practiced by ruling families in Hawaii and by the Inca of Peru without noticeable harmful effects. (Such marriages were generally forbidden to the rest of the population in these societies, although brother-sister marriages seem to have been allowed in Egypt during the period of Roman rule.) In some cases, inbreeding may be positively advantageous, which is why it is deliberately brought about by animal breeders. Thus, it has been argued, favorable cases should offset negative ones.

Until recently this seemed to be a good criticism of the inbreeding theory, but studies in population genetics have shown it to be invalid, for the ratio of deleterious and lethal recessive genes to selectively advantageous genes turns out to be high. Close inbreeding over many generations is possible in lower mammals, such as rats, but not in more advanced, slow-maturing mammals that produce only one or two offspring at a time, with widely spaced births. Thus, close inbreeding in humans would have biological disadvantages after all, particularly in the mating of primary relatives (Aberle et al. 1963; Parker 1976:287).

While this strengthens the case for the inbreeding argument, it seems unlikely that primitive humans could have figured it out, particularly since some nonliterate peoples such as the Arunta of Australia and the Trobriand Islanders of Melanesia do not fully understand the connection between sexual intercourse and pregnancy and have quite different explanations for conception. If we adhere to the inbreeding explanation for the incest taboos, we have to resort to an argument in terms of natural selection: those societies that developed incest taboos were more likely to survive than those that did not.

The childhood association theory

The other usually rejected theory explains the development of incest taboos on the grounds that people who have been brought up together from childhood, like brother and sister, are not apt to feel erotic attraction toward one another. The theory seems to be disqualified by the fact that cases of brother-sister incest do come to the attention of social workers. One may also cite the brother-sister marriages in the ruling families of Egypt, Hawaii, and Peru.

There may be some basis for the argument, nevertheless. Arthur P. Wolf has described a form of marriage among Chinese in northern Taiwan in which a girl is adopted by a boy's parents at often less than a year and seldom more than three years of age. They grow up together like brother and sister but marry when the girl becomes old enough. In the same community the more traditional form of arranged Chinese marriage is also found, in which the bride and groom are often strangers when they meet on the wedding day. Wolf presents evidence that the former type of marriage works out much less successfully than the latter and that much distaste is expressed for it. He also cites the Israeli *kibbutz*, to be discussed later, in which children who have been raised together from infancy claim to feel no erotic attraction for one another. Love affairs within such a group are very rare (A. P. Wolf 1966).

One difficulty in applying such findings to the problem of the origin of incest taboos is that, if lack of erotic feeling resulted from siblings growing up together, there would seem to be no reason for any society to have brother-sister incest taboos since there would be no need to proscribe behavior that was unlikely to occur.

Freud's theory

Sigmund Freud made the opposite assumption, that strong erotic impulses are experienced within the family circle, primarily by a boy toward his mother. This is the basis for the *Oedipus complex* postulated by Freud: an erotic attachment to the mother accompanied by feelings of hostility toward the father. (In the case of a girl, the attachment is to the father.) These feelings and impulses have to be renounced or repressed but may continue to exist in the individual's unconscious. The horror generally shown at the idea of incest is interpreted, in this view, as an unconscious defense against temptation. Incest taboos, then, are regarded as reactions to the existence of incestuous desires. One advantage of this theory, in contrast to the one previously discussed, is that it does offer an explanation for the taboos.

A weakness of the theory is that among nonhuman primates that have been closely observed over long periods, mother-son sexual relations do not seem to take place, although there may be frequent grooming behavior between mother and son (Parker 1976:290).

Life-span considerations

Mariam Slater has made calculations of the possibilities of incestuous relations in family groups living under primitive conditions. The life-span is generally short in hunting-gathering societies. If the life-span is from 25 to 35 years and if puberty starts from 13 to 16, there is not much likelihood of a boy having sexual relations with his mother. If a woman has five children and lives to be 35, only an oldest male child who lives to maturity could become the father of one of her children—the last one. By the time most of the children are old enough to mate, their parents are dead; so they have to seek mates outside the family if they are going to mate at all. According to Slater, these patterns of mating-out existed before (and became the basis of) the development of incest taboos (Slater 1959). This seems convincing, although some of the assumptions about the life-span and length of breeding periods of early humans may be incorrect. The analysis shows why early human beings had to find mates outside the family unit, but it does not exactly explain why incest taboos were subsequently formulated.

Functional interpretations

There are some interpretations which do not suggest any mechanism whereby incest taboos were brought about in the first place but which do try to show that incest taboos had to be established if human society was to endure. If there were no incest taboos, it has been argued, there would be such disruptive sexual rivalry and tension within the family that it could no longer function as a family unit. This view has been countered by the argument that the sharing of sexual partners does not necessarily lead to conflict. Later in this chapter, some forms of polygamous marriage will be discussed in which there does not usually seem to be marked rivalry or tension, although sexual partners are shared. However, none of these marriage forms involve families in which both father and son have sexual access to the son's own mother or sister.

Another functional argument is that incest taboos are required to maintain roles in the family appropriate to the socialization process (Coult 1963). Still another interpretation is that incestuous family units would become isolated and culturally stagnant, while marriage into other social groups provides social contacts, allies, and channels for cultural diffusion. Groups developing such extrafamilial bonds would thus be more apt to survive than those without them. This explanation really has to do with exogamy, rather than with incest. Robin Fox has commented on this point:

In some societies fathers are allowed sexual intercourse with their daughters, and the daughters subsequently marry other men without, seemingly, any problems arising. . . . If, then, it is possible to have incestuous relationships and still marry out, the advantages of marrying out do not explain the prohibition on sex (Fox 1967:57; Fox does not specify which societies allow father-daughter incest).

Forms of marriage

In different societies, families vary greatly in size and composition. There are monogamous families and polygamous ones, small conjugal units and large consanguine family households. One way of classifying forms of family is in terms of the numbers of spouses involved. There are four general possibilities: (1) *monogamy,* a form of marriage involving one man and one woman; (2) *polygyny,* a form of marriage involving one man and more than one woman; (3) *polyandry,* a form of marriage involving one woman and more than one man; and (4) *group marriage,* involving more than one man and more than one woman. It must be emphasized that these are all socially recognized forms of marriage in the societies where they occur, in contrast to adulterous, bigamous, or temporary "illicit" relationships. The term *polygamy,* a general term for marriage with plural spouses, is more widely known than *polygyny* and *polyandry,* but the latter are more specific in meaning.

	Males	*Females*
Monogamy	1	1
Polygyny	1	X
Polyandry	X	1
Group marriage	X	X

Note: X stands for more than one.

Monogamy and polygyny are the two most common forms of marriage, both having had a wide distribution among the societies of the world. Even in polygynous societies most marriages must be monogamous, for there are not enough women to go around. Since the sex ratio tends to be about even, it would not be possible for every man to have two or three wives; so, in polygynous societies, it is usually the wealthier or more powerful men of high status who can afford additional wives, while the common man must be satisfied with one.

Monogamy

Monogamy is the form of marriage with which the reader will be most familiar, since it is the form characteristic of the Western world. However, in Murdock's "World Ethnographic Sample" only about 24 percent of the 565 societies listed were described as monogamous (Murdock 1957:686). This form, which seems so natural to us, is thus relatively rare if one considers societies as wholes. Monogamy is found not only in advanced civilized societies but also occurs as the preferred form in such hunting-gathering groups as the Semang, the Veddas, and the Andamanese. Agricultural southwestern Pueblo Indians such as the Hopi have monogamous families, as did the aboriginal Iroquois of New York. This form of marriage, therefore, occurs at different levels of socioeconomic development. Since the sex ratio is about the same in most human groups, monogamy is an understandable development, particularly in rather egalitarian societies.

Murdock has suggested that "Where the productive accomplishment of the two sexes is approximately equal, and a small unit is as efficient as a larger one, monogamy may be economically advantageous" (Murdock 1949:36). This hypothesis seems reasonable, although it cannot always be easy to judge how nearly equal the productive accomplishments of the two sexes may be in particular societies, or in which cases small units are as efficient as larger ones, particularly when there are seasonal variations involving different kinds of activities in the course of a year.

Polygyny (meaning "many women" in Greek) involves a recognized marriage between a man and two or more women. It would not be considered polygyny if a man has a secret mistress or a concubine not recognized as a spouse, or if, in our society, a man is guilty of bigamy, supporting two separate wives who are not known to one another. Polygyny has been a favored form of marriage in most parts of the world: in Africa, the Near East, formerly in India and China, Melanesia, Polynesia, and among various aboriginal tribes of North and South America. **Polygyny**

We have seen that monogamy is characteristic of many egalitarian hunting-gathering societies. While polygyny may also be found in such societies, as among the Eskimos, Ojibwa, and Sirionó, it seems to be generally related to a more advanced, productive type of economy. Remi Clignet has suggested that in Africa general polygyny tends to prevail in societies with a subsistence basis depending on roots, tubers, and aboriculture, which encourages the maintenance of large households. He concludes: "Rare among societies characterized by a lack of social stratification or, alternatively, by a large number of social levels, plural marriage is most frequent among societies divided into age grades or in which a hereditary aristocracy is separated from the bulk of the population . . ." (Clignet 1970:21). Clignet claims that polygynous societies are characterized by a division of labor in which women carry out much of the agricultural production. The economic advantages of plural wives will be discussed further later.

In view of the roughly equal sex ratio in most societies, how are enough females made available so that most of the less-fortunate males in a polygynous society are able to have at least one wife?

This may be explained by the fact that girls tend to be married when they are quite young, while the men marry at a later age. Younger husbands may be monogamous, older ones polygynous. In a survey of a Gusii community in Kenya, Robert and Barbara LeVine found that the number of monogamous and polygynous adults was about the same. However, more than two thirds of the community's children had polygynous parents, since many monogamous men were young husbands whose wives had not yet given birth or had done so only once. As these young men get older and have more children, they take on additional wives (LeVine and LeVine 1963:39).

Tax registers for the Nyakyusá of Tanzania (then Tanganyika) in the 1930s showed that in parts of the district, in a population of 3,000 men of 18 years of age or older, 34 percent were bachelors, 37 percent monogamists, and 29 percent polygynists. It was the young men who proved to be bachelors and monogamists, while men over 45 were polygynists. There was a difference of 10 years or more in the average marriage age of women and men (Wilson 1950:112).

Polygynous family relationships

It is very common for the first wife to have the highest status in a polygynous household. Linton says that secondary wives are drawn from women who are not attractive enough to be chosen as first wives and from widows and divorcees (Linton 1936:185). However, secondary wives tend to be younger than the first one and are often preferred by the husband. Wife Number One at least has the compensation of her higher status.

Different strategies are possible in the organization of a multi-wife menage. A man may either live in one household with all of his wives together, or else he may set up separate households, one for each wife. The Sirionó who live in the forests of eastern Bolivia follow the first system. Each wife occupies a separate hammock in a communal dwelling, placed with reference to the husband's hammock in order of status; so that Wife Number One has her hammock to the husband's right; Wife Number Two, to his left; Wife Number Three, at his head; and Wife Number Four, at his feet. In a more advanced kind of dwelling, a Yoruba male in Nigeria may have three or four wives living in a house containing about a dozen rooms.

On the other hand, in many African tribes a man sets up a separate household for each wife, sometimes located within a walled compound. Each wife has her own collection of pots and cooking vessels and brings up her own children. She may have her own field, separate from those of her co-wives, and a granary of her own. In such circumstances a dutiful husband follows a rotation system, perhaps spending Monday nights with one wife, Tuesday nights with another, Wednesday nights with a third, and so on. The Fon of Bafut in Cameroon, West Africa, had too many wives to follow such a system. In his case the Fon's two top-ranking wives made out a schedule for him, allotting different wives for different nights. It was not up to the Fon but up to these social secretaries to handle the arrangements (Ritzenthaler 1966:171). Some such rotation system reduces friction and disputes among the wives. But it is not simply a matter of tact on the part of the husband; the rights of the wives are often supported by local law. In Madagascar, if the husband spends one wife's day with another wife, it constitutes adultery under native law. The injured wife may demand a divorce with alimony amounting to one third of the husband's property (Linton 1936:186).

The women in a polygynous household are not necessarily browbeaten creatures, although they sometimes are. They often seem to be self-confident and self-assertive. There is frequently strong rivalry and jealousy among co-wives, but this is not invariable, for

A polygynous family. A Bakhtiari man with three wives.

they may share a cooperative relationship. From the point of view of the women involved, there are various advantages in having co-wives. Many hands make light work. The co-wives may form an efficient working team. As a collective union they may face their husband with a set of joint demands. In the Western world a man can be henpecked by only one wife; in Africa, by five or more. As Elenore Smith Bowen (1964:128) wrote, concerning a West African family:

> ... what man can stand up against five united women? If Ava's husband raised his voice to any one of his wives, all of them refused to cook for him. If he bought one of them a cloth, he had to buy four other identical cloths. Discipline of the wives was in Ava's hands, and stayed there. When the poor man got drunk one day and struck one wife for nagging—well, until he had given many and expensive presents to all his wives, the five of them slept barricaded in one hut.[1]

Sexual rivalry is not an inevitable problem. Indeed, in *Six Chapters from a Floating Life*, the autobiography of a Chinese gentleman of the early 19th century, the author writes about how his wife kept badgering him to add an attractive young concubine to their household. He attributed his wife's premature death to disappointment in her failure to bring this about. This is not to deny that sexual rivalry and jealousy may flourish under polygyny. There is ample evidence in ethnographic accounts that they do. But the women also have the compensations mentioned—companionship, extra help with routine chores, and also the prestige that comes from being part of a polygynous household, since it is usually the wealthier or more powerful men in a community who can support two or more wives.

From the man's point of view there are sexual advantages, not only in the sense of variety but also in the fact that sexual intercourse is often tabooed during pregnancy, for a year or two after childbirth, or during menstrual periods. If Wife Number One is thus disqualified, the husband can turn to Wife Number Two or Three. The husband in a monogamous family in the Western world has no legal alternatives in such cases.

Polygyny makes possible the production of many children, and both children and wives are sources of prestige. In some cases, extra wives provide clear economic advantages as well. Mention was made in Chapter 6 of the Trobriand chief who might have 60 wives drawn from different villages. Since it was customary for brothers to provide their sisters with yams and other garden produce, the chief was continually supplied with a food surplus by his brothers-

---

[1] This is from a novel, but it seems to be closely based on realities; the author is an anthropologist.

in-law, and he was able to give lavish feasts. Another Melanesian tribe, the Siwai, have feasts involving pigs. Pigs are a source of prestige in this society—the more pigs you have, the higher your reputation. But women are needed to raise pigs, so the more wives you have, the more pigs you can raise, and the larger your gardens will be. A great increase in polygyny took place among the Blackfoot Indians of the Western Plains when the fur traders began to buy tanned hides. Since women did the tanning, they were in great demand. The more wives a man had, the more hides he could sell, and the richer he became. In some societies, therefore, there have been definite economic advantages in polygyny for the men, as well as the advantages of prestige and sexual satisfaction.

How do children fare under a polygynous system? There are differences in patterns of child rearing in different polygynous societies, so it is difficult to make generalizations; but in many such societies there may be strong emotional ties between mother and child, with much weaker ties between a child and its father, whose attentions are naturally divided among several wives and all of their offspring. In many polygynous societies there is a taboo on sexual relations between husband and wife for a year or two after childbirth. During this time the child sleeps with the mother.

A child has no lack of age-mates in such a society; in addition to his own siblings he may have many half-brothers and half-sisters, children of the father's other wives. In some African societies there may be an element of rivalry in a boy's relations with his half-brothers. They and their mothers are in competition for inheritance from the father; rivalry between the co-wives may foster rivalry between half-brothers. LeVine (1961:61–62) writes that in such a society there are often tense relations between co-wives involving accusations of witchcraft and sorcery:

Children understand these hostile relationships while still young, and boys come to feel their personal stake in the struggle. Usually, good surface relations among half-siblings are maintained so as not to antagonize the family head, but there is likely to be considerable underlying aggression.

One form of polygyny that has had a wide distribution is *sororal polygyny,* a form of marriage in which a man marries two or more women who are sisters. It seems that in such cases there is a greater likelihood for the co-wives to share the same dwelling than in families where the wives are unrelated to one another. Some statistical support for this generalization has been provided by Murdock (1949:31). Among the Crow Indians, the wives lived in one tepee if they were sisters but had separate tepees if they were not.

As we have seen in the foregoing pages, polygyny may have

various advantages both for the man and the women involved in such a union. Nevertheless, despite these benefits and the wide distribution of polygyny, this system of marriage seems to be on its way out in many parts of the world. The most influential industrialized nations of Europe, the United States, the USSR, the People's Republic of China, and Japan all require monogamous marriage. In societies now becoming more industrialized and influenced by Western culture, there are often feminist movements on behalf of monogamy. It is true that the Islamic religion supports polygyny, but it limits the permissible number of wives to four, and most Muslims can afford only one. In 1937, when Egypt was more traditional than today, only 0.02 percent of Egyptian marriages involved four wives, while 96.86 percent of the marriages were monogamous (Ammar 1966:201).

Polyandry

Polyandry (from a Greek term meaning "many men") is a form of marriage in which one woman lives with two or more husbands. It is generally said to be a rare form of marriage, but Prince Peter of Greece and Denmark (1963) has listed a fairly sizable number of societies that practice it, including some tribes in the former Belgian Congo and northern Nigeria, the Paviotso Indians of North America, the Marquesans, the Kandyans of Ceylon, the Da-La of Indochina, and various peoples in India, Tibet, Kashmir, and Sikkim. Just as there are many monogamous families in societies that favor polygyny, so monogamy is also apt to be found in societies having polyandry. In Tibet and in the adjoining areas influenced by Tibetan culture, which make up the largest single continuous area where polyandry has flourished in recent times, cases of group marriage and polygyny may also be found.

Two types of polyandry may be distinguished: fraternal and nonfraternal. *Fraternal polyandry* is a marriage relationship in which a woman has two or more husbands who are brothers, the converse of sororal polygyny. In the second type of polyandry, the husbands are not related. Tibetans who practice fraternal polyandry sometimes explain it in terms of land inheritance. If two or more brothers share their land and share a wife there is no need for division of property and land fragmentation, such as has plagued India, where holdings become progressively smaller whenever sons divide land inherited from their father. In western Tibet, where fraternal polyandry is common, there has been an impressive stability in the number and size of landholdings over many generations (Carrasco 1959:30). We cannot say that this explains why fraternal polyandry developed in Tibet, but one function of the system has been to preserve landholdings intact from one generation to the next.

We do not find, in the case of polyandry, a situation quite comparable to the African compound where each wife has a home of her own and the husband visits each in turn. In polyandrous households the wife and her husbands generally share the same menage. But, in the homes of some wealthy Tibetan aristocrats, each husband has his own bedroom, and the wife sooner or later visits each room, following decisions made by the men (Peter 1963:449).

In Jaunsar-Bawar in the state of Uttar Pradesh in northern India, the oldest brother in a fraternal polyandrous household has a definite priority over the others. It is he who goes through the marriage ceremony; his brothers then automatically become co-husbands. But, whenever the oldest brother is in the house, the younger ones may not have intercourse with the wife (Saksena 1962:20).

In Jaunsar-Bawar all the brothers of a polyandrous household are called "Father" by their children; they are not distinguished by separate kinship terms, despite the priority of the oldest brother. Among the Todas of the Nilgiri Hills in southern India, a child has a socially designated father. Social anthropologists use the term *pater* to designate a socially recognized father as distinguished from the *genitor,* or biological father. In our society the genitor and pater are expected to be the same person, except in the case of stepfathers. The Todas are not concerned with identifying the genitor of a child— something that would be hard to determine, in any case, in a polyandrous household. In the seventh month of pregnancy, a Toda woman goes through a ceremony with a man that makes him the *pater* of her forthcoming child and also of her succeeding children until such time as she decides to go through the ritual with another man, who then becomes the pater of those who follow.

Group marriages

Group marriages occur only rarely; they sometimes develop from polyandrous households in Tibet, among the Todas, the Marquesans, and the Kandyans of Ceylon. To illustrate one way in which this might occur, let us say that the wife of three brothers from western Tibet fails to give birth to a child. If they suspect she is barren, they may add another wife to the household. The two wives are not divided among the brothers but are the common wives of all.

If a man and his brothers have in common three living wives and yet no child they may not marry another wife but may call in to their family circle another man as an additional husband. If he too begets no child still another man may be called in. If he too is childless the original husband and wife must resort to adoption (Carrasco 1959:36).

Group marriages may also develop if one of the husbands in a polyandrous family takes a fancy to a girl and asks his brothers to

A "polygynandrous" family, Jaunsar-Bawar.

bring her into the family circle. It is possible that special alliances and preferences form in such a setting, but they must not become too marked if the group marriage is to remain intact. Group marriage occurred among the Todas during the period of British rule in India. In former times the Todas practiced female infanticide, which kept down the female population and thus helped to perpetuate polyandry. The British took strong measures to discourage infanticide. When the Todas gave it up, the number of women increased, which is said to have led to a rise in group marriages.

Both polyandry and group marriage occurred among the Marquesans in past times. Polyandry was not of the fraternal type. Ralph Linton wrote:

A chief or head of a rich family would sometimes arrange a marriage with a young woman because she had three or four lovers whom he wished to attach. The men would follow the woman; in this way the family head could build up the manpower of his household (Kardiner and Linton 1939:152).

Secondary husbands lived in a separate house and were called over by the wife or the chief when it was felt to be their turn. A wealthy chief might add a second wife and the secondary husbands attached to the latter. The various husbands were said to have had equal sexual rights to the women. Thus a polyandrous union was turned into a group marriage.

The Muria *ghotul*

The Muria are farming people who live in the hills of Orissa in eastern India. In the years before marriage, Muria young people live in coeducational dormitories (*ghotul*) in what resembles group marriage in some ways. One might say that it *is* group marriage, except that the dormitory group is not, except incidentally, a reproductive unit. If a girl becomes pregnant, she must leave the *ghotul* and get married; marriages, preferably a form of cross-cousin marriage (see p. 119), are arranged by parents. Infants are not brought up and cared for by the group, although the younger children who join the *ghotul* are supervised by dormitory officials, who are older members.

Dormitories for unmarried young people are found in many societies. Very often there are separate ones for boys and girls. This is the case among the Bondo, another hill tribe in Orissa. Bondo boys visit and court girls in the girls' dormitories, but they do not have premarital sexual relations. Among the Muria, however, there is a single dormitory for the boys and girls of a particular village. One joins the *ghotul* at about the age of six and leaves it at the time of marriage.

The Muria dormitory is not just a place to spend the night. The *ghotul* group constitutes a work gang. The young people labor in turn in the fields of their parents and other villagers. They may be hired to work for a prosperous farmer. They also perform well-rehearsed dances on ceremonial occasions or for the benefit of visitors to the village. The *ghotul* is considered to be a religious sanctuary dedicated to a god. Quarrels and discord are not supposed to break out within its walls.

Two types of *ghotul* are found among the Muria. In one, which is held to be the older type, a boy who joins the group is given a *ghotul* wife. A kind of mock marriage ceremony is performed in imitation of an adult wedding. From that time on the boy and girl are expected to sleep together. It sometimes happens that a girl prefers to sleep with another boy and deserts her *ghotul* "husband." Such cases are investigated by the dormitory officials, who may either persuade the girl to return to her spouse or else arrange for "divorce" and "remarriage." At any rate, in this type of *ghotul* everyone is assigned a mate. The latter is not the person whom one marries after leaving the *ghotul*.

The second type of *ghotul* is the one that resembles group marriage. In this kind of *ghotul* no mock weddings are celebrated and no spouses are assigned. Instead, every effort is made to break up close attachments between a boy and girl. The dormitory officials choose which boy and girl spend the night together, making sure that they do not sleep together for more than three nights in a row. The reason for this is that the Muria believe that pregnancy occurs only when a couple cohabits over a long period of time. They consider it unlikely that a girl could become pregnant after sleeping with a boy for only three nights. Hence, by changing partners, they imagine that some birth control is being effected. Verrier Elwin, who made a voluminous study of the *ghotul* system, has shown that the Muria are mistaken about that, for as many pregnancies occur in the second type of *ghotul* as in the first (Elwin 1947:344).

Levirate and sororate

There are some kinds of secondary marriage reminiscent of fraternal polyandry and sororal polygyny. The *levirate*, as it is usually defined, is the custom whereby, when a man dies, his widow is expected to marry one of her dead husband's brothers. There is, however, another meaning for the term *levirate*, which Radcliffe-Brown refers to as the "true levirate." This is the custom, followed by the Hebrews of biblical times and by the present-day Nuer and Zulu tribes of Africa, whereby a man is required to cohabit with a dead brother's widow so that she may have children who are counted as children of the deceased. In this system the surviving brother is not considered to be the husband of the woman or the father of her children (Radcliffe-Brown 1950:64).

The sororate is the custom whereby, when a woman dies, her husband is expected to marry one of his dead wife's sisters. Thus, the terms *levirate* and *sororate* are used for secondary marriage with a sibling of a deceased spouse. The question may be raised, What if the deceased spouse has no sibling? The answer is that there may be a general sense of obligation on the part of the lineage or clan of the deceased to provide a substitute—if not an actual sibling, then some other appropriate member of the kinship line. For example, in some African tribes a man is given a wife's brother's daughter as a wife. Such customs show that, in societies where they occur, a marriage is not just a bond between individuals but serves to link two lineages or clans.[2] The relationship is not terminated by the death of a spouse; a substitute is supplied to maintain the linkage.

The levirate and sororate are widespread institutions. Of the 250 societies studied by Murdock in his *Social Structure* (1949:29), 127 were reported to have the levirate and 100 to have the sororate.[3]

---

[2] Lineages and clans are defined and discussed in the next chapter.

[3] The numbers should probably be higher, since relevant data were not available for many societies.

Anticipatory levirate

The phrase "anticipatory levirate" has been applied to situations where an unmarried man may have sexual access to his older brother's wife. Such a man might reason thus: If he is eventually going to inherit his sister-in-law as a wife in the event of his older brother's death, why not exercise some conjugal rights in advance, while the woman is still young? This practice is said to occur among some Jat communities in northern India, where many songs are sung that touch upon the romantic possibilities of the relationship between a woman and her husband's younger brother. Some Comanche and Shoshone tribes had the anticipatory levirate. The institution, of course, borders on fraternal polyandry.

From time to time utopian movements have tried to establish alternative institutions and do away with family units. These attempts have usually not lasted long, but we need not assume that they cannot be made to work. An at least temporarily viable alternative has developed in some of the *kibbutzim* in Israel. Whether or not "the family" exists in such cases is a matter of definition. The kibbutz "family," at any rate, does not fit the definition given in the beginning of this chapter. **The *kibbutz* family**

A *kibbutz* (plural, *kibbutzim*) is a largely self-sustaining, collective, agricultural community in Israel having common ownership of property, collective production, and communal care of children. There are about 300 *kibbutzim* in Israel. Not all of them have the features to be described below, which are characteristic of the more radical type of *kibbutz*, based on Marxist ideology and affiliated with the Mapam, or Socialist United Workers Party.[4]

Premarital sexual relations are not forbidden in this society, although there is a generally austere ideology with an emphasis on hard work and communal responsibility. When a couple decides to live together, they apply to the *kibbutz* authorities for a room. The granting of this request gives social recognition to the union. The room serves as a bedroom and living room, but the couple does not eat there. Meals are provided in a communal dining room, which is also a recreation center and meeting hall.

When a baby is born, it is taken to the Infant's House and taken care of by trained personnel. The mother visits the child periodically for suckling for about nine months, when weaning is completed. As she cuts down on time spent in nursing, she resumes her work, which was interrupted by childbirth.

---

[4] The main sources of information drawn upon here are Spiro 1954, 1956, 1958.

Children in an
Israeli *kibbutz.*
Young people who
have been raised
together from
infancy in an
Israeli *kibbutz*
seldom marry one
another, and love
affairs between
them are said to be
rare.

The child does not live with its parents. After a year in the Infant's House the child is moved to a house for toddlers and later to
other children's houses, according to age level. Nurses and teachers
provide most of the early social interaction and education. The child
is in school during the day, while the parents are working in the
fields or otherwise engaged. But, in the evenings, the child visits
its parents for a two-hour period in their room, and on Saturdays it
may spend the whole day with the parents.

The *kibbutz* "family" is a continuing social unit but one that
lacks some of the usual attributes of a family. There is no economic
cooperation between husband and wife, although both are engaged
in work for the larger social unit, the *kibbutz.* Meals are not eaten
together in their own home. The child does not live with its parents
and is mainly socialized and educated by nurses and teachers. In a
sense the *kibbutz* has itself become a kind of family, fulfilling family
functions on a larger scale. Spiro has made an interesting observation in this connection:

It is a striking and significant fact that those individuals, who were born
and raised in the *kibbutz* tend to practice group exogamy, although there
are no rules that either compel or encourage them to do so. Indeed, in the
kibbutz in which our field work was carried out, all such individuals married outside their own *kibbutz.* When they are asked for an explanation of
this behavior, these individuals reply that they cannot marry those persons
with whom they have been raised and whom they, consequently, view as
siblings.

Whether or not "the family" is a universal institution depends upon how one defines the term. Later we shall consider another type of "family" that is marginal in the sense of not fitting in with the definition given at the outset of this chapter. That is the *"sambandham* union" of the Nayars in southern India (p. 136). It should be noted, however, that both the Israeli *kibbutz* and the Nayar are part-societies, subdivisions of larger societies in which families are the general rule.

A good, brief introductory essay is provided by Claude Lévi-Strauss, "The Family," in *Man, Culture, and Society,* ed. Harry L. Shapiro (New York: Oxford University Press, 1960), pp. 261–85.

Three good books on the family, each having much cross-cultural data are: Ruth Nanda Anshen, ed., *The Family: Its Function and Destiny* (New York: Harper & Bros., 1959); Stuart A. Queen, Robert W. Habenstein, and John B. Adams, eds., *The Family in Various Cultures* (Philadelphia: J. B. Lippincott Co., 1961); William N. Stephens, *The Family in Cross-Cultural Perspective* (New York: Holt, Rinehart & Winston, 1963).

A good analysis of polygynous family systems in Africa is Remi Clignet, *Many Wives, Many Powers: Authority and Power in Polygynous Families* (Evanston, Ill.: Northwestern University Press, 1970).

An insight into the workings of a polygynous household may be obtained from a collection of life histories in Edward H. Winter, *Beyond the Mountains of the Moon: The Lives of Four Africans* (Urbana: The University of Illinois Press, 1959). See also the same author, *Bwamba: A Structural-Functional Analysis of a Patrilineal Society* (Cambridge, England: W. Heffer & Sons, 1956). Also recommended is the novel by anthropologist Elenore Smith Bowen, *Return to Laughter* (New York: Doubleday & Co., 1964). The best general survey of polyandry is that by H. R. H. Prince Peter of Greece and Denmark, *A Study of Polyandry* (The Hague: Mouton & Co., 1963). A classic early ethnographic account of a particular polyandrous society is W. H. R. Rivers, *The Todas* (London: Macmillan & Co., 1906).

Suggestions for further reading

8

Descent and kinship

We are all related to some other persons through descent, marriage, or adoption, and we use kinship terms to designate these relationships. Persons related to us through birth or descent are *consanguine* or "blood" relatives; those related to us through marriage ("in-laws") are *affinal* relatives. Although all societies have terms for different kinds of relatives, like "mother," "father," and "uncle," societies differ in the relationships they distinguish and the ways in which relatives are lumped together or separated. There are some common basic principles, however, that are used to distinguish between different categories of relatives. These principles are set forth below (Kroeber 1909).

Principles of classification

1. *Generation.* Most English kinship terms make use of the criterion of generation. "Father," "mother," "uncle," and "aunt" belong to the parental generation. "Grandfather" and "grandmother" are in the generation before that. "Brother" and "sister" are in Ego's generation. "Son," "daughter," "nephew," and "niece" are of the generation below Ego, the person from whom the relationships are reckoned.

2. *Relative age.* A criterion we do not use in our system but which is employed in some other kinship systems is distinction of age levels within a generation. Different terms are used for one's older and younger siblings or for one's father's or mother's older and younger siblings.

3. *Lineality versus collaterality.* Lineal kin are related in a single line, as grandfather-father-son, while collateral kin are related through a linking relative, such as father's brother or mother's

110

brother. In some kinship systems, known as *merging,* such distinctions are not made. Father's brother may be addressed by the term for father, and father's brother's sons may be equated with siblings and addressed as "brother" in such a system.

4. *Sex of relative.* The English terms for mother, father, brother, sister, uncle, aunt, nephew, and niece all make distinctions in the sex of the relative, but our term "cousin" does not.

5. *Consanguine versus affinal kin.* Kinship based on descent (mother, sister) is contrasted with relationship through marriage (mother-in-law, sister-in-law).

Except for the second criterion of relative age, our system makes use of the above principles. But there are some other widely used principles not employed in our system:

6. *Sex of speaker.* In some societies different kinship terms are used by males and females.

7. *Sex of linking relative.* Distinctions between collateral relatives may be made on the basis of the sex of the connecting relative. This serves to distinguish cross cousins from parallel cousins (see p. 119).

8. *Status or life condition.* Distinctions may be made between relatives on the basis of whether a linking relative is alive or dead, married or single.

Bilateral descent

In our society we have what is called *bilateral descent,* that is, we feel we are equally related to the mother's and father's people, although there is a unilineal principle in the passing-down of the family name through males. Our society is not alone in having bilateral descent, nor is this principle limited to the more advanced civilizations of the world. It is also found among some of the technologically simplest hunting-gathering societies. About 60 percent of the hunting-gathering societies listed in Murdock's "World Ethnographic Sample" have bilateral descent. But bilateral descent also occurs among agricultural societies at different levels of technological advance.

Why should it be that both the most and least technologically advanced societies so often have this kind of descent-reckoning rather than unilineal clans and lineages? The answer seems to be that flexibility and mobility are required in both hunting-gathering societies and modern industrial societies. In both cases it is adaptive for nuclear families to be able to move in search of game resources or new job opportunities without first getting clearance from large family councils.

In the United States we speak about an individual's *kindred,* which consists of relatives on both sides—both maternal and paternal relatives. A kindred group can never be the same for any two persons unless they are brothers or sisters. As Murdock (1949:60) has written, "Since kindreds interlace and overlap, they do not and cannot form discrete or separate segments of the entire society." Kindreds play functional roles in other parts of the world besides the United States, even in some societies that have unilineal descent groups. An example is the Kapauku of New Guinea, among whom a person's kindred, traced bilaterally, is an important kinship group, which contributes to the price paid for his bride, exchanges mutual help, and exacts blood revenge, if need be.

A functional weakness is that a kindred cannot act as a corporate group; it cannot hold land or other property and has no continuity over time. These functions may, however, be assumed by clans and lineages.

Unilineal descent

A *clan* is a unilineal descent group, the members of which believe that they are related to one another through descent from a common ancestor or ancestress. The same definition could be given for a *lineage*, except that in a lineage the members are able to trace their descent to known forebears, while in a clan the common ancestor is more distant and usually mythical. A clan may contain many lineages.[1] Unilineal descent means that kin relationship is traced through one line, either through males, in which case we speak of *patrilineal* descent, or else through females, in which case we speak of *matrilineal* descent. In a society with unilineal descent, one is either a member of one's father's lineage or clan, or a member of one's mother's lineage or clan, but not of both, although there are some exceptions in cases of "double descent," which is discussed later in this chapter. In societies having patrilineal descent, property and titles are passed from father to son; in matrilineal societies, they are handed down from a man to his sister's son. Thus, property remains within the lineage or clan.

In clan societies a man and wife almost always belong to different clans. This is due to the rule of clan *exogamy*, the requirement to marry outside of one's clan. Clans can be identified by the fact that they have names. Very often they are named after animals such as Bear, Wolf, or Fox, or after plants or other aspects of the environment. If a man belonging to the Bear clan meets a girl who says that

---

[1] In his *Social Structure*, Murdock used the word *clan* for quite a different social unit and uses the word *sib* for what is here called clan. The usage followed here is a traditional one in British and American social anthropology.

she is a Bear, he knows that he cannot marry her, even though they may be unable to trace their genealogical relationship to one another.

A clan, a subclan, or a lineage may be a landowning unit. As a group it can be responsible for blood vengeance, if a member has been killed, and may demand indemnity. Religious cults may be associated with the unilineal group, such as the ancestor worship of traditional Chinese culture. Sacred objects or places of worship may be in charge of a particular clan, as among the Hopi. A named social unit that has a certain unity and special identity, which may own land, and may serve as a focus for collective economic or religious activity can be called a *corporate* group. Members of such a group show their solidarity by coming together on ceremonial occasions such as initiations, weddings, and funerals. They often have the obligation to extend hospitality or financial aid to other members of the group. Myths are sometimes told about the origin of the kinship group, serving to reinforce its corporate character and identify it as a unit set apart from others. Sometimes members of a lineage group occupy a single, large dwelling, as in the Iroquois longhouse or the large communal dwellings of the Tupinambá of the tropical forests of eastern Brazil. Or they may live in several homes grouped closely together. The degree to which unilineal groups manifest corporate qualities varies in different societies. The Chippewa, for example, had clans, but they were not strongly corporate groups like the clans of the Hopi. But the potentiality for the development of corporate features is inherent in unilineal kinship systems. This may be why unilineal systems are so common among the societies of the world, numbering about 60 percent of the societies in Murdock's "World Ethnographic Sample."[2] Unilineal systems are often found in horticultural and agricultural societies in which land rights are held by kin groups.

Patrilineal descent

When unilineal descent is traced in the male line, we speak of patriliny, or patrilineal descent. In this case, one belongs to one's father's clan, not to one's mother's clan. This is illustrated in the accompanying diagram. In kinship charts like the one presented here, a triangle designates a male and a circle represents a female. An equal sign indicates a marriage. Siblings, brothers and sisters, are linked by a bar. *Ego*, from the Latin word for "I," is the person from whom the relationships are reckoned.

---

[2] William Davenport (1959) has pointed out that some nonunilineal descent groups may also have corporate features: being named, having identifying emblems, and ownership of land.

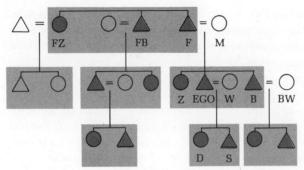

Diagram showing
persons related
through patrilineal
descent.

Note: B is Ego's brother; Z his sister. F is Ego's father; FB is his father's brother; FZ is his father's sister. M is Ego's mother.
S and D are son and daughter.

One's patrilineal kinsmen include one's father's father and his siblings (brothers and sisters), one's father and his siblings, the children of father's brothers, one's own brothers and sisters, and the children of one's brothers. Patriliny affiliates a person with kinsmen related to him through males only.

The majority of societies having unilineal descent are patrilineal. They range from hunting-gathering societies, such as the Chippewa, to advanced civilizations, like that of traditional China. Most of India, except for parts of the south, has patrilineal descent. Patrilineal American Indians included both some Siouan-speaking and Alonquian-speaking tribes. There are many patrilineal tribes in East Africa, among the Nagas of Nagaland in India, and among tribes in New Guinea.

Incidentally, it may be noted that there is another way of diagramming kinship relations than the one given above. Another system is shown below. Students are likely to encounter both of these kinds of

Diagram of a
nuclear family.

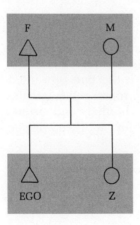

diagrams in works on anthropology. In the second system a husband and wife are connected by a bar beneath the symbols, while brother and sister are linked by a bar above them.

This diagram shows Ego's relationship to his parents and sister. In this chapter the first system of diagramming kinship relations will be used henceforth, rather than the latter.

Matrilineal descent

Matriliny, or matrilineal descent, affiliates a person with kinsmen related to him through females only. In this case, one belongs to one's mother's, not one's father's, clan. One's matrilineal relatives include one's mother's mother and her siblings, one's mother and her siblings, the children of mother's sisters, one's own brothers and sisters, and the children of one's sisters.

This system of descent is relatively restricted in range. Only about 15 percent of the societies in Murdock's "World Ethnographic Sample" are matrilineal. Among American Indians the Navaho, Hopi, Zuñi, Hidatsa, Crow, Cherokee, Iroquois, Tlingit, and Haida were matrilineal. So are the people of Truk and the Trobriand Islands. The Nayar, Tiyyar, and Mappilla of Kerala in southwestern India follow matrilineal descent, as do the Minangkabau of Indonesia. In Africa the Ashanti, the Plateau Tonga, the Bemba, and the Yao have matrilineal descent.

Double descent

Another possible way of tracing descent is through double descent, a combination of the patrilineal and matrilineal principles. In this system the individual belongs to both his father's patrilineal group and his mother's matrilineal group. Early in this chapter it was stated that there are such exceptions. Double descent has been de-

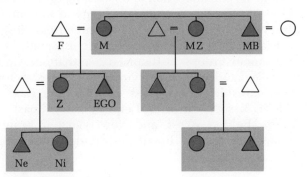

F M MZ MB

Z EGO

Ne Ni

Note: Ne is nephew; Ni is niece.

Diagram showing persons related through matrilineal descent.

scribed for some societies in Africa, India, Australia, Melanesia, and Polynesia. Of 565 cultures listed in the "World Ethnographic Sample," 29 are cited as having double descent.

One society with such a system is the Yako of Nigeria. Residence is patrilocal; that is, the married couple live in the husband's community (see p. 134). The women who marry-out are dispersed. All movable goods, such as money and livestock, are inherited matrilineally, while immovable goods, such as house and land, are handed down from father to son. There is consistency here, since the men do not move upon marriage and thus transmit the immovable property, while the movable goods are transmitted through the line of the movable women.

There are still other possible ways of tracing descent. For example, among the Apinaye of Brazil, females follow matrilineal descent and males, patrilineal descent; while, in some tribes of Celebes, odd-numbered children are affiliated with the mother and even-numbered ones with the father.

Phratries and moieties

In some societies two or more clans are linked together to form a *phratry*. The member clans may feel that they have particularly close ties with the other clan or clans of the phratry. They may perform reciprocal services on ceremonial occasions. Sometimes, as among the Hopi of Arizona, the phratry is an exogamous unit, so that one may not marry members of the other clans within the phratry.

In some societies the clans form two groups in which each half is called a *moiety*. These are usually exogamous; a man must marry a woman of the opposite moiety. Sometimes the moieties are associated with contrasting abstract concepts or different phenomena of nature. The conceptual universe of the Murngin, a hunting-gathering society in northeastern Arnhem Land in Australia, is divided into a dual system in which plants, animals, stars, and people belong to either one moiety or the other. Myths and folklore supply rationalizations for the allocation of objects to particular moieties, explaining why a spear, for example, belongs to one moiety while a spear-thrower belongs to the other (Warner 1958:30).

Elaborate systems of contrasting associations are found in many exogamous groups in Indonesia, so that one side, for example, may be associated with such symbolic features as Right, Male, Land or Mountainside, Above, Heaven, In Front, East, and Old; the other side is associated with Left, Female, Coast or Seaside, Below, Earth, Behind, West, and New (van der Kroef 1954:852). Bororo villages in eastern Brazil are divided into exogamous matrilineal moieties known as Weak and Strong. In some communities these moieties are cross-cut by moieties called Upstream and Downstream (Steward and Faron 1959:386).

Dual divisions like these facilitate patterns of reciprocity, not only in relation to marriage but also in the exchange of special services. For example, members of one moiety among the Seneca performed mourning services for those of the other. Such symbolic contrasts as Right and Left and North and South serve to emphasize the complementary roles played by the two divisions.

The Zuñi Indians of New Mexico associated their clans and societies with the different directions — North, West, South, and East — as the accompanying table shows. This symbolism also reinforced feelings of mutual interdependence and reciprocity among these subdivisions of Zuñi society.

Directional symbolism in Zuni mythology

	North	West	South	East	Up	Down
Colors	Yellow	Blue	Red	White	Many colored	Black
Seasons	Winter	Spring	Summer	Autumn		
Elements	Wind/air	Water	Fire	Earth		
Time of day		Evening		Dawn		
Institutions	War/destruction	War cure, hunting	Husbandry, medicine	Magic, religion		
Clans	Crane	Bear	Badger	Turkey	Sky	Toad
	Grouse	Coyote	Wild tobacco	Antelope	Eagle	Water
	Evergreen-oak	Spring-herb	Corn	Deer		Rattlesnake
Societies	Ice-wand	Bow Priest	Great Fire	Priesthood, priests	Nekwewe	Rattlesnake
	Knife	Coyote	Little Fire	Cottonwood-down	Scavenger	
	Cactus			Bird-Monster		

Source: Based on ethnographic data given in Cushing 1896:368–70.

Totemism

Similar ideas may be associated with clans or other unilineal units in some societies. Among central Australian aborigines, members of the Kangaroo clan have the idea that the remote ancestor of their clan was a kangaroo and that they have a special affinity with kangaroos. Where beliefs of this kind exist, there may be a taboo on eating the meat of the clan animal. A complex of beliefs and customs relating to such ideas is called *totemism*.

The Bondo, hill tribesmen in the state of Orissa in eastern India, have totemistic concepts relating to their moieties, Cobra and Tiger. Members of the Cobra moiety cannot kill a cobra, "for it is our brother." Similarly, members of the Tiger moiety never kill a tiger. They say, "When we go out hunting, we feel very embarrassed if we meet a tiger; we just don't know what to do and our weapons fall of their own accord from our hands. The tiger also feels awkward and goes away." Verrier Elwin, who recorded this statement, adds, "But I suspect a certain apprehension on the part of the Bondo that, while he himself may be strictly orthodox, the tiger may not be equally observant of the rules" (Elwin 1950:29).

Segmentary lineage systems

Unilineal descent is of particular importance in societies with *segmentary lineage systems,* such as the Tiv of Nigeria, the Nuer of the Sudan, and the Bedouins of Cyrenaica. These are patrilineal tribes lacking centralized political organization. The segments that make up the society are not ranked in a hierarchy but are roughly equivalent duplicates of one another. In these "tribes without rulers," as they have been called, the lineage is a political unit, having collective responsibility in blood vengeance; a good deal of feuding goes on between lineage groups.

Unilineal systems are normally in process of segmentation. Two brothers of one family may become the heads of two new lineages. They usually remain close allies, however, and one will come to the aid of the other if he is attacked. Usually, one's sense of loyalty is greatest to those kinsmen most closely related, although one may also acknowledge ties to more distant kin. Feuds are more common and more bitterly fought with more remote kinsmen, but, in case of attack from without the tribe, feuding kinsmen will unite against the outsiders. When a quarrel breaks out between two segments, closely related groups are apt to be drawn into the affair on both sides, for there is no organized political machinery for dealing with internal conflicts. The normal tendency in these societies is toward a kind of social atomism. Political consolidation occurs only to meet a threat from outside the tribe, and, once that danger is over, the atomistic condition is resumed.

The Tiv are conscious of their tribal unity through descent from a common ancestor, and this awareness enables them to make common cause against another tribe, when that is necessary.

In societies of this type, the lineages should have roughly equal status, but there are also societies with more political centralization in which one lineage, that of the king or chief, is more important than the others. Some illustrations of this type are given in Chapter 14.

So far we have dealt with kinship ties determined by consanguinity. But kinship ties are also achieved through marriage. Indeed, for Claude Lévi Strauss (1969a) these are the most significant relations in human societies. According to Lévi-Strauss, men in primitive societies brought about alliances through marrying their daughters or sisters to other men. The resulting network established social cohesion, tying families or bands more closely together. This was probably a necessary stratagem in hunting-gathering days, when the use of weapons, unknown to nonhuman primates, heightened the potential dangers of strange groups. In a pioneer discussion of exogamy in 1888, E. B. Tylor wrote that savage tribes faced the alternatives of marrying out or being killed out, and he quoted these lines from Genesis 34:16: "Then will we give our daughters unto you, and we will take your daughters to us, and we will dwell with you, and we will become one people." This biblical passage illustrates the process of establishing peace and broadening social bonds through intermarriage.

A widespread form of marriage which links small family groups together is cross-cousin marriage. It is found among many peoples in southern India, parts of China and Melanesia, and among many tribes of Australian aborigines, African tribal groups, and North American Indians.

The kinship system of the Western world does not distinguish between cross cousins and parallel cousins, but the distinction is important in many of the world's kinship systems since it may designate which "cousins" are marriageable and which are not. In defining these types of cousins it is useful to use the word *sibling*, which is a general term for brother or sister, without specifying the sex. Parallel cousins, then, are children of siblings of the same sex, while cross cousins are children of siblings of opposite sex. In other words, a man's parallel cousins are his father's brother's children and his mother's sister's children; they are children of siblings of the same sex. A man's cross cousins are his father's sister's children or his mother's brother's children; they are children of siblings of opposite sex.

It is quite common for parallel cousins, such as father's brother's children, to be equated with siblings and termed "brother" and "sister," while quite different terms are employed for cross cousins.

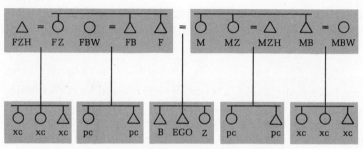

Kinship chart showing cross and parallel cousins.

Note: In this chart xc stands for cross cousin; pc stands for parallel cousin.

Among the Chippewa (Ojibwa) Indians of former days, a man's potential mates were to be found among his cross cousins. He could marry a mother's brother's daughter or a father's sister's daughter. Since a man could have two or more wives in former times, he might marry several of them. A man would also be expected to marry an unmarried sister of his wife after his wife's death. A man's range of marriage choices was greater than that indicated by our kinship chart, since there would be other women whom he would address by the term for cross cousin. These "cousins" were not necessarily related to him genetically. It was customary to address people by kinship terms in those days. Let us suppose that a young man joined a Chippewa community and was allowed to camp with a particular family. If he were accepted, he might address the older man of the family as "father" and the latter's wife as "mother." Their children would then be called "brother" and "sister," and their relatives would be addressed in appropriate terms. In this fashion, nonrelatives could become incorporated into the kinship network.

The Chippewa had the custom of cross-cousin joking, that is, if a man met a woman whom he called by the term for cross cousin, it was more or less expected that they would exchange bawdy wisecracks, risqué repartee. A man would never bandy such rough remarks with a female parallel cousin, who would be treated like a sister. Cross cousins, however, were potential mates. Similar practices occur in some other parts of the world where cross-cousin marriage is practiced — for instance, among the Tswana of Botswana, in southern Africa.

Cross-cousin marriage and exogamy

Let us suppose that two adjacent hunting-gathering bands, A and B, have gotten into the practice of exchanging women in marriage and have come to form "one people" as in the biblical passage quoted earlier. This might be one way in which moieties were

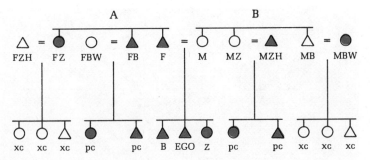

Two exogamous moieties, A and B.

formed. The accompanying diagram shows a patrilineal moiety system in which Ego belongs to his father's moiety A (*shaded*). Note that his cross cousins automatically fall in the opposite moiety B (*unshaded*), while his parallel cousins are in his own moiety. This means that a man's female cross cousins are in the category of marriageable women, while his female parallel cousins are the equivalents of sisters.

In ethnographic accounts when it is stated that a man in Society X must marry a cross cousin, this often means that a man must marry a woman in the marriageable category which includes, among others, his own mother's brother's daughter and father's sister's daughter.

Three forms of cross-cousin marriage

The Chippewa had what is called *bilateral* cross-cousin marriage, meaning that a man could marry either a mother's brother's daughter or a father's sister's daughter. But there are some peoples, including some of the Rājpūts in India, who require or prefer a man to marry a mother's brother's daughter but not a father's sister's daughter. This is called *matrilateral* cross-cousin marriage. Some societies, much fewer in number, require a man to marry a father's sister's daughter, which is known as *patrilateral* cross-cousin marriage. This was done, for example, among higher-status families in the Trobriand Islands in Melanesia.

There has been a good deal of argument among social anthropologists about why matrilateral cross-cousin marriage is more common than the patrilateral variety. Lévi-Strauss's explanation for this is in terms of the social solidarity principle mentioned earlier. Some differences between the two systems are illustrated in the accompanying chart from Needham 1962:15.

Here we see that in the matrilateral system "exchanges" of women are made in the same "direction," whereas there is an "alternating current" in the patrilateral system. The second form lends itself to

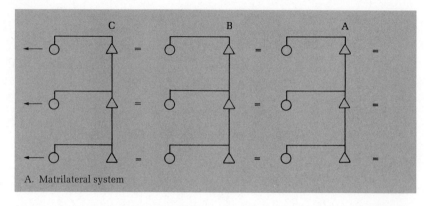

A. Matrilateral system

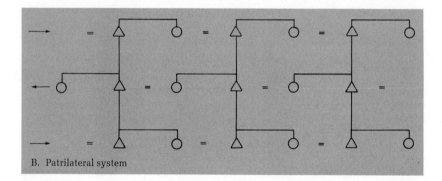

Matrilateral and
patrilateral
cross-cousin
marriage.

B. Patrilateral system

an egalitarian, reciprocal exchange of women; but the first form, the matrilateral one, does not permit a direct exchange. In the first diagram, line **A** gives women to line B but does not receive any in return. Similarly line B gives women to line C without reciprocal exchange. Lévi-Strauss (1969a) believed that matrilateral cross-cousin marriage establishes a wider social network, with greater cohesion, than does the patrilateral form.

George C. Homans and David M. Schneider (1955) offered an alternative explanation for the greater frequency of matrilateral cross-cousin marriage. They pointed out that this form is usually associated with patrilineal descent, while patrilateral cross-cousin marriage tends to be associated with matrilineal descent. Since patrilineal descent is much more common than matrilineal descent, it is not surprising that mother's brother's daughter marriage should be more common than marriage with a father's sister's daughter.

But why, in any case, should there be an association between patrilineal descent and matrilateral cross-cousin marriage? Homans and Schneider offer a psychological explanation derived from an essay by Radcliffe-Brown, "The Mother's Brother in South Africa" (1924). In a patrilineal system the father has jural authority over his son and consequently becomes a somewhat austere and distant figure. The boy's mother, on the other hand, is apt to be seen as warm and nurturant. The warm feeling that a son feels for his mother tends to become extended to her brother, who is seen as a sort of "male mother." (In some patrilineal societies he is called by such a term.) This positive attitude makes marriage with a mother's brother's daughter "sentimentally appropriate." This is also true on the girl's side, for she tends to be close to her father and his sister.

For the boy, the father's sister is a sort of "female father" and hence is a more distant person associated with the authority invested in the father and his lineage.

In a matrilineal society like that of the Trobriand Islands a boy is not a member of his father's lineage or clan, and the father is not so much an authority figure as is the maternal uncle, who does belong to the same clan or lineage as the boy. A Trobriand father's relations with his son tend to be relaxed and indulgent. The son's positive attitude toward his father is apt to be transferred to the father's sister, and so marriage with her daughter would be sentimentally appropriate in a matrilineal society.

In opposition to this set of arguments, it has been noted that the assumed psychological process of extending sentiments from primary to secondary relatives has not been proven to occur. If it does take place, however, one would think that positive attitudes would be extended toward a mother's brother in a matrilineal society, since warm feelings must also be felt by boys toward their mothers in such societies. Despite the statistical associations presented by Homans and Schneider, most patrilineal societies do not prescribe marriage with a mother's brother's daughter, nor do most matrilineal societies prescribe marriage with a father's sister's daughter. Indeed, the latter form of marriage is very rare (Needham 1962).

Parallel-cousin marriage

The Tswana of South Africa practice cross-cousin marriage. They regard marriage with a mother's brother's daughter as the preferred form, while father's sister's daughter marriage is a second choice. But the Tswana are unusual in also practicing marriage with a father's brother's daughter or mother's sister's daughter. Members of this tribe are divided into nobles and commoners. I. Schapera has pointed out that there is a difference in the incidence of marriage types in these two social strata. Fifty percent of the commoners practice matrilateral cross-cousin marriage, with roughly equal distributions in the other three brackets. But nearly 48 percent of the nobles have father's brother's daughter marriage. The Tswana have a proverb, "Child of my father's younger brother, marry me, so that the (*bogadi*) cattle may return to our kraal." This suggests an economic motivation in such marriages. Schapera, however, believes that the main motive in the upper class is not the acquisition of cattle but maintenance of status and political advantages within the family (Schapera 1950:151, 157, 163).

Marriage with a father's brother's daughter is a widespread form of alliance among Muslims in North Africa, the Near East, Pakistan, and India, having Islamic religious support. Among some Arab peoples, if a family wishes to marry their daughter to someone other than her father's brother's son, the cousin must be handsomely paid for his permission. Among the Arabs, as among the Tswana, marrying among close kin may serve to conserve property and status, and it may also maintain family solidarity among pastoral tribesmen such as the Bedouins, who have to be ready to defend themselves against sudden attack from other groups.

Fictive kinship

We have considered kinship relations through birth (consanguine) and through marriage (affinal). There is another way in which persons may be related—through adoption or fictive kinship.

The godparent is an important figure in many societies. In Latin America the institution of *compadrazgo* not only provides a child with a godparent but also establishes mutual ties between the co-parents, or *compadres*.

Patterns of "blood brotherhood" or institutionalized friendship are found in some societies. Among the Jimdars of eastern Nepal two men or two women may go through a simple ceremony that commits the partners to a quasi-familial relationship. This brings about incest barriers between a man and members of his friend's family, and an avoidance relationship develops between the man and his friend's wife.

Types of kin terminologies

Murdock has drawn up a typology of kinship systems on the basis of the terminology applied to cousins. These are ideal types; particular societies may be said to have one or the other system if enough criteria are met in their terminologies.[3]

---

[3] Robert Lowie argued that each kinship system should be analyzed separately. "There is no Hawaiian *system*, no Dakota *system*. But we can legitimately speak of the principle of generations and the bifurcation principle of merging collateral and lineal kin . . ." (Lowie 1929:123; Needham 1974:50–55). There does, however, seem to be a good deal of parallelism in the ways in which kinship systems have developed in different parts of the world. There has also been diffusion of kinship principles from one society to another.

The Sudanese system

The Sudanese system, associated with patrilineal descent, has a particularizing emphasis, with different terms for each type of cousin and sibling, aunt, niece, uncle, and nephew. This system occurs mainly in a band across central Africa from west to east, including the Dahomeans, the Dinka, and the Azande, but it is also found among the Batak of Sumatra, the Gilyak and Yakut of Siberia, and some scattered societies in other parts of the world.

The Eskimo system

The Eskimo system is found not only among the Eskimos but also among ourselves. Cross cousins are not distinguished from parallel cousins. We use the term "cousin" to include all of them, which would seem strange to people with some other kinship systems. We distinguish between siblings and cousins. This is a bilateral, not unilineal, system found in societies that usually lack corporate descent groups. It is found among such varied societies as the Andaman Islanders, Ruthenian peasants in eastern Europe, and Taos Pueblo in New Mexico.

The Hawaiian system

The Hawaiian system is more common in Murdock's sample of societies than the Eskimo type. Female cross cousins and parallel cousins are called by the same terms as those used for sisters. This is sometimes called a generational system, because classificatory terms are used for many relatives within a generation. Thus, one term is applied to mother, mother's sister, and father's sister, and one term is used for father, father's brother, and mother's brother. This system is found among the Samoans, the Maori of New Zealand, the Ifugao of the Philippines, the Kaingang of Brazil, and the Shoshone Indians of North America, among others.

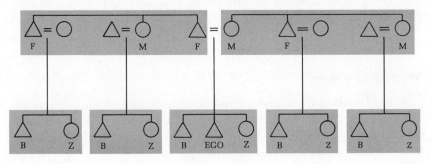

Diagram of Hawaiian kinship system.

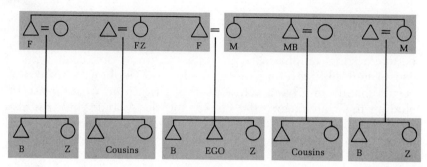

Diagram of Iroquois
kinship system.

The Iroquois system

This system, associated with matrilineal or double descent, equates female parallel cousins with sisters but has a different term for cross cousins. If we look at the kinship diagram we note that in this system, Ego applies the same kinship term to father and to father's brothers. It used to be said that this term was "extended" from father to include his brothers, but this involves making an unwarranted assumption about unknown past events. It is safer to say that the term in question has the meaning "male of the previous generation on the father's side." The same term is not applied to males on the mother's side.

Note, next, that Ego uses the same kinship term for mother and mother's sisters. We need not conclude that Ego does not know which woman is his biological mother or that he feels equally close to all the women whom he calls by this term.

It is perhaps a logical next step to find that father's brother's children are called "brother" and "sister" by Ego and so are mother's sisters children. In other words, Ego's parallel cousins are equated with his siblings.

In this system some relatives are separated or bifurcated, while others are merged. Hence it has been called a *bifurcate-merging* system, which is also true of the Omaha and Crow systems to be discussed next. Besides the Iroquois, this system is found among the Navaho, the Nayar of the Malabar coast of India, the Vedda of Sri Lanka, the people of Dobu, and the Minangkabau of Indonesia, as well as many other societies.

The Omaha system

What is called the Omaha kinship system applies not only to the Omaha tribe after which it is named but also to various other patrilineal peoples: the Osage, Winnebago, and Miwok Indians and some tribes in Africa, Melanesia, and India.

Diagram of Omaha kinship system.

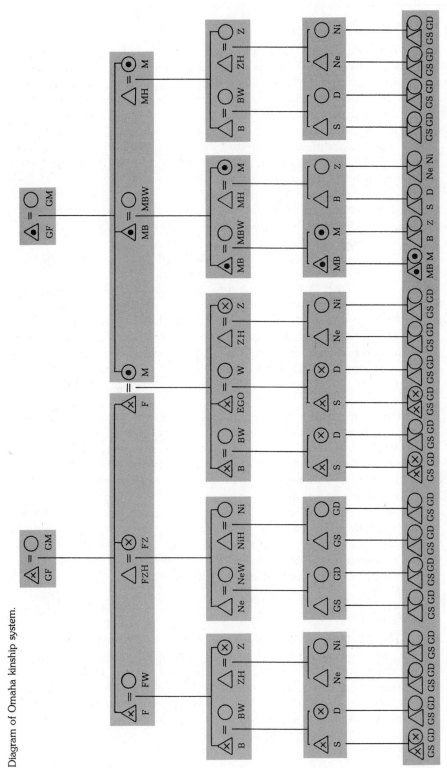

Note: Symbols are the same as in the chart on page 114. Here GF is grandfather, GM is grandmother, GS is grandson, and GD is granddaughter. An X designates members of Ego's clan; a dot designates members of Ego's mother's clan.

The bifurcate-merging principles described for the Iroquois system reappear here. The same terms are used for father and father's brother and for mother and mother's sister; there is an equation of parallel cousins with siblings but separate terms for cross cousins. Ego calls his brother's children by the terms he applies to his own children, corresponding to "son" and "daughter," while he calls his sister's children by different terms, corresponding to "nephew" and "niece." It is, again, consistent to find that terms applied to these children are also applied to the children of Ego's "classificatory" brothers and sisters of both sides. Putting it in our own terms, the following persons would be called "sons" by Ego: his own sons, his brother's sons, his father's brother's son's sons, and his mother's sister's son's sons.

While parallel cousins are equated with siblings, different terms are applied to cross cousins. Father's sister's children are called "nephew" and "niece." But now we come to a big surprise: The son of Ego's mother's brother is called "mother's brother," while mother's brother's daughter is called "mother." (It is understandable that the children of this "mother" are called "brother" and "sister," although they may be below Ego's generation.) But the children of mother's brother's son are called — guess what?: "mother's brother" and "mother." Ego may apply these terms to children of four or five years of age.

Up to this point the system has seemed very orderly and consistent. It may be unfamiliar to a citizen of the Western world, but it must be granted that there is logic in the scheme, at least until one comes to the cross-cutting of generations in the terms for "mother" and "mother's brother." It must now be remembered that this is a patrilineal system. The males whom Ego calls "mother's brother" are members of his mother's patrilineal lineage. Ego has close, often affectionate, dealings with these people whose lineage is second only to his own. To them, as a group, he is "sister's son." The kinship terminology employed here thus expresses the unity of the patrilineal lineage (Radcliffe-Brown 1950:32–33).

The Crow system

The Crow system is often described as a mirror image of the Omaha system. It is found among some matrilineal peoples, including the Choctaw, Cherokee, Crow, Hidatsa, Tlingit, Haida, and Hopi Indians, the Banks Islanders of Melanesia, and one Twi-speaking community in West Africa. In this system, Ego belongs to his mother's clan, not his father's. In both systems, incidentally, the terms "grandfather" and "grandmother" are applied bilaterally to the parents of both mother and father.

Here again the term applied to the father is also used for the father's brothers, while that for the mother is applied to her sisters. Parallel cousins are once again equated with siblings. Children of "brothers" are called "son" and "daughter"; children of "sisters" are called "nephew" and "niece." Different terms are used for cross cousins than for parallel cousins. So far, everything is similar to the Omaha system.

Now, in the matrilineal lineage of Ego's father's sister we find a situation that parallels the patrilineal lineage of Ego's mother's brother in the Omaha system. In Crow terminology, a term comparable to "father's sister" is applied not only to a father's sister but also to her daughter and daughter's daughter. It has the meaning of "female member of father's matrilineal lineage." The men married to these women are called "grandfather," even though they may be younger than Ego. A father's sister's son is called "father." This term also overrides generations, so that it has the significance of "male member of father's matrilineal lineage." This is not Ego's group, for he belongs to his mother's clan; but he has close ties with his father's people, just as, in societies with the Omaha system, a person has close ties with his mother's people. Thus, the Crow system is a true mirror of the Omaha system.

Kinship and behavior

It should be kept in mind that a kinship system is not just a collection of words or names for different kinds of relatives. There are characteristic ways of behaving toward different categories of relatives, so that one may have a joking relationship with cross cousins, as among the Chippewa Indians, or else there may be a relationship of extreme deference, as in the case of a Jat or Rājpūt bride in northern India in relation to the elder members of her husband's family. Respect may be emphasized to the extent of avoidance. Among the Chiricahua Apache, brothers and sisters practiced an avoidance relationship and would not remain alone together at home, while a man also avoided his mother-in-law and father-in-law and both of their mothers.

If two or more persons are called by the same kinship term, a person's behavior toward these persons should be roughly similar, although there are exceptions. Among the Tswana, a Bantu-speaking tribe of Botswana, the same kinship term is used for sister, father's brother's daughter, and mother's sister's daughter. In other words, female parallel cousins are equated with sisters, as is the case in the Omaha and Crow systems described above. But a Tswana may marry a parallel cousin and he may not marry a sister. Again, Tswana use the term *rrakgadi* for both father's sister and father's father's brother's daughter. Marriage is permitted with the latter but not with the former. A man may marry his wife's sister but not her mother; yet the same kinship term is used for both (Schapera 1950:161). While there are such exceptions, there is normally a good deal of consistency in behavior toward categories of relatives designated by particular kinship terms.

This kind of patterning may be illustrated by some ethnographic data about the Hopi Indians of Arizona.

The Hopi, farmers in a bleak desert environment, provide an illustration of the ways in which the kinship network structures some interpersonal relationships within the tribe. The Hopi have the Crow system described above. A child belongs to its mother's clan but has strong ties with the father's clanfolks. The mother of a child's father becomes its godmother. A ceremony is performed on the 20th day after the birth in which the godmother, after sprinkling a line of cornmeal to the east, presents the baby to the rising sun. Her daughters bring baskets of cornmeal as presents. These are the women whom the child will call "father's sister" and whose husbands will be called "grandfather."

These women have a friendly, teasing, joking relationship with a growing boy. Their husbands, on the other hand, behave in a severe, jealous manner toward him. They pretend to believe, or perhaps sometimes actually do believe, that the boy is having sexual relations with their wives, and they may threaten to castrate him. Don Talayesva, a Hopi, tells about experiences of this sort:

After I was four or five nearly all my grandfathers, father's sisters' and clan sisters' husbands, played very rough jokes on me, snatched at my penis, and threatened to castrate me, charging that I had been caught making love to their wives, who were my aunts. All these women took my part, called me their sweetheart, fondled my penis, and pretended to want it badly. . . . I liked to play with them but I was afraid of their husbands and thought that they would castrate me. It was a long time before I could be sure that they meant only to tease (Simmons 1942:40).

One of these men once tied up Don, took out his knife, sharpened it on a stone, and said, "I am going to castrate him." But then he let the boy go. In winter these men sometimes rolled their wives' nephews naked in the snow. It was traditional for young men to "get even" with their tormentors when they were old enough to do so. After he came back from school, Don met the man who had pretended to castrate him, and, without saying a word, Don lassoed him and dragged him down the mesa. On another occasion Don threw the old man into some wet mortar (Simmons 1942:57–58, 76, 108, 280, 368).

Among the Chippewa Indians a sexual joking relationship was associated with potential marriage, as among cross cousins, but among the Hopi there could be no marriage between a man and a woman of his father's clan. Nevertheless, there seems to have been a tradition of investing erotic overtones in this relationship, with concomitant jealousy, whether real or feigned, on the part of the "father's sisters'" husbands. These relationships are structured by the kinship system and by the customary attitudes and behavior directed toward these categories of relatives.

Suggestions for further reading

Two recent paperback books provide brief introductions to the study of kinship: Roger M. Keesing, *Kin Groups and Social Structure* (New York: Holt, Rinehart and Winston, 1975), and Burton Pasternak, *Introduction to Kinship and Social Organization* (Englewood Cliffs, N.J.: Prentice-Hall, 1976).

A good general work is Robin Fox, *Kinship and Marriage: An Anthropological Perspective* (Baltimore: Penguin Books, 1967). Three well-written essays on the study of kinship and unilineal descent are: A. R. Radcliffe-Brown, "The Study of Kinship Systems," in A. R. Radcliffe-Brown, *Structure and Function in Primitive Society: Essays and Addresses* (Glencoe, Ill.: Free Press, 1952), pp. 49–89; A. R. Radcliffe-Brown, "Introduction," in *African Systems of Kinship and Marriage,* ed. A. R. Radcliffe-Brown and Daryll Forde (London: Oxford University Press, 1950), pp. 1–85; Meyer Fortes, "The Structure of Unilineal Descent Groups," *American Anthropologist,* vol. 55 (1953), pp. 17–41.

George P. Murdock's *Social Structure* (New York: Free Press, 1949) makes difficult reading, but it has been a very influential book. The same is true of Claude Lévi-Strauss, *The Elementary Structures of Kinship,* trans. from the French by James H. Bell, John R. von Sturmer, and Rodney Needham (Boston: Beacon Press, 1969). For a criticism of this work, see Francis Korn, *Elementary Structures Reconsidered: Lévi-Strauss on Kinship* (Berkeley and Los Angeles: University of California Press, 1973). Both Murdock's and Lévi-Strauss's contributions to the study of kinship are assessed in J. A. Barnes, *Three Styles in the Study of Kinship* (Berkeley and Los Angeles: University of California Press, 1973).

Two readers may be recommended: Jack Goody, ed., *Kinship: Selected Readings* (Harmondsworth, England: Penguin Books, 1971), and Nelson Graburn, ed., *Readings in Kinship and Social Structure* (New York: Harper & Row, 1971).

9

Marital residence and affinal relationships

Now that we have reviewed some different types of kinship systems and considered some of the various ways in which relatives may be aligned, let us return to the subject of marriage and family life. A newly married couple has to set up residence somewhere. There are different customs concerning this in different societies, which may be influenced by whether the kinship system is patrilineal, matrilineal, or bilateral. Marriage involves relationships with affinal relatives or in-laws. Especially in patrilineal societies, payment may have to be made to members of the wife's lineage to compensate for her loss. Some matrilineal societies have this custom, too—for example, the Trobriand Islanders. Various ways of handling these matters have been developed in different societies.

Economic exchanges in relation to marriage

In Chapter 7, the point was made that levirate and sororate practices show that marriage in such societies is not just a union between individuals but one between lineages or clans. Relationships between such unilineal groups are continuing, fostered by patterns of etiquette and reciprocity.

In many societies a girl leaves her own community when she gets married and goes to live with her husband's people. Her own lineage group thus loses a useful worker. The groom's lineage may make up this deficiency by marrying one of its daughters into the other group, thus evening matters and further strengthening mutual ties.

Sometimes payment is made by the groom or by his family to the girl's family at the time of marriage. Although this is called "bride price," it is not purchase; the girl is not considered a slave or market-

132

able commodity. (For this reason the term "bridewealth" is sometimes used instead in ethnographic accounts.) Rather, the payment is a kind of restitution to the girl's family for the loss they have incurred. The payment is also a kind of insurance that the girl will be well treated. If she is not, she may return to her parents, and her husband is often unable to get the bride price back, especially if it is felt that he is to blame for the breakup.

In many African tribes that have cattle, the traditional medium of "payment" is cows. The cows are used by the girl's family to finance the marriage of one of their sons. A boy who wants to marry may have to wait until his sister's bride price has been paid and the cattle driven into the kraal.

Sometimes a man cannot acquire enough wealth to pay the bride price. In some societies where such problems have come up, an institutionalized solution is at hand, namely, bride service or suitor service. The young man goes to the home of the girl and works for her parents, as Jacob worked for Rachel in the Old Testament. This practice is found in many societies, for example among the Reindeer Chukchee of Siberia and the Kaska Indians of British Columbia. Since the young man lives with the girl's family in such cases, he is more or less her husband from the beginning.

In some societies, payments go the other way—from the bride's family to the groom's. In present-day India, the bride's parents pay a sum of money to the groom, despite the fact that their daughter leaves her community and moves to her husband's paternal residence. The dowry is particularly high in the case of young men who have studied in England and who are therefore thought to have promising futures. Even in small rural villages the dowry paid by the bride's parents may represent the savings of many years. Families often go in debt on this account.

Forms of marital residence

The possible forms of postmarital residence are rather limited; a newly married couple can live alone, with the man's relatives, with the woman's relatives, or they can shuttle back and forth between her family and his. There are some other possible arrangements and combinations, but there is a limitation of possibilities for the options.

In many societies there is a dominant or usual form of marital residence, as in some examples that follow. But there may be differences in residence in different segments of a population, as in a heterogeneous, modern, industrial society. And there may be different patterns for older and younger sons, as among the Nambudiri Brahmans discussed later.

Neolocal residence

The custom we are familiar with in the United States is for the newly married couple to set up a separate home, living with neither the husband's nor the wife's parents. This is called *neolocal* residence. It is consistent with the bilateral emphasis in American kinship and with our traditions of individualism, romantic love, and individual choice in the selection of a mate. It is a useful pattern in a highly industrialized society like ours, since it permits of much individual mobility. This form of residence is associated with a small conjugal family having rather weak ties to the relatives of either husband or wife. It is a rare form of residence among the societies of the world, being found in only 27 of the 565 societies in Murdock's "World Ethnographic Sample."

Patrilocal residence

The custom whereby a bride goes to live with or near her husband's patrilineal kinsmen is called *patrilocal* residence.[1] This is far more common than neolocal residence, being found in 314 societies in Murdock's "World Ethnographic Sample." It is also more common than *matrilocal* residence, to be described later, which is found in 84 societies, and *avunculocal* residence, which is found in only 18 societies (Stephens 1963:133).

To give an example of arrangements relating to patrilocal residence, let us consider conditions in northern India, where patrilineal descent is followed. In northern India, marriages are arranged by parents. The bride and groom usually have not met before the first wedding ceremonies, for the bride does not come from the same village as the groom. A man must marry a girl from another village. Indeed, in some parts of northern India one must marry outside of a complex of about 20 villages. Marriage is not completed all at once, in one ceremony, but involves various stages drawn out over a period of about three years. In the first years of marriage, the bride still spends a lot of time in her native village, but, as time goes on, she comes to spend more and more time in her husband's community, which before long becomes her main place of residence. There, she lives with her husband in his parents' home. If he has married

---

[1] I have followed Murdock's terms for residence, as set forth in his "World Ethnographic Sample" (1957). The terms *virilocal* and *uxorilocal* are sometimes used to have the same meanings as *patrilocal* and *matrilocal*, respectively. Sometimes a distinction is made so that the latter terms are used for societies having localized lineages, while *virilocal* and *uxorilocal* are applied to those that lack them. Only a few of Murdock's categories of marital residence are presented here.

Young Indian
mother.

brothers, they and their wives and children all share the same joint household. A young bride in such a household must show great respect to her father-in-law and to her husband's older brothers, covering her face with her veil in their presence. They rarely exchange conversation. She is freer in the presence of her husband's younger brothers. Among the Jats, who allow leviratic marriages, a joking relationship exists between a man and his older brothers' wife.[2]

Matrilocal residence

Matrilocal residence involves residence of the married couple with or near the wife's female matrilineal kinsmen. This is the custom among the Hopi Indians of Arizona who, as we have seen, have matrilineal clans, with the Crow kinship system. The Hopi have individual courtship before marriage, and there is a good deal of premarital intercourse. The boys visit girls at night in their homes but leave before dawn. If a girl becomes pregnant, she names the boy she wants to marry, and a match is arranged. Marriages are monogamous. The Hopi girl continues to live in the household into which she was born. This household includes her parents, her

---

[2] See the section on anticipatory levirate, p. 107.

unmarried brothers, her sisters, and their husbands and children. In the north Indian household it is the bride who must adjust to her in-laws; among the Hopi it is the groom who must adapt himself. However, their situations are not the same. The Indian bride is a stranger in her husband's village, while the Hopi groom normally comes from the same community. He courted his wife and knew her and her relatives before marriage. His mother's home, which he continues to visit, is apt to be in the same village; so he is less isolated than the bride in north India, and he enjoys a higher status.

The Hopi woman's status is also high, however, since she, or her clan, owns the house and fields where the men work. In his autobiography, Don Talayesva thus describes his wife's situation:

She owned the house and all the property that her relatives gave her, including orchards, stock, water holes, land, and personal possessions. She also owned any property she made with her hands, such as pots, baskets, milling stones, and clothes, or anything that she earned for work or purchased with our money. She owned the fuel and the foodstuffs that I brought into her house, as well as all household equipment and utensils (Simmons 1942:272).

The husband's status in this home is weakened by the fact that his wife's brothers and other maternal kinsmen have important roles in authority and decision making.

Nayar *sambandham* unions

In some cases, matrilineal societies seem to be almost able to dispense with husbands altogether. The Nayars of Kerala, in southwestern India, are a case in point. The Nayars made up a group of castes, some having high status, associated with the royal lineage, while others were associated with chiefs, village headmen, and commoners. The description that follows is based on a reconstruction by Kathleen Gough (1959) of conditions in Kerala during the 18th century. The patterns she describes no longer exist.

Every few years or so a ceremony was held at which the prepubescent girls of a Nayar lineage were ritually married to men of a "linked" lineage. A girl stayed together with her ritual husband for about four days. After that she was unlikely to see him again. The male had fulfilled his role in legally marrying her.

After puberty the girl might accept as visiting lovers or "husbands" men who were usually members of her own subcaste but not of her lineage. These relationships were known as *sambandham* unions. The men usually gave presents of cash, cloth, and other gifts. If the girl became pregnant, one of the men of her subcaste acknowledged his probable paternity by giving some cloth and vegetables to the midwife. Although the men gave presents, they did not really support the woman or her child, who received their food and maintenance from the woman's matrilineal group. Guardianship and discipline of the child came from the male members of her lineage.

Castes in India are *endogamous:* one is required to marry a person of the same caste or subcaste (see p. 169). This rule, which is usually strictly adhered to, was circumvented in *sambandham* unions between some Nayar women and younger sons of Nambudiri Brahman households. Nambudiri Brahmans were the highest caste in Kerala, outranking the Nayar. They traced descent patrilineally. Nambudiri Brahmans maintained their landed property intact through generations by following the custom of primogeniture, inheritance by the oldest son. Younger sons could neither inherit property nor marry Nambudiri Brahman girls. What they did was to enter into *sambandham* unions with Nayar women. Since they were of ritually higher rank, these men could not eat with their *sambandham* consorts but could have sexual relations with them. A man did not establish a household with the Nayar woman but continued to live in his own parental home. Any children that came of such a union did not belong to the Nambudiri Brahman's patrilineal line but to the Nayar woman's matrilineal family group; they were her children, not his.

This represents an extreme example of the attenuated role of husband in a matrilineal system. One cannot speak of it as exemplifying matrilocal residence since the "husband" does not really live with his "wife."

One cannot point to a single cause to account for the development of arrangements such as these, but an important contributing factor was the involvement of Nayar men in warfare. The Masai and the Chagga, African tribes engaged in warfare, did not allow their younger adult men to marry, but they were allowed to have extramarital sexual relations. A similar permissive attitude occurred in the Nazi armed forces during World War II; it has often been associated with societies on a military footing (Lévi-Strauss 1960:263).

Avunculocal residence

Residence of a married couple with or near the husband's male matrilineal kinsmen, particularly his mother's brother, is called *avunculocal* residence. The Trobriand Islanders of Melanesia provide an example. Most Trobriand Islanders are monogamous. Descent is traced matrilineally. There is individual courtship and much premarital intercourse, although some of the higher-status families arrange patrilateral cross-cousin marriages for their sons, marriage with a father's sister's daughter. Such marriages, arranged in infancy, are considered binding. Otherwise, most Trobriand marriages are the outcome of courtship. At the time of marriage, or soon thereafter, the husband leaves the village of his father, where he has grown up, and moves to a village owned by his mother's subclan, where his mother's brother lives. From the point of view of the bride, Trobriand postmarital residence may be said to be virilocal, residence at the husband's home, or community. But it is classed as avunculocal because of the husband's shift to his maternal uncle's village.

In a matrilineal society the mother's brother is an important figure, since he belongs to Ego's lineage or clan. Property and titles are inherited from him rather than from the father, who does not belong to Ego's lineage or clan. Among the Trobriand Islanders the maternal uncle is the principal authority figure, a source of discipline. It is the maternal uncle who teaches his nephew the traditions of his clan.

We find residential customs like those of the Trobriand Islanders among the matrilineal Tlingit of the American Northwest Coast. Among the Tlingit a boy left his home at around the age of eight to ten and moved to the house of his maternal uncle, who was responsible for the boy's training. This type of residence resembles the patrilocal residence of patrilineal societies in the sense that it maintains in association some male kinsmen who belong to the same unilineal group. Avunculocal residence would seem to give the husband a stronger position in the household than is the case in matrilocal residence.

Other forms of residence

Bilocal residence involves either patrilocal or matrilocal residence with about equal frequency. In some societies a married couple starts off living with the bride's parents or in their community and later moves to live permanently in the home or community of the husband. Murdock calls this shifting kind of residence *matripatrilocal*.

The Islanders of Dobu in Melanesia had a combination of matrilocal and avunculocal residence. Their society has been described by Reo F. Fortune in *Sorcerers of Dobu* (1932), but they are best known from Ruth Benedict's synopsis of that work in Chapter 5 of her *Patterns of Culture* (1934). A Dobuan married couple lives in alternate years in the villages of the husband's and wife's lineages. For one year the husband is an unwelcome outsider in his wife's village; in the next year she is an unwelcome outsider in his. Then they return to her village, and so on, year after difficult year. The fact that this arrangement *is* difficult is suggested by the high divorce rate, which Fortune found to be five times as frequent as among the Manus, another Melanesian tribe in which he worked. It does not follow, of course, that all people practicing such shifting patterns of residence must be miserable.

Many societies cannot be said to have any one particular type of marital residence. For example, the Dogrib Indians, hunting people in northwestern Canada, have many options, marrying either within or without the band, living with the parents of either husband or wife or with a brother of the husband, and so on. Many changes in residence may occur over a period of time. June Helm, who has described this fluid pattern, states that it also occurs in other hunting societies such as the Nambikwara of the Matto Grosso of Brazil, the !Kung Bushmen, and some Australian tribes (Helm 1968).

Why does a society come to "prefer" one form of residence over others? Many considerations must be involved. It has been argued that there is a stress on patrilocal residence in the case of hunting-gathering band societies where there is a premium on a man's knowing his hunting area where he, his father, and his brothers have hunted. Patrilocal residence also keeps together males who have grown up together and learned to defend themselves against outside attack. For reasons such as these, the claim has been made that all hunting-gathering societies in the past were patrilocal (Service 1962). This view is no longer generally held. As we have seen, there are hunting societies like the Dogrib and !Kung Bushmen that have no one consistent pattern of marital residence. This does not seem to be an aberrant modern development; the flexibility of such a system would have had advantages in the past as well as now (Lee and DeVore 1968:7–8).

Any aspect of a society's economy that enhances male status or favors male cooperation would seem, nevertheless, to strengthen the chances of patrilocal residence. Thus, pastoralism favors patrilocality; so does plough agriculture. Conditions favoring matrilocal residence would be those that foster cooperative work among women in gathering, fishing, or horticulture. Absence of herds and other forms of property associated with males and a low degree of political organization also seem to give weight to the matrilocal side. According to Kathleen Gough (1961:560) ". . . avunculocal residence seems most likely to occur where the descent group jointly owns an estate of relatively high productivity, in relation to which the products of the men require redistribution, and their labor, regular coordination, on the part of an authority." Neolocal residence seems

Determinants of marital residence

to be favored by factors that result in the isolation of the conjugal family and strengthen monogamy. An emphasis on individual private property and personal freedom would have the same result. Bilocal residence may be favored by migratory habits and appear in societies where the sexes have relatively equal status. The foregoing suggestions are largely hypothetical, since residence rules in most societies are very old and one cannot see them in process of formation.

Some possible determinants of kinship forms

It seems reasonable to suppose that kinship systems with patrilineal descent developed as a result of patrilocal residence. In such cases, the men form a permanent corporate group; the women are marrying-in outsiders. Pastoralism, warfare, and political centralization have probably contributed to patrilineality as well as to patrilocality.

Matriliny, on the other hand, has probably developed from matrilocal residence. Matriliny often seems to be related to horticulture at a low level of productivity. Except in the case of some groups in southern India, the Minangkabau of Indonesia, and a few other societies, matriliny is not found in areas having plough agriculture and extensive agricultural works.

Problems involved in matriliny and matrilocality

Since patriliny and patrilocality have a much higher incidence than matriliny and matrilocality, there seem to be some inherent disadvantages in the latter institutions. Perhaps marrying-in males who are outsiders from different communities form a less effective team for cooperation and defense than members of a patrilineal lineage who have grown up together. On the other hand, Kalervo Oberg (1955:481) has argued that matrilocality provides for effective mobilization of manpower among lowland tribes in South America. A man gets economic assistance from his sons-in-law; but his sons, who marry into nearby villages, can also be called upon for help when needed. If the sons remained at home and the daughters married-out, the sons-in-law could be called upon for help, but their ties to him would be weaker. Of course, the advantages of the matrilocal system depend upon the villages being rather close to one another.

Authority is usually in the hands of males. In patrilineal societies, there is consistency in the tracing of descent and exercise of authority by men. In matrilineal societies, however, there is some discontinuity. Marrying-in males do not have much authority in the wife's

Hopi women. The Hopi have matrilocal residence and matrilineal descent.

lineage, and, initially, at any rate, are placed in a position of relative inferiority. But a girl in northern India, trained to be submissive, is more easily kept in her inferior status than a marrying-in male in a matrilineal society. This creates some strain and tension for men in the latter case. Perhaps it is not surprising that a high rate of divorce has been reported for some matrilineal, matrilocal societies, such as the Hopi and Minangkabau. Max Gluckman (1950:190) has suggested that patrilineal tribes in Africa tend to have lower divorce rates than matrilineal or bilateral tribes.[3] Strong conjugal ties between husband and wife are probably more compatible with patrilineal than with matrilineal systems.

Matrilineal societies face other problems. If a woman gets married and moves to her husband's community, her kinfolk have to find

---

[3] The same point has been made for Indonesia (Loeb 1935:68 ff). David M. Schneider (1961:16) has observed: "The institutionalizing of very strong, lasting or intense solidarities between husband and wife is not compatible with the maintenance of matrilineal descent groups."

ways to maintain control over her children. Authority is divided between her brothers and her husband. But if there is matrilocal residence and her husband moves to her community, her brothers move out upon their marriages. Either way, it is difficult to secure discipline for the children from the maternal uncles (A. I. Richards 1950:246). If the clans have political functions, it may be harder for the male members of the clan to get together. These dilemmas are less pressing if the husband's and wife's families live near one another, as among the Hopi. The problem facing a matrilineal family group or lineage is how to maintain control over both its male and female members. In patrilineal, patrilocal societies, females are lost to the group, but this is less of a disadvantage since they are not needed to fill authority roles, while men must fill such roles in matrilineal societies.

Suggestions for further reading

Good studies of matriliny and matrilocality are available in A. I. Richards, "Some Types of Family Structure among the Central Bantu," in *African Systems of Kinship and Marriage,* ed. A. R. Radcliffe-Brown and Daryll Forde (London: Oxford University Press, 1950), pp. 207–51; and in the more comprehensive survey of matrilineal societies, David M. Schneider and Kathleen Gough, eds., *Matrilineal Kinship* (Berkeley and Los Angeles: University of California Press, 1961). For speculations on patrilocal bands as an allegedly basic type in hunting-gathering societies, see Elman R. Service, *Primitive Social Organization: An Evolutionary Perspective* (New York: Random House, 1962), chap. 3.

Patrilocal residence in a joint family household in northern India is well described in Leigh Minturn and John T. Hitchcock, "The Rājpūts of Khalapur, India," in *Six Cultures: Studies of Child Rearing,* ed. Beatrice B. Whiting (New York: John Wiley & Sons, 1963), pp. 203–362.

Once again, George P. Murdock's *Social Structure* and Robin Fox's *Kinship and Marriage* are recommended.

10

Male-female relations

The various forms of family organization reviewed in previous chapters represent different ways of combining males and females, parents and children. In many of these systems men seem to have higher status than women, although women have higher status in some arrangements than in others, a topic which forms the subject of this chapter. In most societies men carry out occupational and political roles which are conceived to be more important than those of women. At present there are women's movements which protest against the condition of male dominance. Others defend male dominance as a natural state of affairs resulting from the biological differences between men and women. A variant of this viewpoint is that male dominance stems from the long period during which human beings lived by hunting and gathering. It is argued that the greater strength of males gave them leadership positions in hunting and defense of the group. Women were tied to the home base by the demands of childbirth, suckling, and child rearing. They consequently engaged in such domestic tasks as cooking, fetching food and water, making clothing, and bringing up children. Although this was clearly essential work, women's tasks carried less prestige than the activities of men. Our culture today seemingly retains traces of our long hunting-gathering heritage in these respects.

While there are myths in some societies about a former state of matriarchy, in which women were dominant and held political power, anthropologists have found no society in which women actually control the political system. (Perhaps the nearest approach to such a state of affairs is the former society of the Iroquois, to be discussed later.) Men seem to have always been dominant in the

143

Indira Gandhi.

political sphere, despite the occasional appearance of a Golda Meir or Indira Gandhi. Although queens have reigned, their advisors have usually been male councillors; their generals and soldiers were males.

In opposition to those who hold male dominance to be natural and inevitable are those who consider it to be essentially arbitrary, not supportable by the biological distinctions between the sexes or past cultural conditions. One way to approach this subject is through a comparison with other primate species.

Primate comparisons: Dominance and aggression

Some primate species, particularly terrestrial ones, are marked by *sexual dimorphism*, differences in size and strength between males and females. In such species males are generally dominant over females, and in multi-male groups some males are often dominant over others. Dominant animals display more aggression, win most of the fights, and have priority in access to food, sexual relations, or other advantages of limited availability. Male primates generally show more aggression than females. This is true of our closest primate relatives, the chimpanzees. It is adult chimp males who kill animals of other species, although this is a relatively uncommon practice. Male chimpanzees eat much more meat than females do, and adult males have at least twice been seen to kill and eat immature chimpanzees (Bygott 1972).

Juvenile male primates engage in more rough-and-tumble play than do juvenile females. The sexual distinction in such behavior is probably influenced, though not completely determined, by the action of endocrine glands. This is suggested by laboratory experiments in which the male sex hormone testosterone was administered to pregnant female rhesus monkeys. Their "masculinized" female offspring showed more threatening behavior and rough-and-tumble play than did an untreated control group of females (Young, Goy, and Phoenix 1964). Experiments have been carried out in various animal species to change the structure of a group's dominance hierarchy by administering male hormones to its more submissive members. Thus, for example, when ringdoves ranking lowest in a pecking order were injected with male hormones, they rose to the highest positions in the dominance hierarchy (Hinde 1974:255; Ardrey 1970:113).

Both men and women have both male and female hormones in their systems, but a man secretes 2–2.5 times as much of the male hormone as a woman does. Women have a more variable endocrine balance. "At times, a normal woman may produce even less of the female hormone than an average man does, but at other times her production shoots up to much more than ten times as much" (Scheinfeld 1947:134). Since the endocrine glands form an interconnected system, it would be oversimplified to relate the male hormone directly to aggression. Besides, the term "aggression" is often used loosely, sometimes to cover all expressions of self-assertion. Should predatory behavior against other species be termed "aggression"? Perhaps not. The word should probably be limited to attacking behavior intended to cause injury to another individual; the injury may be either physical or symbolic, such as a threat to status.

Cross-cultural studies of aggression

The Six Cultures project described later (p. 312) was a well-designed cross-cultural investigation in which six communities were studied in some detail, particularly in relation to child-rearing practices. One by-product of this project was a study by Beatrice Whiting and Carolyn Pope Edwards of aspects of child behavior in the six communities, plus a seventh community, Ngecha, 20 miles north of Nairobi in Kenya, East Africa. The original six communities studied were: a Gusii community in Kenya, East Africa; a Rājpūt community in northern India; a village in Okinawa; a town in Mexico; a barrio in the Philippines; and a New England town in the United States.

On the basis of observation of children's behavior in the seven settings, it was stated that boys from three to six years old generally engage in more rough-and-tumble play than do girls. Insulting and dominating egoistically are also common male traits in this age group. Girls, on the other hand, exhibited more passive, dependent, and nurturant behavior than do boys. These observations are in accord with the usual stereotyped expectations about boys and girls. That, indeed, is what Whiting and Edwards believe is responsible for their findings. They attribute the contrasts in behavior not to any inborn predispositions but, rather, to early training for the expected roles of males and females. They found fewer sex differences in the case of the Gusii, where half the boys aged five years and over were assigned to take care of younger siblings and to help with domestic chores. Here the girls were rated aberrantly high in rough-and-tumble play and assaulting behavior (Whiting and Edwards 1973). In another East African tribe, the Luo of Kenya, boys are also often assigned "feminine" chores. Here a study showed that boys who did a good deal of such work were less aggressive than other boys, but still more aggressive than girls (Ember 1973).

Another cross-cultural study by Barry, Bacon, and Child (1957) which examined data from 110 societies, found a widespread pattern of stressing nurturance, obedience, and responsibility in girls, while emphasizing self-reliance and achievement motivation in boys.

In all these cross-cultural studies the emphasis of the authors is on socialization and training for adult life rather than on the influence of biological factors in causing contrasting patterns in the behavior of boys and girls. But if socialization is all that is involved, one wonders why parallel contrasts appear in so many species of higher primates as well as in so many human societies. It must be that biological reasons underlie the divergent training patterns that direct

Boys fighting

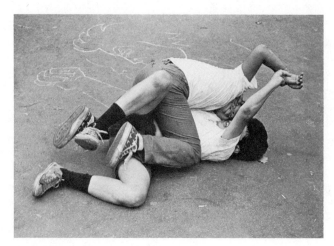

boys and girls toward different goals. There should be good reasons why boys and girls receive the contrasting kinds of socialization they do.

In still another cross-cultural study, Ronald P. Rohner examined data from 101 societies and found, as usual, that boys were invariably more aggressive than girls. In none of the societies were girls said to be more aggressive than boys. However, Rohner also found that the amount of aggression varied considerably from one society to another and that the level of aggression in one sex within a society tended to approximate that of the other sex, although boys always showed at least slightly more aggression than girls. Among the Chenchu of southern India, for example, the ethnographer never saw any quarrels or show of bad temper among the children within a six-week period. In a Colombian village in South America, on the other hand, constant displays of aggression among both boys and girls were observed. The level of aggression, then, is obviously influenced by general sociocultural conditions (Rohner 1976).

Rohner cites an unpublished cross-cultural study of 125 societies by Herbert Barry III and associates in which it is claimed that in only 20 percent of the societies were young boys *encouraged* to be more aggressive than girls. There would seem, then, to be some "natural" predisposition toward greater aggression on the part of boys, which, again, is apt to be considerably modified by sociocultural conditions and by particular child-rearing practices.

There are some societies where differences between males and females are not greatly emphasized; there are others in which they are stressed. In the latter group fall societies in which large animals are hunted and pastoral societies in which large animals are herded. In both cases male roles must be distinguished from female ones; correspondingly different training practices are therefore developed for boys and girls.

The following sections of this chapter present features of societies having different patterns of subsistence: hunting-gathering, horticultural, agricultural, and industrial societies.

Hunting-gathering societies

The argument that male dominance stems from our long hunting past has been advanced by such male writers as Lionel Tiger, Robin Fox, and Robert Ardrey. Tiger and Fox believe that there is a natural and universal tendency, which they call *male bonding*, for men to form cooperative groups that exclude women. Male bonding first developed during mankind's hunting phase, during which territoriality and defense of the group became vital concerns (Tiger and Fox 1971; Ardrey 1976).

A contrasting view of human evolution has been offered by two female anthropologists, M. Kay Martin and Barbara Voorhies (1975), who claim that in foraging (hunting-gathering) societies women are economically dominant and have a status equal to that of males. The basis for this contention is that in over two thirds of the foraging societies in a sample of 90, hunting provides only 30–40 percent of the diet. Gathering by women is therefore the mainstay of such a society. The authors admit that the recently studied groups that make up their sample are marginal peoples who do not have the rich game resources enjoyed by our Paleolithic forebears, but they claim that there is no evidence that the hunting-to-gathering ratio has been significantly altered. Naturally, no evidence for that is available from the remote past. Martin and Voorhies fail to mention an important consideration: the likelihood that there was much less gathering of plant foods in the days before cooking was developed. Plant foods of any caloric value generally need to be cooked before they can be digested by human beings, and many plants are poisonous in the raw state (Leopold and Ardrey 1972).

There is evidence of the use of fire in southern France 750,000 years ago and in northern China by 500,000 years ago, but fire may not have been used for cooking plants until a considerably later period, when adequate containers were made. A few million years of foraging preceded such an invention. Early humans must have collected fruits, nuts, seeds, and edible roots and shoots, but much of the plant food now consumed by marginal foragers was not yet utilizable. This is not to deny the claim that the sexes generally have an egalitarian, complementary relationship in hunting-gathering societies. Ernestine Friedl has noted that in such societies each sex controls resources and services required by the other, and both men and women enjoy a good deal of autonomy. On the other hand, male hunters often control extra-domestic exchanges of meat, which gives them some additional authority and prestige. According to Friedl (1975:31–32), dominance is least and equality between the two sexes is greatest in societies, such as the Washo of the Great Basin of North America, where men and women share the same subsistence tasks. Male dominance is greatest in societies, such as the Eskimo, where hunting is almost the sole source of food. Yet even in traditional Eskimo society there seems to have been a complementary, mutually dependent relationship between the sexes. A quotation from Franz Boas' early ethnographic work, *The Central Eskimo*, gives a vivid picture of what that relationship was like and what work was expected of the two sexes. Boas (1884:561–65) describes a typical day in wintertime:

At this time of year it is necessary to make use of the short daylight and twilight for hunting. Long before the day begins to dawn the Eskimo prepares for hunting. He rouses his housemates; his wife supplies the lamp with a new wick and fresh blubber and the dim light which has been kept burning during the night quickly brightens up and warms the hut. While the woman is busy preparing breakfast the man fits up his sledge for hunting. He takes the stone block which closes the entrance of the dwelling room during the night out of the doorway and passes through the low passages. Within the passage the dogs are sleeping, tired by the fatigues of the day before. . . . The sledge is iced, the harnesses are taken out of the storeroom by the door, and the dogs are harnessed by the sledge. Breakfast is now ready and after having taken a hearty meal of seal soup and frozen and cooked seal meat the hunter lashes the spear that stands outside of the hut upon the sledge, hangs the harpoon line, some toggles, and his knife over the antlers, and starts for the hunting ground. Here he waits patiently for the blowing seal, sometimes until late in the evening. . . .

Meanwhile the women, who stay at home, are engaged in their domestic occupations, mending boots and making new clothing, or they visit one another, taking some work with them, or pass their time with games or in playing with the children. While sitting at their sewing and at the same time

Eskimo hunter.

watching their lamps and cooking the meat, they incessantly hum their favorite tunes. About noon they cook their dinner and usually prepare at the same time the meal for the returning hunters. As soon as the first sledge is heard approaching, the pots, which have been pushed back during the afternoon, are placed over the fire, and when the hungry men enter the hut their dinner is ready. While hunting they usually open the seals caught early in the morning, to take out a piece of the flesh or liver, which they eat raw, for lunch. . . .

After the hunters reach home, they first unharness their dogs and unstring the traces, which are carefully arranged, coiled up, and put away in the store room. Then the sledge is unloaded and the spoils are dragged through the entrance into the hut. A religious custom commands the women to leave off working, and not until the seal is cut up, are they allowed to resume their sewing and the preparation of skins. . . .

When the men have finished their meal the women take their share, and then all attack the frozen meat which is kept in the store rooms. The women are allowed to participate in this part of the meal. . . .

All the work being finished, boots and stockings are changed, as they must be dried and mended. The men visit one another and spend the night in talking, singing, gambling, and telling stories. The events of the day are talked over, success in hunting is compared, the hunting tools requiring mending are set in order, and the lines and dried and softened.

Here there seems to be a rather egalitarian relationship between men and women, although the men are the focus of more attention. But we will see later in Chapter 18 that Central Eskimo myths and tales often depict women as negative and dangerous beings. A devaluation of women is also suggested by the formerly common Eskimo practice of female infanticide. On the other hand, Jean L. Briggs (1974), who spent 30 months in the Central Arctic, saw no conscious, institutionalized conflict between the two sexes.

Horticultural societies

The difficulty of generalizing about horticultural societies, which show much variability, is stressed both by Friedl and by Martin and Voorhies, but both studies make some general statements. In a worldwide sample of 515 horticultural societies, Martin and Voorhies (1975) claim that women dominate cultivation activities in about 41 percent of the cases. In only 22 percent of the societies are men the exclusive cultivators. In societies where the two sexes contribute equally (37 percent), the men usually have the responsibility of clearing the garden plots, while the women tend and harvest the crops. As dependency on crops increases, so does the role of men in cultivation.

Although the range is great, most horticultural societies are small; in about 79 percent of the sample the populations are less than 400.

In societies with larger populations than that, there is an increased male share in cultivation.

Despite the important economic roles of women, patrilineal kinship systems predominate in horticultural societies. Matrilineal societies make up only one quarter of the sample. Ernestine Friedl notes that warfare is endemic in many horticultural societies. That would tend to strengthen male status. Men also engage in extra-familial food distributions, a source of prestige. Separate men's houses are found in many horticultural societies. Furthermore, polygyny occurs in 55 percent of the Martin and Voorhies sample. If several wives are busy cultivating plants, a man's wealth and prestige multiply. Hence there are many factors that bolster the status of males in horticultural societies. On the other hand, women also have certain advantages. They often engage in trade in such societies and enjoy a good deal of autonomy and influence, particularly in matrilineal and matrilocal systems.

Yolanda Murphy and Robert F. Murphy (1974) have focused on women's roles in a study of the Mundurucú, a South American Indian horticultural tribe located east of the upper Tapajós River in Brazil. A Mundurucú village contains from 50 to 100 persons. The men occupy a men's house, and there are three to five dwellings where the women and children live. Houses are set in a circle grouped around a village plaza. There are two moieties, subdivided into clans; extended cross-cousin marriage is practiced. Descent is patrilineal, but residence is usually matrilocal, which results in a scattered dispersal of clansmen. Women, on the other hand, form compact, continuing groups held together by collective labor. Men's work—hunting, fishing, and formerly warfare—takes them outside the village; women's work is done within it. Although men clear the fields, women do most of the horticultural work.

A group of village women—mothers, daughters, sisters, and others —makes up a collective team for processing manioc and controls its distribution. Moreover, a woman distributes the game brought back by her husband. Women seem to have a secure position in village life. A senior woman is the acknowledged head of her dwelling. Men do not challenge her authority; they live in their separate men's house and play no role in women's domestic activities. There is little economic cooperation between husband and wife; the nuclear family is not a productive unit in this society. It is the cooperative women's group that controls production.

However, in Mundurucú ideology women are considered inferior to men. A myth recounts that women were formerly dominant and played sacred trumpets which men took away from them and now store in the men's house. The Murphys suggest that the myth expresses the men's insecurity about their own current dominance. Women are supposed to be passive and submissive; those who violate the standards are subject to mass rape by the men. The women resent this practice and do not acknowledge the male claims of superiority. Under the circumstances it is hard to define the status of women in Mundurucú society. The men judge it to be low, but the women do not accept the males' definition of the situation.

Another horticultural society, in which women had a more acknowledged high status, was that of the Iroquois in the 18th century. Descent was matrilineal; residence was matrilocal in longhouses which contained several family units in separate compartments. An elder woman in charge of a longhouse could evict a man for misbehavior. As among the Mundurucú, women had control over the production, storage, and distribution of food. Communally owned land, inherited matrilineally, was held by the women, who also owned the farming implements and seeds. Horticultural work was organized under the supervision of an elected female leader chosen by the women who worked together.

A council of chiefs headed the confederacy or League of the Iroquois. Selection of these chiefs was determined by matrons of the matrilineal clans, who could also impeach a chief whose actions met with their disapproval. Iroquois matrons had a role in council deliberations and veto power in declarations of war, for since men could not hunt while on a war party they had to depend on dried rations provided by the women. Women also controlled such assets as wampum. Moreover, in contrast to the Mundurucú, they played important roles in the religious life. Iroquois ideology does not seem to have pictured women as inferior. The high status of Iroquois women may be attributed to the combination of matrilineal descent, matrilocal residence, and women's control of both production and distribution (Martin and Voorhies 1975:225–28; J. K. Brown 1970).

Agricultural societies

In agricultural societies, including peasant societies, male authority is heightened and female status is often considerably depressed. Men are usually the main cultivators, since the ploughing and irrigation connected with agriculture involve strenuous work in which male strength is clearly advantageous. Since farming is mainly men's work, polygyny ceases to be adaptive as it was under horticulture, and this type of family becomes much less common (Martin and Voorhies 1975:288).

In a review of 46 peasant community studies, Evalyn J. Michaelson and Walter Goldschmidt (1971) found that economic control and authority are in the hands of men. Fathers tend to be authoritative and mothers indulgent. In patrilineal families, which are common, marriages are usually arranged, and there are weak affective ties between husband and wife; although strong bonds usually develop between mother and son. A common feature of peasant life is social segregation of the sexes.

The custom of *purdah*, or seclusion of women, is found in Muslim households, primarily in cities, in Pakistan and northern India and also among many Hindus in northern India. According to the purdah system a woman generally stays within special women's quarters in the home. If she leaves its confines, she must cover her face with a veil or part of her sari. The Rājpūts in northern India have separate houses or sleeping quarters for men and women. Husbands may visit their wives in the women's courtyard at night. Patrilocal residence is practiced. A married girl covers her face in the presence of her husband's older male relatives and other visitors and she sits at a lower level than her in-laws. Strictly speaking, she should cover her face in front of her mother-in-law and older sisters-in-law until the birth of her first child, but since this custom involves so much inconvenience, it is often omitted. Ideally, a man and his wife should not talk to one another in the presence of older members of his family — who are usually present (Minturn and Hitchcock 1963:240–41, 266).

Sexual segregation is also practiced in rural Egyptian towns. In Silwa, in upper Egypt, women are expected to stay within the home. A woman who often leaves her house is called a "strayer." Women keep to the wall when walking down the street, while men walk

Veiled women in Morocco.

down the middle. If she should meet a man, a woman turns her head away or pulls her head covering over her face (Ammar 1966).

This kind of sexual segregation finds support in the Koran, where it says of women: "They should not go out of the house lest they commit a grave sin." Therefore a pious woman should first get her husband's consent before leaving the house. Urban Egyptian women were generally veiled until the 1920s, when that custom was ended by a liberalizing feminist movement, but until then veiling was common in much of North Africa and the Near East.

Veiling and purdah were not practiced in precommunist China, but the position of women was comparable in many ways to that of northern Indian women, since arranged marriages, patrilineal descent, and patrilocal residence were customary. As in India, a young bride was under the domination of her mother-in-law and had to be on her best behavior in her husband's family. The low status of women was expressed by the high incidence of female infanticide in traditional China. However, it seems that accounts about submissive daughters-in-law in the literature about China have given Westerners an oversimplified conception of the Chinese woman. That is suggested by the work of Margery Wolf, who gives an intimate picture of women's life in rural Taiwan. She shows that women were not just passive pawns at the mercy of a stern mother-in-law. They were not confined to walled courtyards, but spent much time washing clothes by the river, cleaning vegetables at a pump, or sewing under a tree in the company of other women. These groups formed gossip centers where a bride had an opportunity to complain about her mother-in-law's behavior. Since a mother-in-law knows about the force of local gossip, that should act as a check on her behavior. From Margery Wolf's account we learn that the women in rural Taiwan do not fit the usual stereotype. "A truly successful Taiwanese woman is a rugged individualist who has learned to depend largely on herself while appearing to lean on her father, her husband, and her son" (Wolf 1972:41).

Industrial societies

If agricultural societies emphasize that women's place is in the home, industrialism brought women out of the home, first into factories as machine workers and later into offices as typists and stenographers. The greater strength of males was of less significance in a factory where muscle was provided by machines; and since women's labor was cheaper than men's, it was in great demand. By 1860 one third of all factory workers in New England were women. During the Civil War, women not only became nurses and took factory jobs but also got clerical work in business offices which had formerly employed only men. After the war, women became the dominant sex in teaching.

The factories that employed women often produced goods that replaced the traditional kinds of work women had done in earlier agricultural times, such as prepared cereals, canned vegetables, and factory-made clothing. The new kinds of work ultimately affected women's dress too. Long skirts were dangerous in a factory; skirts became shorter and dresses simpler after 1890 (Degler 1964).

There were over 1 million female factory workers by the 1890s, most of whom were young and unmarried. But married women, including those with children, increasingly sought employment, particularly during and after World War II. Between 1948 and 1967 the rate of employment for mothers of young children nearly doubled. In 1969 a government publication stated that women made up 37 percent of the work force in the United States; more than one third of the working women had dependent children.

Accompanying the changes in women's roles were demands for equal treatment with men. American women got the right to vote in 1920. Since then demands have been made for equal pay and equal employment opportunities with men. Although many women are not satisfied with the advances made so far, there have been remarkable changes in these respects since World War I.

This brief review has dealt with the United States as an example of an industrial society, but comparable developments have taken place in the other industrial societies of the world. The sex ratio is in favor of women in the Soviet Union, since so many men were killed in World War II. Fifteen years after the war there were 20 million more women than men in the Soviet population. There are proportionately even more female school teachers in the USSR than in the United States, and the elected leaders of peer collectives in schools are likely to be girls (Bronfenbrenner 1970:73). However, women do not hold prominent administrative posts in either the government or the Communist Party. Apart from education, they figure prominently in the field of medicine, making up 75 percent of the total, but 92 percent of the women hold lower-ranking positions. In education, too, women teachers are mainly found in the lower grades (Martin and Voorhies 1975:379).

Despite the very different political systems and ideologies of Russia and the United States, there has been a good deal of convergence in the experiences of women in moving from a mainly domestic realm into factories, hospitals, schools, and other contemporary spheres of occupation.

**Suggestions
for further
reading**

The question of how or to what extent males and females differ in person-ality is discussed in two collections of articles: Dirk L. Schaffer, ed., *Sex Differences in Personality: Readings* (Belmont, Calif.: Brooks/Cole, 1971), and Eleanor E. Maccoby, ed., *The Development of Sex Differences* (Stanford, Calif.: Stanford University Press, 1966).

The view that male dominance stems from the hunting tradition is presented in Lionel Tiger and Robin Fox, *The Imperial Animal* (New York: Holt, Rinehart, and Winston, 1971) and also in Robert Ardrey's books, the latest of which is *The Hunting Hypothesis* (New York: Atheneum, 1976).

A more feminist approach to the evolution of culture is expressed in M. Kay Martin and Barbara Voorhies, *Female of the Species* (New York: Columbia University Press, 1975) and in Ernestine Friedl, *Women and Men: An Anthropologist's View* (New York: Holt, Rinehart, and Winston, 1975).

Some interesting reading is provided in two collections of articles by female anthropologists: Michelle Zimbalist Rosaldo and Louise Lamphere eds., *Woman, Culture, and Society* (Stanford, Calif.: Stanford University Press, 1974), and Carolyn J. Matthiasson, ed., *Many Sisters: Women in Cross-Cultural Perspective* (New York: The Free Press, 1974).

For a good account of women's life in a hunting-gathering society, see Jane C. Goodale, *Tiwi Wives: A Study of the Women of Melville Island, North Australia* (Seattle: University of Washington Press, 1971). For a horticultural society, see Yolanda Murphy and Robert F. Murphy, *Women of the Forest* (New York: Columbia University Press, 1974). For an agri-cultural society, see Margery Wolf, *Women and the Family in Rural Taiwan* (Stanford, Calif.: Stanford University Press, 1972).

part five

Age grades, associations, castes, and classes

11

Age grades and voluntary associations

As we have seen, kinship is an important organizing principle not only in tribal societies but also at higher levels of socioeconomic integration. However, it is not the only organizing principle. Societies are knit together in other ways than through kinship.

Just as all societies have kinship terms for different relatives, they also have terms for persons of different age levels, corresponding roughly to our words: infant, baby, child, boy, girl, adolescent, young man, young girl, man, woman, old man, old woman — to which various other terms could be added. These refer to different *age grades*.

The term *age set* is used for a group of persons of the same sex who are of about the same age, such as the members of a particular class in school. Together they advance from one grade to another. Members of an age set may develop strong bonds of solidarity, supporting one another in everyday activities and in marriage and other ceremonies. Like kinship units, they may be corporate groups, although they do not usually own property or have special religious cults or shrines.

Initiation ceremonies

In some societies, movement from one age grade to another is celebrated by elaborate rituals, especially at puberty. Indeed, boys' initiation ceremonies at puberty receive far more emphasis in some societies than do marriage ceremonies.

159

This is the case among the Arunta of central Australia, whose initiation ceremonies go on for weeks or months and are marked by various stages. The boys are first segregated from the women and children and are made to fast and stay awake at night. Then the old men throw the boys up in the air and beat them when they come down. The men sit around an initiate and bite his scalp and chin until they bleed (which makes the hair grow and is good for the scalp, they say). Then the boys are circumcised and subincised. In a final ordeal they have to lie on some leaves over a smoldering fire. A boy who has gone through all that is surely entitled to feel that he is now a man.

Circumcision and other genital operations have a wide distribution in the puberty ceremonies of Africa, Melanesia, and Australia. In some Australian societies, a tooth gets knocked out instead. In the tropical forest area of South America, youths are often tested by fasting, exposure to ant bites, scarification, and whipping. A girl may

Initiation among the Iatmul of New Guinea. The boy, clasped and comforted by his mother's brother, is cut by a member of the moiety opposite to that of the boy.

be hoisted in a hammock up to the ceiling of the large communal house in which she lives, where she is exposed to smoke from fires within the house.

These ordeals are reminiscent of the hazing that accompanies initiation into secret societies, and, in a sense, that is what is involved. The boys who are admitted into the ranks of the older males are often given instruction about matters hitherto kept from them, and they may be warned on pain of death or severe punishment never to reveal these secrets to the women or uninitiated children.

Arunta men have sacred objects of stone or wood, decorated with simple designs, called *churingas*. These are kept in secret storage places and taken out on solemn occasions, passed from hand to hand among the men, and sometimes rubbed on their bodies. These *churingas* must never be seen by women or children, but, after a boy has been initiated, he may be shown them and told something about the mysteries associated with them.

In the Chaga tribe in East Africa, the adult men are not supposed to defecate. At least, that is the impression they try to give to the women. They say that at the time of initiation a man's anus is stopped up by a plug, which he retains until old age. Defecation must be done very secretly, and severe punishments are threatened to any man who should be so disloyal as to spill the secret. However, the women know what is going on. In *their* initiation ceremonies, the older women tell the young girls that the men pretend not to defecate, and they are warned not to laugh about the matter.

So, initiation into adulthood involves learning all kinds of things one did not know before. For the boys, initiation involves separation from their mothers and closer association with the adult men. Such ceremonies celebrate and reinforce male social solidarity. They often occur in warring polygynous societies in which male solidarity is an important desideratum. Upon initiation the boy may be given a new name, new accouterments, and new privileges that designate his enhanced status.

Some different explanations have been offered by anthropologists to account for why there are initiation ceremonies in some societies and not in others. In some Pacific islands there are no such transition rites; so socialization of the young can take place without them. Explanations for this range from psychological to sociological in nature. John W. M. Whiting and some of his colleagues have offered a series of interpretations based on cross-cultural correlations in 56 societies. It was hypothesized that societies likely to have initiation ceremonies for boys at puberty are those in which mother and child sleep exclusively together for at least a year after the birth and which have a taboo on sexual relations between husband and wife during that period. The reason first put forward for this hypothesis was that the mother-son sleeping arrangement establishes a strong, dependent relationship of the boy upon the mother and Oedipal hostility toward the father, both of which need to be counteracted by the time of puberty. An initiation ceremony serves these functions by separating the boys from their mothers and bringing them into the ranks of the adult males. A later interpretation by Whiting, which was felt to be more satisfactory than the earlier one, was that one consequence of exclusive mother-child sleeping arrangements is a boy's cross-sex identification with his mother that needs to be overcome and replaced by male identification through the drama of the initiation ceremony. Whiting and his colleagues found correlations in support of their hypotheses linking exclusive mother-child sleeping arrangements and postpartum sex taboos with initiation ceremonies. Of 20 societies where both antecedent variables were found, 14 had initiation ceremonies and 6 did not. Where both of the antecedent variables were absent, only 2 of the 25 societies had the ceremonies (Whiting, Kluckhohn, and Anthony 1958; Burton and Whiting 1961).

Interpretations of a more sociological, less psychological sort have been offered by Yehudi A. Cohen and Frank W. Young, both of whom have also made use of the cross-cultural correlation approach. In a sample of 65 societies, Cohen distinguished between those in which socialization is directed toward establishing the individual in a larger kin group stressing interdependence (28 societies) and those in which socialization is directed toward independence anchored in a nuclear family (37 societies). Initiation ceremonies were found in 18 of the 28 societies of the first type (about 65 percent) but in only 1 of the second type. This suggests that initiation ceremonies are more apt to occur in societies in which the interdependent action of clan or lineage members is important (Cohen 1964:113).

Frank W. Young claims that initiation ceremonies serve to dramatize and reinforce male solidarity in "middle-level" societies "where the variety of food exploitation patterns is limited and where the resources may be exploited by cooperative groups. Moreover, it is among such societies that intergroup hostilities conducive to male solidarity are possible" (Young 1962:380).

In another cross-cultural study, Judith K. Brown finds that no initiation ceremony takes place for girls in societies where they leave home upon marriage since the act of leaving marks that change. But, in societies where the girl remains in the same social setting after marriage, a ceremony may be performed to mark her change of status, especially in societies in which women make a notable contribution to subsistence (J. K. Brown 1963).

Men's house in
New Guinea.

Men's houses

Many societies have a special men's house where unmarried men sleep. It also frequently serves as a ceremonial center and military stronghold. Among the Rengma Naga of northeastern India, boys move to the men's house when they are six or seven years old and sleep there until they get married. Older men come there to sit and gossip and to instruct the young boys. In former days, when fighting was frequent, men kept their knives, spears, and shields in the men's house. This place was regarded as a sanctuary. No fugitive criminal could be harmed if he sought protection there. Corresponding to the men's house there was a "dormitory" for unmarried women, which girls entered at the age of six or seven and left at marriage.

Men's houses are found in various societies in Africa, Indonesia, Melanesia, Micronesia, Polynesia, and South America. The character and functions of such houses differ in different cultures, but their existence in any society serves to symbolize and strengthen male solidarity. The bonds among the adult men cross-cut kinship lines, enabling the men of a society to act in concert, whether they are related by kinship ties or not.

Nyakyusa age-set villages

An unusual arrangement emphasizing age sets has been worked out by the Nyakyusa, a Bantu-speaking tribe in East Africa. Until around ten years of age, boys live in their fathers' homes, but, after that, they leave and start a new village with other boys of their age set and build little huts of reeds in which they sleep. Later, when they are older, the boys build more substantial houses with better thatch. At first, two or three friends share a hut, but, eventually, each builds his own house. Unmarried youths continue to eat at their fathers' houses, which they visit in small groups in turn.

When a young man of about 25 gets married, he brings his wife to his village. Then, for the first time, he is able to have fields of his own and eat his own produce, for cultivation requires the cooperation of a man and a woman, and cooking is women's work.

Eight or ten years after the young men from the chief's village have begun to marry, their fathers hand over the government of the country to them, following an elaborate series of ceremonies. Each Nyakyusa village, then, is composed of men of different age sets with their wives and children.

This system should lead to considerable autonomy and independence on the part of young men. Although bonds with age mates are emphasized, kinship ties are still important, for property, such as cattle, circulates within the kinship group rather than within the age-set village (Wilson 1951).

The solidarity of an age set may be brought about by other means, such as the coresidence of boys and girls in the Muria dormitory (see p. 105) or by membership in school classes or fighting groups. In all of these systems the age grades cross-cut kinship lines and provide for wider social ties.

Voluntary associations

So far we have been dealing with society-wide categories according to age. Some societies also have voluntary associations not joined by all members of the society, although they are not limited by kinship. These include men of different age sets and different kin groups. Some societies may have several parallel, roughly equivalent social units of this kind, which are competitive in some respects. An example is provided by the military societies of Plains Indian tribes such as the Cheyenne.

Cheyenne military societies

The equestrian, buffalo-hunting Cheyenne Indians of the early 19th century on the Great Plains had six military societies: Fox, Elk,

Shield, Bowstring, Dog, and Northern Crazy Dogs. The members in each of these came from all the bands that made up the summer-camp circle, with the exception of the Dog soldiers, who were from a single band. Except for the latter, the military societies could function only during the summer months when all the Cheyenne bands came together. In wintertime the camp circle was dispersed and the component bands hunted in separate territories.

It was an honor to belong to a military society, and each claimed to be the best and bravest. Each society had special ways of painting the body and personal possessions and maintained some special traditions. The military societies had the responsibility of keeping order when the tribe was on the march, during communal buffalo hunts, and on tribal ritual occasions. They represented a kind of police force under the authority of the tribal council of 44 chiefs and could punish persons who violated the rule against unauthorized hunting of the buffalo and broke other tribal laws. These social units obviously had much political importance in regulating social order among the Cheyennes. They cross-cut kinship, age, and band divisions.

Secret societies

In some societies there are voluntary associations whose membership is secret. Some American Indian tribes, including the Hopi, Kwakiutl, and Iroquois, have had such societies; they are also important in West Africa and the Congo. Sometimes, as among the Hopi, the Iroquois, and the Mende of Sierra Leone, secret societies are associated with the curing of particular ailments. Sometimes they have political functions. African secret societies help to maintain social order, backed by strong religious sanctions. Since secret societies sometimes perform in public dances or rituals, it is not surprising that many have developed the use of masks or other forms of disguise, like the Ku Klux Klan.

Among the Mende, secret societies play roles in the education of the young, regulation of sexual conduct, supervision of political and economic affairs, and the operation of various social services, including medical treatment, entertainment, and recreation. In the Poro society, boys undergo a long initiation which involves both ordeals and instruction. They learn something about native law, crafts, agricultural techniques, drumming and singing, bridge building, and the setting of traps. There is a parallel society for girls, who receive training in housework and child care and are given sex instruction. The Humoi society is concerned with the regulation of sexual conduct. The Mende have many taboos concerning sex, and there are many relatives with whom sexual intercourse is forbidden; it is believed that transgression of such rules results in sickness. A person must be treated by the society concerned with the taboos he has broken; so those who violate sexual regulations report to the Humoi society. Illness may also be explained as being due to a person's having entered that part of the bush where secret society meetings have been held. Confession to the society is required, followed by medical treatment and purification. Those who have been so treated become members of the secret society, since they have learned something about the society's operations in the process.

The Poro society has important political functions. No one can hold office among the Mende without being a Poro member; no chief can be appointed without its approval. There are dangers of autocracy here, but the Poro may, at the same time, act as a check on the autocracy of rulers. The Poro society also has economic functions in fixing prices for certain commodities and regulating trade (Little 1949).

Secret societies have sometimes played political and economic roles in the Western world as well—witness the Ku Klux Klan and the Mafia. Anthropologists have not done much work on secret societies, but that is understandable, for if an anthropologist can learn the secrets of such a society, it's not a very secret society.

Religious cults

Religious cults that require periodic ceremonies bring members together and emphasize their common ties. Among many possible examples, let us consider the Drum Dance, or Dream Dance, of the Chippewa Indians in northern Wisconsin. This dance was borrowed from the Sioux in the 1870s, after peace was made between these Indian groups. It is said to have originated from the vision of a young Sioux Indian girl who was instructed by the Great Spirit to spread the dance as a means of reconciling the Chippewa, Sioux, and other Indian groups. Not all Chippewa Indians are members of this cult. In the 1940s (the period for which the following description applies), there were three drum groups at the Lac Court Oreilles reservation, each consisting of about 30 people. Such a group tries to meet at least once very season to drum, sing, and pray. Members also assemble on various emergency occasions—to remove mourning from a person who is initiated into the group, to install new members, or to effect curing through the presence of certain powerful individuals who relate dreams of their buffalo or grizzly-bear spirits.

The drum groups also visit other communities and act as hosts to visiting drum groups from outside. Not only do the Chippewa In-

Chippewa Drum
Dance drum.

dians from different reservations pay mutual four-day visits to each
other but the Drum Dance network also includes Menomini, Pota-
watomi, and Winnebago Indians, for the Drum Dance aims to cut
across local and tribal ties and to establish friendly relations everywhere. This intercommunication is fostered by the practice of giving
drums away every few years. Such a cult provides an in-group for its
members, taking on some of the attributes and functions of a kinship
unit.

Voluntary associations in the United States

The United States is a nation in which all kinds of voluntary associations flourish—clubs, including women's clubs (unheard of in
some nations), learned societies, Rotarians, Lions, Moose, Elk, nud-
ist groups, bird-watching societies, veterans associations, alumni,
chess players, societies for helping the American Indian or Negro
Americans, associations for aiding museums, conserving nature, and
many other causes. This aspect of American life must have developed early in our history, for it was commented upon, with his usual
penetrating attention, by Alexis de Tocqueville in the 1830s.

Tocqueville (1954:117–18) found that voluntary associations were
much more numerous here than in other countries, and he related
this to the democratic traditions of the United States:

As soon as several of the inhabitants of the United States have taken up an
opinion or a feeling which they wish to promote in the world, they look out
for mutual assistance; and as soon as they have found one another out, they
combine. From that moment on they are no longer isolated men, but a power

seen from afar, whose actions serve for an example and whose language is listened to.

Impressed by this phenomenon, Tocqueville (1954:118) concluded, "If men are to remain civilized or to become so, the art of associating together must grow and improve in the same ratio in which the equality of conditions is increased."

Suggestions for further reading

Puberty ceremonies, especially those involving genital operations such as circumcision and subincision, have lent themselves to various Freudian and sociological analyses, of which the following references provide a variety of interpretations: Theodor Reik, *Ritual: Psychoanalytic Studies* (New York: International Universities Press, 1958), pp. 99 ff.; Bruno Bettelheim, *Symbolic Wounds: Puberty Rites and the Envious Male* (Glencoe, Ill.: Free Press, 1954); John W. M. Whiting, Richard Kluckhohn, and Albert Anthony, "The Function of Male Initiation Ceremonies at Puberty," in *Readings in Social Psychology*, ed. Eleanor E. Maccoby, Theodore M. Newcomb, and Eugene L. Hartley, 3d ed. (New York: Henry Holt & Co., 1958), pp. 359–70; William N. Stephens, *The Oedipus Complex: Cross-Cultural Evidence* (Glencoe, Ill.: Free Press, 1962): Yehudi A. Cohen, *The Transition From Childhood to Adolescence: Cross-Cultural Studies of Initiation Ceremonies, Legal Systems, and Incest Taboos* (Chicago: Aldine Publishing Co., 1964); Frank W. Young, *Initiation Ceremonies: A Cross-Cultural Study of Status Dramatization* (Indianapolis: Bobbs-Merrill Co., Inc., 1965).

12

Castes and classes

Caste and class stratification are found mainly in advanced civilizations. Although some exceptions can be cited, there is usually not much internal ranking in hunting-gathering bands. Hereditary social classes appear in many advanced horticultural and agricultural societies. In this chapter we shall consider some aspects of the caste system in India and similar features in some other societies. After that, concepts of class and class stratification will be discussed.

Hindu castes

A Hindu caste is an endogamous, hierarchically ranked social group, which is sometimes associated with a particular occupation. Rules determine whether or not one may accept food or water from persons of different caste. Usually, one may accept food from one's own and from higher, but not lower, castes. Concepts of pollution are associated with the lowest-ranking castes, termed "untouchables," who often have separate wells and live in separate quarters in a town or village.

Endogamy

Endogamy is the requirement to marry within a particular group. Like the opposite rule of exogamy, it may apply to different kinds of social units. Among the Inca of Peru there was a requirement to marry a person of one's own village or community; this could be called village or local endogamy. In the Hindu caste system one must marry within the caste or subcaste. A caste resembles a clan in that membership is determined by birth. However, clans are

169

Hindu villager by
pond.

exogamous; husband and wife are members of different clans but
must always belong to the same caste. Although clans and castes
seem to be very different kinds of social units, Lévi-Strauss believes
that the latter may in some cases, at least, have developed from the
former. He points to some similarities between totemistic clans and
Hindu castes, such as food prohibitions, the function of marriage
regulation, and the complementary exchange of certain goods or
services. He believes that some tribes in southeastern North America, such as the Creek and Chickasaw, were in the process of trans-
forming their clan units into castes (Lévi-Strauss 1966a:113 ff). While
this may have occurred, it would seem that a caste system of the type
found in India must depend upon a more complex economic specialization and division of labor.

Hierarchical ranking

Castes in India are ranked. Some castes are considered to be purer
and higher than others. The Brahmans, associated with the priest-

hood and with education, are accorded the highest rank, while Chamars (leatherworkers) and Bhangis (sweepers) are the lowest. In some of the intermediate ranks, there may be disagreement about relative position in the system, but there is a rough consensus about the structure of the hierarchy and placement of castes within it.

The relative rank of a caste group is related to its traditional occupation. Those engaged in work that is considered defiling, such as handling leather or cleaning latrines, are low in the social order. Some low-caste groups have tried to raise their collective status by refusing to follow traditional occupations, tabooing the eating of meat, and being meticulous in the observance of orthodox Hindu rituals.

Because of the stratification in the caste system, some people have regarded castes as frozen classes. One theory about the origin of the caste system is that it resulted from efforts of the light-skinned Aryan invaders after 1500 B.C. to maintain social distance between themselves and the dark-skinned peoples they conquered. Yet another equally plausible view is that a caste system was already in operation in India before the arrival of the Aryans. Contrary to the usual assumptions, a caste system does not preclude social mobility. The hierarchy is not absolutely frozen. Some Hindu untouchables are wealthy; many Brahmans are poor. An untouchable, B. R. Ambedkar, was India's first minister of law. Status in India is affected by criteria other than caste membership alone.

Traditional occupation

Not all Hindu castes are associated with particular occupations. Exceptions occur in the case of some groups, such as the Jats of northern India, that originated as tribal groups. Many hill tribes, which formerly constituted separate social units with distinctive cultures, have become absorbed into the Hindu caste system, often, though not always, with low rank.

To give an example of a particular Indian village, let us consider the caste composition of the village of Rampur, 15 miles west of Delhi, with a population of about 1,100. This village, like many in northern India, has a "dominant caste" —a caste that not only has numerical superiority but also owns all the land in the village. In Rampur the dominant caste is that of the Jats, who number 78 families. They have the reputation of being hard-working farmers.

There are 15 Brahman families in Rampur. The men of these families are farmers, whose actual status is no higher than that of the Jat landlords. None of them are priests.

Not far below the Jats in status are the four Khati (carpenter) families and one Lohar (blacksmith). There is one Baniya (merchant) family. There are three Nai (barber), two Chipi (tailor), seven Kumhar (potter), five Jhinvar (water carrier), and four Dhobi (washermen) families. At the bottom of the hierarchy are the 20 Chamar (leatherworker) and 10 Bhangi (sweeper) families.

Most of the houses of the Jats are clustered in the center of the village, along with some Brahmans, the Nais, and the Baniya families. Most of the other castes are on the outskirts of the village.

Not all persons carry on the traditional occupation associated with the caste. Many Chamars refuse to do so because of their desire for higher status. But many persons do follow the traditional work (Lewis with Barnouw 1958: chap. 1,2).

The *jajmani* system

In villages like Rampur there is a system whereby goods and services are exchanged that has come to be known as the *jajmani* system. It is helpful to understand how this system works in a rural Indian village, since it serves to make the caste system more comprehensible to a person from the Western world.

To contrast jajmani practices with our own, let us consider the problem of getting a haircut. In the United States a man who wants to get a haircut goes to a barbership, waits for his turn, has his hair cut, pays for it, and gives the barber a tip. If he lives in a city, he may go to many different barbershops in the course of a year, not being obliged to patronize the same one all the time. In Rampur, however, there are no barbershops. If you are a Jat, a barber comes to your home or visits you in the fields. Payment is made, not when he has finished but later, at harvest time. You can expect him to come around in about a month to cut your hair and give you a shave once more. It is always the same barber or a close relative of his, a brother or son, who cuts your hair. Maybe he is not a very good barber and you would rather have another one, but the rules do not permit it.

A barber has hereditary ties with certain Jat families whose hair he cuts. He does not serve all Jat families, for the barbers of a particular area have to divide up the clientele. The client who is served in this system is called a *jajman;* the person performing the service is termed a *kamin.* A particular kamin family may have served a jajman family for many generations. The barber's father cut the hair of the jajman's father, and the barber's son will cut the hair of the jajman's son or grandson. At harvest times, when the kamins present themselves at the fields, stipulated amounts of grain are handed out by the jajman to his kamins. There may be many of the latter, for the jajman has similar relations with families of other castes. A particular potter family presents him with clay vessels when needed during the year. Members of a particular Chamar family drag off his dead cows, skin them, and make sandals and other leather objects. A particular Bhangi family sweeps the jajman's courtyard and cleans his latrine. Thus, many goods and services are exchanged with little exchange of money.

Besides grain, kamins receive various other benefits from the system: a virtually free house site; some free food, fodder, and timber; and credit facilities and legal advice and aid from their jajmans. They are tied to their client families in various ways. Nais (barbers), for example, used to be marriage go-betweens and helped to arrange the marriages of their jajman's children. Chamars did various kinds of fieldwork, repaired roofs, and dug wells, among other things. Each caste has a particular role to play at a wedding and may expect to receive some food and other handouts on the occasion. Lower castes exchange some goods and services among themselves.

The jajmani system is now breaking up in Rampur and in many other villages through an increasing involvement with the money economy from outside the village and because of the refusal of some lower caste groups, particularly Chamars, to perform their traditional services (Lewis with Barnouw 1958).

One might suppose that if the jajmani system is breaking up, the caste system itself might be disappearing in India, especially since

Hindu barber shaving customer in Rampur.

the government has passed much legislation against the observance of untouchability and caste discrimination. However, that is not the case. Caste endogamy is still the rule. A small minority of well-to-do westernized persons are willing to marry across caste lines, but, otherwise, this is seldom done. In elections, castes tend to vote in blocs. There has probably been an increase in caste solidarity in recent years among low-caste groups, such as the Chamars, who are campaigning for better treatment. Caste journals are published. There are caste hostels, banks, hospitals, and cooperatives. Separate seats are set aside for "Ex-Untouchables" in Parliament and state legislatures, and there are separate scholarships for them in schools and universities. These institutions paradoxically emphasize and perpetuate caste distinctions.

Castelike systems outside of India

Many societies, as in Egypt, Iran, Europe, and Japan, have at various times developed rules confining certain occupations to particular social groups. In itself this regulation does not bring about a caste system, but it does combine the rule of endogamy with a traditional hereditary occupation.

From the 12th to the middle of the 19th century A.D., Japan had a system of five ranked social groups headed by the military Samurai. At the bottom of the social order were groups like the Eta, leather-workers whose position was remarkably like that of the Hindu Chamars of India.

The Eta of Japan

Like the Chamars and similar groups in Tibet and Korea, the Eta traditionally work with dead animals in removing carcasses, butchering, and shoemaking and other leatherwork. The Hindu notion that work with dead animals and hides is defiling was evidently diffused along with Buddhism to Tibet, Korea, and Japan. In the 7th, 8th, and subsequent centuries in Japan, legislation was passed forbidding hunting and slaughtering, and Shinto notions of uncleanness became associated with meat eating; but it was apparently not until the Tokugawa period (1603–1868) that the Eta became distinguished as a kind of untouchable caste, required to marry within their own group and to live in separate Eta villages. They were sometimes obliged to wear a patch of leather sewn on the kimono, to walk on one side of the street, and to observe various other restrictions like those affecting the Chamars in India.

The Eta were officially emancipated by government edict in 1871, but their lot has not greatly improved, and they still live in ghettoes.

Like Chamars in northern India, many Eta have refused to remove the carcasses of dead animals and to continue leatherwork. Self-improvement and protest movements and demands for integration provide parallels with such developments in India and the United States. Although the Eta are racially indistinguishable from other Japanese and hence "invisible," they are not unidentifiable. Since their homes are restricted to Eta neighborhoods, their addresses give them away, and "passing" is very difficult (De Vos and Wagatsuma 1966).

Castelike groups in Africa

The term *caste system* has been applied to the African kingdom of Ruanda, which has a population of nearly 2 million. The situation is different from that of India with its thousands of caste groups, for in Ruanda there are only three main castes: (1) the Tutsi, who are the wealthiest and who own most of the cattle in the country; (2) the Hutu, the agriculturalists; and (3) the Twa, who are hunters and potters. The Hutu make up 85 percent of the population, the Tutsi 10 percent, and the Twa 5 percent. The three groups have somewhat different physical appearance, the Tutsi being Nilotic, while the Hutu are of Forest Negro type and the Twa are pygmylike, although taller than the Pygmies.

The term *caste* seems justifiable here, since these groups are mainly endogamous, hierarchically ranked, and associated with different occupations. The Tutsi constitute the dominant group, exerting political control over the larger Hutu caste (Maquet 1960).

In Somalia some groups are treated in ways reminiscent of untouchability in India. Tanners and hunters, known as Midgan, are regarded as unclean and are tabooed in marriage. Similar attitudes are held concerning blacksmiths, who are considered inferior and defiling by the Masai.

Black-white relations in the United States

In the 1940s some writers compared black-white relations in the Deep South of the United States with caste relations (Davis, Gardner, and Gardner 1941; Dollard 1949; Myrdal 1944). Although ideals of racial endogamy were upheld by both blacks and whites, the frequency of interbreeding shows that this particular criterion of caste was rather weak. The authors, however, pointed out that black-white marriages were not recognized in the South at the time of their research and that illegitimate offspring of a white man and a black woman were always classed as black.

Entrance to waiting
room, train station,
Atlanta, Georgia.

Differences in occupation held to some extent between blacks
and whites, and this is still much the same today, since many blacks
are of low socioeconomic class, poorly educated, and face barriers
of prejudice (H. P. Miller 1964:90, 94, 95).

Emphases on endogamy and hierarchy are castelike features of a
society. Orthodox Hindu religious traditions about the inherent
inferiority of low castes find their American parallels in biblical texts
that have sometimes been cited to support segregation. There is
even a concept of untouchability or pollution, suggested by the
separate washrooms and drinking fountains formerly characteristic
of the South. Davis, Gardner, and Gardner (1941:16) write:

. . . there remains a strong feeling that the color of the Negro is abhorrent
and that contact with them may be contaminating. There is generally a
strong feeling against eating or drinking from dishes used by Negroes, and
most of the whites provide separate dishes for the use of their servants.

Although the application of the concept of caste to black-white
relations is loose in some respects, there seem to be striking parallels
with Hindu caste attitudes and practices and with Japanese-Eta
relations, suggesting regularities in social and psychological patterns

in hierarchically structured societies.[1] It was the coexistence of this tendency toward hierarchic attitudes with American democratic traditions that led Gunnar Myrdal to term this problem an "American dilemma."

With the development of castes and classes, the vertical axis acquired an interesting symbolic significance in human thought. Certain attitudes are built into some Indo-European languages and are expressed in several English words used in preceding pages, such as *super*ordinate and *sub*ordinate, *upper* class and *lower* class. We distinguish between *high-* and *low-*ranking persons, *over*lords and *under*lings, *top* dog, and *low* man on the totem pole. This kind of hierarchy is often expressed in myths and religious traditions. For example, according to one of the hymns of the Rig-Veda of the Aryans, the four *varna,* or social divisions of India, sprang from different parts of a primeval man, the Brahmans (priests) from his mouth, the Kshatriya (warriors) from his arms, the Vaishya (peasants) from his thighs, and the Shudra (serfs) from his feet. (Basham 1954:35). Here, the ranking of the *varna* corresponds with the vertical order.

Cognitive aspects of hierarchy

Differences between castes in India are symbolized by sitting arrangements. In a North Indian village, if a low-caste man, such as a potter or water carrier, approaches a group of higher-ranking Rājpūts who are sitting on string cots, he should not sit at their level but should squat on the ground some distance away. Similar practices are followed on the Indonesian island of Bali, where there are caste divisions based on the Hindu *varna.* A low-caste person should never be at a higher level than a high-caste person. Note how this "vertical" symbolism contrasts with the more "horizontal" and reciprocal symbolism concerning moieties discussed on page 116.

Class differs from caste in lacking a kinship basis. Since a child is usually assigned to the class of its parents, and since persons often marry within their own class, the distinction may not seem clear. But in societies with class stratification it is possible for a person to move either up or down the class hierarchy and to marry someone of a different class. In India, a Chamar is always a Chamar, even if he changes his occupation and becomes well-to-do; a Brahman always remains a Brahman. Caste membership is more explicit and unalterable than class membership, although, in some societies, classes

Class

---

[1] Another somewhat parallel situation is to be found in Ladino-Indian relationships in Guatemalan communities (Tumin 1952).

may be distinguished by different speech patterns and clothing and may thus seem quite distinct from one another and separated by marked social distance.

Class has been variously defined or determined by different writers. Some have used income or occupation for assigning class membership, while others have made use of additional criteria, such as type of housing, residence area, and prestige rating. Karl Marx, whose system of ideas made such important use of the concept of class, defined class in terms of relationship to the means of production. The bourgeoisie are owners of the means of production, such as factories. Members of the proletariat, or working class, have no such ownership and must work for the bourgeoisie to earn a living. Although Marx also referred to other class groups in his writings, these two were the crucial ones from his point of view, for he believed that the future conflict between the workers of the world and the bourgeoisie would ultimately usher in the communist society.

Classes in Middletown

In their well-known study *Middletown,* Robert and Helen Lynd presented a view of class membership that was similar, if not identical, to the bourgeois-proletarian dichotomy. Middletown (a pseudonym) in Indiana was considered to be a "typical" U.S. community, with about 36,500 inhabitants, when it was studied by the Lynds in the 1920s. They saw Middletown, then, as being made up of two groups: the Working Class and the Business Class. The workers made things and performed services, while the businessmen sold and promoted things, services, and ideas. There were two and a half times as many people in the Working Class as in the Business Class. To quote the Lynds (1929:23–24):

The mere fact of being born upon one or the other side of the watershed roughly formed by these two groups is the most significant cultural factor tending to influence what one does all day long throughout one's life; whom one marries; when one gets up in the morning; whether one belongs to the Holy Roller or Presbyterian church; or drives a Ford or a Buick; whether or not one's daughter makes the desirable high school Violet Club; or one's wife meets with the Sew We Do Club or with the Art Students' League . . . .

In 1937 the Lynds published the results of a restudy of Middletown, whose population had since increased to almost 50,000. They found that conditions, including the class structure, had changed somewhat. Without altogether giving up their former two-class division, they now set forth a series of six occupational groups, which in some ways resemble the six classes based on prestige rating, style of living, and other factors that W. L. Warner described for the New England town of "Yankee City" (Lynd and Lynd 1937:443–61). If both Middletown studies are valid, it seems that classes can change or differentiate rapidly within a ten-year period, at least in some parts of the United States.

Defining class membership

Analyses like those of the Lynds raise the question: Is a class something that exists in the minds of members of the society or something that exists in the mind of the sociologist? Middletowners often denied the reality or significance of class differences; nevertheless, according to the Lynds, their whole lives were being shaped by them. In this case, then, classes were distinguished by the observer rather than by the people themselves.

This is not always the case in class-stratified societies. Reporting on a questionnaire given to large numbers of persons in England, Goeffrey Gorer writes: "Nine out of ten English people feel no hesitation in assigning themselves to a social class. Five of them call themselves working class and three middle class. . . . (Gorer 1955:34).[2]

Self-assignments to class groups are not always determined by income or occupation; subjective factors are often involved. Thus, one woman wrote: "I was born in the slums of London of working class parents and although I have attained a higher standard of living I still maintain I am working class" (Gorer 1955:34). Conversely, people who consider themselves to be middle class sometimes live in the slums and have low incomes. Identification with a particular class stems from family background as well as from occupation and income.

Warner took such subjective factors into account in drawing up a sixfold prestige-rank classification of 99 percent of the families in Yankee City, the name he gave a New England town with a population of about 17,000. His classifications were as follows:

1. *Upper-upper.* Wealthy old families who have lived in the best neighborhoods for several generations; 1.4 percent of the population.

2. *Lower-upper.* Slightly richer in average income than the upper-upper but with less prestige, because they are relative newcomers or because their wealth has been recently acquired; their

---

[2] Here we note a contrast with the United States, where public opinion polls (like the *Fortune* magazine poll in 1940) have found that about 80 percent of Americans describe themselves as "middle class."

manners are held to be less polished and their families less well established; 1.6 percent.

3. *Upper-middle.* Families of moderately successful business and professional men; 10.2 percent.

4. *Lower-middle.* Families of clerks, skilled and semiskilled workers, and wholesale and retail dealers; 28 percent.

5. *Upper-lower.* "Respectable" working-class families; 32.6 percent.

6. *Lower-lower.* Low-prestige working-class families; 25.2 percent (Warner and Lunt 1941).

This, then, is a partly subjective ordering of social classes, in contrast to Marx's distinction of classes in terms of relationship to the means of production. However, Warner's six groupings seem to correspond to social realities. This is suggested by another study made by Warner et al. (1949), that of a Midwestern town he called Jonesville, with a population of about 6,000. The same town was studied by August B. Hollingshead (1949), who named it Elmtown. Both sociologists, using different procedures, made prestige ratings of the community's families and came out with very similar results. Each distinguished five social classes. Since a number of such studies have yielded similar results, it seems that at least some U.S. cities and towns are stratified along some such lines.

Warner's system of classification would not seem to be applicable cross-culturally in non-Western stratified societies, where other models would have to be devised. Nor would it apply to the Soviet Union, which also has class stratification, though of a different order.[3]

The power elite

One potential way of studying stratified systems cross-culturally would be to determine which people within a particular society make the important decisions. Except for atomistic societies in which there is little political centralization, most societies have people in positions of authority whose decisions affect many other persons. These are not exclusively political or governmental leaders; in the United States, for example, leaders of large corporations form part of the power elite. An upper class may be much larger than the core of leading decision makers, but it may be assumed that there is some sort of relationship between the core and the broader upper class; this relationship may be examined in any particular society.

---

[3] One interpretation distinguished eight social classes in the Soviet Union in rank order as follows: the ruling elite, the superior intelligentsia, the general intelligentsia, the working-class aristocracy, the white-collar workers, the well-to-do peasants, the disadvantaged workers, and the forced-labor group (Inkeles 1950).

In an effort to identify the power elite in the United States, G. William Domhoff has used both social and economic criteria, such as listing in the *Social Register,* attendance at one of a select group of prep schools such as Choate, membership in one of a select group of men's clubs, and substantial family wealth. Although friendships and marriages are apt to occur within this social level, it is an open class into which newcomers keep being admitted. The problem is to show that members of this wealthy class make important political decisions. Domhoff points out the predominant representation of its members in the universities, the big foundations, the Council on Foreign Affairs, the Foreign Policy Association, and the National Association of Manufacturers. This upper class, according to Domhoff, provides the main financial support for both the Republican and Democratic parties, and from its ranks often come the men who fill cabinet posts and act as presidential advisers. But there are many other sources of power on the American scene (labor unions, local politicians), and the upper class obviously does not control all aspects of American life. Moreover, it does not seem to share a unified viewpoint; one could not predict how "it" would act in any given situation (Domhoff 1967).

Despite the differences in economic and political systems in the Soviet Union and the United States, there are special rewards in both nations for people with advanced, specialized education and those in managerial positions. Such persons receive much higher salaries in the Soviet Union than do common laborers. The top elite level consists of *apparatchiki,* full-time Communist Party functionaries and their families. H. Gordon Skilling (1971:379–80) roughly estimates the numbers of the Soviet elite as follows: ". . . 100,000 to 200,000 *apparatchiki,* 100,000 managers in heavy industry, several 100,000 military officers, perhaps the same number of military police, 100,000 lawyers, 300,000 economists (including planners and statisticians), and 6,000 writers (members of the Writer's Union)." Like the American power elite, these groups do not share a unified viewpoint but often have conflicting interests and goals.

The culture of poverty

There are different ways of defining poverty or deciding which persons make up "the poor." One way is to establish a particular income level. One writer, for example (Gallaway 1973), uses a salary of $3,000 per year per family as a standard, below which families are said to be poor. That is close to the poverty income line of $3,335 for a nonfarm family of four, established in the late sixties by the Social Security administration. Another way of defining poverty is to arbitrarily take the families in the bottom fifth of the income distribution. In 1958 the lowest fifth of U.S. families had 4.7 percent of total personal income, while the highest fifth had 45.5 percent. One might also gauge poverty in terms of the presence or absence of certain goods or facilities, such as baths and inside toilets, but this may give conflcting evidence since there are families that lack baths and inside toilets but nevertheless have automobiles or TV sets.

Whatever index is used to define poverty, the poor must be considered numerous. In *The Other America* (1964), Michael Harrington estimates that the poor make up about one fourth of our population, somewhere between 40 million and 50 million people. If such a high estimate surprises the reader, it may be because much present-day poverty is invisible, at least to some of the population. As Harrington put it, poverty is often off the beaten track, away from the freeways, hidden in rural areas like Appalachia; and urban slums may be bypassed or only briefly glimpsed by suburban dwellers.

Although there are traditions that idealize poverty, most people seem to regard it with disfavor. Several books and articles have presented evidence that there is more mental disorder among the poor than among higher classes. Best known among these studies is one by August Hollingshead and Fredrick Redlich (1958), who divided the population of New Haven into five socioeconomic classes. They found that in the lowest class (Class V) the incidence of psychoses was almost three times greater than in the two highest classes (I and II) and twice the rate for Class IV.

Some writers have argued that poverty is not just a condition but a way of life that tends to perpetuate itself. A "culture of poverty," according to Oscar Lewis, is apt to appear in societies that have a cash economy with low wages and a high rate of unemployment for unskilled labor. It appears in societies having a bilateral kinship system rather than corporate lineal ones. Other features that encourage the development of a culture of poverty are the absence or weakness of government aid to the poor and lack of concern about them among the better-off segments of the population.

According to Lewis (1968:xliii–xliv), some aspects of the culture of poverty are: lack of participation by the poor in the institutions of the larger society, except for jails, army, and public relief; absence of savings, shortage of cash, and, hence, much pawning and borrowing; low levels of literacy and education; hatred of police and mistrust of government; briefness of protected childhood; early experience with sex; lack of privacy; consensual marriages; illegitimacy; wife abandonment; and mother-centered families. On the part of the individual there are feelings of inadequacy and dependence, maternal deprivation, a poorly developed ego, confusion about sexual identity,

a habit of living for the moment and absence of planning, fatalism, and absence of class-consciousness.

Since many of the features listed have often been reported for poor communities, it would seem to be a plausible hypothesis that a particular kind of culture has developed in many different areas in response to similar conditions as a sort of cross-cultural regularity. If this is indeed a separate culture or subculture, it might help to explain the persistence of poverty in rundown areas. By the age of six or seven, according to Lewis, slum children have usually absorbed the dominant values and attitudes of the culture of poverty, and they are not psychologically prepared thereafter to take advantage of new opportunities. Some anthropologists who have worked in slum areas see the matter differently, however. Elliot Liebow, for example, has written (1967:223):

No doubt, each generation does provide role models for each succeeding one. Of much greater importance for the possibility of change, however, is the fact that many similarities between the lower-class Negro father and son (or mother and daughter) do not result from "cultural transmission" but from the fact that the son goes out and independently experiences the same failures, in the same areas, and for much the same reasons as his father.

Suggestions for further reading

A standard work on caste is J. H. Hutton, *Caste in India: Its Nature, Function, and Origins,* 3d ed. (Bombay: Oxford University Press, 1961). For comparisons between India's untouchables, the Eta of Japan, and American Negroes, see George De Vos and Hiroshi Wagatsuma, eds., *Japan's Invisible Race: Caste in Culture and Personality* (Berkeley: University of California Press, 1966).

For cross-cultural studies of class stratification, see Gerhard E. Lenski, *Power and Privilege: A Theory of Social Stratification* (New York: McGraw-Hill Book Co., 1966); Joseph A. Kahl, ed., *Comparative Perspectives on Stratification: Mexico, Great Britain, Japan* (Boston: Little, Brown & Co., 1968). For class stratification in the United States, see the studies by the Lynds, Warner, and others cited in the chapter, and Joseph A. Kahl's *The American Class Structure* (New York: Rinehart & Co., 1957).

See also Charles A. Valentine, *Culture and Poverty: Critique and Counter-Proposals* (Chicago: University of Chicago Press, 1968).

part six

Political organization, law, and warfare

13

Political organization, social control, and conflict resolution

A political unit occupying a particular territory is faced with two requirements: to preserve order within its ranks and to regulate relations with outside groups. All societies have rules of conduct, but rules are not automatically obeyed. They have to be enforced in some way by someone or other, if the rules are held to be important for the society's continuance and well-being.

Societies are also characterized by internal conflict and competition between persons and groups, which need to be worked out or controlled in some way.

Conflicts occur in all societies, and this is not necessarily unfortunate or harmful. In some cases, conflict within a group may help to establish, or reestablish, unity. Indeed, Lewis A. Coser (1956:151) has argued that such conflicts may be positively functional for the social structure when they concern goals, values, or interests that do not contradict the basic assumptions on which the relationship is founded. However, conflict may be experienced as stressful and dangerous by members of a society, especially by supporters of the status quo. It is to their interest, and often to the interests of most members of the society, to resolve conflicts and prevent their further spread. Whether we label it as law or not, some means of conflict resolution must exist. This is another function of political authority.

Social control and conflict resolution concern internal order. But a political community must also deal with outside groups and may engage in warfare, which may strengthen the authority of the political leadership, at least temporarily. Some societies have developed different leadership offices for the two spheres of internal and external relations, having both a "peace chief" and a "war chief"; but

187

more often the political locus of authority deals with both internal control and external affairs.

In this chapter and the next we will examine how these issues are handled in societies with different bases of subsistence. Following the general approach employed in Chapter 5, we will deal in turn with hunting-gathering societies, simple horticultural societies, pastoralists and mounted hunters, advanced horticultural societies, agricultural societies, and industrial societies. This chapter will deal with the first three categories. The following chapter concerns state societies. While these categories do not always permit neat generalizations, they do provide a rough evolutionary framework that can help us to look for possible cross-cultural regularities. There are problems in doing so, however. One is that hunting-gathering societies that have been studied in recent times may not be very similar to hunting-gathering societies of the past. Some of the hunters referred to in this chapter may have had more complex political institutions in former days. It has been argued, for example, that the nomadic Sirionó of eastern Bolivia, who are now mainly hunting-gathering people who also practice some horticulture, had a more sedentary advanced culture in former times. European colonization in North and South America and elsewhere not only uprooted native peoples but also increased the scale of warfare among them through the introduction of rifles and, sometimes, horses. This led, in some cases, to increasing political centralization among the tribes that acquired these advantages and increased social atomism among those that lacked them and were thus at the mercy of their better-equipped enemies. Reconstruction of social and political organization in such societies before the coming of Europeans is difficult. We can at any rate study how some hunting and gathering peoples live today. The generalizations that follow are based on recent ethnographic work; they are not necessarily meant to depict timeless "aboriginal" patterns but patterns that at least have had some duration.

Although reasons have been given above for the need for political organization, we will examine some societies in this chapter in which there is little political authority, in which headmen have little power. Nevertheless, these societies are viable systems. One reason for this is that proper behavior on the part of a society's members is not determined by fear of punishment alone. There are other deterrents to antisocial behavior.

Sanctions

According to Radcliffe-Brown (1952:205), "A sanction is a reaction on the part of a society or of a considerable number of its members to a mode of behavior which is thereby approved (positive sanctions) or disapproved (negative sanctions)." Praise is a positive sanction: applause, awards, medals, the good opinion of one's neighbors. Disapproval is a negative sanction: ostracism, blacklisting, unpopularity. Fear of sorcery is a negative sanction which may serve to inhibit aggression. Fear of ghosts, punitive ancestors, or eternal damnation after death may also contribute to good behavior during this life in different societies. Laws that punish offenders are negative sanctions, but sanctions are a more inclusive category, found in all societies, whether they have law courts and prisons or not. These sanctions are learned in the process of socialization as one grows up. Children gradually become informed about the various values, taboos, and anxieties current in their culture: ethical concepts, beliefs in gods, ghosts, sorcerers, and the dangers of sickness and death. Children also learn what they must do to be liked and approved of by others. These positive and negative sanctions help to bring about a relatively orderly way of life in any society.

Hunting-gathering societies usually have little political organization. A band may have a headman or chief, but he does not normally exercise much authority over its members. The term *atomistic* has sometimes been used to describe groups such as the Canadian Ojibwa (or Chippewa), the Great Basin Shoshones, and the Central Eskimos. These peoples lived under ecological conditions that favored dispersal at certain seasons; their groups were small and scattered. It was not difficult for the component units, such as families, to break away from the larger group. Hence, it would often be hard for a headman to apply social sanctions against an errant band member.

Hunting-gathering societies

Among the Canadian Ojibwa there was village life during the summer months when between 3 and 15 families came together; during the winter months these families broke up to take maximum advantage of the game resources. The families did not always return to the same village sites. Villages were not stable in numbers or location over any considerable period of time.

Pygmy bands in the Congo have been described as frequently breaking up and regrouping in different patterns. This fission and fusion has the function of maintaining peace; if a quarrel threatens, the band may split. This shifting band composition would make it difficult for a headman to wield much authority.

Headmen among the Bushmen of Botswana have responsibilities such as planning the band's movements, but their authority is relatively weak. Lorna Marshall (1967:38) writes: "Headmanship is not especially advantageous to the individual. Among the !Kung, each person does his own work, carries his own load, and shares meat.

Headmen are as thin as the rest. No regalia, special honours, or tributes mark them out."

According to Allan Holmberg (1950:59), among the Sirionó of eastern Bolivia ". . . there is no obligation to obey the orders of a chief, no punishment for nonfulfillment. Indeed, little attention is paid to what is said by a chief unless he is a member of one's immediate family."

Under such circumstances, informal sanctions must operate to control aggression. There seems to have been little murder, theft, or open show of hostility among the Canadian Ojibwa. A. Irving Hallowell (1955:278) attributed this to a widespread fear of sorcery, which served to check the expression of aggression. Some Eskimo bands, on the other hand, had high rates of homicide. Knud Rasmussen reported of one Eskimo band that all the adult males of its 15 families had been involved in a homicide, either as principal or accessories; usually this was due to quarrels over women. Female infanticide was common among the Eskimos, but this was not considered a crime by them; nor was the killing of old people who were unable to keep up with the rest of the band when it moved from place to place. If a man is murdered, a kinsman of his may kill the murderer. A danger here is that a blood feud may develop between the two families.

Among the Eskimos an alternative to murder and the inception of a blood feud is a challenge to a singing contest. Two enemies face one another in a circle of onlookers and alternately sing songs of derision in which each insults the other with such charges as stinginess, incest, cannibalism, or murder. Public opinion has a chance to express itself in the responses of the surrounding crowd, whose applause or jeers help to elect the winner. At the end of the song duel, the enemies are supposed to put aside their quarrel and resume normal relations.

Not all hunting-gathering societies lacked political organization. With the emphasis on relative rank in Northwest Coast Indian tribes, high-ranking chiefs seem to have had more political power than in most hunting societies. Another exception was found among mounted hunters such as the horse-riding Indians of the Great Plains and their counterparts in Patagonia and the Gran Chaco in South America.

Simple horticultural societies

As indicated in Chapter 5, simple horticultural societies are those in which the digging stick is the chief farming tool; hoes, plows, terracing, and irrigation are not relied upon. Such societies have been found in parts of North and South America and in Pacific islands, including New Guinea, but not Australia. Simple horti-

A Samoan chief.

cultural societies are not very different from hunting-gathering societies in community size and other features, but they are sometimes larger and less egalitarian. Gerhard E. Lenski (1966:139) has argued that, in simple horticultural societies, headmen have more prerogatives than they do in hunting-gathering bands:

Often they wear special insignia or clothing, setting them apart. In addition, they are often shown special deference, as in the case of the Manasí chiefs, whose people address them only in a very formal manner and in whose presence the young people are not permitted to sit. . . . Jivaro chiefs are entitled to first choice among women captives, Chiquito chiefs are permitted to practice polygamy, and Boro chiefs are given larger and more convenient garden plots. Quite commonly these chiefs are exempted from manual labor and have their material necessities supplied by their people.[1]

This increase in power may sometimes be due to the chief's role as an agent in the redistribution of goods.

---

[1] Footnotes have been omitted in this quotation.

Horticultural societies in South America, Polynesia, and New Guinea frequently engage in warfare, which may contribute to the relatively high status of the headman or chief. This warfare is sometimes over land resources, but this is not always the reason for such fighting (Vayda 1961; Chagnon 1968).

There are also simple horticulturalists among whom chiefly distinctions are not in evidence. The appearance of chiefly prerogatives is thus a potentiality, not an automatic consequence of the adoption of horticulture. Gertrude E. Dole has pointed out that in Tropical Forest tribes of South America there is a relationship between effective political organization and the presence of lineal kinship systems. The tribes that have cognatic or bilateral descent systems tend not to have strong leadership (Dole 1966). Thus, among the variables influencing leadership patterns in horticultural societies there are the chief's role in redistribution, patterns of warfare, and the degree of emphasis on lineal kinship. A chief in such societies, as among hunting-gatherers, is often expected to be generous, an expectation that should serve to restrain exploitative tendencies to some extent. Moreover, slash-and-burn (or swidden) horticulture has a centrifugal influence on settlement patterns, which should discourage political centralization and the influence of chiefs (Sahlins 1968:31).

Pastoralists and mounted hunters

Since societies classified as pastoral live in different kinds of environments (grasslands, deserts, steppes) and herd different kinds of animals (cattle, camels, sheep, goats, horses, reindeer, yak), this forms a heterogeneous category difficult to generalize about. Moreover, pastoral societies differ widely in population density, and it seems likely that there would be more political centralization in pastoral groups which have the greater density (Krader 1965). Some pastoralists are mounted horsemen; others are not. Despite this heterogeneity, many pastoral societies in both Asia and Africa have segmentary lineage systems with little political organization.

Most pastoralists are forced to be mobile, since their herds eat grass and must move on to new pasture grounds as the area becomes overgrazed. Moreover, the herds need water, and as they trample and soil water courses, they must be moved to unspoiled areas. The nomadic way of life of pastoralists often has atomistic tendencies, making it possible for groups to segment and split off. Fredrik Barth (1961:25–26) has described the situation among the Basseri tribe of South Persia, in which camp members are faced with daily decisions about whether to move or stay put, and which routes to follow next:

These decisions are the very stuff of a pastoral nomad existence; they spell the difference between growth and prosperity of the herds, or loss and poverty. Every household head has an opinion, and the prosperity of his household is dependent on the wisdom of his decision. Yet a single disagreement on this question between members of the camp leads to fission of the camp as a group — by next evening they will be separated by perhaps 20 km of open steppe and by numerous other camps, and it will have become quite complicated to arrange for a reunion.

On the other hand, a factor leading to political centralization in pastoral societies is organization for warfare. Cattle-herding pastoralists often engage in fighting and raiding. In such societies, the main form of wealth is cattle, and cattle are easy to steal. If herds become depleted by disease or enemy raids, they must be replenished. A member of the Karimojong tribe said, "A Karimojong loves his cattle above all other things, and for these cattle he will give his life." He went on to detail the various uses of cattle in his tribe (for milk, meat, feasting, sacrifices, bride wealth) and concluded:

Everyone wants to find a wife, friends, happiness; to become a man of importance and influence. Without cattle he cannot achieve any of these things. So each person thinks to himself, "Where shall I find cattle?" (And the answer is) "From foreigners." So he resolves to go to enemy country, and kill for cattle (Dyson-Hudson 1966:102–3).

So pastoral societies, such as the Karimojong and the Nuer of the Nilotic Sudan, go in for much fighting over cattle. As far as the Nuer are concerned, there is almost no political centralization. There are other pastoral tribes, however, in which a militant ruling group has developed aristocratic traditions and established itself as a political elite.

The Bahima of Uganda are a pastoral people who have overpowered and dominate the Bairu, who are farmers. The Bahima have become a ruling class, the Bairu are serfs. The Bahima developed some feudal tendencies; thus a man swears loyalty to his king and promises to follow him in war, when called upon. He was also obliged to hand over some of the cattle acquired in a private raid. In return, the king protected his subject's cattle from outside raiders, and he would help him start a new herd if all of his cattle were stolen or died of disease. Only the Bahima were allowed to own productive cows; Bairu could own only barren cows. These two groups were endogamous and could not intermarry. Hence they had a kind of caste system, to which was added a still lower class or caste of slaves; they thus formed a stratified society comparable to that of the Tutsi, Hutu, and Twa of Ruanda, discussed in the preceding chapter.

The Bahima king was believed to be sacred, the supreme authority. He had a chief military adviser and an entourage of warriors. Subordinate chiefs carried out his orders and supervised the collection of tribute. A Bahima chief acted as a redistributive agent, giving to his followers articles made for him by Bairu craftsmen as well as some of the beer and millet porridge which came to him as tribute (Oberg 1940).

A parallel to some of these features may be seen in the ancient Aryans, who also had hard-fighting aristocratic traditions, and who conquered and dominated the agricultural peoples of northern India from around 1500 B.C. According to Ralph Linton, the Aryan chief was the head of the wealthiest and most important family, who attracted to his following both kinsmen and unrelated supporters. Bodyguards like these, who fought with the king, formed the prototype of King Arthur's round table. Indeed, Linton (1955:265) wrote, "Perhaps the most important contribution of the Aryans to later civilization was the establishment of the aristocratic pattern which survived in Europe until recent times."

Social stratification like that of the Bahima and the Aryans has been found in some other pastoral societies. The Marri Baluch of Baluchistan, for example, are headed by a *sardar* who levies taxes from his tribesmen and owns much land. He is supported by members of the dynastic lineage and by other prominent men. Below them are the common people, serfs, and slaves. There are traditional rates of compensation to be paid for wrongful killings, which reflect the relative status of these groups. If a *sardar* or other member of his lineage is killed, the compensation must be 8,000 rupees; but if a serf or slave is killed, the compensation is only 1,000 rupees, and for a commoner, 2,000 rupees (Pehrson 1966:28).

Political organization of the Cheyennes

The Cheyenne Indians present a problem in classification. Before their movement into the Plains, they had lived for some time as horticulturalists in earth lodge villages. Toward the end of the 18th century, having acquired horses, the Cheyennes took up the nomadic buffalo-hunting way of life of Plains tribes. Since they were so dependent upon the horse, they could be called herders or pastoralists, or else they could be classified as mounted hunters. However we label them, their technological adjustment to Plains life made it possible for them to live in large social groups, much larger than those generally characteristic of hunters.

The large summer-camp circle of the Cheyennes numbered 500 or 600 lodges. In the center on certain occasions there was a double-sized chiefs' lodge. The Cheyennes had a council of 44 chiefs which functioned only during the summer months. At the approach of winter the various bands which occupied traditional places around the camp circle broke up and moved to separate winter hunting grounds, reconvening again at an appointed place in the spring. The headmen of the various bands were also tribal chiefs; each band was thus represented in the Council of Forty-Four. Each chief in the council appointed his own successor for a ten-year term of office. Chiefs were expected to be dignified and self-controlled men. The Council of Forty-Four had executive and judicial functions, directing camp movements, making peace, and banishing murderers from the camp.

A kind of police force was supplied by the military societies described in Chapter 11: the Fox, Elk, Shield, Bowstring, Dog, and Northern Crazy Dogs. These military societies acted to police the camp, regulate the buffalo hunt, prevent individual raids on buffalo, and keep order on the march. This was a complex, well-functioning political system (Llewellyn and Hoebel 1941). Their culture was similar to that of cattle-pastoral societies in their pattern of raiding for horses and in the development of military traditions which exalted courage in war.

It is interesting that some parallels in the use of the horse and in patterns of culture and social organization developed among the Indians living on the plains of South America, after the Spaniards introduced the horse. In this case, instead of the buffalo, the Indians hunted wild cattle, which had originally been brought over by the Spaniards. Mounted Tehuelche bands in Patagonia became larger than aboriginal bands; some included about 500 persons. Collective hunting, making use of the surround, was employed by the horsemen, as on the Great Plains of North America, and there was warfare between different Indian bands. Military societies were formed by the mounted Abipón and Mocoví of the Gran Chaco (Steward and Faron 1959:408–24).

We have seen that something like a state system exists in some pastoral tribes, while others have little political centralization. At the more advanced level there may be formal court procedures and the announcement of decisions by a judge or judges. In societies which lack such features there must be some other means of conflict resolution, such as resort to blood feuds, payment of compensation, and employment of a go-between.

The Tiv of Nigeria and the Nuer and Dinka of the Nilotic Sudan **Blood feud** have segmentary lineage systems. As mentioned in Chapter 8, the **and com-** lineage is a political unit, having collective responsibility in blood **pensation** vengeance in these societies; much feuding goes on between lineage groups. A murder is not punished by a superordinate state; instead, there is retaliation by members of the dead man's lineage. If, in such a society, a member of lineage A kills a member of lineage B, someone of lineage B is likely to kill either the murderer or some other member of his lineage. This retaliation need not be seen as punishment; rather, in some societies, it restores balance between lineages that should have equal status. John Beattie (1964:175) has written:

> Only one life should be taken for one life, and in some societies, such as that of the Berbers of North Africa, the requirement of exact equivalence demands that the person killed in revenge must be of the same standing as the original victim. So if a man in one group kills a woman in another, the object of the injured group will be not to kill the murderer, but to kill a woman on their opponent's side.

The very existence of the institution of blood feud must serve to restrain aggression to some extent, since a potential murderer knows that either he or a relative will die if his victim dies.

To prevent a blood feud from developing, a murderer may try to offer compensation to the offended lineage. Among the Nuer, who are horticulturalists as well as pastoral people, a murderer goes to the home of an official called leopard skin chief. Since the latter is believed to have some sanctity, his home is a haven for the murderer; the dead man's kinsmen cannot attack him there. After performing some sacrifices and purification rites for the murderer, the leopard skin chief may act as a go-between or mediator between the two lineages. He will find out how much cattle the murderer's kinsmen possess, what they are willing to pay in compensation, and whether the murdered man's relatives will accept it. The leopard skin chief has no judicial or executive authority; he cannot compel anyone to accept a settlement.

In some African societies where cattle are accepted in compensation, they serve the role of replacement. The cattle may be used to acquire a wife who will bear children for the lineage.

Go-betweens

The Nuer leopard skin chief is an example of the go-between, an institution which is often found in societies that are politically decentralized. Another example is afforded by the Ifugao of the Philippines, who also lack political organization. They do not have clans but have close-knit bilateral groups of kinsmen who support one another in quarrels with other groups. When a man seeks compensation for a wrong or an insult, he goes to a member of the Ifugao upper class and asks him to act as go-between. If he agrees, the mediator goes back and forth with claims, proposals, counterclaims and counterproposals. Like the Nuer leopard skin chief, he has no authority to impose a settlement; he is more like the arbitrator in a labor dispute who tries to get both parties to agree on a compromise.

If the go-between fails, a feud develops—a serious matter, for the Ifugao of former times were headhunters. In the cases of the Nuer and Ifugao, there are no courts of law, but there are methods of conflict resolution.

In societies with more advanced political organization, the state may insist upon the right to punish murderers, and the institution of blood feud declines. The degree of political centralization may be gauged by this factor. The Shilluk of the Nilotic Sudan had a "divine king" who was an important symbol of unity for his tribe but who otherwise was no more than a figurehead, having no real political authority. This is expressed in the fact that blood feud flourished among the Shilluk. This "kingdom" was more like a segmentary lineage system with a symbolic but powerless ruler at its head.

Suggestions for further reading

A well-written general essay on the development of political organization in human societies is Morton H. Fried's *The Evolution of Political Society: An Essay in Political Anthropology* (New York: Random House, 1967). Another thoughtful work on the subject is Georges Balandier, *Political Anthropology*, trans. from the French by A. M. Sheridan Smith (New York: Pantheon Books, Random House, 1970). See also Ronald Cohen and John Middleton, eds., *Comparative Political Systems: Studies in the Politics of Pre-Industrial Societies* (New York: Natural History Press, 1967).

For the hunting-gathering stage, see Richard B. Lee and Irven De Vore, eds., *Man the Hunter* (Chicago: Aldine Publishing Co., 1968).

For horticulture, see Marshall D. Sahlins, *Tribesmen* (Englewood Cliffs, N.J.: Prentice-Hall, 1968). For the African scene, see Meyer Fortes and E. E. Evans-Pritchard, eds., *African Political Systems* (London: Oxford University Press, 1940); Lucy Mair, *Primitive Government* (Baltimore: Penguin Books, 1964).

The best work on the cross-cultural study of law is E. Adamson Hoebel, *The Law of Primitive Man: A Study in Comparative Legal Dynamics* (Cambridge, Mass.: Harvard University Press, 1954). See also Laura Nader, ed., *The Ethnography of Law*, Special Publication, *American Anthropologist*, vol. 67, pt. 2 (1965); Paul Bohannan, ed., *Law and Warfare: Studies in the Anthropology of Conflict* (New York: Natural History Press, 1967), and Laura Nader, ed., *Law in Culture and Society* (Chicago: Aldine Publishing Co., 1969).

14

Political organization and social control in state societies

 State societies exist at the level of advanced horticulture and agriculture. They are associated with systems of hierarchy and stratification and involve a high degree of political centralization and integration.

Advanced horticultural societies

In advanced horticultural societies where hoes and irrigation are used, political organization has sometimes been highly developed, particularly in parts of Africa. In New World horticultural societies the populations were generally smaller, and political organization was less advanced. For example, although the Hopi Indians of the Southwest lived in permanent settlements, they had little in the way of organized government, and each Hopi village was politically autonomous. Making an exception for the Incas, parts of Mesoamerica, and southeastern North America, Robert H. Lowie (1967:83) has argued that, in contrast with Africa, American Indian societies were generally separatistic and democratic. "Generalizing for the whole of America, there were sundry gropings toward centralization of power, but counteracting trends made them fall short of permanent results."

Advanced horticultural societies in Africa often had a high degree of political organization. Both Ralph Linton and George P. Murdock have stressed the autocratic aspects of such African kingdoms as Uganda and Dahomey. Some of these were large states numbering hundreds of thousands of persons. The king was often believed to be divine and had the power of life and death over his subjects. He lived in ritual isolation, held court, surrounded by attendants, officials, and symbols of office, and maintained a harem. He dis-

198

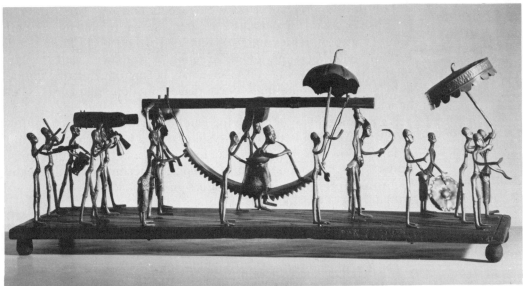

Chief of Dahomey and entourage. Bronze casting from Benin, West Africa, showing symbolic attributes of high status — litter, umbrellas, and attendants.

pensed justice and was the court of last appeal. Under the king there was a bureaucracy that collected taxes and supervised corvée labor. The leading ministers formed a council to advise the king (Linton 1955:463; Murdock 1959:37–39). This political centralization may perhaps be interpreted in terms of the chief's or king's exploitation of his control over redistribution. It may be, however, that some aspects of African kingdoms were influenced by 19th-century contacts with European and Arab traders relating to the slave trade (Service 1968:164–65).

Royal lineages

When a kingdom becomes established, it is likely that the king's lineage will come to be seen as more important than other lineages. In such cases, measures may be taken by the royal lineage to retain its power and authority.

Among the Swazi of southeastern Africa there is a royal couple who act as the symbolic parents of the people. They appeal to their royal ancestors to help the nation, just as an ordinary Swazi household head appeals to his own ancestors to aid his family. Although clan exogamy is normally practiced in this society, the royal clan is segmented into subclans, which enables the king to marry closely related women and which keeps the ruling line restricted in numbers. Sisters and daughters of the king are sent as wives to important chiefs, to spread the influence of the royal family (Kuper 1950:86–87, 110).

The development of a royal lineage is one way for a ruler to establish a group of persons on whom he can count for support. Another way of achieving the same goal would be to forge bonds with unrelated persons, a body of retainers who owe loyalty to their ruler. Since closely related kinsmen may become rivals to the throne, more trust has sometimes been placed in dependent, unrelated henchmen.

An important way of resolving conflicts in advanced horticultural societies in Africa is the court system, with a judge, such as a chief or king, witnesses, the hearing of testimony, and the announcement of decisions. A common aspect of court procedure is taking oaths to ensure truthfulness. Ordeals are sometimes administered to test the honesty of the accused.

Agricultural societies

As was noted in Chapter 5, agricultural societies with more advanced farming techniques than horticulture developed in Mesopotamia, Egypt, the Indus Valley, Shang China, Southeast Asia, Peru, and Mexico. The advanced techniques in the Old World involved the use of irrigation, the plow, and draft animals. Terracing and fertilization were used in Peru, and irrigation and *chinampas* in Mexico. These were areas in which city life and class stratification developed, along with much political centralization. The strengthening of political control in these societies may have been partly due to the increased density of population and conflict with neighboring groups.

The hydraulic theory

One view, that of Karl A. Wittfogel, is that political centralization was related to the practice of irrigation. Wittfogel's *Oriental Despotism* (1957) is a comparative study of what he has called "hydraulic societies," including the ancient civilizations of Mesopotamia, Egypt, India, China, and Peru of the Inca. He believes that in these societies, where the state controlled the irrigation network, the ruling bureaucracy became an upper class with despotic power. In contrast to the situation in feudal societies of Europe and Japan, there were no countervailing forces that could be balanced against the government, and the dominant religion was closely attached to the state. The absence of any other center of power gave such states the despotic hold they maintained over their subjects. The monumental constructions, pyramids, tombs, and ziggurats raised in such societies testify to the power of the state and its dominant religion and to the ability of the state to control large masses of labor.

Wittfogel's ideas seem convincing; they appear to show the operation of cross-cultural regularities in the development of early civilizations and to draw together several interrelated aspects of culture in one explanatory framework. There have been some criticisms made of the hydraulic theory, however (Eberhard 1958, 1965). First of all, there are despotic societies that have had no connection with irrigation, and there are societies that make much use of irrigation that have not become despotic (such as Holland, Belgium, northern Italy). Wittfogel felt obliged to link Russian despotism in some way with irrigation and did so in a peculiarly roundabout manner. Patterns of despotic rule, he explained, were introduced into Russia (which lacked an irrigation economy) by the 13th-century nomadic Mongols (who also lacked it) (Wittfogel 1957:191–93, 205).

Wolfram Eberhard does not agree with the assertion that there were no other important sources of power besides the state in China and India. He refers to secret societies, the Buddhist church, organized artisan groups, federations of landowning gentry in China and castes in India. He does not agree that the governments were always so powerful or effective in these countries.

Eberhard claims that the impetus to construct irrigation works in China, from Sung times on (and, thus, perhaps earlier), often came from individuals rather than from the state, as Wittfogel's theory would assume. Religious organizations and village assemblies also undertook such projects. In northern China, where the Shang Dynasty developed and where wheat and millet were raised, irrigation was not really vital. It became more important, after Chinese civilization had already developed, in the later rice culture of the south.

A similar criticism has been made by Robert McCormick Adams (1966:66–69), who argues that irrigation developed on a large scale in Mesopotamia only *after* the appearance of strongly centralized state systems. This criticism has in turn been challenged by William Sanders and Barbara Price (1968:177–88), who have argued for the importance of irrigation in both Mesopotamia and Mesoamerica. They point to the fact that in societies using irrigation there are frequent conflicts over water rights, such as between upstream and downstream communities. This conflict stimulates a need for central authority to supervise the irrigation network, as Wittfogel suggested. There are thus both critics and defenders of the hydraulic theory. It would seem, at any rate, that irrigation was an important concomitant of most of the first Bronze Age civilizations and that most of these societies had strong political centralization.

The circumscription theory

Robert L. Carneiro (1970) has argued that a state system develops most readily in a geographically circumscribed area, hemmed in by desert or mountain walls. In a developing agricultural society, population expands. In more open, uncircumscribed settlements, groups can bud off and exploit more distant land resources, but this cannot be done in a circumscribed setting. What happens, then, is that conflict over the limited land resources takes place, and one group finally becomes dominant over the others. It is then able to exact tribute or taxes from the defeated groups, which cannot escape. Thus, class stratification and political centralization develop simultaneously.[1]

Warfare, which seems to increase at the level of "civilization," can also be seen as strengthening political centralization and state control.

Court systems

Court systems developed in advanced urban centers in both the Old World and the New. In Mexico, Aztec courts adjudicated market disputes. There were also local courts in each quarter of the city and one for each district outside the city, all in session daily. The ruler's palace was a court of appeals and for commoners a court of last resort. Noblemen could appeal to a supreme court consisting of a war leader and a council of 13 elders. This system resembled that of modern states in several ways but lacked professional lawyers and trial by jury.

In Bronze Age Mesopotamia, when political centralization in city-states exerted control over progressively larger populations, the invention of writing made possible the first written codifications of laws, culminating in the Code of Hammurabi. Written laws increased the stability of the legal system and provided for a quick examination of precedents and previous rulings in any contingency. In later periods, after the diffusion of the alphabet, when a larger percentage of the population became literate, public tabulation of the laws had a democratizing influence. This happened in Greece in the 7th century B.C., when the open publicizing of the laws served as a check on the arbitrary authority of the ruling class.

A law differs from a custom in the quality of obligation. A person who deviates from custom may be considered eccentric, but one cannot punish him for an infraction. I may not approve of a young man who has long hair down to his shoulders and who walks about barefoot, but he is not doing anything against the law. But, if the young man rides his motorcycle beyond the prescribed speed limit or if he decides to undress in front of a policeman, he is liable to arrest. These distinctions may seem arbitrary, since some societies

---

[1] For some criticisms of the circumscription theory, see Dumond 1965.

allow what others do not, and a society may change its laws over a period of time. But laws are customs that persons *must* abide by. This means that laws must somehow be enforced; they are enforced by an agency that is recognized as having political authority within the society.

Some anthropologists hold that law is universal, found in all societies, while others say that law is associated only with state societies. Law can be defined to suit either view.

Donald Black (1976:2–3) defines law as governmental social control and contrasts it with other kinds of social control such as were discussed in the section on sanctions (p. 188). Black (1976:6) has advanced the proposition: "Law varies inversely with other social control." This means that there is more law in societies where other forms of social control are relatively weak. Within a society, too, law fills a vacuum when other forms of social control are lacking. There is more juvenile law, for example, in societies where family discipline is weak.

Black (1976:4) also distinguishes four styles of law: *penal, compensatory, therapeutic,* and *conciliatory,* which have different ways of defusing deviant behavior. The penal approach prohibits certain kinds of behavior and punishes infractions. The initiative in judging the innocence or guilt of the offender is made by the group. In the compensatory style, the initiative is taken by a victim who demands some restitution. In the therapeutic and conciliatory styles of law, punishment or payment is not the issue; instead it is the mending or improvement of an unfortunate situation. The deviant is seen as someone who needs help. In conciliation two parties meet to patch up a dispute and to restore a former balance, perhaps with the help of a mediator.

Black (1976:29) claims that these styles vary in different societies according to aspects of social organization and culture. There is more penal law in a "downward" direction in stratified societies, but more compensatory and therapeutic law in an "upward" direction. Thus a poor man who steals from the rich is found guilty and punished, but a rich man who expropriates property of the poor may be asked to make restitution or else may be judged to be mentally ill; he is not so likely to be punished. Punishment is more severe in socially differentiated societies than in simpler ones with much face-to-face interaction, where there is more remedial law.

Ruling elites

Estimates for the size of ruling groups in preindustrial agrarian societies have indicated very small minorities. The governing class in the last days of the Roman republic is estimated to have been about 1 percent of the capital's population. During the first half of the 19th century the Chinese gentry who made up the ruling class constituted about 1.3 percent of the population. A similar figure is given for Russia of the mid-19th century (Lenski 1966:219). How could such a small ruling class dominate such a large population? One explanation is that a ruling elite is apt to be highly organized, while the majority is not. The elite in an agrarian society is usually supported by a somewhat larger retainer class consisting of army officials, soldiers, servants, and others close to the ruling elite. Another reason for the continuing authority of the small ruling group is that it has many sources of power and influence. As an example, let us consider the sources of wealth of the 19th-century Chinese gentry.

The Chinese gentry were not engaged solely in political activity. It is estimated that in 19th-century China only 1.6 percent of the gentry held office in the central government at any given time, while about two thirds of the gentry got some of their income from holding governmental positions at the local level. Another large source of income was land ownership. In the late 19th century, about one quarter of all arable land in China was owned by the gentry. They also received some income from mercantile activity and money-lending (Lenski 1966:225–27; Fei 1953:98–99). The gentry thus occupied strategic positions both in government and in the economic system of the country.

The concentration of power and wealth in a small ruling class has been characteristic of many agrarian societies. In Mexico, before the revolution, 1 percent of the population owned 97 percent of the land, while 96 percent of the people owned only 1 percent of the land (Stern and Kahl 1968:6).

Traditional patterns of authority

Ever since the period of the Bronze Age civilization, Western people have been conscious of status differences and privileges that go with authority and power. It is a familiar experience in the Western world that a person, A, who is in a recognized authority position, has the power to direct the actions of B, who is under the obligation to obey the directions. A has higher prestige than B, and, in some cases, may be more splendidly dressed with "robes of office" or military insignia. Interaction between A and B may be accompanied by symbolic acts of deference on B's part, such as saluting, bowing, standing at attention, and using such expressions as "Sir," "Your Honor," or "Your Highness." Failure to act in such expected ways may bring a reprimand or punishment, since A has access to more power than B. But this state of affairs need not be resented by B, who may be full of admiration for A and consider it a privilege to serve him. The cognitive aspects of hierarchy (see p. 177) may be deeply ingrained.

It is because such patterns of authority were so familiar to Europeans of the 17th and 18th centuries that many were surprised by their absence among some North American Indians whom they encountered. Concerning some Central Algonkian "savages," Nicolas Perrot, a fur trader wrote: "Subordination is not a maxim among these savages; the savage does not know what it is to obey. . . . It is more necessary to entreat him than to command him. . . . The father does not venture to exercise authority over his son, nor does the chief dare give commands to his soldier. . . (Perrot 1911:145).

Walter B. Miller (1955:271–72), who quotes this passage, gives three other similar quotations from Europeans about Central Algonkians. They all describe the absence of submissive behavior in much the same way, with an implicit bewilderment which reveals that European traditions and practices were quite different from the Central Algonkian ones.

Despite the American revolution, democratic traditions, and the relatively recent experience of frontier life, present-day Americans seem to have maintained the European traditions to a greater degree than one might expect, judging from the experiments of Stanley Milgram (1974). Milgram asked volunteers in a psychological experiment on learning to administer progressively stronger electric shocks to another volunteer when he made mistakes. Despite the howling protests of the strapped victim at the stronger shocks, a high percentage of subjects continued to give the shocks at the direction of the psychologist. (The victim was the psychologist's confederate and actually received no shocks at all, but the subjects did not know that.) Out of 40 subjects in one series of experiments, 26 obeyed the psychologist's instructions to the end, which involved giving a shock of 450 volts. After this shock had been given three times, the experimenter concluded the session. Relatively few subjects refused to continue the experiment.

This seems to reveal a remarkable deference to authority. Some subjects appeared to be anxious and unhappy about what they were doing but continued to press the shock keys anyway. Milgram devised a number of ingenious modifications of this experiment. The results suggest that people who normally do not want to cause suffering to others will readily do so at the command of an authority, even when he is a stranger with no real power over them, as in this case. Milgram's experiments also suggest that this readiness is not due to a wish to release sadistic impulses; rather, an authority's order often carries more weight than individual conscience and human sympathy.

Feudalism

Feudalism is one of those vague but useful terms which have been defined in various ways. Here we will follow the view of Rushton Coulborn (1965:4–8,364), who sees feudalism as primarily a method of government, not an economic or social system; a method of government in which the essential relationship is between lord and vassal and in which the agreements between leaders and followers usually emphasize military service. Feudal tendencies are apt to develop in prevailingly agricultural societies, not in societies with highly organized commerce. Coulborn also sees feudalism as a mode of revival of a society that has experienced disintegration.

We know that in western Europe feudalism developed after the

Marksburg Castle in the Rhine Valley, begun in the 11th century.

collapse of the Roman Empire and the subsequent failure of Charlemagne's heirs to keep western Europe united in a new empire. Coulborn suggests that similar feudal revivals, building on a contracted local scale, may have taken place in other societies that formerly controlled wider areas but suffered dismemberment and collapse. Here we have another hypothesis about cross-cultural regularities.

The best parallel with western European feudalism is provided by Japan in the period between the 14th and 19th centuries A.D. During this time, effective government was on a local basis. Feudal lords (*daimyō*) commanded the services of armed knights (*samurai*) to defend and control a particular area. The imperial family and court nobility had little real political power, but, as in Europe, the concept of a larger centralized state was remembered from the past. In both areas an earlier, wider polity had become weakened, and local magnates—landlords, fighting men, clan or tribal chiefs—had assumed responsibility for local control and defense. Both Europe and Japan had its "barbarians" who influenced the character of the feudal period. In the case of Japan, the barbarians occupied the northeastern half of the central island of Honshu.

The true period of feudalism in Japan is said to date from the collapse of the Kamakura regime in A.D. 1333. The era of "high feudalism" runs from the 14th to the 16th century A.D., corresponding

Hirosaki castle, Aomori, Japan.

to the period in France between the later 10th to the 12th centuries. During the second half of the 16th century in Japan there was a rash of castle building, in which there appeared many similarities to the castle architecture of Europe. Castles were defended by masonry-faced earthworks and surrounded by moats. Parallel to the medieval European code of chivalry, there were strong traditions of feudal loyalty and a code of honor among samurai. Religion played an important role in both feudal regimes, and it is a curious parallel that a "universal" church with a monastic order was present in both. Buddhist monasteries owned much land and controlled large groups of warriors in Japan.[2]

The many parallels indicate that some cross-cultural regularities were at work in these two widely separated regions. Coulborn has suggested that two other areas exemplify a similar feudal development, although not in so clear-cut and striking a fashion: Chou China to about 700 B.C. and Mesopotamia in the 500 or 600 years after Hammurabi.

Not all disintegrating empires give birth to feudal regimes. In many cases, successful attempts are made to restructure the old political order. Feudalism cannot be seen as an inevitable stage of development in the evolution of human culture. It is one possibility, which seems to have occurred in a number of different times and places.

Industrial societies

The great increase in business enterprise of the 19th century associated with the Industrial Revolution was followed by a corresponding expansion of the state in the 20th century. In 1901 there were fewer than 240,000 employees of the U.S. federal government, but by 1975 there were 2,882,000, while the number of employees of state and local governments increased by 200 percent between 1940 and 1970. Much of the federal bureaucracy is concerned with military affairs, related to which, too, is the space program. About half the federal civilian employees are connected with defense. Much of the bureaucracy is also involved in control and regulation of trade, transportation, and communication, and the fields of education, job training, and social security.

Consider our relationship to the state in connection with just one aspect of our culture, the automobile. The automobile has become so much a part of our lives that Americans can hardly imagine life without it. It has transformed the appearance of the country, which is now crisscrossed with highways that have gasoline stations and

---

[2] Some qualifications about the classification of feudalism in relation to Japan are given in John W. Hall (1968).

motels strung along at intervals. These highways are built and kept in repair by the state or federal government, which establishes laws about speed limits.

In order to drive an automobile, one must pass a test, buy and renew a driver's license, and yearly license the car one has bought. One must drive on the prescribed side of the street, stop at red lights, and obey other traffic signals. If one drives through a red light, exceeds the speed limit, or otherwise breaks the law, one may be arrested by a police officer and be given a fine or a jail sentence, depending on the nature of the offense. The police officer is a recognized agent of government, identifiable by badge and uniform. Police have legitimate power, acknowledged by members of the society, whether they like it or not.

What applies to the automobile applies to many other aspects of our lives. If we transgress our nation's laws, a host of legal institutions may be brought into play: police officers, law courts, judges, prisons, and parole boards. Legal machinery is also resorted to in conflict resolution, in the adjustment of disputes, arguments over property or contracts. The agencies that deal with these matters have to do with the nation's internal law, the regulation of its own affairs. But a modern state also deals with other nations and has institutions for dealing with them: ambassadors, consuls, state departments, agents of espionage, and the armed forces.

The expansion of the modern state in the past century came on the heels of the expansion of industry, and there has been some mutual influence in these two spheres of action. A large industry like General Motors is itself a kind of political system, but it must work in harmony with the larger political system of the United States, in accord with the prevailing legal code. A corporation may also derive advantages from the state in the form of mineral depletion allowances, tax benefits, large defense contracts, tariff and quota considerations, and so forth.

Since a modern state is such a powerful institution, with nuclear bombs at its disposal in many cases, the state has often been regarded with fear and apprehension, as in George Orwell's novel *1984.*

There are potential dangers of dictatorship and authoritarianism in the state. At the same time, the incorporation of so many people within the ranks of modern government may have a democratizing tendency. We have seen that preindustrial agrarian societies were ruled by very small elites, which were often authoritarian. By comparison, many modern industrial nations are more democratic. All have elaborate codes of written laws that are meant to apply impartially to all citizens, although this often does not work out in practice. Modern industrial nations tend to have high rates of literacy and well-developed media of communication, which at least have the potentialities for making citizens well informed. Of course, the same instruments can also be used for propaganda. At the time of Hitler's rise to power, Germany was the best-educated nation in Europe. The Soviet Union emphasizes education but also maintains the harsh labor camps described by Alexander Solzhenitsyn in *The Gulag Archipelago*. Even so, there seem to be grounds for optimism in the presence of a high literacy rate and good educational facilities, features that were generally lacking in preindustrial agrarian societies.

Politics

This chapter and the preceding one have been about political organization rather than about politics. That is to say, they concern institutions or systems for dealing with social control and conflict resolution, such as go-betweens and courts. Politics, on the other hand, deals with the analysis of competitive political processes rather than with structural analysis. Following Swartz, Turner, and Tuden (1966:4–7), we may say that politics concerns public goals desired by members of a group or faction relating to the allocation of power. These authors describe some political processes as follows: During a preliminary phase of organization, competing groups try to win support and allies through persuasion and influence, promising rewards for support and spreading adverse gossip about the opposing faction or factions. Attempts may be made to win over or bribe members of an opposing group and to split it. This preliminary phase is succeeded by an open encounter or showdown which precipitates a crisis, signaled by violating a norm of usual ethical behavior. The crisis is apt to produce countervailing tendencies toward restoration of harmony. After resolution of the conflict, there must be some restoration of peace. Swartz, Turner, and Tuden refer to such sequences as "political phase developments." They have stimulated cross-cultural processual studies of politics along these lines (Swartz, Turner, and Tuden 1966:32–39). Detailed studies of factional struggles involve a multiplicity of factors and relationships. It may be necessary, for example, to sketch the personalities of particular leaders and their sources of influence. Such studies become, in effect, essays in history (e.g., Turner 1957).

Warfare

A society must not only preserve order within its borders but must also regulate relations with other social groups, making treaties or agreements about boundaries and spheres of influence, acting as host to visiting strangers, carrying on trade, and so forth. Failure to regulate such matters adequately may result in warfare.

Warfare scene, highlands of New Guinea.

Warfare has been reported for societies at all levels of cultural evolution. Some tribes, such as the Jivaro of Ecuador, live in a state of endemic warfare. In some societies, for example the former Plains Indian tribes, warfare was a seasonal matter, taking place in summer. In some societies, warfare has acquired ritualized aspects, with some of the qualities of a game.

Warfare may claim many lives in societies at all levels of technological development. Among the hunting-gathering Murngin of Australia, there was an estimate of 200 deaths from fighting in a population of 700 adult males. About 25 percent of adult males died in warfare among the Enga of New Guinea and about 24 percent among the Yanomamö of Venezuela, both horticultural societies. A similar percentage has been recorded for the Piegan of the northern Plains. For the more advanced civilization of the Valley of Mexico before the Spanish conquest, there were estimated to have been about 15,000 deaths a year due to warfare and human sacrifice.[3]

---

[3] These figures are drawn from Livingstone (1968).

The scale of warfare has, of course, increased in the course of cultural evolution as population density became greater, state control wider, and weapons more efficient.

In view of our long history as fighters, from Paleolithic times to the Atomic Age, some writers have concluded that humans have an aggressive instinct. Robert Ardrey (1966) believes that humans, like many other animals, have an inborn urge to defend the territory in which they live. Konrad Lorenz (1967) gives many examples of territorial behavior, but most of it is about birds and fishes, animals not closely related to us. Lorenz does devote a whole chapter to rats, which inhibit fighting within the pack but viciously attack the members of other packs in humanlike fashion. But there are many mammals that do not defend territories, such as caribou, elephants, and sea otters. Many mammals lead busy, largely peaceful lives, with little show of aggression (Carrighar 1968:48).

Our closest relatives, the orangutan, gorilla, and chimpanzee, do not have territories. Clashes may take place with strangers, but this is usually in the form of threat displays rather than actual combat. Desmond Morris (1969) believes that the early hominids who adopted a carnivorous diet and a cooperative hunting way of life had to have a fixed base and hence acquired a common territory to defend. This would account for our differences from our ape relatives with regard to territoriality; it would also accord with Ardrey's picture of humans as aggressive carnivores. One would assume, if this explanation is right, that all hunting societies would engage in war, but this is not the case. Warfare is reported to be absent for the Semang of the Malay Peninsula, the Congo Pygmies, some Eskimo groups, the Yahgan of Tierra del Fuego, and the western Shoshone.

Even if Ardrey is right and we all have inborn impulses of territorial defense and aggression, it seems that modern states cannot count on these instincts to fill up their armies but must resort to military conscription and enforce stiff penalties on draft dodgers and pacifists.

Human instinctual nature is probably not the best explanation for the long record of warfare and aggression of the human species. Our actions are determined more by learned behavior, by culture, than by instincts or drives. And this is a source of hope, if not of actual optimism, for culture and cultural traditions can change. Since Lorenz puts the emphasis on instinct, he recommends ways of sublimating aggression in order to avoid war: more Olympic games, competitive sports, and the competition of the space race. But it seems unlikely that such maneuvers could prevent war as long as there are powerful governments that see some advantage in it. Our problems lie not in the genes of the common man but in the ambitions of those with power.

My two chapters on political organization have been influenced by Gerhard E. Lenski, *Power and Privilege: A Theory of Social Stratification* (New York: McGraw-Hill Book Co., 1966). A more recent work along similar lines is Gerhard Lenski and Jean Lenski, *Human Societies: An Introduction to Macrosociology*, 2d ed. (McGraw-Hill Book Co., 1974). **Suggestions for further reading**

Different theories about the origin of the state are examined and assessed in Elman R. Service, *Origins of the State and Civilization: The Process of Cultural Evolution* (New York: W. W. Norton, 1975).

The hydraulic theory is set forth by Karl A. Wittfogel, *Oriental Despotism: A Comparative Study of Total Power* (New Haven, Conn.: Yale University Press, 1957).

The processual approach to the study of politics is exemplified in two readers: Marc J. Swartz, Victor W. Turner, and Arthur Tuden, eds., *Political Anthropology* (Chicago: Aldine Publishing Co., 1966); and Marc J. Swartz, ed., *Local Level Politics: Social and Cultural Perspectives* (Chicago: Aldine Publishing Co., 1968).

There are review articles on political anthropology, law, and warfare, by, respectively, Ronald Cohen, Laura Nader, and Barbara Yngvesson and Keith Otterbein in John J. Honigmann, ed., *Handbook of Social and Cultural Anthropology* (Chicago: Rand McNally and Co., 1973), pp. 861–958.

Anthropologists have not paid much attention to the cross-cultural study of warfare, but a special symposium has been devoted to the subject: Morton Fried, Marvin Harris, and Robert Murphy, eds., *War: The Anthropology of Armed Conflict and Aggression* (New York: Natural History Press, 1968).

part seven

Religious ideology and ritual

15

Animism, magic, and shamanism

In George P. Murdock's list of universal aspects of culture that have been reported for all societies for which we have ethnographic descriptions, there are several items that concern religion. According to Murdock (1945:124), all societies have the custom of propitiating supernatural beings and have religious rituals. All known cultures contain beliefs of some sort about the soul and life after death. Funeral rites and mourning customs are universal. Divination is practiced in all cultures, according to Murdock, and belief in magic is also found everywhere.

These universals apply to cultures rather than to individuals. There are, of course, many persons in the United States, Europe, the Soviet Union, and elsewhere who do not believe in spirits, gods, or life after death; but these ideas are part of the cultural tradition and are accepted by great numbers of people, even in the Soviet Union, where the favored official view on religion is atheistic.

Culture patterns that are so widespread, found in all parts of the world and among societies at different levels of technology, must be very old. This applies to all of the "universals" and must apply to religious patterns as well. In the first volume of this work (Chapter 10) we noted some evidence for religious belief on the part of the Neanderthals. Here is archaeological testimony supporting the age of such beliefs, which probably go much further back in time. But, even without archaeological evidence, we can be sure that religious beliefs and practices have great antiquity on the basis of their universality.

Nineteenth-century writers who wrote about "primitive religion" hoped to figure out how religious beliefs originated in the first place and what were the characteristics of the earliest primordial religion. This was part of the general 19th-century interest in origins and evolution, applied also to the origin of the family, the state, and other institutions. The problem as they saw it was to find out how the institution got started and then to trace it through different stages of cultural evolution to the present. These 19th-century writers tended to be rationalists, with an optimistic faith in reason, science, and the future of mankind. They often regarded religion as the product of erroneous reasoning. In some cases, there was an implication that, as society advanced and people learned to reason more effectively, religious faiths would be supplanted by a more rational outlook.

The chief representative of 19th-century rationalism in this field was Edward B. Tylor. About half of his two-volume work *Primitive Culture* (1877) is devoted to religion. Later writers who concerned themselves with religion generally felt obliged to either agree or disagree with Tylor's views. It is convenient, therefore, to start our discussion of religion with an examination of his theories.

Animism

Tylor wanted to find a "minimum definition" of religion which would apply to all religions in different parts of the world and different stages of development. He ruled out certain features that are not universal, such as belief in a supreme being, the notion of reward and punishment after death, worship of idols, and the practice of sacrifice. These are found in many societies but not in all, Tylor observed. What he chose as his minimum definition was "the belief in spiritual beings," to which he gave the name *animism*. It encompasses belief in souls, ghosts, gods, demons, and other supernaturals. For Tylor, animism was the core of religion from which all of its other aspects sprang. Once this idea was implanted in people's minds, various other beliefs and practices followed as a rather logical consequence.

But how did the belief in spirits arise in the first place? Theologians would answer that it stemmed from revelation, a view Tylor rejected. His own way of accounting for the origin of animism was in the experiences, shared by humans everywhere, of having dreams and reflecting about such phenomena as trance states, disease, and death. When a person wakes up he remembers that he has had various experiences during the night, traveling about and having conversations with others. Yet his companions will assure him that he has been asleep all night and has not moved. Reflecting about this paradox, humans would reach the dualistic conclusion that there is a soul that inhabits the body and animates it but is able to leave the body at night and communicate with other souls. When the soul returns to the body, the person wakes up again and is reanimated. But, when the person dies, it is because the soul has left the body for good. Tylor argued that these beliefs need not be derived from revelation but are more likely to have arisen from the natural process of reasoning about universal experiences.

There are further natural consequences that follow upon a belief in spiritual beings. One conclusion would be that, once the soul has left the body, it may continue an existence after death or may be reborn in another bodily form. It was only natural to assume that other animals and plants also had souls. A cult of ancestor worship was still another likely consequence; this is not universal, but such cults could easily arise on the basis of animistic assumptions.

The belief in *possession* is another possible consequence, which is not universal, being not much developed among American Indian tribes although widespread in the Old World. This is the idea that a discarnate entity, spirit or soul, can take possession of a living body, temporarily dislodging its rightful occupant. In societies that have such beliefs, where people become "possessed," it is understandable that rites of *exorcism* have often developed to drive out invading spirits. But, often, as among spiritualist mediums and Siberian shamans, possession is voluntary, sought after. In other cases, as in devil possession in medieval Europe, it is considered evil, involuntary, requiring exorcism.

If a spirit can invade a living organism, then perhaps it can also take up lodgment in an object such as a piece of wood. This idea Tylor termed *fetishism* (not to be confused with sexual fetishism), the fetish being an object that is worshiped because it is conceived to be inhabited by or associated with a spirit.

Nature worship may also stem from animistic beliefs. Trees, rivers, animals, and plants may all be seen as having souls and may be worshiped. From this pattern arose the polytheistic pantheons of civilized and near-civilized peoples in which different gods were believed to control different aspects of nature: the rain, thunder, earth, sea, sun, and moon.

Tylor saw *monotheism* as being a late development in the evolution of religion, which could arise in various ways. One god might be elevated to dominance over the others. In a society having a king and aristocracy, it might be assumed that the supernatural realm had the same political organization as the known earthly world. A supreme deity, supported by an aristocracy of lesser gods, might then be assumed to rule the universe.

Tylor's work had great influence; it is still considered a classic in anthropology, but in time his views about religion attracted criticism from various angles. Tylor's explanation of the origin of animistic beliefs has the weakness that it cannot be proven. Other, perhaps equally plausible, explanations for the origin of religion were offered by some of his contemporaries. How can one choose between these alternatives? It becomes a matter of personal taste. This is part of the reason why later anthropological works on religion turned from speculation about origins to a study of the functions of religions in living cultures.

One criticism of Tylor's theories about the origin and development of animism was that they overemphasized the role of reason and the conceptual side of religion. R. R. Marett (1914:xxxi) argued that ". . . savage religion is something not so much thought out as danced out." It involves awe and other emotions as well as thought.

Animatism

Marett pointed to a widespread religious concept that could not logically be derived from belief in spirits and might be just as old as, or older than, animism. This is belief in an impersonal supernatural power.

Mana is a word used in both Melanesia and Polynesia for impersonal supernatural power. Marett gave the term *animatism* to belief in such a power, which is conceived to pervade the universe but is stored up more in some objects or persons than in others. Chiefs, priests, men of high status, have more mana than ordinary folk. An odd-shaped stone may be thought to have mana. If a man plants such a stone in his garden and if the yield of yams subsequently increases, he may become convinced that there is mana in it. Such ways of thinking are not foreign to the conceptions of the Western world. We regard the altar of a church as being somehow qualitatively different from a lamppost on the corner; it is more "sacred," just as holy water is thought to be different from ordinary water.

Like electricity, mana may be dangerous as well as beneficial. An object handled by a Polynesian chief may be considered perilous for a commoner to touch. Hence, the concept of *taboo* in Polynesia was closely associated with that of mana. The word *taboo* has implications of sacredness as well as of the forbidden. Idols, temples, members of the ruling family, priests, canoes of the gods, and many other objects were taboo to commoners, a practice that served to widen social distance between the ruling family and the common people.

As Ruth Benedict (1938a) pointed out, conceptions about the supernatural may be based on two kinds of contrasting assumptions. On the one hand, one may conceive of supernatural things as having the attributes of objects, such as color and weight. On the other hand, one may attribute personality to all segments of the universe, to stars, plants, animals, storms, and other aspects of nature. To attribute mana to a stone, seeing it as being full of power, would be the first alternative, that of animatism. To assume that a spirit lives within the stone would be the second alternative, that of animism. Benedict made a distinction between an *amulet,* an object that is believed to automatically radiate supernatural power or good luck but is not personified, and a *fetish,* an object that is worshiped because of its indwelling spirit. Both objects are regarded as sacred but for different reasons. In Africa the fetish is talked to, cajoled or pleaded with, and otherwise addressed as a person. This is not done with an amulet. If the emphasis in a religious system is on animatism, men try to tap, build up, and increase supernatural power. If the emphasis is on animism, men try to establish contact with the gods and offer petitions and sacrifice. The former system tends more in the direction of manipulation and magic; it operates with cause and effect sequences and, in that respect, is similar to science. The second system tends more in the direction of personal religion involving interpersonal relationships with gods and spirits. In practice, however, most religious systems represent a complex mixture of animism and animatism, religion and magic.

Magic

There have been different ways of distinguishing between magic and religion. One has just been referred to; Ruth Benedict, following James G. Frazer, saw magic as being manipulative, while religion is supplicative. Frazer regarded magic as "primitive man's science," although it is based on two erroneous principles which Frazer termed the "Law of Similarity" and the "Law of Contact." The former is the belief that like produces like, while the latter is the notion that things that have once been in contact continue to act on each other at a distance. According to the first principle, the magician imitates the effects he desires. For example, he jabs pins into a doll and thus wounds his enemy. According to the second principle, the magician assumes that what he does to a material object will affect the person with whom it was once associated. Thus, sorcery can be worked against a person if one has acquired some of his fingernail parings, feces, teeth, or clothing (Frazer 1943:11–45). In either case, the effect is conceived to be brought about more or less automatically through the will and ritual actions of the magician; he does not appeal to a higher authority for help.

Émile Durkheim, who emphasized the social, collective nature of religion in his book, *The Elementary Forms of the Religious Life* (1912), claimed that magic is mainly an individual affair in which no lasting social bonds are established, while religion is a collective enterprise that involves a church or community of fellow believers.

Hindu ritual.

Bronislaw Malinowski (1954:17–90) made a series of distinctions between magic and religion: magic is a means to an end, while religion is an end in itself; belief in magic is simple and its aim is straightforward and definite, while religious belief is more complex, involving pantheons of supernatural beings. He argued that humans resort to magic when faced with the possibility of failure. The hunter cannot find game, the lover cannot win over his beloved. Despite one's best efforts, one cannot attain the valued goal through normal, rational means. A natural recourse in such blocked circumstances, according to Malinowski, is resort to magic. Moreover, this has an effect, for it gives the magician confidence. Feeling that something has been done to bring him closer to his goal, he perseveres with renewed effort. Religion also gives humans the confidence to carry on, but on a more long-range basis, establishing positive attitudes and values.

Although much of this seems convincing, Francis L. K. Hsu (1952) has subjected Malinowski's contrast between magic and religion to severe criticism and has shown that in practice, when dealing with a particular religious system, it is very difficult to separate magic and religion from one another or even sometimes to say which is which. Perhaps it is useful for analytical purposes to distinguish between magic and religion, as Frazer, Durkheim, and Malinowski have done in their different ways, but magicians may make use of religious practices and appeal to spirits for help, while religious bodies may make use of magical techniques, as in sprinkling holy water, and in pursuit of immediate practical ends, as in a prayer meeting for rain. Magic is not always individual, nor religion always collective; the young Ojibwa Indian, fasting alone in the woods, is engaged in a religious quest.

In visions, dreams, states of trance, and "possession," human beings receive convincing support for the existence of the gods and spirits in which they believe.

Unusual psychological states

Visions may sometimes be induced by lack of food. Early humans must often have gone hungry and then experienced unusual psychological states. Young men among the Ojibwa and other American Indian tribes deliberately fasted in order to have visions of their guardian spirits. We may assume that hunting-gathering people who ate a wide variety of vegetable foods must occasionally have swallowed hallucinogenic plants. After the discovery of their properties, these were often eaten deliberately for their effects. This is the case, at any rate, among some Siberian tribes of the Kamchatka Peninsula, some Mount Hagen natives of Northeast New Guinea, and some of the peoples of Mexico. In each of these areas, hallucinogenic mushrooms are eaten for their visionary effects. It is very likely that the intoxicating *soma* juice often referred to in the Vedas of the ancient Aryans was derived from hallucinogenic mushrooms. In northern Mexico and the southwestern United States, the peyote "button" was consumed for the same purpose. In South America, datura was used; in wide areas of the Old World, opium, *bhang,* or hashish have been smoked, with similar effects. In recent years in the United States, there has been a vogue for experimenting with LSD and other "mind-changing" drugs. Besides fasting and drugs, there are other methods used in various parts of the world to induce states of dissociation, including the repetition of rhythmic motor activities, drumming, singing, or dancing to the point of exhaustion.

The purposes of seeking visionary experiences are many, but one of them is to learn about matters not accessible to the normal conscious mind. A shaman goes into trance to find where game is located or to find the whereabouts of a missing person. Whether or not this can be done, the belief in such faculties is widespread. The pattern of crystal gazing or of staring at a flame or into water or some other liquid to gain information about unknown matters is almost universal. It has been reported among Canadian Indians, Iroquois, Apaches, Polynesians, Maoris, the Malagasy of Madagascar, the Zulus, and the

Inca of Peru, as well as among the peoples of modern Europe (Lang 1909:83–87).

Tylor referred to the experience of visions and hallucinations as being a contributory factor in the development of animistic beliefs. He also briefly alluded to the belief in "second sight," or what we now call extrasensory perception. Andrew Lang took Tylor to task for not inquiring into the possible validity of such experiences:

. . . it might seem to be the business of Anthropology, the Science of Man, to examine, among other things, the evidence for the actual existence of those alleged and supernormal phenomena. . . . About the psychical condition of the savages who worked out the theory of souls and founded religion we necessarily know nothing. If there be such experiences as clairvoyance, telepathy, and so on, these unknown ancestors of ours may (for all that we can tell) have been peculiarly open to them, and therefore peculiarly apt to believe in separable souls (Lang 1909:44, 56).

Lang presented some anecdotes to show that telepathy is widely believed in by "primitive" peoples. Here is one example which Lang culled from *Among the Zulus* (1875) by David Leslie, who was brought up in Zulu country and could speak the native language. Leslie went to meet his Kaffir elephant hunters at an appointed place, but they did not show up. A servant suggested that he consult a local "doctor" or medicine man, which he did, largely to pass the time. The doctor made eight fires (the number of hunters). Into each he cast some roots and a stone, shouting the name of the hunter to which the stone was dedicated. Then he ate some "medicine" and fell into a brief trance. After he got up again, he went to one of the fires, raked the ashes, looked at the stone, described the man in question, and said, "This man has died of fever, and your gun is lost." At the next, "This man has killed four elephants." The next, "This man has been killed by an elephant, but your gun is coming home." And so on. Each man was described correctly in detail. The doctor told where the survivors were and what they were doing and said that they would come out in three months. Leslie took note of all this information at the time. All of it, reportedly, turned out to be true. The men were scattered about in a country 200 miles away (Lang 1909:68–69).

There are too many unknown factors in this anecdote for us to evaluate it adequately. Lang presented it partly to show that there was at least a problem worth examining. His plea that anthropologists undertake cross-cultural psychical research has been largely ignored since his day, perhaps because most anthropologists, like most psychologists, do not believe in extrasensory perception and therefore do not think there is anything to investigate. The writer made a small attempt in this direction, giving a series of 48 runs of Rhine's ESP (extrasensory perception) card-guessing test to an old Chippewa religious leader in the summer of 1944. The Rhine test makes use of a pack of cards with five symbols, each card having one of the five: circle, star, wave, cross, and square. The subject, often seated in a separate room from the examiner, is asked to guess the order in which the symbols appear after the pack has been shuffled. The old Chippewa, who certainly believed in telepathy, did not score significantly above chance. The most ambitious attempt along these lines has been Ronald Rose's administration of the ESP test to Australian aborigines, who did score better than chance. Rose and his wife recorded 16,625 guesses; chance would have been 3,325 "hits," but they recorded 3,870 correct hits (Rose 1956:227). Rose thought this was evidence that Australian aborigines had ESP abilities, but most psychologists would probably not agree.

Shamanism

The *shaman,* or medicine man, is mankind's first specialist, although not on a full-time basis. In a hunting band he is a hunter like anyone else. In most hunting-gathering societies and among many simple horticulturalists, there are religious practitioners of this sort. They are also to be found in advanced civilizations, but then they coexist with another type of religious specialist, the priest, who will be discussed later. The shaman is an intermediary between the members of his society and the supernatural world, with which he communicates either by talking to the spirits and listening to their replies or through possession. Edwin M. Loeb (1929) has made a distinction, on this basis, between the *seer* and the shaman. The seer has visions of spirits, who talk to him, but the true shaman is possessed; the spirits speak *through* him. Loeb believes the seer is the older type of religious specialist, being found among American Indian tribes and among the more primitive and isolated peoples of the Old World, such as the Australian aborigines and Andaman Islanders. Possession shamanism is widespread in the Old World. Another writer, Mircea Eliade (1950:299), makes a distinction between shaman and medicine man, restricting the term *shaman* to those who make "an ecstatic trip to Heaven, to the Lower World, or to the depths of the ocean." Most anthropologists, however, use the terms *shaman* and *medicine man* interchangeably; there seems to be no harm in doing so.

Medicine men fill various functions; they "communicate" with spirits and learn about hidden matters, and they are sometimes believed to influence the weather and to make the rain fall or stop.

As the term implies, a medicine man is also concerned with curing. Various medical techniques are used by shamans in different societies, including the administration of herbs, roots, brews, poultices, salves, ointments, enemas, massage, and sweat baths. Many of these are valid curative practices, but even when that is not the case, the curing process itself provides reassurance to the patient and often helps him get well, especially if the ailment is of psychosomatic origin. The cure may be helped along by drum-beating, singing, dancing, and impressive, dramatic behavior on the part of the medicine man, which assures the patient that he is in good hands.

The sucking cure

A widespread, probably ancient, technique is the sucking cure, in which the shaman goes through the motions of sucking a disease from the patient's body. Usually he "extracts" something, which he shows to the patient and other persons present as proof that the sickness has been removed. This, again, must have a reassuring, sometimes therapeutic, effect upon the patient. Of course, it does not always work, just as modern medical practices sometimes do not work. But even if the patient dies, that does not necessarily lead to a loss of faith in this curing method, for the shaman may have a ready explanation, such as, for example, that a powerful sorcerer was responsible for the death and that he was summoned too late to prevent it. Some variant of the sucking cure is found among the Jivaro Indians of Ecuador, the Ojibwa of the Great Lakes region in North America, the Cochiti Indians of New Mexico, the Kwakiutl Indians of the Northwest Coast, the St. Lawrence Island Eskimos, and the Arunta of Australia.

The objects "extracted" from the patient's body may be stones, pieces of wood, and other objects that the shaman has probably kept in his mouth, although it is sometimes difficult to see how he has managed to do that. Harry B. Wright (1957:14–15), a dentist and explorer from Philadelphia, recorded that a Jivaro medicine man spat out the following objects in succession during the course of a cure: a splinter of wood, a mouthful of ants, a grasshopper, and a lizard. (Both the grasshopper and the lizard were dead.) This cure, incidentally, was for a toothache and was a complete success.

Edwin T. Denig, who entered the fur trade in 1833, married the daughter of an Assiniboin chief and lived among Indian tribes of the Upper Missouri for 21 years, twice made physical examinations of a sucking doctor to find where the worms and snakes were hidden. The shaman, who was naked, was not forewarned about the search, and the Indians had never engaged in such investigations themselves.

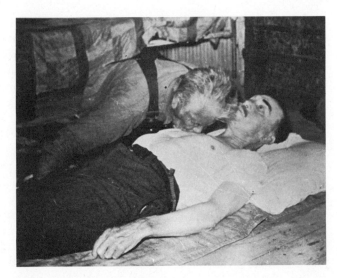

A Chippewa
sucking doctor
at work.

Yet he acquiesced cheerfully, afterwards continued his performance, and
repeated it in our presence, drawing and spitting out large worms, clots of
blood, tufts of hair, skin, etc., too large to be easily secreted, and leaving
no visible mark on the patient's body. The trick was well done and not yet
known to any of us (Denig 1928–29:424).

There is a recorded case of a Kwakiutl informant who was initiated
as a shaman and taught how to perform a sucking cure. George Hunt,
the Kwakiutl, wrote the details of his shamanistic practice to Franz
Boas. Here is one case where we know how the "cure" was done,
although it does not seem to be so impressive a feat as the Jivaro's
alleged expectoration of splinter, ants, grasshopper, and lizard.
George Hunt was taught to place some eagle down between his
inner upper lip and gums. While sucking the patient's body, he bit
his tongue, so that the down became saturated with blood. At the
end of the sucking process he spat out the bloody eagle down and
showed it to the impressed onlookers. Hunt became a huge success
as a shaman and aroused much envy and hostility among other
Kwakiutl medicine men who were not familiar with his particular
technique. They begged him to tell them how he did it, but Hunt
refused (Boas 1930).

Magic tricks

The term *magic* has more than one meaning. In previous pages it
has referred to supernatural manipulation, as in love magic, hunting
magic, garden magic, or sorcery. But the term has another, colloquial
meaning, referring to sleight of hand, the magic of performers like

Houdini. It is interesting that medicine men have often been magicians in both senses of the word. The sucking-out of objects is itself quite a good trick, but shamans have often performed other marvels, sometimes as a prelude to a cure, as a way of establishing a receptive, trusting attitude on the part of the patient. By demonstrating that he can perform miracles, the shaman shows his credentials, demonstrates his power, and wins assent from his clientele. Many such performances must have been very crude, but some that have been described by travelers are impressive.

Jane M. Murphy (1964) has reported on some of the magic tricks performed by St. Lawrence Island Eskimo shamans. W. F. Doty, a missionary on that island in 1898, was present at a seance when a shaman sank into the ground until only the hair of his head was visible. The Russian ethnographer Bogoras watched a shaman, with arms crossed on his bare chest, make a walrus skin stick to his shoulders so tightly (without visible attachments) that he was able to pull Bogoras, who was hanging onto it, out of the room. Another shaman was said to make a parka rise from the ground and stand up without visible support. Murphy gives various other examples of such tricks, including ventriloquism.

One of the most impressive reports along these lines is one by E. Lucas Bridges, included in an autobiographical account of his life in Tierra del Fuego, at the southern tip of South America, where he was born, the son of a missionary.

Bridges described the performance of a medicine man named Houshken which took place outdoors on a clear moonlit night. Houshken began by chanting, then brought his hands to his mouth and produced a strip of guanaco hide about 18 inches long. He shook his hands violently and gradually separated them until the strip was about 4 feet long. Then Houshken called his brother, who took one end of the strip, which now doubled its length. After this, however, the strip began to diminish and soon disappeared into Houshken's hand.

With the continued agitation of his hands, the strip got shorter and shorter. Suddenly, when his hands were almost together, he clapped them to his mouth, uttered a prolonged shriek, then held out his hands to us, palm upward and empty.

Even an ostrich could not have swallowed those eight feet of hide at one gulp without visible effort. Where the coil could have gone to I do not profess to know. It could not have gone up Houshken's sleeve, for he had dropped his robe when the performance began (Bridges 1950:285).

Later, Houshken produced a small, semitransparent object that rapidly revolved between his hands, less than 2 feet from Bridges' face. When his hands drew to about 3 inches apart, it disappeared.

Leather seems to have played a role in tricks of the type just cited, both among the Eskimos and the Ona. And the mouth is important in the episodes described by Wright, Denig, and Bridges. But, perhaps, there are few other places where a naked shaman could hide something.

Sincerity of shamans

Some of the foregoing data suggest that some medicine men must be deliberate frauds who deceive their patients. This, at least, was the case of the Kwakiutl, George Hunt, who became a shaman in order to find out whether shamans really had supernatural powers and soon discovered they did not. Kwakiutl shamans, who were leagued in groups, gained much wealth and status from their profession. In this they were assisted by spies, whom Hunt called "the eyes of the shamans," for they reported to them about current ailments in different communities. This enabled a shaman, when he appeared on the scene, to seem clairvoyant, already knowing all about a patient's sickness and where it was located (Boas 1930:9–11).

Paul Radin (1957:41–51) believed that in food-gathering societies like the Yokuts of California, shamans were leagued in a conspiracy with the chiefs to terrorize the other members of the society and maintain control over them. This may sometimes have happened, but neither the Yokuts nor the Kwakiutl seem typical of hunting-gathering societies. The tribes of California and the Northwest Coast were unusually concerned with wealth and status. The cynicism and opportunism of the Kwakiutl shamans do not seem to have been general traits of medicine men.

It is true, nevertheless, that the sucking cure involves deception in the production of twigs, stones, and other objects that cannot possibly have been sucked from the patient's body. This could be excused on the ground that the visible presentation of the object adds to the patient's sense of security. More than that, the shaman often seems to really believe in his powers, despite his knowledge of his own deception, and, when he is sick, he goes to another medicine man who uses the same techniques (Elkin 1954:281). A variable combination of fraud and sincerity seems to have been characteristic of medicine men.

Wrangel, a late 18th-century traveler in Siberia, denied that Siberian shamans were impostors:

Anyone who has observed a *true* shaman at the height of ecstasy will certainly . . . admit that he is neither able to practice deception, at least at that moment, nor desirous of doing so, but that what is occurring to him is a consequence of the involuntary and irresistible influence of his intensely stimulated imagination. A true shaman is certainly a very remarkable psychological phenomenon (quoted in Oesterreich 1930:295–96).

Becoming a shaman in three cultures

Let us see how one becomes a shaman in three hunting-gathering societies for which there are good ethnographic data: the Eskimos, the Ojibwa, and the Arunta. As will be seen, there are many similarities in the shamanism of these three groups.

Both men and women can become shamans among the Eskimos, but most of them are men. Among the Central Eskimos, a candidate who wishes to study under a shaman must present him with something valuable, perhaps some wood, which is scarce. Then the candidate and his parents must confess to all the breaches of taboo they have committed. The training period involves exposure to cold and fasting. A Caribou Eskimo gave Knud Rasmussen a doubtless exaggerated account of having fasted for 5 days; then being allowed a mouthful of warm water and then going another 15 days without food. Again he was given a mouthful of warm water; then he fasted for 10 days more, after which he was allowed to eat but had to avoid entrails and other tabooed foods. The informant claimed that he sat alone in a cold snow hut in wintertime for 30 days; then, he finally had visions of the spirit he sought (Rasmussen 1930:51–54).

In East Greenland, candidates started training at the early age of seven or eight. They had to sit for hours in a deserted place rubbing one stone against another. It is believed that if the boy keeps this up long enough, a bear will come up from the lake and swallow him. Then, he will spit him out again, and the novice's body parts will become reassembled. After this experience, the young man can declare that he is a shaman and may start to practice, but the novitiate usually lasts from five to ten years (Thalbitzer 1931:430–36).

Among the Central Eskimos, as soon as a young man has become a shaman, he is given a special shaman's belt, to which are attached various bone carvings of human figures, fishes, and harpoons. These are presents from people who hope to thereby be protected or, at least, not harmed by the shaman's helping spirits (Rasmussen 1929: 111–14).

Among the Ojibwa, or Chippewa, there was no training for novices. The power to become a shaman came from a dream or vision of a guardian spirit. All Ojibwa children fasted in former days, beginning from between four and six years of age. In the morning a parent smeared some charcoal over the child's face; seeing this, a neighbor would know that the child should not be given food. The boy was sent out to play in the woods without breakfast; he might

be given some food during the day, but not much. He could, however, break his fast at nightfall. Fasting of this kind might continue
for a few days and then stop, to be resumed later. Thus it was kept
up sporadically throughout childhood until the sacred dream finally
came. This dream or vision should come before puberty. Sometimes,
eager for their dream experience, boys fasted for as much as ten days
or more on a kind of platform built high in the treetops, where they
sometimes chewed on a piece of lead or deer fat to keep their mouths
from getting dry.

Girls also fasted and might get a dream or vision, but it was much
more important for boys to succeed in this quest since their lives
involved the risks and uncertainties of hunting and warfare, while
women's work was more routine and dependable. Shamanism was
men's work, although women sometimes became shamans, particularly after the menopause. Not all dreams or visions were sacred. A
sacred dream had to have some rather stereotyped elements, mainly
a meeting with a guardian spirit that could assume either human or
animal form. In the case of boys destined to be shamans, the guardian spirit gave instruction about their practice. Usually, they were
not supposed to embark upon their shamanistic careers until many
years after the vision.

There were two kinds of medicine men: sucking doctors and tent
shakers. Some shamans were both. The sucking cure has already
been briefly described. Tent shaking was a specialty, also known as
conjuring, which involved the construction of a barrel-shaped lodge,
which was entered by the medicine man. It was put up on occasions
when people needed information about something not accessible to
their normal conscious minds: the whereabouts of a lost person, the
location of game or, in former days, the enemy. It could also be used
for diagnosis of an ailment or the identification of a sorcerer. The
conjuring lodge is called a shaking tent because, after the medicine man gets into it, it starts to vibrate. It probably does so because
the shaman is shaking it, but the Indians believe that the vibration is
caused by a strong wind inside the structure. Voices issue from the
tent, doubtless produced by the shaman but attributed by the Indians to the various spirits that enter the lodge. Since the power of
conjuring supposedly comes from a fasting vision, there could be no
instruction in this technique, or at least it could not be admitted
that there had been any. It is not known how the knowledge was
passed on from one generation to the next (Hallowell 1942; Landes
1968).

Among the Arunta of central Australia, a man who wants to become a medicine man wanders away from his camp until he comes
to a cave, in front of which he goes to sleep. At daybreak a spirit is

Ojibwa shaman beside conjuring lodge. During a seance the framework is covered by hides, cloth, or blankets.

supposed to come from the cave and throw an invisible lance through his head, making a hole in his tongue. This hole is the badge of shamanhood, and it should remain open as long as the shaman practices. It is probably made by the shaman himself, but he would never admit that. The spirit that spears him is believed to take the novice into the cave, remove his entrails, and replace them with a new set. He also places some magic stones in the novice's body, which are later used in shamanistic practices.

There is another way to become a medicine man and to acquire the sacred stones and the requisite hole in the tongue. A novice may be initiated by some medicine men who perform the tongue operation for him and press rock crystals into his skin, supposedly forcing them into his body (Spencer and Gillen 1927).

Some parallels may be noted in these three societies. Women could become shamans in all three cultures, but most shamans were men. Fasting was an important approach to shamanism among the Eskimos and Ojibwa. Ojibwa and some Arunta novices purportedly received no training or instruction from shamans, while Eskimos and some Arunta did receive training. The novitiate generally involves the inducement of dissociated states. The Greenland Eskimo novice is swallowed by a bear and his body parts are reassembled; the Arunta has his entrails removed and gets a new set. The idea of dying and being reborn with a somewhat different body is implicit in these ways of acquiring shamanistic power.

The sucking cure is practiced by the Ojibwa, Arunta, and the Eskimos of St. Lawrence Island. Clairvoyant and telepathic abilities are attributed to shamans in all three societies. Arunta and Ojibwa shamans are feared as sorcerers and are believed to be able to assume the forms of birds or animals. It is evident that the shaman is regarded with some ambivalence. Since he cures the sick and helps the members of his society in various ways, his services are naturally valued. But the very fact that the shaman is believed to have so much supernatural power makes him a potentially dangerous man, capable of killing others through sorcery, if he is so inclined.

Mythology

Even though it may contain internal contradictions and inconsistencies, the mythology of a society expresses a kind of world view and presents a set of answers for some of the riddles of life — such as why people have to die or why hunters sometimes cannot find game. In ceremonies, the gods and spirits may be appealed to or their roles may be enacted. Ceremonies may, in part, be dramatizations of myths.

Let us consider a crucial part of Central Eskimo mythology, which also finds expression in some of their ceremonies. This myth answers the question of why hunters sometimes cannot find game. This is certainly a vital matter for the Eskimos in wintertime, when they largely depend upon sea mammals for food, especially upon the seals, whom they harpoon through blowholes in the ice when the seals come up to breathe.

Sedna

The Central Eskimos formerly believed in the existence of a woman at the bottom of the sea, often known as Sedna. Her story is told with local variations, but goes roughly like this: Sedna was once an Eskimo girl; she married a bird and went to an island to live with her husband. Her father and brothers did not approve of this match, so they went to the island in a boat and rowed away with Sedna. Angered, the bird called up a storm and great waves on the sea. Sedna's father threw his daughter overboard, but she clung to the side of the boat. Her father then chopped off the first segments of her fingers, but she hung on. Father next chopped off the second segments; Sedna still hung on. After one more blow of the knife, Sedna sank to the bottom of the sea, where she remains to this day. The different segments of her fingers turned into different sea mammals, seals and walrus.

Sedna sometimes gets angry at human beings for breaking taboos. Eskimo life is hedged about by so many taboos that it is difficult not to break some of them. There are more taboos affecting women than men, especially concerning menstruation, stillbirths, and food. When a woman breaks a taboo, a kind of smoke or vapor rises up from her body, sinks through the sea, and settles in Sedna's hair in the form of dirt or maggots, which Sedna cannot comb from her hair since she has no fingers. Angered at human beings, she calls down all the sea mammals, former segments of herself, to the bottom of the sea. The Eskimos then face the possibility of starvation.

Here we see an explanation for the hunters' failure to kill game. They have been out by the blowholes, on the ice, all day but have had no luck. The story tells us that it is not their fault; it is their wives who are to blame for breaking taboos. We will never know whether it was men or women who made up this story, but one would suspect that the men would find it a satisfactory explanation, providing for displacement of possible feelings of guilt or failure. Apart from this, any explanation is better than none, especially when a course of action is made available once the cause of failure is known.

The person who comes to the rescue in this case is the medicine man; he arranges a seance and the lights are put out. The shaman's voice in the darkness gets fainter as he sinks to the bottom of the sea. Some Eskimos believe that the shaman goes to the bottom of the sea in his bodily form, while others hold that only his spirit travels there. At any rate, when he reaches Sedna's home, he appeases her, combs her hair for her, and persuades her to release the sea mammals. Then he surfaces, returning to the Eskimo dwelling from whence he came.

Upon his return, all the persons in the dwelling must confess the taboos they have broken. They may be reluctant to admit them, of course, but fear of famine and of Sedna's anger forces them to confess. In this way, everyone learns about everyone else's secrets. Women may be sent for who are not present; the young wives who come in, crying and penitent, also confess. After this, the men return to their blowholes with renewed confidence (Rasmussen 1929: 123–29).

Sedna is not a very benevolent deity; she has to be placated and coaxed to help mankind and not bring on starvation; and the Eskimos seem to feel some hostility toward her. Boas described a ceremony in which Sedna was harpooned by two shamans who stood on either side of a coil of rope, which represented a seal's breathing hole. The shamans proudly displayed the blood-sprinkled harpoon to their audience (Boas 1884:604).

In the seance, when the shaman dives to the bottom of the sea, the people present are made aware of the reality of Sedna, who, in the absence of such dramatizations, might seem to be a rather abstract concept. Similarly, when the Ojibwa shaman brings spirits into the shaking tent, one can hear their voices, and their immediate reality is brought home to the onlooker.

Bronislaw Malinowski's *Magic, Science and Religion and Other Essays* (New York: Doubleday-Anchor Books, 1954) is recommended. **Suggestions for further reading**

An interesting collection of readings is available in Ari Kiev, ed., *Magic, Faith, and Healing: Studies in Primitive Psychiatry Today* (London: Free Press of Glencoe, 1964).

Two good readers on the effects of hallucinogenic drugs and their relation to religion are also recommended: Peter T. Furst, ed., *Flesh of the Gods: The Ritual Use of Hallucinogens* (New York: Praeger Publishers, 1972); and Michael J. Harner, ed., *Hallucinogens and Shamanism* (New York: Oxford University Press, 1973). See also Erika Bourguignon, ed., *Religion, Altered States of Consciousness, and Social Change* (Columbus: Ohio State Press, 1973); and R. E. L. Masters and Jean Houston, *The Varieties of Psychedelic Experience* (New York: Holt, Rinehart, and Winston, 1966).

16

Communal and ecclesiastical religious cults

 Anthony F. C. Wallace (1966:84–88) has drawn up a typology of cult institutions as follows: (1) individualistic, (2) shamanic, (3) communal, and (4) ecclesiastical.

A typology of cult institutions

The individualistic type refers to rituals performed by persons who are not specialists, such as an Ojibwa boy's vision quest or a person's private prayer at a family shrine.

The second category refers to shamanism, in which distinction is made between the magico-religious specialist and ordinary laymen.

Communal cults are performed by groups of laymen in rites of transition, calendrical ceremonies, ancestor cults, or other ceremonies. No full-time priesthood is involved.

Ecclesiastical cult institutions, however, do have priests, professional religious specialists who are neither shamans nor lay officials.

There is an implicit evolutionary progression in Wallace's scheme. "In societies containing an ecclesiastical cult institution, there will also be communal, shamanic, and individualistic institutions. Where there is no ecclesiastical institution, but a communal one, there will be also shamanic and individualistic varieties. And when there is neither ecclesiastical nor communal, there will be shamanic and individualistic" (Wallace 1966:88). The presumably earlier forms are retained in the later. There seem to be no societies that have only individualistic cult institutions, but there are some, such as the Eskimos, that have both individualistic and shamanic types. Shamanism was discussed in the previous chapter. In this chapter we will deal with communal and ecclesiastical cults.

236

Rites of transition, or rites of passage, are ceremonies performed at certain stages in the life cycle of an individual when he or she moves from one status to another. A ceremony may be performed at birth to greet the new baby and welcome it into the world of the living. This ceremony also involves a change of status for the married couple, especially if it is their first child—they now become parents. **Rites of transition**

Initiation ceremonies mark the transition from childhood to adulthood at puberty. These were discussed in Chapter 11, where there were brief accounts of Arunta and Chaga initiations. Some societies lack puberty ceremonies. Margaret Mead explained the absence of female initiation in Samoa in terms of the smooth transition from childhood to womanhood with little change in roles.

The Arunta initiation of young boys is under the supervision of the older men, who also go through ceremonies involving the *churingas* and totemic rites.

In societies that have ecclesiastical cults, rites of transition may be presided over by priests, rather than a group of laymen.

Marriage is an important transition point, although it does not involve ceremonial behavior in all societies. Among the Kaingang, Murngin, Papago, and Sirionó, there are no marriage ceremonies, and there is very little ceremony at the time of marriage among the Ifaluk, Kwoma, and Trobriand Islanders (Stephens 1963:221). At the other extreme, in northern India, the marriage cycle is drawn out over a period of two years or more, with various ritual stages before the final consummation of the marriage.

Death is another occasion for rites of transition, usually accompanied by mourning. This reaches an acute pitch among the Arunta, who gash themselves with knives and sharp, pointed digging sticks at a funeral, the women "battering one another's heads with fighting clubs," as Spencer and Gillen reported. Among the Arunta there is not only sadness at a death but also a kind of rage or anger, probably because deaths are seen as being due to sorcery.

Why do people mourn and weep at a funeral? The answer seems simple: because they have lost a loved friend, spouse, or relative. Durkheim, in analyzing Spencer and Gillen's data, rejected this apparently obvious explanation. He pointed out that in the midst of mourning, if someone speaks of some temporal interest, the mourners' expressions may suddenly change and the people may assume a laughing tone before going back to their weeping. "Mourning is not a natural movement of private feelings wounded by a cruel loss; it is a duty imposed by the group," concluded Durkheim (1965:443). No member of the group is allowed to be indifferent; by collectively mourning, the members express their solidarity, and in doing so they overcome and repair the loss that has befallen them. Durkheim's view seems a bit cynical in denying to the mourners spontaneity of feeling, which must often be real enough, but he is no doubt right about the function of mourning in unifying the group.

Freud also had a theory about mourning. It was his belief that a person is invariably ambivalent in his emotions, particularly among neurotic individuals. One does not only love one's wife or husband; one also hates him or her, although the hatred may be repressed and only partially conscious. At one point or other, according to Freud, one has wished for the death of one's spouse. Thus, when the death actually occurs, it may trigger a sense of guilt in the survivor. Freud accounted in this way for the deep depression and self-blame that sometimes follows a death. The survivor may accuse himself of not having been attentive enough to the deceased, even though his record on that score may have been excellent. Freud explained in these terms the fact that recently deceased persons, in many non-Western societies, are often regarded as malevolent spirits, hostile to the living; for the survivor, plagued with his feelings of guilt, projects his own aggression onto the ghost. Freud noted that modern humans no longer fear the recent dead. His explanation for this was that primitive peoples must have been more ambivalent in their emotions than modern humans (Freud 1938:852–58; see also Opler 1936).

Calendrical rites

Calendrical rites are found in relatively advanced agricultural societies that have developed sufficient knowledge about the sun, moon, and stars to have an idea of the yearly cycle and its different seasons. The Hopi Indians of Arizona have a communal cult of the *katcinas*, which involves both a calendrical cycle and initiation ceremonies for the young. The katcinas are ancestral spirits, believed in by the Hopi, who are also spirits of the rain clouds. They are said to spend half the year in the San Francisco Mountains and the other half among the Hopi. During the latter period they are impersonated by men who wear large masks.

According to Hopi mythology, friendly katcinas accompanied the Hopi in their emergence from the underworld and helped them with rain dances when the Hopi began to plant crops. They left the Hopi to go and live in the San Francisco Mountains but left behind their masks, rattles, and other paraphrenalia. Since then, the Hopi have impersonated the katcinas and worn their masks in order to bring rain and fertility to their fields.

The masked impersonations are held between the winter and

Hopi Snake Dance at Walpi, Arizona. From mural by George Peters, Milwaukee Public Museum.

summer solstices, beginning late in November. Dances are performed in *kivas*, underground chambers. At the Powamu ceremony in February, beans are grown in heated kivas, a seemingly miraculous event in the middle of winter, and the bean sprouts are distributed among the people. When the weather gets warmer, katcina dances are held outside in the plaza. These are impressive, well-rehearsed performances. At the end of their half-year's stay, there is a final ceremony to bid goodbye to the departing katcinas.

Adults, of course, know that the masked beings are Hopi men in disguise, but children think that the katcinas are real spirits, and they do not discover the true identity of the men in disguise until their initiation into the katcina cult. The katcinas sometimes give presents—rattles or bows and arrows to boys and katcina dolls to girls. If a boy has been unruly, his parents may decide to frighten him into better behavior by calling in a giant katcina impersonator. The masked man enters the house saying he wants to carry off the little boy and eat him since he has been behaving badly. The parents offer the katcina some meat as an alternative, but he rejects it and chases after the little boy. After having thoroughly frightened him, the katcina grudgingly accepts the substitute meat but warns that he will be back again if the boy continues to act badly.

The katcina initiation, held every fourth year, is for boys and girls between the ages of six and ten. On this occasion the boys are naked, but girls wear dresses. They are taken into a kiva, the underground ceremonial chamber, which becomes filled with masked katcinas. A boy, held by a ceremonial godfather, is whipped by one of the katcinas. The children are thus whipped in turn, the girls receiving gentler treatment than the boys. If a boy has been unruly, as Don Talayesva, the author of *Sun Chief* was, he may get a severe flogging; indeed, Don received permanent scars from his whipping.

Four days later, in another ceremony in the kiva, the boys and girls see the katcinas without their masks and discover that they are their older brothers, fathers, uncles, and neighbors. The children are then warned never to tell this secret to uninitiated children lest they be flogged more severely than before — perhaps even to death. This experience has been described by some Hopi informants as extremely disillusioning. Nevertheless, it seems to have the intended effect, for Don Talayesva writes in his autobiography, "I thought of the flogging and the initiation as an important turning point in my life, and I felt ready at last to listen to my elders and to live right" (Simmons 1942:87).

The katcina cult is a very complex institution and serves many functions. Children are taught to be obedient by live, masked bogeymen, perhaps more effectively than by purely imaginary ones. The carrot is offered as well as the stick; the katcinas bring presents and reward good children, like benevolent Santa Clauses. The whipping at initiation is a powerful incentive to obedience and cooperation with the village elders in community enterprises. The katcina dances unite the community and provide much color and entertainment. Of course, they probably have some negative, dysfunctional consequences as well.

One might think that the disillusionment of the initiation and the new knowledge that the masked gods are only men would lead to an agnostic, skeptical attitude among the young adults, but this does not seem to happen. They continue to believe in the katcinas. After his second initiation, into the Wowochim society, Don Talayesva wrote that he had learned a great lesson, that the ceremonies handed down among the Hopi meant life and security, and that ". . . the Hopi gods had brought success to us in the desert ever since the world began" (Simmons 1942:178).

Priesthood   Priests are religious specialists who are found in relatively advanced agricultural societies, including the Bronze Age civilizations of the Old World, and the Inca, Aztec, and Maya Indians of the New.

Priesthood depends upon the existence of an organized cult worshiping a god or pantheon of gods and having definite doctrines and rituals. The job of the priest is to learn the rituals properly; as a novice he undergoes training in this and other matters until he is declared by his superiors to be a qualified priest. The priest differs from the shaman in various ways. He does not have to see spirits or be possessed by them or have any particular dreams or visions. He succeeds to an office, while the shaman is more of a self-made man, or a man who has acquired spirit helpers. The priest does not depend upon spirit helpers. His authority comes from the religious order of which he is a part; he is an organization man. He is also more apt to be a full-time specialist than the shaman.

In societies where priests and shamans coexist, there may be rivalry between them, with the shaman as a freewheeling individualist trying to bypass the authority of the cult organization, while the latter tries to monopolize religious activities under its own control.

The foregoing generalizations about shamans and priests do not always hold. Although the Ojibwa were hunting-gathering people, they had a kind of priest, the Mide priest, or priest of the Medicine Dance. He was often a shaman as well, but he did not need to be, and he was not required to have had a fasting dream or vision. A man who became a Mide priest learned ritual and Mide lore as an assistant and understudy to a Mide priest.

Wallace, whose typology of religious cults we have been following, distinguishes between two kinds of ecclesiastical institutions in which priests officiate: *Olympian,* which recognizes a pantheon of gods; and *monotheistic,* in which there is worship of one supreme being. As an example of Olympian religion, he cites precolonial Dahomey, a west coast African kingdom based on advanced horticulture. In the Dahomean Great Gods cult, each deity was responsible for a particular aspect of nature; each had its own temple, priests, ritual, and mythology. Similar Olympian cults existed in the American Indian civilizations of the Inca, Maya, and Aztecs, and in such East Asian societies as Burma, Indonesia, Korea, and Japan.

As examples of monotheistic, ecclesiastical cults, Wallace lists Hindu-Buddhist, Judeo-Christian, Islamic, and Chinese monotheism. But the characterization of Hinduism as monotheistic is questionable; insofar as traditional village practices are concerned it is better characterized as Olympian. Monotheism seems to be associated with political complexity. Guy E. Swanson (1969), at any rate, found this association in a cross-cultural study of 50 societies, as well as an association between monotheism and food production rather than food collection.

**Bellah's
evolutionary
scheme**

An evolutionary sequence of forms of religion, different from Wallace's, has been proposed by Robert N. Bellah (1964). This has five stages: Primitive religion, Archaic religion, Historic religion, Early modern religion, and Modern religion.

The first stage, *Primitive religion,* is based on data about the Australian aborigines, since Australia was the only major culture area that was largely unaffected by the cultural developments of the Neolithic period. According to Bellah, this kind of religion has two main features: (1) the high degree to which the mythical world is related to features of the actual world, and (2) the fluidity of organization. Rather than worshiping supernaturals, people identify with them and participate with them. Ritual involves acting out rather than praying or sacrificing, and there is little distance between humans and the supernatural beings. There are no priests as mediators, and there is no religious organization.

In the second stage, *Archaic religion,* there is a more definite distinction between humans and gods and more distance between them. Worship and sacrifice are now offered, and there are many different cults. Much of what is usually called primitive religion falls under this heading.

Australian
aborigines in
religious ritual.

The third category, *Historic religion,* is relatively recent and found in more or less literate societies. Historic religions stress the theme of world rejection; they are dualistic and transcendental and have a pessimistic view of the human condition but a potentially better (or worse) conception of the afterlife. Salvation is now regarded as the main purpose of life, and a religious elite, a priesthood, is committed to helping people attain it.

The main example Bellah offers for the fourth category, *Early modern religion,* is the Protestant Reformation. At this stage, salvation no longer needs to be mediated but is potentially open to anyone. There is a stress on faith rather than on ritual behavior, and there is more individualism.

Finally, in *Modern religion,* the tendencies set in motion during the preceding stage are carried further. There is a collapse of orthodoxy, and there is still more individualism. Indeed, freedom increases at each of these five stages.

It would be difficult to synthesize Wallace's and Bellah's schemes, since they emphasize different things. Because the religious system of the Australian aborigines is both shamanic and communal, it appears relatively late in Wallace's scheme, but it represents the earliest stage of religion in Bellah's outline, earlier than the development of shamanism, which presumably developed as part of the Archaic religion.

Sigmund Freud, the founder of psychoanalysis, suggested that concepts about gods may be modeled after a child's relationships with its parents. We are relatively defenseless creatures who need reassurance against anxiety. Freud has written (1957:39–40): **Religion and projection**

> Now when the child grows up and finds that he is destined to remain a child for ever, and that he can never do without protection against unknown and mighty powers, he invests these with the traits of the father-figure; he creates for himself the gods, of whom he is afraid, whom he seeks to propitiate, and to whom he nevertheless entrusts the task of protecting him.

Abram Kardiner, a later psychoanalyst, carried this notion further. He believed that in societies with good parental care, idealized deities will appear in the pantheon, modeled after the benevolent parents. But in societies where the parental care is poor and where children are neglected, it will be difficult for the members of the society to idealize their gods. A case in point is Alor, an Indonesian society studied by Cora DuBois, where children suffer much maternal neglect and where little is expected of the deities, whose effigies are carelessly made and soon discarded. In the Western world, on the other hand, we have long traditions of good parental care and also belief in an idealized, loving God the Father, from whom all blessings flow (Kardiner 1945).

In some societies there are beliefs in gods who are hostile and threaten human beings. This is hard to account for in terms of the familiar notion that religion is a solace, a source of reassurance. While it may supply reassurance, religion also often adds to human fears and anxieties. Christianity gives people belief in a loving God and the hope of Heaven but also a Devil, Hell, and the prospect of eternal damnation. Thus, religions sometimes seem to take away with one hand what they give with the other.

The religious pantheons of some societies contain more frightening gods and spirits than benevolent ones. Jules Henry (1944:95) writes of the Kaingang of the jungles of Brazil that ". . . the emphasis in the supernaturalism is not on the beneficence of the supernaturals but on their vindictiveness if thwarted and on the danger inherent in any contact with them." Similarly for the Aymara of Peru: ". . . the great majority of supernatural beings are at best ambivalent toward mortals, if, indeed they are not actively malevolent" (Tschopik 1951:190). In the list of deities believed in by the Ifugao of the Philippines, R. F. Barton gives the names of 31 gods who send dysentery, 21 "boil and abscess producers," 20 "liver-attacking deities," 4 "headache deities," 14 that cause wounds, 5 that send arthritis, 50 "harpies," and 10 "spitters" (Barton 1946:62–74).

An attempt has been made to relate such fears to patterns of socialization in a cross-cultural survey undertaken by William W. Lambert, Leigh Minturn Triandis, and Margery Wolf. The authors rated 62 societies described in ethnographic accounts in terms of (1) general benevolence or aggressiveness attributed to supernaturals, and (2) children's experience of pain or relative lack of pain from their nurturing agents. Their statistical analysis showed that in societies where infants were treated punitively, there tended to be beliefs in aggressive supernaturals. This would be in harmony with the Freud-Kardiner theory of projection. Lambert, Triandis, and Wolf (1959), however, have a somewhat different interpretation of their correlations. They reason that anxiety is produced in a child through its conflicting anticipations of pain and nurture. This conflict is reduced by conceiving of a god or gods as aggressive, which is in keeping with the anticipation of harm. Their findings must be considered as only preliminary. More investigations should be made into the contrasting belief systems in different societies about benevolent and malevolent supernaturals.

Reference was made in Chapter 12 to the cognitive aspects of hierarchy on the Indonesian island of Bali, where there is a *varna* system that evidently diffused from India. It was mentioned that a low-caste person should not be seated above a high-caste person. Notions of hierarchy dominate Balinese conceptions about the world in general and are expressed in many aspects of their religion. The main roads in Bali run from the mountain to the sea. The mountain symbolizes holiness, while the sea is regarded as a zone of danger and evil spirits. Height is associated with purity. Thus, one should sleep with one's head (the highest and most sacred part of the body) toward the mountains and one's feet toward the sea. Family shrines are located on the inland part of house compounds, toward the mountain, while kitchens and latrines are on the coastward side, toward the sea. Village cemeteries are located on the coastward side. In Bali there is disapproval if a child is seen crawling on the ground; hence, children are generally carried until they are able to walk (Belo 1935).

Cognitive patterns in Balinese religion

A concern with spatial symbolism is evidently widespread in Indonesia and not limited to Bali. Clark E. Cunningham (1964) has documented the importance of spatial symbolism in house construction among the Atoni of Timor in Indonesia. Here, there is a consistent association between male activities and the right-hand side, female activities and the left-hand side. The upper direction is held to be male and spiritual, while the lower direction is female and secular. These ideas enter into details of house construction to a remarkable extent.

Religious movements of great dynamism have often swept quickly over large populations, sometimes crossing national and linguistic borders. Very often they are started by visionary prophets. They may be a response to contact with peoples having a more advanced culture, and the religion may then represent a kind of nationalistic protest, as in the Shawano cult of the Woodland Indians in 1808, the Ghost Dance of the Plains in the 1870s and again in 1890, and the Cargo cults of Melanesia from 1913 to recent years. Let us consider these three movements briefly.

Religious movements

The prophet of the Shawano cult was the brother of the Indian leader Tecumseh, and his religion was related to the latter's struggle against the whites. The prophet called for a return to Indian ways and a boycott of the trader's goods—beef and pork, flint and steel, guns and traps. The Indians were urged to give up sorcery, to throw away their medicine bags, and to stop drinking liquor. We see here something reminiscent of India's anti-British, noncooperation movement under Gandhi's leadership, an effort to break away from dependence on the enemy through boycott and to return to some earlier, simpler conditions of life during the struggle. Although it did not succeed, since the whites were already so well entrenched, the Shawano cult was a practical, realistic movement, in contrast to the Ghost Dance, which relied more heavily on magic.

The Ghost Dance found many converts among the Paiute and some tribes in California and Oregon in the early 1870s, since it promised that adherents to the cult would be reunited with their dead parents and other relatives and that the whites would disappear and the Indians become rich. There was some disillusionment when these prophecies did not come true, but in 1889 and 1890, there was a revival of the Ghost Dance, which this time affected the Indians of the Great Plains. The culture of these Indians was being destroyed by the disappearance of the buffalo herds on which they had depended. Added to the earlier prophecies of the white man's extinction and the return of the Indian dead, there was also included the return of the buffalo. The religion involved prolonged dancing, until some members fell into trance states. Members wore supposedly bullet-proof "ghost shirts," some of which (sometimes with bullet holes in them) are now on display in our museums. The ghost shirt exemplifies the magical, unrealistic nature of this cult, which quickly died out, although there is still an Indian group in Canada that adheres to a Ghost Dance cult.

Many Cargo cults, as they have been called, have flourished in Melanesia at different times and places. The most common element is a prediction that ships or airplanes will soon appear, bringing all kinds of valued goods to the natives, including refrigerators and other things possessed by the whites. Sometimes the cultists are enjoined to throw away their old belongings, otherwise the new goods will not come. These movements sometimes have antiwhite predictions, like those of the Ghost Dance.

The Melanesians have seen Europeans enjoying the use of all kinds of equipment that have come by ship; they have no idea of how or where they are made. It is apparently a kind of magic, which some Melanesians have tried to divert to themselves by engaging in cult activities that imitate magical European behavior, such as marching, drilling, and performing rituals with flagpoles. In the Vailala movement of Papua from 1919 to 1929, it was thought that flagpoles were the media through which messages came from the dead. These heavily magical cults usually have a short life, since the promised cargoes do not materialize; their ship does not come in.

These three examples of religious movements show that religion does not necessarily remain stable and may be affected by economic crises, contacts with other cultures, a sense of relative deprivation and resentment and of "nationalistic" feelings.

A very good source is William A. Lessa and Evon Z. Vogt, eds., *Reader in Comparative Religion: An Anthropological Approach,* 3d ed. (New York: Harper & Row, 1972). It contains well-chosen selections from the writings of Tylor, Frazer, Durkheim, Malinowski, Radcliffe-Brown, Rasmussen, Linton, Kluckhohn, Opler, and many others.

Suggestions for further reading

Three general works can be recommended: Edward Norbeck, *Religion in Primitive Society* (New York: Harper & Bros., 1961); Anthony F. C. Wallace, *Religion: An Anthropological View* (New York: Random House, 1966); Annemarie de Waal Malefijt, *Religion and Culture: An Introduction to Anthropology of Religion* (New York: Macmillan Co., 1968).

An outstanding work is Victor W. Turner, *The Ritual Process* (Chicago: Aldine Publishing Co., 1969).

The account of Hopi katcinas presented in this chapter draws upon Mischa Titiev, *Old Oraibi: A Study of the Hopi Indians of Third Mesa,* Papers of the Peabody Museum of Archaeology and Ethnology (Cambridge, Mass.: 1944); Laura Thompson and Alice Joseph, *The Hopi Way* (Chicago: University of Chicago Press, 1944). See also Frank Waters, *Book of the Hopi* (New York: Ballantine Books, 1963).

part eight

Recreation, folklore, and the arts

17

The enjoyment of life

Life brings much disappointment, frustration, and tragedy. This may seem like an odd way to start a chapter entitled "The Enjoyment of Life," but the point is that there are usually sufficient incentives to go on living, in spite of sickness, deformity, debts, taxes, loneliness, boring work, unhappy marriage, feuds with neighbors, military service, and all the other miseries that may assail us. Religion and other compensations give some people the strength to carry on, but many others break down, fall ill, go mad, or commit suicide. Even so, most people seem to find life worth living. "Life can be beautiful," as the saying goes. In this chapter, we shall briefly examine some of the pleasures of life that men and women have enjoyed in different times, places, and cultures. Since all-inclusiveness is impossible, only a few universal aspects of behavior, found in all cultures, will be considered. This means that some currently widespread but not universal patterns of enjoyment are omitted, such as reading, tourism, watching television, tobacco smoking, and the drinking of intoxicating beverages. There is some pathos in drawing up a brief catalog of universally recognized pleasures of life, for we must admit that many persons have killed themselves in spite of having known these satisfactions. For some, they were not enough.

Food

Eating is something we have to do to stay alive. Most people find it enjoyable, too, although there are children with feeding problems and some persons who do not seem to get much pleasure from it. Cultures vary, as individuals do. The French and Chinese are noted for their cuisine, the variety of their dishes, and their interest in food,

251

whereas English cooking has a low reputation. Oscar Lewis (1951: 187–91) writes that the basic diet of the people of Tepoztlán, Mexico, is corn, beans, and chile. Corn provides from 10 to 70 percent of the family diet. For most people, breakfast consists of black coffee and tortillas; the midday dinner generally features tortillas and chile, and sometimes, on good days, there is meat and vegetables and rice or noodles cooked in broth. For supper there are tortillas or bread, with perhaps some cheese. This sounds like a monotonous diet to a middle-class American. But Lin Yutang (1937:253–54), the Chinese writer, in turn, finds American cuisine "dull and insipid and extremely limited in variety," especially in its treatment of vegetables and soups.

Lin Yutang, who holds eating to be "one of the very few solid joys of human life," remarks that it is fortunate that it is less hedged about with taboos than sex, and that "generally speaking, no question of morality arises in connection with food" (Yutang 1937:48). Here, he seems to forget that food taboos of one kind or another are universal. There are millions of Hindus and Jains in India who, for religious reasons, will not eat meat. The idea of eating beef is particularly abhorrent to them, as is the eating of pork to Muslims and Jews. The Apache Indians will not eat fish, although edible trout are available in their streams.

Lin Yutang lists with evident gusto some dishes he particularly enjoys, including carp's head, pig's tripe, ox's tripe, and large snails, which pious Hindus, and perhaps many Americans, would not dream of eating.

Certain foods are unavailable in some societies for geographical, climatic reasons. The Eskimos are at the opposite pole (no pun intended) from vegetarian Hindus in that they live mostly on meat and fish. We are taught that a balanced diet should include such things as fruit, green, leafy vegetables, and cereals, but the Eskimos have none of these. They evidently get the vitamins they need by eating the whole animal, including entrails. Edward Weyer (1932: 72) gives a rather grim list of some items eaten by Eskimos: "raw intestines of bird and fish, swallowed like oysters; live fish, gulped down whole, head first; slime scraped from a walrus hide together with some of the human urine used in the tanning process; fatty soup thickened with the blood of seal or caribou. . . ." Although their diet is limited, the Eskimos seem to be hearty eaters, judging from travelers' descriptions and such films as *Nanook of the North*. Food tastes good to a hungry person, even if it is not served up in special style. In that case, maybe, the pleasures of eating balance out, with hungry nomads ultimately enjoying food as much as French gourmets do.

VICTOR BARNOUW

Hindu woman
cooking.

On the other hand, the pleasure of eating is surely enhanced or diminished by the nature of the social setting in which it takes place and by cultural traditions about food. In Europe, the United States, China, Japan, and many other regions, there is a tradition of the family meal, where all the family members eat together. When men are away all day at work and the children have lunch at school, this is not always feasible, but the tradition is still maintained, when possible. This custom strengthens the sense of family unity and may be (although it often is not) an occasion for pleasant conversation and relaxed enjoyment. While the tradition of the family meal may seem to be a natural, almost inevitable, invention, it is not found in all societies. Among the Rājpūts of Khalapur in northern India the men eat separately from the women and children. Minturn and Hitchcock write (1963:244):

Each man eats either at his own hearth or men's quarters. Each woman takes her food into her own room or into a corner of the courtyard where she can turn her back toward the other women. Children are fed when they demand food and may eat together or separately. . . .

There is no set dining hour. The custom of turning one's back to others while eating, sometimes associated with feelings of embarrassment or uneasiness about food, is found in some other cultures, including those of Bali and the Trobriand Islands.

Japanese tea
ceremony.

The Sirionó of eastern Bolivia do much of their eating individually, late at night. This is partly because they spend most of the day hunting and gathering, but also because they do not want to be forced to share food with others who come around begging for scraps. So they have furtive late-night snacks while others are asleep (Holmberg 1950:36).

One cannot be sure that individualistic eating patterns such as those of the Rājpūts of Khalapur and the Sirionó diminish the enjoyment of food; perhaps, instead, they enhance it. But they would seem, at least, to shorten the meal and to lessen opportunity for relaxed sociability in connection with it. Like the hurried chompers of frankfurters at a quick-lunch counter, they may be missing something.

The Chinese are notable not only for the variety of their food and their interest in eating but also for the development of aesthetic attitudes about it. Lin Yutang devotes many pages to the pleasures of drinking tea, which has been popular in China since at least the 4th century A.D. and perhaps earlier. The Japanese have developed an elaborate ceremony around tea drinking. In both China and Japan, the sipping of tea is associated with quietness, reflection, and aesthetic contemplation. Since the Sung Dynasty, Chinese tea lovers have considered a cup of *pale* tea to be best, ". . . and the delicate flavor of pale tea can easily pass unperceived by one occupied by busy thoughts, or when the neighborhood is noisy . . ." (Yutang 1937:226). Where such aesthetic and gastronomic traditions are present, the satisfactions of food and drink are probably much increased. It would seem that if food is one of the main pleasures of life, some societies allow greater scope for such enjoyment than others.

Desmond Morris has stated that man is "the sexiest primate alive"; **Sex** in this case, "man" embraces woman, as the proverbial professor of anthropology told his class. "Sexiest" does not refer to physical appeal; Morris means that humans have a stronger sexual drive than other primates. He notes that copulation in apes and monkeys is often very brief, lasting only a few seconds in baboons. It seems unlikely that the females are capable of orgasm, as women are, although orgasmic reactions have been reported for some female chimpanzees. If field reports are representative, it would seem that our closest relatives, the apes, do not engage in much sexual activity, although it may be that some of this behavior occurs at night or at other times when fieldworkers are not around. At any rate, Morris (1969:53) writes: ". . . we can see that there is much more intense sexual activity in our own species than in any other primates, including our closest relations. For them, the lengthy courtship phase is missing. Hardly any of the monkeys and apes develop a prolonged pair-bond relationship." If the human sexual drive is so strong, its satisfaction must be correspondingly intense, although the intensity varies from one individual to another.

Human variability

One of the surprising discoveries of the first Kinsey report was the great variability in the number of orgasms experienced by males. One man was reported to have had over 30 orgasms a week for over 30 years, while another said that he had had only one ejaculation in 30 years. The mean frequency for white American males under 30 years of age is reported to be about 3.3 per week (Kinsey, Pomeroy, and Martin 1948:195). Great variability is also reported for women in the second Kinsey report: ". . . 22 percent of the married females between the ages of sixteen and twenty, and 12 percent of the married females between the ages of twenty-one and twenty-five, had never experienced any orgasm from any source . . ." (Kinsey, Pomeroy, Martin, and Gebhard 1953:532). On the other hand, about 14 percent of the females in the married sample regularly had multiple orgasms during coitus (Ibid:375). It is evident that the satisfactions derived from sex vary enormously among individuals.

The Kinsey report on American males also showed that sexual behavior is influenced by economic class membership and by the extent of education. Conditions may have changed since 1948, but the following generalizations were made at that time: Between the ages of 16 and 20 there was nearly twice as much masturbation among college students as there was among the young men who did not go beyond grade school. There was also much more heterosexual petting to the point of orgasm among college students than among those who had not gone beyond grade school, while premarital intercourse was more frequent in the grade-school and high-school groups than among college-level students. There was more foreplay, kissing, and manipulation of the woman's breasts in the lovemaking of upper-level males than in that of lower-level males (Kinsey, Pomeroy, and Martin 1948:326–71).

There are even greater differences in lovemaking among the various cultures of the world. If love is a universal language, it has many dialects. Kissing, so important in American lovemaking, is not a trait of nonhuman primates and is not found in all human groups. Clellan Ford and Frank Beach list the following societies where kissing is said to be unknown: Bali, Chamorro, Lepcha, Manus, Sirionó, and Thonga (Ford and Beach 1951:58). The position assumed in intercourse is often culturally determined. Kinsey, Pomeroy, and Martin estimated that 70 percent of American couples have never experimented with any other position than the most common one, in which the woman lies on her back and the man lies above her. Among the Trobriand Islanders, on the other hand, the man is usually in a squatting position, while among the Murngin the woman lies on her side with her back to the man.

Attitudes about sex also differ greatly in different societies, ranging from great permissiveness and acceptance to feelings of guilt and disapproval. As in the idea of Original Sin, such attitudes may be associated with religion. Many Hindus, for example, believe that semen is stored in the head and that to accumulate the supply leads to physical and spiritual power; so there is reluctance to lose semen.

The setting and circumstances in which sexual behavior occurs also affect the nature and degree of sexual satisfaction. In many villages in northern India the men sleep in a separate men's quarters. If a man wants to have intercourse with his wife, he gets up during the night and goes to the women's quarters, where many women and children may be sleeping. These arrangements do not allow for much privacy. Privacy is lacking in many societies where a family shares a single-room dwelling, such as a wigwam, tepee, igloo, mud hut, or log cabin. Under such circumstances it is difficult to keep children from observing adult intercourse. It may be partly for this reason that in many such societies no effort is made to prolong the sex act or to delay orgasm. The Berens River Ojibwa, for example, make no effort of this sort. They engage in little or no fore-play or petting, little kissing, and no manipulation of breasts. Oral-genital contacts are taboo. The couples seldom undress to the point of nudity. The man's aim is to achieve orgasm as quickly as possible, and the woman's role is purely passive. A. Irving Hallowell (1949), who provides this information, points to the similarity of these patterns to those of lower-class Americans, as described in the Kinsey report.

Attitudes toward children's sexual behavior

Ford and Beach have assembled data about societies that have different degrees of restrictiveness or permissiveness toward sexual behavior in young children. Some societies, which Ford and Beach label *restrictive,* try to deny young children any form of sexual expression. These societies include, among others, the Apinaye, Ashanti, Chagga, Chiricahua, Dahomeans, Haitians, Kwoma, Manus, Murngin, Penobscot, and Trukese. Some of these peoples, such as the Trukese, later allow considerable sexual freedom to adolescents. Despite severe punishment of children for masturbation in these societies, it seems to take place anyway. In most of the restrictive societies, efforts are made to keep young children from learning anything about sex. In most of the African societies in the Ford and Beach sample, boys are strictly forbidden to have intercourse before going through the male puberty ceremony, a taboo found in some other culture areas as well, for example among the Jivaro of Ecuador.

In many societies there is a very tolerant, permissive attitude toward sexual expression in childhood. Grouped under the *permissive* rubric there are, among others, the Alorese, Copper Eskimos, Hopi, Ifugao, Kwakiutl, Lepcha, Maori, Marquesans, Masai, Samoans, Sirionó, Tikopia, Trobrianders, and Zulu. In some of these societies, such as the Sirionó, parents may masturbate their own children. The open self-masturbation of children is accepted and taken for granted, and in some of these societies children are allowed to watch the copulation of adults. These are two different ways of being consistent, one in restrictive and the other in permissive terms. In between these two polar types, there are many less consistent societies, which are restrictive in some ways, permissive in others (Ford and Beach 1951:187–99). Until recently our own society favored a largely restrictive policy, but there is now a tendency among many middle-class parents to be relatively permissive in regard to children's sexual behavior.

If we compare the two polar groups of societies singled out by Ford and Beach, can one group be said to be happier than the other?

Do the permissive societies, let us say, produce better-adjusted adults than the restrictive ones, or vice versa? These questions would be hard to answer, since we have no easily applicable yardstick by which to measure happiness or adjustment. Happiness is the product of many factors, not just sex. As Ford and Beach point out, there are American women who consider their marriages to be happy, although they do not enjoy having sexual relations with their husbands. There are also persons who function well sexually but who are neurotic and unhappy in other ways. The Alorese are on the permissive list, but they seem to be quite unhappy people, judging from the ethnographic description by Cora DuBois, the life history material she collected, and the analyses of their Rorschach tests and children's drawings. Much of their unhappiness, apparently, stems from the maternal neglect experienced in childhood. The masturbation of a child by caretakers is done to pacify it, as a substitute for the breast. Among adults, relations between the sexes are poor. Despite the burdensome monetary negotiations attendant upon divorce, the Alorese studied by DuBois averaged about two divorces apiece (DuBois 1960:28–115).

The Lepchas of Sikkim, also in the permissive group, seem to be happier people, judging from Geoffrey Gorer's description of them in *Himalayan Village* (1938), but relations between the sexes are relatively shallow or brittle. Gorer writes that the Lepchas whom he studied ". . . had rates of outlet in their early adult life which would make Dr. Kinsey's high scorers look like pikers. For the Lepchas, sex was a satisfaction no more important than food; they did not believe in love, made no allowance for it, and the exclusive possession of a spouse was legally impossible" (Gorer 1948:284). On the other hand, the Trobriand Islanders, also found in the permissive group, were described by Malinowski to have stable, monogamous marriages that followed after a period of sexual freedom, living with different partners in adolescence. Husband and wife lived "for the most part, in excellent harmony and with mutual appreciation" (Malinowski; 1929:109). Malinowski described the Trobrianders as being well-adjusted people, lacking in neuroses or perversions. They had no nervous tics, obsessive compulsive behavior, or homosexuality, although some of Malinowski's data suggest that there were some sadistic tendencies among the Trobrianders (Barnouw 1973:113–28).

There is evidently much variation with regard to emotional well-being and stability of marriage in the permissive group, judging from this brief examination of three societies. This is also true of the restrictive group. Despite the sexual restriction, Manus children, in 1928, gave evidence of having a happy, carefree childhood. There

Manus children, Admiralty Islands, New Guinea. Manus children were described by Margaret Mead as having a happy, carefree childhood, while adult life was seen as a grim routine.

was so little supervision by adults that the sexual taboos were probably easily broken. But adult life was described by Margaret Mead as being grim. Marriages were arranged by parents, and husband-wife relationships were difficult. Men were involved in a rat race of hard work and trading, paying off debts, and striving for financial success (Mead 1930). The Manus do not sound happy, but they seem to have been more so than the Alorese, although we do not have Manus Rorschachs or life histories for comparison.

We do, however, have life histories, Rorschachs, Thematic Apperception Tests, and good ethnographic description for the Trukese. Although they were placed by Ford and Beach in the restrictive group, they seem to have an essentially permissive attitude toward sex. When a child is punished for sexual experimentation, it is not with the idea that sex is bad, but rather that such behavior is premature; it will be all right later on, when the child reaches puberty. From puberty on, there is much preoccupation with sexual liaisons, both premarital and extramarital. The fact that a permissive period follows after a restrictive one may account for some of the anxiety concerning sex that Seymour B. Sarason saw reflected in Trukese projective personality test responses. Sarason described the Trukese as being unspontaneous people whose interpersonal relations are superficial and who lack strong ties of love or friendship. The men have a sense of inadequacy, which they try to overcome in their sexual affairs, but the women are subtly dominating, which makes the man's victory over them only temporary (Gladwin and Sarason 1953:232–34; see also Goodenough 1949).

A society faces some difficulty if it follows a consistently restrictive policy with young children and later permits freer sexual behavior. The individual must then unlearn what he has previously learned. Ruth Benedict drew attention to this problem in her article. "Continuities and Discontinuities in Cultural Conditioning" (1938b). If, in its formative years, a child is given the impression that sex is wicked, it may be difficult for him to unlearn that lesson as an adult.

As in the case with food, we may conclude that the enjoyment of sexual experience is much affected by attitudes and values, and that some societies allow much greater possibilities for such enjoyment than others.

Play, sports, and games

A general primate trait, play is, of course, a very important activity among human beings, not limited to childhood. The most frequent social activity among young apes and monkeys is play fighting, which finds especially elaborate expression among chimpanzees. Young monkeys may spend four or five hours a day playing in groups. Play is inhibited by some factors and facilitated by others. Exposure to unfamiliar objects or conditions may depress play, while moderate novelty encourages it. The amount of play activity varies in different primate species; the chimpanzee seems to be one of the most playful primates and the gorilla one of the least (DeVore 1965:528–30, 619). It seems likely that humans evolved from a more playful and imaginative chimpanzee-like ancestor, rather than from a forerunner like the dull, businesslike gorilla.

"Athletic sports" and "games" both appear in Murdock's list of universal aspects of culture, found in all cultures about which there is adequate information (Murdock 1945:124).[1] Simple athletic sports, such as chasing and wrestling, seem to be carry-overs from the social play of young primates; it is easy to understand their universality. Games may be more complex phenomena and more remote from bodily activities, as are checkers or chess. Both sports and games involve traditional rules, unlike the spontaneous play of children who are involved in a world of make-believe.

---

[1] According to Roberts and Sutton-Smith (1962-169), there are some societies, such as the Murngin of Australia, that do not have games. There may be gaps in the ethnographic reporting on such societies, although the authors report "complete information" for the Murngin.

Johan Huizinga, who has discussed the importance of play in the development of human culture, describes some of the characteristics of play as follows (1955:13):

..., we might call it a free activity standing quite consciously outside "ordinary" life as being "not serious," but at the same time absorbing the player intensely and utterly. It is an activity connected with no material interest, and no profit can be gained by it.

Huizinga does not distinguish between play, sports, and games. He regards play (or a game) as having a definite beginning and end and as taking place within a circumscribed area. For Huizinga, the play-area boundary forms a magic circle within which a different order of reality exists and where special rules apply. The squares for marbles or hopscotch, the tennis court, and the chessboard all have their separate kinds of order. He also believes that people who have played a game together feel they have shared something important that continues to bind them to one another, for they have momentarily been in, and can again return to, a magic world apart from the realm of everyday life.

These features ally play to ritual, which also requires a marked-out area that is separate and different, with rules of its own. Huizinga suggests that festivals, holidays, mysteries, and sacrifices may all be seen as forms of play. The men of primitive tribes who dress up in masks are, in a way, "only pretending"; there is some deliberate "make-believe" in their performance.

These speculations suggest that elements of play may enter into spheres where we might not expect to find them. Huizinga notes that some uses of the word *play* (and its parallels in other languages) show that play is involved in still other activities, as in *play*ing music, the stage *play*, and sexual fore*play*.

Games

Societies differ not only in the kinds of games that are played but also in the degree of involvement in games. This is also true of individuals within a society. Different kinds of games are often played by people of different age and sex. It would be interesting to know why particular individuals or groups become attracted to particular games and participate actively in them, while others show little interest. It cannot be said that we have the answers to these questions, but a beginning has been made in two studies (Roberts, Arth, and Bush 1959; Roberts and Sutton-Smith 1962).

Roberts et al. define games as recreational activities characterized by organized play, competition between two or more sides with agreed-upon rules and criteria for determining the winner. In these respects games are distinguished from unorganized "amusements," such as swimming or making string figures. The authors subdivide games into three main types: (1) physical skill (races, boxing, hockey); (2) strategy (chess, checkers); and (3) chance (dice, roulette). Games of physical skill may be subdivided into those in which physical skill is the only relevant attribute, as in weight lifting, and those in which strategy is also involved, such as fencing or football. Other combinations of types are also possible, but the above are the classifications of games used by the authors in their cross-cultural surveys of games.

In the first study, 43 societies were rated on the basis of the ethnographic literature as having either low political integration or high political integration and as having games of strategy or not having them. In the statistical analysis it was found that games of strategy tend to be associated with high political integration; they are more apt to be found in societies having complex social organization:

... among the adequately-covered tribes, the four hunting and gathering groups lacked games of strategy, only one out of five fishing groups had such a game, and only one out of three pastoral groups. On the other hand, no truly complex society appears to have lacked them (Roberts, Arth, and Bush 1959–601).

We see here an implication of cultural evolution. Games of physical skill are found in societies at all levels of social organization, but games of strategy appear mainly where political integration is more advanced. There may be significance in the fact that symbolism of royalty and relative rank is evident in the king, queen, bishop, knight, and pawn of the strategic game of chess and in the king, queen, and jack of the card deck.

Team sports

Team sports are so familiar to us in the United States that we might assume they are universal, but such is not the case. The Olympic games of the ancient Greeks seem to have emphasized individual athletic competition rather than teams. In Europe, before the 16th century, there were semiritualistic team games symbolizing the conflict between darkness and light, winter and spring, but these do not seem to have involved much cooperative team play.

In the pre-Columbian New World, team games were widespread, and it seems likely that the idea of team sports was carried to Europe after the discovery of America. Shinny and hockey were played over

Maya ball court,
Zaculeu,
Guatemala.

a wide area in eastern North America; hockey was also played in
central Mexico and in the Gran Chaco area of South America. La-
crosse also had a wide distribution in central and eastern North
America. But the most interesting of American Indian team sports
was the rubber ball game, which had a distribution from Arizona
in the North, through Mesoamerica and the Circum-Caribbean area
to as far south as San Salvador. This game involved something
unknown in Europe before the discovery of America: the bouncing
rubber ball. The game was played in a ball court flanked by sloping
walls. The two opposing teams varied in composition from two or
three members to 10 or 11. The men were not allowed to touch the
ball with hands or feet but could bounce the ball from elbows, knees,
or hips, all of which were padded. Points were made when the ball
touched the opponents' end zone, but the climax of a game, out-
scoring all other points, came if a player sent the ball through a
vertical stone ring affixed in the center of either side wall. That
brought the game to an end and entitled the scorer to collect jewels
and clothing from the audience. There was betting for high stakes
among the spectators. This was a very violent game in which the
participants often died; moreover, the captain of a losing team was

sometimes sacrificed to the gods. On the other hand, a winning captain was greatly honored. Religion and sport were closely intermingled in the rubber ball game.

In 1528, Hernando Cortés brought some Aztec ballplayers to the court of Charles V in Spain, where they staged several demonstration games. The use of rubber balls considerably influenced European sports, and the team principle may also have been copied, leading to the present forms of some of the sports we know today, such as volleyball, soccer, and football. In basketball we also have the idea of sending a ball through a ring or hoop, although the basketball hoop is horizontal and much wider than the narrow, vertical ball court ring (Borhegyi and Borhegyi 1963; T. Stern 1948).

The diffusion of team sports throughout the world in recent years shows how readily they appeal to people of different cultures. Perhaps, on a small scale, they represent a moral equivalent of war, a relatively safe arena for the expression of competition and aggression.

Gambling

Gambling is a widespread activity among the societies of the world, but it is not universal. A. L. Kroeber lists among nongambling peoples the Australian aborigines, the Papuo-Melanesians, most of the Polynesians and Micronesians, and many Indonesians. In the pre-Columbian Americas, most of the northern continent gambled, while most of the southern did not. Gambling takes place in most of Asia, except for some marginal fringes. Nongamblers are found in East Africa, while many tribes in West Africa and the Congo Basin gamble. Kroeber finds no consistent, worldwide correlation of gambling with subsistence economy, wealth system, or type of religion. Roberts, Arth, and Bush found some statistical support for a hypothesis that games of chance will occur in societies where supernatural beings are considered to be benevolent, nonaggressive, and coercive in human affairs. But not all games of chance are associated with gambling for stakes; they may be played just for the fun of it. Kroeber (1948:552–53) points out that the areas of both gambling and nongambling are rather large and compact, which suggests the operation of diffusion, although he considers this to have been the diffusion of attitudes rather than diffusion of specific games.

Joking

Joking appears on Murdock's list of universals. It is nice to know that people joke in all societies. In some societies there are structured joking relationships, so that a man is expected to joke with persons related to him in a particular way, as in the bawdy badinage that used to take place between cross cousins of opposite sex among the Ojibwa Indians.

There are many theories about the nature of humor and why some things are considered funny while others are not. The problem is made more difficult by the relativistic nature of humor. What is held to be funny at one time or place may not draw a smile in another. It is often impossible to translate a joke from one language to another, especially, of course, in the case of puns. Well known is the story about how Abraham Lincoln, at a tense moment during the Civil War, took time out to read aloud to the members of his cabinet a passage from the writings of Artemus Ward. The President evidently thought the passage was very funny, and it was probably so regarded by his listeners. Both Stephen Leacock and Max Eastman quote the passage in their books on humor; as they point out, it is hard to see how anyone could find the passage funny today.

One of the efforts made to explain the nature of humor is Eastman's analysis. He believes that one must be in a playful spirit to perceive something as funny and that anything seen as funny would have an unpleasant aspect if one were *not* in a playful state. A joke, then, contains potentially unpleasant experiences playfully enjoyed. Eastman asks what most jokes have been about through the ages in Western culture, and his answer is: "Mothers-in-law, unpaid bills, drunks, taxes, tramps, corpses, excretory functions, politicians, vermin, bad taste, bad breaks, sexual ineptitudes, pomp, egotism, stinginess and stupidity!" (Eastman 1936:25). It would be interesting to have a cross-cultural survey of humor in different societies to see if such topics form the subject matter of joking in other cultures. Oddly enough, anthropologists have not investigated this question.

Another view of humor, not at odds with Eastman's, would see it as a form of one-upmanship, a way of feeling superior to others. This is true of at least some humor. The ancient Greeks had "dumb peasant" jokes like this one quoted by Stephen Leacock (1935:221): "A peasant, having heard that parrots live for a hundred years, bought one to see if it was true." Another example is of a peasant who wanted to see if his horse could live without food. A while after he stopped feeding him, the horse died. "Alas," said the peasant, "just as he was learning to live without food, he died." We feel superior to the peasant; so we smile. Similar "Polish" jokes are told today in Milwaukee and other cities that have Polish minorities. (Poles tell them, too.)

Minority groups form the subject matter of much joking in our own society. We have jokes about the irrationality of Irishmen ("Lucky are the parents who have no children"), the stinginess of Scots, and the wiliness of Jews. Such jokes help to reinforce group stereotypes and perhaps make the narrator and hearers feel comfortably superior for a moment. It would be interesting to know whether similar jokes are current in other societies that have minority groups.

Other pleasures

There are, of course, many more pleasures in life than the few touched on in this chapter: dozing, sleeping, scratching, sitting in the sun, bathing, sipping cool drinks, looking at a view, having conversation with friends, and many others. There are also the satisfactions of work and achievement, the solution of a puzzle, the attainment of a goal. There is the pleasure of social acceptance within a group, initiation into a society, entrance into a club, or the experience of a religious rite. There are also the enjoyments of storytelling, folklore, and the arts, to which we turn in the next two chapters.

18

Oral literature

In all known societies, people have told stories to one another. There may be some peoples, like the nomadic Sirionó of eastern Bolivia, who are reported not to tell many stories, but all societies have at least some traditional tales. Such stories are often referred to as *folklore,* although this term is sometimes given a much wider scope to include such matters as costume and dance (Dundes 1965:3). Hence, the title "Oral Literature" has been chosen here. It is a somewhat paradoxical term, since we usually think of literature as being written. Perhaps "Oral Narrative" would have been a better label, but it has not been so widely used.

Oral literature has sometimes been divided into various categories, such as *myth, folktale,* and *legend.* Although the word *myth* has acquired the connotations of error and wishful thinking in modern speech, a myth may be defined as a sacred story that is usually accepted as true in the society where it is told; it may explain how the world and people and various human institutions came into being. A *folktale* is a more secular story, dealing with the adventures of a hero, trickster, or other character. *Legends* are set in the world of the present in localized places (although they may deal with creatures like ghosts and supernatural beings), while myths are set in the distant past, and folktales in no particular time or place (Bascom 1965). These distinctions are often blurred. Franz Boas long ago pointed out that it would be difficult to make clear-cut distinctions between folktales and myths in an area like the Northwest Coast of North America. A more useful distinction to make, in a particular culture, would be what categories of stories are distinguished by the members of the society themselves. In some

267

Bushman story
teller, Botswanaland.

societies, for example, there are categories of tales that may be told
in certain seasons of the year or on particular occasions.

Oral literature differs from written literature in various ways. The
writer does not directly confront an audience. He writes a work that
is, or should be, original; and, when it is published, it appears in a
fixed, usually unalterable form, unless and until it is reprinted with
minor corrections or issued in a revised edition. The narrator of a
story, on the other hand, faces an audience, even though it may consist of only one or two persons. He is usually not the inventor of the
story and is often telling a tale which his hearers have heard many
times and may know as well as he. Among the Central Eskimos, if a
narrator makes a mistake in what should be a perfectly memorized,
stylized account, the audience is quick to correct him. In this case,
exact repetition is valued, but in some societies there is more room
for improvisation, and, over a period of time, the story may change
markedly in character. An example is provided by the Italian story
of "The Cock and the Mouse," which Frank H. Cushing (1965) told

to a group of Zuñi Indians. A year later, Cushing revisited Zuñi and heard the story, which had now become transformed and adapted to the Zuñi scene and Zuñi traditions.

The narrator in a non-Western culture does not simply tell a story; he may also enact it, dramatize it, and even dance it. Moreover, members of the audience often participate by giving responses, promptings, or encouragement. The more isolated writer does not experience this kind of direct feedback, although he or she may receive comments in reviews and letters from readers.

Folklorists and anthropologists have filled many volumes of folktales. In most cases, these collections consist simply of the stories themselves, without observations on the setting in which the story is told, the composition of the audience, the occasion for the narration, or the nature of the audience response. It is now realized that such observations should be included in the presentation of a narrative. Boas took down texts in the native language and trained his students to do the same. We have a text in Kwakiutl, for example, set forth on one page with a concurrent English translation on the facing page. This provides for both linguistic analysis and analysis of the story itself. Ideally, this should give some insight into the ways in which the world appears to the native speaker. The use of tape recorders now facilitates the collection of such texts.

A classification of folktales has been made by a Finnish folklorist, Antti Aarne, with revisions by Stith Thompson, the latest appearing in 1961 with the title *The Types of the Folktale: A Classification and Bibliography*. But these deal with only Indo-European tales; 2,000 synopses are given, with a code number for each. Stith Thompson has also compiled a six-volume *Motif-Index of Folk Literature* (1955–58), which has worldwide coverage.

Folktales may be combed by ethnologists for historical clues — for evidence of past migrations and contact with other cultures. Tales and motifs may be mapped and their areas of diffusion traced. Some myths and folktales have an almost worldwide distribution. The story of a flood is one example; it is often associated with the motif of a diving animal that brings up some grains of soil from the bottom of the sea, from which the earth is made. Various explanations have been put forth to account for the wide distribution of flood myths. It used to be argued that once there must have been a great flood or several floods, the memory of which has been preserved in the myths. A psychoanalytic view would be that water has an unconscious symbolic meaning for all peoples and, hence, is apt to appear in dreams and become embodied in myths. Flood myths probably diffused from one or more centers, from one society to another.

Collection and interpretation

A widespread but not universal story is the Magic Flight. A hero who is pursued by some kind of ogre magically causes obstacles to form behind himself by throwing three objects in turn: a stone, which causes a mountain to rise; a comb, which creates a forest; and a liquid, which forms a lake or river. This story has probably spread by diffusion, being told in a continuous area from Europe, through northern Asia, to North America.

The legend of the hero

Otto Rank (1956), Lord Raglan (1937), and Joseph Campbell (1949) have all been struck by certain recurrent themes in the lives of legendary heroes, some of which are as follows. The hero is the son of a king and queen. Before his birth a prophecy is made about him, which leads to an attempt, often initiated by his father, to have him killed. Instead, the child is spirited away and reared by foster parents. When he reaches manhood, the hero goes to his future kingdom, where he wins a victory over the king or else over a giant, dragon, or wild beast. He then marries a princess and becomes king.

Lord Raglan made a list of 22 items, including most of the themes just mentioned, together with several others. He then found that 20 of the items applied to the story of Oedipus, 20 to that of Theseus, 17 to Romulus and Heracles, 16 to Perseus, Bellerophon, and King Arthur, and 21 to Moses. Other heroes who were scored included Jason, Pelops, Asclepius, Dionysus, Apollo, Zeus, Joseph, Elijah, Siegfried, and Nyikang, a Shilluk hero. Raglan concluded that the lives of the various heroes could not be historical but must reflect a bygone ritual involving birth, initiation, and death. Rank, on the other hand, saw the stories as reflecting the Oedipus complex posited by Freud, in which a young man unconsciously wishes to marry his mother and do away with his father. The area dealt with by Raglan consisted mainly of western Europe and the Near East, but it has been shown that essentially similar hero myths are found in the Far East. Roughly analogous tales are told by the Navaho, where the parallels are less close (Kluckhohn 1965).

Myths and dreams

Some writers have argued that myths often originate in dreams. This seems likely, especially when the content is somewhat bizarre. Clement Wood gives the account of a woman who dreamed of being followed by a large white horse which finally turned into a man.

I told him to go inside a barbershop and shave off his mane, which he did. When he came out, he looked just like a man, except that he had a horse's hoofs and face, and followed me wherever I went. He came closer to me, and I woke up.

I am a married woman of thirty-five with two children. I have been married for fourteen years now, and I am sure my husband is faithful to me (Wood 1931:92–93).

This is a dream that did not become a myth, but one can see how a dreamer might well impress others with such a tale, so that it might get to be repeated often enough to become part of a traditional repertoire. At the same time, this dream may reflect mythical stories about centaurs that the lady had read about in childhood.

If there is a tendency toward similar symbol formation in different cultures, as Freudians and Jungians assert, one might expect to find similar dreams and myths in different culture areas. For example, J. Stephen Horsley, an English neurologist and psychiatrist, claims that in treating patients with soneryl narcosis, he has been struck by the fact that certain dreams are common to the human species, especially that of being swallowed by a whale and the dream of spiritual or psychological rebirth (Horsley 1943; see Woods 1947:474). It is interesting that this dream was considered a bad sign by Sushruta, a Hindu commentator who lived around 600 B.C. Sushruta referred to ". . . the patient who dreams of being eaten by a fish, or who fancies himself again entering into the womb of his mother, or thinks that he is falling from the summit of a mountain or into a dark and dismal cave . . ." (Woods 1947:55).

In Old World mythology we have not only Jonah and the whale but also the Greek hero Herakles, who was swallowed by a monster sent by the sea god Poseidon. In the New World the Ojibwa culture hero Wenebojo was swallowed by a giant fish, while the Bering Straits Eskimos tell how their trickster hero Raven was swallowed by a whale-cow (Campell 1949:90–94). All of these heroes came out alive.

Abram Kardiner regards the mythology of a society as part of its "projective screen," the nature of which is influenced by the patterns of child rearing current in the society (see p. 243). From this point of view the differences in oral literature between societies take on as much psychological significance as the similarities, which were stressed by the more orthodox Freudians and Jungians.

Myths and rituals again

In Chapter 15, we referred to the close connection that sometimes exists between rituals and myths. As mentioned, Lord Raglan argued that the parallels between the various hero tales were best explained by the hypothesis that they were formerly related to a ritual involving birth, initiation, and death. There have been other attempts to derive particular myths from posited early rituals. For example, it has been suggested that the familiar story of The Three Bears originated in a northern Eurasiatic bear sacrifice ceremony (Dundes 1965:84–87). Similarly, some children's games, such as London Bridge and counting "eenie, meenie, miny, moe," have been explained as being the survivals of techniques for choosing victims of human sacrifice. However, even if there is a relationship between certain myths and rituals, there is no way of proving that the rituals came before the myths or vice versa. There are some recently documented cases, like that of the Ghost Dance of the Plains, where we know the history of the myth and the ritual and can point to their "origin" in the visions of a prophet. ("Origin" is in quotation marks because the vision in itself would not have been enough to start a religious movement.) But, where old myths and rituals are concerned, theories about origins must remain hypothetical.

Functions of myths

It was characteristic of Malinowski's functionalist approach that he rejected the effort to find origins of myths and rituals but emphasized, instead, the functions they serve. The most obvious, immediate function of all oral literature is entertainment. People enjoy hearing stories, and the narrator, who becomes the center of attention, gets satisfaction from the telling. But Malinowski pointed out that myths also provide a "charter" of belief, explaining how things came to be as they are. Unacculturated Ojibwa, for example, believe that their myths are true—that they are not just entertaining tales. Myths provide an explanation of, and support for, traditional customs and correct behavior. On the other hand, some characters in myths do shocking things that are normally taboo, such as committing murder and incest. There is some inconsistency here, but it can be argued that even these immoral episodes serve useful functions in letting off steam and bringing normally repressed material into the open.

Malinowski (1922:328) stated that ". . . myth possesses the normative power of fixing customs, of sanctioning modes of behavior, of giving dignity and importance to an institution." He thus emphasized the stable, conservative aspect of mythology. In this respect, Malinowski was challenged by Raymond Firth and also by Edmund Leach. Firth (1968:175) wrote that ". . . *very often traditional tales are divisive, not unitive* for the society at large. . . ." The mythology of a society is not always homogeneous and consistent; it may contain conflicting traditions that are appealed to by different segments of the society (see Leach 1968).

How well does the oral literature of a society reflect its culture? Certainly, it is never a complete mirror image. Folklore is selective; important aspects of the culture may not appear in the narratives at all. For example, the pig, which plays so important a role in Melanesian culture, does not figure in Melanesian mythology. W. H. R. Rivers (1968), who drew attention to this fact, suggested that familiar and uniform aspects of culture are less likely to be dealt with in mythology than elements that have some variety and inconstancy. If the moon inspires more mythological elaboration than the sun, it is because it undergoes more changes of appearance, while the sun, especially in tropical countries, is much the same from day to day, year after year.

Content, themes, and world view

But the element of variety is not enough, in itself, to account for the presence of an item in folklore. Among the Clackamas Chinook Indians, there was much interest in girls' puberty ceremonies, marriage negotiations, sorcery, and shamanistic cures, but there were few stories dealing with these topics. Melville Jacobs (1959:130) has explained this by saying that these were conscious concerns that were much discussed and also resolved in ritual performances. It was the repressed tensions that became expressed in Clackamas Chinook mythology, including tension about women, in-laws, and other relatives.

In Chapter 16 it was stated that the religious pantheons of some societies, such as the Kaingang and Aymara, contain more frightening, malevolent supernatural beings than benevolent ones. Similarly, the oral literature of a society may emphasize depressing themes and content. It does not necessarily follow that all the members of such a society are gloomy persons, but the belief system presented by such a body of folklore would seem to encourage the formation of a depressing world view at the same time that it expresses such a view. An example is, again, provided by the Aymara, who live in the semidesert *altiplano* of the Lake Titicaca region in the Andes.

Aymara folktales

One of the ethnologists who has worked among these Indians is Weston La Barre, who made a collection of Aymara folktales. These seem to depict a dog-eat-dog universe. A brief summary of some of these stories follows.

1. A fox and a condor meet in the snow-covered mountains. The fox makes a bargain, saying, ". . . whoever sitting in the snow best resists the cold will eat the other." He thinks that his tail will keep him warm; but it is the fox who freezes to death, and the condor eats him.

2. A vixen envies the beautiful white color of a gull's children and asks how they got it. The gull replies that she puts her children in a hot stove. When the vixen does the same, her children are cooked to death. She vows to eat the gull and her children in revenge, but they swim out to safety on a lake. The vixen proceeds to swallow up the lake to trap the gulls, but her belly swells up, and she dies.

3. A skunk used to play with a shepherdess in the field, but then the girl died. The skunk went to her funeral, taking some food and coca. The skunk apparently meant well, but when the people opened his food bundles, they found only black scarabs, gray lizards, and leaves.

4. A hawk who wants to kill a sparrow waits for him at the latter's front door. While offering excuses for his delay in coming to the door, the sparrow makes a hole in the back of his house and escapes.

5. In a time of famine, a mouse and a sparrow agree to hoard their food in the mouse's house. When the hungry sparrow goes to get some of his food, he finds that the mouse has eaten it all. The sparrow asks that at least his empty food bags be returned; whereupon the mouse hits him on the head with one of them.

Aymara Indians in Bolivia, 1953.

6. A condor successfully courts the daughter of a chief and takes her away to a high cliff. The chief does not know where she is and looks for her in vain. A hummingbird not only tells the chief where his daughter is but also helps him bring her back home. The condor returns to an empty house.

7. The Inca told the people of a certain town that if they did not obey him, he would destroy the town. The people did not listen, so the Inca destroyed the town and killed all its inhabitants.

8. Some foxes play a joke on a burro by untying him at night, leaving him free to eat crops, for which he is beaten by the people. The burro pretends to be dead. The foxes decide to truss him up with ropes and haul the carcass away. Then the donkey springs up and drags them to the house of the chief, who kills all the foxes.

In analyzing these tales, La Barre points to the "almost obsessive emphasis on food" and the themes of deceitfulness and trickery. In a concluding sentence, La Barre remarks (1966:143):

If the Aymara, as evidenced in their folktales (and indeed throughout the rest of their culture) are apprehensive, crafty, suspicious, violent, treacherous, and hostile, one important reason for this may be that such a character structure is an understandable response to their having lived for perhaps as long as a millennium under rigidly hierarchic and absolutist economic, military, and religious controls.

Recurrent themes in Central Eskimo folklore

In Chapter 15, the story of Sedna was presented, the woman who sits at the bottom of the sea and controls the movements of the sea mammals which came into being when the segments of her fingers were chopped off. She is sometimes called by a name that means Meat Dish, since she is the ultimate source of the Eskimos' principal food. In some versions of the Sedna myth, she is said to be living with her father at the bottom of the sea. Sedna is large and tall, but her father, who is crippled, with only one arm, is no larger than a ten-year-old boy. In some versions, Sedna is said to have been blinded in one eye by her father. She has, of course, no fingers, and she can barely move. As a nutritive Meat Dish and in her large size, Sedna seems to be a Magna Mater figure, although she is not always generous and nurturant.

According to Rasmussen (1929:66,98), Sedna's father is described as being habitually ill-tempered. After death, people who have committed sexual sins have to pay penance by living in his place for one year or more before they can go on to the land of the dead. They have to lie beside him and let themselves be pinched or beaten by him. In the case of persons who have committed bestiality, Sedna's father strikes them continually on the genitals for a year or more. According to Boas, who describes him in more favorable terms, Sedna's father is called "the man with something to cut (with a knife) . . ." (Boas 1884:583 ff).

This suggests fear of castration; note, too, that Sedna's fingers have been chopped off, and her father has only one arm. If this interpretation seems fanciful, consider another prominent female supernatural being, the woman who lives in the moon. She is called "the one with the *ulo*," a knife used by women. When men visit the moon, she tries to make them laugh by dancing in a ludicrous, sensual manner. If a man so much as smiles, she immediately slits his belly, tears out his entrails, and dumps them into a dish. Behind her hover a crowd of pale men whom she has disemboweled but who laugh at everything she does (Rasmussen 1929:76).

Here we have two instances of supernatural beings with knives. In an analysis of Nunivak Island Eskimo folklore, far to the west, Margaret Lantis (1953:131) noted that the most frequently mentioned physical dangers were cutting or stabbing, biting, and eating. When supernaturals are involved, it is the spirits who cut and bite the protagonist, not the other way around. Among the Central Eskimos, however, human beings may stab supernaturals. The harpooning of Sedna by a shaman was described earlier (p. 234). Of course, the Eskimos are always using knives to cut up the animals on which they depend for food. Eskimos have sometimes expressed guilt about living at the expense of animals, which they believe have souls, just as humans do. The fear of cutting may thus represent fear of retaliation. But there may also be a sexual element involved. The woman in the moon disembowels a man only when she has forced him to laugh or smile. There is one other reference to a taboo on smiling among the Central Eskimos. This occurs at a festival, described by Rasmussen (1929:241–43), at which men and women are paired for sexual relations. Two masked figures preside, one a woman with a snowbeating stick, the other a man with a huge artificial penis. Each paired couple has to pass by these masked beings who make all kinds of grotesque, lascivious gestures, trying to make them laugh. The couples have to keep their faces set and stiff, while the onlookers roar with laughter and try to get them to smile. Perhaps the taboo has something to do with the close quarters in which Eskimos sleep, sharing a sleeping platform, huddled close together. The same close proximity may also provide temptation for incest, which might in turn lead to castration anxiety.

Rasmussen (1929:300–301) tells one incest story about some women whose husbands had been murdered and who lived alone with their little sons, whom they carried in their *amauts*, the hoods in back of their jackets. The women had such a need for men that they had sexual relations with their sons. As a result, the latter never grew. The women did the hunting but were instructed by their sons from the *amauts*.

Another fearsome female supernatural being is the *Amaut* witch, a great ogress whose *amaut* is filled with old, rotten seaweed and the human beings whom she has captured (Rasmussen 1929:212).

Eskimo folklore seems to express a bias against women. Sedna, the moon woman, and the *Amaut* witch are all rather unpleasant. Of course, so is Sedna's father, but the moon woman is paired with a moon man who has benevolent traits. He helps young men hunt and protects those who die in accidents or commit suicide. If a woman is barren, she lets the light of the full moon shine on her bare lap, and he thus helps her have children. The moon man warns people about the moon woman and turns her out of his house when she tries to do harm (Rasmussen 1929:76). It will be recalled that, when men fail to kill seals, it is not their fault but the fault of women who have broken taboos. Women, then, seem to be seen as dangerous trouble-makers.

The Caribou Eskimos have a story about a man named Kivioq who was carried out to sea on the ice and reached a strange land, where he met an old woman and her daughter. He married the girl, but, one day, while Kivioq was out hunting, the old woman killed her daughter, flayed her, and pulled the skin over herself. This disguise did not fool Kivioq when he returned, for he could see the black, wrinkled legs of the old woman; so he ran away.

The old hag caused obstacles to rise in front of him. First, he came to two bears fighting. He slipped through them. Then, there were two hilltops that opened and closed. Although he passed safely between them, the tail of his coat was cut off. Then, Kivioq came to a boiling cooking pot, which he also got by.

Freudians might point out that both the cooking pot and the hill-tops that open and close sound like vagina symbols. If so, the symbolism becomes more explicit in the next episode, when the road is barred by the huge underpart of a woman. After Kivioq "lay with the thing," he was able to continue. Another obstacle was some sealhide thongs in his path.

Then Kivioq came to the house of an old woman who had a tail made of iron. When he lay down to sleep, he was careful to place a flat stone on his chest. Laughing, the old woman jumped up in the air to land on top of Kivioq and pierce him with her iron tail. But it struck the stone, was driven into her inner parts, and she died.

Kivioq went on from there, cruising in a kayak. A huge mussel shell almost cut him in two, but he escaped, with only the stern of his kayak cut off. Kivioq finally managed to return to his own country, and he was so happy to see it again that he sang for joy. His mother said, "That sounds like Kivioq's voice." Then, when his parents caught sight of Kivioq, they were so overjoyed that they fell over and died (Rasmussen 1930:97–99).

A remarkable aspect of this story is the applicability of Freudian symbolism, not only in the vagina symbols already referred to but also in the castration motifs. The tail of Kivioq's coat is cut off by the clashing hilltops, and the stern of his kayak is clipped off by the huge mussel shell. Kivioq is in flight from female sexuality; he tries to return to his parents, but that is forbidden, and they die. More examples could be given of Eskimo stories dealing with tension between men and women (Rasmussen 1929:221–22,287–90; 1921: 52–55,90–92).

There seems to be no easy way to account for this emphasis, but some possibilities may be suggested. In wintertime, particularly, the Eskimos are cooped up for long periods of time in close quarters and probably get on one another's nerves, although they seem to be very sociable and philosophical about hardships. Perhaps the men, hunched over the blowholes all day on the ice in winter, resent the fact that the women at home are warm, confortable, and out of danger, just as soldiers in combat resent the safety of those at bases

Elderly Eskimo couple.

behind the lines. The temptations and taboos of incest may also contribute to the male-female conflict expressed in these narratives.

However, it must be admitted that these are only guesses. The difficulty with such analyses has been well stated by Lévi-Strauss (1967:203):

If a given mythology confers prominence on a certain figure, let us say an evil grandmother, it will be claimed that in such a society grandmothers are actually evil and that mythology reflects the social structure and social relations; but should the actual data be conflicting, it would be readily claimed that the purpose of mythology is to provide an outlet for repressed feelings. Whatever the situation, a clever dialectic will always find a way to pretend that a meaning has been found.

Some approaches to the study of folktales

An early approach to the study of folktales was the historico-geographical method pioneered by some Finnish folklorists. Its aim was to reconstruct the life story of a folktale. This could be done, it was thought, by collating and comparing all the variants of the tale and breaking them up into component motifs and traits. This analysis was supposed to uncover the original form or archetype of the story. One could then see what elements had been added in the course of time, and also where, if the distribution of variant themes were plotted geographically.

Another approach to the study of folktales is the intensive study of the oral literature of a single society, noting its recurrent themes and special emphases and seeing how they differ, if they do, from those of other societies. One example of such an approach is Margaret Lantis' study of Nunivak Eskimo mythology, referred to earlier.

Still another approach to the study of folktales is the cross-cultural survey method, making use of the ethnographic data in the Human Relations Area Files (see p. 360), applying scoring systems and looking for statistical correlations. For example, the folktales of a number of societies may be scored for the degree of achievement motivation (*n* achievement) evidenced in the tales. Then one can see if there is any correlation between *n* achievement and certain features in the child-training patterns in the societies selected for investigation (McClelland and Friedman 1952; Child, Storm, and Veroff 1958).

The foregoing approaches involve analyses of *themes*. Studies have also been made of the *structure* of folktales. A Russian folklorist, Vladimir Propp, claimed that most Russian fairy tales follow a standard pattern, divided into a series of what he called *functions,* or components of the tale. Propp (1968) has listed these functions and provided a brief definition and a conventional sign for each, so it is possible to diagram the structure of a tale with his symbols. A Russian fairy tale may begin with an Absentation: one of the members of a family departs. This is accompanied by an Interdiction addressed to the hero ("You must not look into that closet while we are gone"). The Interdiction is always Violated, at which point a Villain is introduced. A function like Interdiction may be performed by various characters in Russian fairy tales, but the functions themselves are stable and limited in number. Although particular functions may be omitted in stories, the functions always follow the same sequence, according to Propp.

Since some European fairy tales are similar to Russian ones, it would be possible to apply Propp's system to them but not to most other bodies of folklore, which have different structures. Alan Dundes, however, has tried to apply Propp's approach to North American Indian folklore. He finds that a common formula in such tales is Lack/Lack liquidated. This means that a hero discovers that he lacks something (food, a wife), goes to get it, and thus liquidates the lack. In American Indian tales few episodes intervene between the statement of a lack and its liquidation, while in European and Russian tales there are many more intervening episodes. Interdiction and Violation episodes occur in American Indian tales, as they do in Russian and European stories, and they frequently intervene between Lack and Lack liquidated. For example, in what have been called "Orpheus" tales in North America, a man loses his wife, but he can get her back if he does not violate a particular taboo. Of course, the man does violate the taboo and loses his wife again (Dundes 1964).

A structural analysis has been applied to Cinderella stories of Northwest Coast Indian tribes, which have been compared to European Cinderella tales. Betty Uchitelle Randall (1949) distinguishes four basic steps common to both Old World and New World Cinderella tales: (1) *The need for change.* Recognition of an inferior status or situation by a mistreated stepdaughter or younger son. (2) *The reason for change.* Behavior of others makes the situation worse: rejection, abandonment. (3) *The process of change.* The means by which the hero attains the goal. (4) *The result of change.* The fulfillment of the goal. (5) A fifth step, *Retribution,* is sometimes added: punishment of those who made the hero or heroine suffer. This last step is more common in European than in American Indian stories, since an ethical dualism of good and bad is prominent in European but not in Indian tales. Another contrast is that the emotions of the hero are given full expression in the Indian stories, while Grimm's Cinderella expresses no feelings. The only outspoken emotion in the story is the hatred of the wicked stepmother.

The most ambitious attempt to analyze folklore in recent years is the four-volume *Mythologiques* of Claude Lévi-Strauss. Whereas Propp's structural approach has been called *syntagmatic* (i.e., concerned with the linear sequence of episodes, as in the analysis of a sentence's syntax), Lévi-Strauss' approach has been termed *paradigmatic,* in search of patterns. He always looks for binary opposition that he assumes underlie myths, such as the contrasts of raw and cooked, nature and culture. Lévi-Strauss claims that the function of a myth is to provide a resolution or mediation of a conflict.

The structural approach of Lévi-Strauss

The first volume of *Mythologiques* deals with the myths of the Bororo and neighboring tribes in South America. In later volumes the author moves up into North America. His analysis is therefore not focused on a single American Indian culture but on a series of them.

Lévi-Strauss starts off with a particular Bororo myth and then tries to show that other South American myths are variations or transpositions of the same story. One myth, for example, is about a boy who has climbed a tree to throw macaws down to his brother-in-law, but he is stranded in the tree when the brother-in-law removes the pole by which he climbed up. Along comes a jaguar, who asks the boy to throw down some birds, which the boy does. The jaguar then asks the boy to jump down, and catches him. Although the boy is afraid, he is not harmed. The jaguar carries the hero to his home and introduces him to his wife (in some versions human), who is unfriendly to the boy. The hero complains about her to the jaguar, who gives him a bow and arrows and two baskets of roasted meat to take back to his village. The jaguar tells the boy how to shoot his wife, if she pursues him. When she follows the boy, he kills her. After the boy's return to his village, an expedition is organized to capture fire from the jaguar. Formerly, the jaguar had had bow and arrows and fire and had cooked meat; but, after giving these things to human beings, the jaguar has had to use his fangs for hunting, has eaten raw food, and has become full of hatred for human beings.

A story told by another tribe, the Opaye, represents an inversion of this tale, according to Lévi-Strauss. A girl expressed admiration for a jaguar's success in hunting. He married her, and, since he regularly supplied his in-laws with grilled meat, he was allowed to live in her village. But the girl began to look like a jaguar, so her grandmother killed her through witchcraft. The girl's brother, afraid of the jaguar's reaction, asked if he would accept another sister in her place. The jaguar said that he meant them no harm and went away, roaring loudly.

Lévi-Strauss sees jaguar and man as polar opposites. The human wife plays a mediating role. Once the jaguar's gifts of bow and arrows and grilled meat have been acquired by man, the mediating female must be destroyed, since she no longer serves a useful purpose. It is the woman who is killed, rather than her husband, in the two stories.

A third story is related to these. A man climbs a tree to catch parrots and throw them down to his wife, at the foot of the tree. But, as she catches the birds, she eats them — unnatural behavior. When the man climbs down, she kills him, returns to her village, eats up her children, and then turns into a jaguar. This myth explains the origin of jaguars, while the first story explains the origin of fire for cooking. In both of these myths a man climbs a tree to throw birds to someone down below. In the first story it is a brother-in-law, who is later replaced by a jaguar. In the second story it is a wife, who turns into a jaguar. In the first myth the animal behaves like a human being; in the second, the human woman behaves like (and turns into) an animal. The stories seem to imply that culture is a valuable but precarious attainment that can easily be lost, as it was by the generous jaguar and the cannibalistic woman.

In his writings about kinship in primitive societies, Lévi-Strauss has emphasized the importance of the idea of reciprocity, which involves mutual relations between families related through marriage. In the South American myths, it is necessary to pay attention to the affinal relationships. In our society we have neolocal marriages and rather weak ties with in-laws. So, when we read a story about a jaguar and his human wife, it is natural for us to wonder how the jaguar and the girl will get along. But a South American Indian might be more interested in learning how the jaguar will get on with his in-laws.

These myths have necessarily been constructed out of materials available in the environment of the South American Indians. Besides human beings, the stories deal with jaguars, wild pigs, vultures, otters, and other animals. One feature of Lévi-Strauss's many-sided analysis of this material is that he presents information about the behavior and characteristics of some of these animals and of the Indians' traditions about them in order to clarify why a particular animal, rather than some other species, was chosen for the role it plays in a particular story. There does seem to be a rather consistent order in the South American tales, as suggested by the few examples given above (Lévi-Strauss 1969b).

Influenced by Lévi-Strauss, Edmund R. Leach has followed his approach and method of interpretation. He points out that myths are characterized by redundancy, as if to make sure that a particular piece of information will be communicated. Important stories recur in several different versions. Leach (1967:4) draws attention to the binary structure of myth: "In every myth system we will find a persistent sequence of binary discriminations as between human/ superhuman, mortal/immortal, male/female, legitimate/illegitimate, good/bad . . . followed by a 'mediation' of the paired categories thus distinguished." Leach proceeds to analyze the stories of the creation, the Garden of Eden, and Cain and Abel as given in the Bible. He then points to some similarities between these stories and the myth of Oedipus. As in Lévi-Strauss's analyses, much of this demonstration seems farfetched. Leach himself (1967:9) concedes that ". . . this kind of algebra is unfamiliar and more evidence will be needed to convince the skeptical."

Despite the difficulty of analyzing myths and folktales, it seems better to try to make some sense out of them than to give up the job as impossible.

Suggestions for further reading

A good, brief introduction to the field is Alan Dundes, "Oral Literature," in *Introduction to Cultural Anthropology: Essays in the Scope and Methods of the Science of Man*, ed. James A. Clifton (Boston: Houghton Mifflin Co., 1968), pp. 117–29.

A classic work is Stith Thompson, *The Folktale* (New York: Dryden Press, 1946).

Valuable for providing insight into the historical development of approaches to oral literature is Robert A. Georges. ed., *Studies on Mythology* (Homewood, Ill.: Dorsey Press, 1968). It contains articles by Boas, Rivers, Radcliffe-Brown, Malinowski, Benedict, Kluckhohn, Firth, Leach, and Lévi-Strauss. Two other anthologies are also recommended: Alan Dundes, ed., *The Study of Folklore* (Englewood Cliffs, N.J.: Prentice-Hall, 1965); John Middleton, ed., *Myth and Cosmos: Readings in Mythology and Symbolism* (New York: Natural History Press, 1967).

19

The arts

Dancing, music, and decorative art are all listed in Murdock's catalog of universal aspects of culture (1945:124). Adumbrations of such activities may be seen in some of the behavior of nonhuman primates, particularly among chimpanzees.

Proto-art in nonhuman primates

As far as dancing is concerned, consider this description by Wolfgang Köhler (1927:314–15) of a group of chimpanzees:

For instance, two would wrestle and tumble near a post; soon their movements would become more regular and tend to describe a circle around the post as center. One after another, the rest of the group approach, join the two, and finally march in an orderly fashion round and round the post. The character of their movements changes; they no longer walk, they trot, and as a rule with special emphasis on one foot, while the other steps lightly, thus a rough approximate rhythm develops, and they tend to "keep time" with one another.

Chimpanzees also engage in rhythmic drumming, which may be accompanied by loud cries and stamping. In this way they sometimes generate a remarkable volume of sound, which has astonished travelers in the jungle. Man's pleasure in rhythmic movement and rhythmic sound must be a heritage from a prehominid level.

Drawing and painting among apes in captivity

Nonhuman primates do not seem to produce decorative art; its universality may thus be somewhat less understandable than that of

284

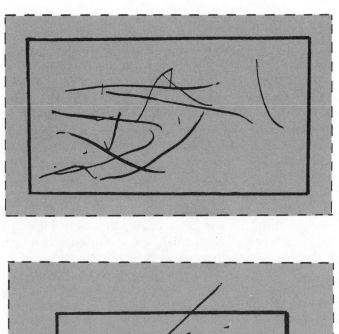

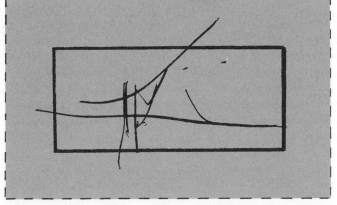

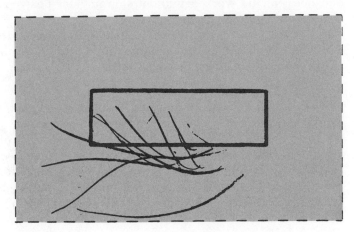

A chimpanzee's reaction to rectangles. (*Top*) all marks are made within the rectangle and none in the one-inch margin. (*Center and bottom*) the rectangles are smaller—with some markings made outside the rectangle (*center*) and markings under rather than inside the rectangle (*bottom*).

dancing and music. But it is interesting that some apes and monkeys in captivity have learned to scribble with pencil on paper and to make fingerpaintings and paint with a brush. When an ape is given a pencil and makes a mark with it, he is very interested in seeing what he has produced, and he continues to make marks. These scribbles are not purely random; they are, first of all, confined to the page and seldom spill over. Desmond Morris presented his chimpanzee subject, Congo, with a sheet of paper on which a large rectangle had been drawn, leaving a one-inch margin; Congo's scribbles remained within this rectangle. Alpha, a young female chimpanzee, always marked the four corners of a blank sheet of paper before scribbling in the center; but she ignored the corners if there was a square, circle, or other form on the page. Then, she placed almost all of her marks within the square or circle, with only a few spots outside. If the square or circle was small, she scribbled over it instead of within. If there was a small, solid figure on the page in an off-center position, Alpha did not mark it but scribbled in the open space in such a way as to balance the figure. Congo did the same. These apes had their individual differences. Congo did not mark all four corners as Alpha did, and he favored a fan-shaped type of composition which Alpha did not produce, although other primates have done so.

A striking aspect of ape art production is the intense interest and motivation shown by the ape while drawing or painting. This work was not rewarded by food or other awards; it was done for its own sake. Indeed, at such times, food was ignored. An interruption could cause a temper tantrum. A female chimpanzee, interrupted in the middle of a drawing, bit her keeper, although she did not usually do such a thing, even when the keeper took attractive food away from her. Congo's drawing sessions usually lasted between 15 and 30 minutes, with between 5 and 10 drawings being produced, but on one occasion he worked without stopping for nearly an hour and turned out 23 drawings and paintings.

If decorative art is a universal feature of human cultures, it may be that a feeling for balance, symmetry, and rhythm was inherited from our prehominid ancestors (Morris 1962).

Design forms

The feeling for balance and regularity may find expression in designs characterized by bilateral symmetry. Franz Boas pointed out that such designs are found even in the simplest forms of decorative art, including Paleolithic geometrical figures and the body paintings of Andaman Islanders and of natives in Tierra del Fuego. Perhaps the stress on bilateral symmetry is ultimately based on the bilateral symmetry of the human body itself. Boas (1955:33) suggested that

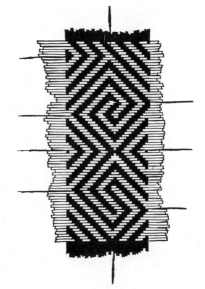

Greek key designs. (*Left*) two pieces of mammoth ivory from the Ukraine, about 15,000 years old, engraved with Greek key design. (*Right*) a Greek key pattern in matwork made by Indians of the Rio Branco in northwestern Brazil.

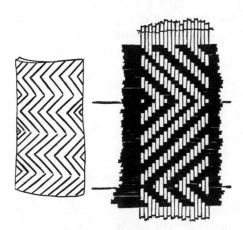

Zigzag herringbone designs. (*Left*) engraved mammoth ivory from the Ukraine, probably 15,000 years old. (*Right*) woven textile made by Bakaïri Indians of the Amazon jungle.

the sensation of the motions of right and left might lead to the feeling of symmetry. At any rate, such patterning is widespread in the decorative arts of the world.

Rhythmic repetition is another fundamental aspect of design. We see it in the regular flaking of a Solutrean flint blade and in the adzing of a Haida canoe, where the adze marks were purposely left unsmoothed for the sake of their texture and patterned effect. Rhythmic repetition often appears in the decoration of pottery, baskets, and textiles.

In some cases, particular design patterns have been imposed or suggested by a process of manufacture. Checkerwork basketry presents a chessboard pattern, especially if the two sets of interlacing strands have different colors or shades. Twilling produces diagonal strips, which may also be combined into diamond forms. The coiling of a basket may suggest a spiral (Lowie 1940:182).

A design form known as the Greek key, fret, or meander, has a very wide distribution, partly because of its association with a particular weaving technique. Its oldest known appearance is on an engraving on mammoth ivory from a site in the Ukraine dating from about 15,000 years ago. On a second piece of such ivory a zigzag herringbone design was engraved. Gene Weltfish has shown that both of these designs develop naturally from the twill-plaited weaving of basketry and matting, such as is made by some Amazon Indians today. On this basis, Weltfish argues convincingly that this weaving technique must have been known 15,000 years ago.

Weltfish (1953) has also shown that the impressive designs painted on pottery by the Mimbres people of the American Southwest (A.D. 900–1150) probably had their origin in a basket-weaving process known as the diagonal-inverted-symmetry pattern. Although there are no remains of basketry in the area, one of the pots in the early style is painted in an almost exact replica of this weave pattern.

Once a design like the Greek key has come into circulation, it may be transferred from one medium to another, as seems to have been the case in both the mammoth-ivory engravings and the Mimbres pottery. It may also be diffused from one society to another.

Problems concerning the diffusion of art motifs

Like folklore motifs, design forms can be mapped, and efforts may be made to trace their diffusion. It seems likely that designs that have been imposed or suggested by processes of manufacture have appeared independently in many different times and places. The same is probably true of relatively simple forms, such as crosses, spirals, and swastikas. But, when design motifs become more complex, and when their component parts do not seem to be obviously related to one another, the possibility of diffusion presents itself whenever similar motifs appear in different culture areas.

Trans-Pacific diffusionists, who believe that much of the advanced culture in the New World was affected by Asian influence, base much of their argument on the similarities of design motifs in Asia and the Americas. Consider, for example, what has been called the *Hocker* motif: a figure with bent arms and legs extended on either

(*Top*) two hockers carved on stone slabs, Ecuador. (*Bottom left*) hocker from Dyak woodcarving, Borneo. (*Below right*) clay stamp from Guerrero, Mexico. (*Bottom right*) painted pottery from Puerto Rico.

side of the body, with dots or disks appearing between the knees and elbows. Similar figures appear in Shang or early Chou China, in Malaysia, Melanesia, Polynesia, Mexico, Peru, Ecuador, Brazil, and on the Northwest Coast of North America. In some of these figures, eyes and faces appear on the joints and hands. This pattern is found in the Northwest Coast, in Aztec reliefs, in the Mississippi Basin, and in parts of Melanesia.

There are many parallel features in the architecture of Mexico,

Guatemala, India, Java, and Indochina, including pyramids with stairways and sometimes serpent columns and balustrades. Serpent balustrades appear in Chichén Itzá of the Mexican period and at Tula in Mexico; they are also found in the Borobudur in Indonesia.

Carved jade for ornaments and funerary offerings were used in Mexico, Guatemala, Costa Rica, and Colombia, but also in early China and New Zealand. Chinese of the Shang and Chou periods used to place a jade cicada in the mouth of a dead person. Miguel Covarrubias (1954:104) writes: "The ancient Mexicans also were in the habit of placing a jade bead in the mouth of their dead, and both Chinese and Mexicans painted their funerary jades with red cinnabar." He also points to some stylistic features common to both Chinese and Mexican jadework.

The foregoing similarities are indeed striking. Since Covarrubias, Ekholm (1953), and others have produced so many apparent linkages like these, they may ultimately convince their skeptical colleagues, who feel that independent invention in the Old World and the New is still the best explanation for these oddly parallel features.

Music

Music is an expressive form of communication found in all societies. Like decorative and plastic art, music is culturally patterned and differs from one society to another. Just as it is often difficult (despite the influence of Picasso and modern art) for an American to appreciate the aesthetic qualities of an African statue or Melanesian mask, it is also difficult to enjoy the music of a Chinese opera as much as we enjoy more familiar Western music. In all societies there are traditions about the patterns of art production with which persons are familiar from an early age. The symbolic meanings attached to particular aspects of art in one society may not be at all understood in another. This was shown in an experiment undertaken by Robert Morey (1940). Pieces by Schubert, Handel, and Wagner that were meant to express such emotions as fear, reverence, rage, and love were played to members of a Liberian tribe, who did not make the emotional associations one would expect of a European or American audience.

This does not mean that we cannot enjoy another style of music. Some styles are sufficiently similar to our own to be easy to assimilate. Music developed by New World Negroes is said to represent a syncretism or blending of African and European-American music. According to Richard A. Waterman (1952), this syncretism was made possible because there is enough similarity between African and European music. But European music is quite different from North American Indian music, making syncretism more difficult. Alan P.

Merriam, who has studied music among the Flathead Indians of Montana, writes that a Flathead child may learn to play the clarinet in a marching band at school, while at the same time he is learning traditional Indian music at home. Here, the result is not syncretism but compartmentalization. The two kinds of music are kept separate for different occasions. Aspects of the traditional music do not appear in a Western performance, nor are aspects of European music introduced into an American Indian performance (Merriam 1964). Of course, some syncretism may develop in time, but it has not done so yet.

Persons who are familiar with a particular style of music may feel a heightened sense of solidarity when they either perform together or collectively listen to music they enjoy, as in the case of a hymn-singing church congregation or a large audience of young Americans at a rock festival. Such occasions may be very important in some societies, as they were among the Plains Indians. It has been estimated that about a third or more of a Ponca's year was devoted to preparing for or participating in dancing and ceremonial activity that involved music (Howard and Kurath 1959:1).

Cultures vary widely in the number and kinds of musical instruments present. Musical instruments have been divided into idiophones (rattles, marimbas, gongs, bells); membranophones (skin instruments, such as drums); cordophones (stringed instruments); and aerophones (wind instruments). Rhythmic instruments such as rattles and drums seem to be the oldest, judging by their wide distribution and presence among many hunting-gathering societies, but flutes are also ancient and widespread. Stringed instruments are more limited; they did not occur in pre-Columbian America.

Integration of the arts

Fine museum displays and beautifully illustrated books have made people familiar in recent years with some of the arts of non-Western societies. At the same time, the influence of abstract and expressionist art has, to some extent, modified earlier aesthetic attitudes and made it possible for many people to now see beauty in African sculpture and other artworks they might formerly have dismissed as barbarous and grotesque. Non-Western art has thus become more acceptable and familiar. However, the context in which we see African masks, Kwakiutl shamans' rattles, and other such objects is very different from those in which they once functioned. We see them atomistically arranged on a wall, in a display case, or on the pages of a book. They have been recreated as something new in their new setting. While it is good that we can appreciate these objects, it is worth keeping in mind that they are quite removed from the world in which they once had a very different function and significance.

The arts are often interrelated and integrated. Consider, for example, a Kwakiutl winter ceremonial, held at night in a huge, dark, gable-roofed, plank-walled house in the light of a crackling fire. Architecture, costumes, masks, music, singing, dancing, pageantry, and oral literature were all combined on such occasions. The costumes were magnificent, including dark mantles of Hudson's Bay blankets bordered with scarlet flannel and sewn with buttons or dentalium shells. The masks, beautifully carved and painted, represented the spirits that were believed to possess the dancers. Some of the masks were huge composite structures with movable parts operated by weights, pulleys, and strings, so that beaks could snap and bite, or so that the mask could split in two and widen to display another mask within. The bodies of the dancers were often hidden under long fringes of cedar bark. These impressive figures danced about the flickering fire to the accompaniment of singing. The men who did this dancing, acting, and singing were also the carvers of the masks. Although some artists were known to be outstanding,

Balinese play scene.

most men did some carving. This widespread familiarity with the arts made possible a high level of sophistication and art criticism that maintained or raised local standards.

Similarly impressive are the masked dances of the Zuñi Shalako ceremony, where, again, there is a combination of impressive setting, colorful costumes, ingenious masks, and well-rehearsed dancing.

One more example of integration in the arts is the Balinese drama, usually enacted in front of an elaborately carved temple with magnificently costumed players, some of whom may be masked, to the accompaniment of a *gamelan* orchestra. The performances are done with such professional skill that it is hard to remember that these dancers, actors, and musicians are peasant farmers who spend much of the day in their rice fields and who meet at night to rehearse and perform their dazzling dramas. The travelers from Europe and the United States who witness such performances realize what we may have lost, in our modern world, in the course of economic specialization and industrial progress.

The artist in social context

In modern industrial society the artist is often considered to be an aberrant individual who may be highly talented but who is somehow set apart from the more practical world of the majority. This is not the case in many non-Western societies, where the practice of art is not held to be either deviant or limited to talented persons. The Anang of Nigeria believe that all people are equal in their innate artistic potentialities; ability is simply a matter of training and practice. "Once an individual commits himself to this occupation by paying the fee and participating in a religious ritual, he almost never fails to develop the skills which will enable him to enjoy success as a professional." (Messenger 1958:22). This applies to all the arts among the Anang: carving, dancing, singing, and weaving.

In such a society a person does not create art for the purpose of self-expression or aesthetic satisfaction alone. The work is more apt to be intended for some general social purpose, such as ceremonial activity, and the artist may work in collaboration with others, so that the finished object is the work of several persons. Since so many people are producers of artwork in such a society, there are commonly shared standards of craftsmanship, and there are apt to be expressions of criticism or admiration of particular products, which help to maintain or improve the level of artistic production.

In some societies where high standards of workmanship prevail, there may be some specialization. Although carving techniques were generally known in the Northwest Coast of North America, some men specialized in carving and were held to be better at it than others. But they engaged in hunting and fishing and other everyday activities like anyone else. Their work sometimes required them to join a secret society and to take part in ceremonies, which brought about an increase in social status. Harry B. Hawthorn (1961:62) has described such a carver: "Martin hums and sings throughout his working day. The songs are those which accompany the presentation of the supernatural figures in the winter dances. He is carving them; in the dances they will be portrayed by masked and costumed performers." Note how this passage reflects the integration of the arts. Hawthorn adds that if Martin, the carver, has an audience, he will tell the myth of the ceremony and execute some of the dance steps.

This particular man, a southern Kwakiutl, became a carver partly because that was his mother's wish. She hoped that he would be a carver and become rich, so she asked his uncle, a well-known carver, to train him, which he did. In this particular society, then, wealth and fame were among the incentives of the artist, but there was also the intrinsic satisfaction of the work itself, as the quotation from Hawthorn attests.

In Bali, where everyone seems to be an artist, according to the gifted artist and ethnographer Miguel Covarrubias (1937:163), wealth and fame were not important considerations. "The artist in Bali is essentially a craftsman and at the same time an amateur, casual and anonymous, who uses his talent knowing that no one will care to record his name for posterity. His only aim is to serve his community. . . ." There are constant demands on artists in Bali, since the soft sandstone used in temple sculpture crumbles after a few years and the sculpture must be renewed. The same is true of wooden sculpture, often eaten by ants, while paper and cloth rot from the humidity. Artists are probably even busier nowadays in Bali than they were in Covarrubias' time, since there are more tourists today than there were in the 1930s, and there are many shops where wooden sculpture and other art products are sold. Moreover, a great many dramas and performances are put on solely for tourists. Thus, there have been changes in the social context and motivation of Balinese artists.

The motives that lead people to engage in art are various. A distinction should first be made between the process of art production and contemplation of the finished product. We have seen how intent and absorbed chimpanzees are when engaged in drawing and painting, but they seem to have little interest in the work of art when it is done. They do not try to hoard it or put it up on the wall. Instead, they may crumple it up or try to eat it. At the opposite extreme are modern collectors of art who do nothing whatever to produce an *objet d'art* but who are proud and pleased to have artworks on display in their homes.

Franz Boas (1955:25–29) believed that the Sauk and Fox Indians were more interested in making and painting their rawhide boxes than in the appearance of the finished product. They made elegant designs on a flat piece of rawhide, but when the hide was folded to make the box, the design was lost. Most artists, however, seem to combine both the pleasures of creation and contemplation of a finished work of art.

Part of the motivation for engaging in art production is the sense of mastery and control, the satisfaction of successfully coping with a challenge. Even when making an arrowhead, basket, or pot, the workman is usually not satisfied with a product that simply does the job. He wants it, of course, to be utilitarian, but he is apt to lavish more attention on the object than purely utilitarian considerations would demand. Vanity and prestige may also motivate art production. Painting the face and body, tattooing, scarification, and elaborate headdress, ornaments, and clothing all draw attention to the self, and so do special clubs, maces, stools, and other objects that may be the prerogatives of kings, chiefs, or other persons of high status. Another motivation in art production has been in connection with religion, in the search for security. Masks that represent the ancestors or the gods must be well made to ensure supernatural aid. Shrines or temples are beautified to enhance the holiness of the place. There is also the pleasure of being surrounded by beautiful things, as in the decoration of a home, its embellishment with objects of beauty. Finally, there is patronage, artwork done upon commission for a king or wealthy person, who may thus employ several artists.

Variation in the emphasis on art

Societies like the Kwakiutl and the Balinese represent a high level of art production and keen interest in the arts. Not all societies reach such high levels of aesthetic interest. Although the arts are universal, there is much more art in some societies than in others. In some societies, certain fields of artistic expression remain unexplored. The Ona of Tierra del Fuego did not model or carve, although they did paint their bodies and perform elaborate dances. The California seed gatherers made no pottery, but they produced very beautiful, intricately woven baskets. These variations may sometimes be due to the level of technology of the society or to the presence or absence of certain materials or resources in the local environment, but such explanations do not always apply.

Alvin W. Wolfe, who did fieldwork among the Ngombe of the Congo equatorial forest, found that they did not produce much art, although there are other African tribes that are famous for their fine artwork. He raised the question of why art becomes developed in some societies and not in others. The Ngombe are patrilineal; some of the art-producing African tribes are matrilineal. Could this be part of the explanation? Wolfe noted that of 20 societies frequently cited in anthropology textbooks to illustrate the artwork of nonliterate peoples, 11 had matrilineal kin groups, whereas, according to Murdock's "World Ethnographic Sample," only 20 percent of the world sample has matrilineal kin groups. Wolfe did not assume that matriliny causes art, but he thought it might be significant that in matrilineal societies men tend to be alienated from their local lineage centers and have no strong solidarity with one another. Wolfe suggested that "cleavages" among the men of a community may result from other causes than matriliny. Whatever their origin, men seek to overcome these barriers through art. Wolfe tried to test these rather vague hypotheses in an elaborate computerized exercise in statistics. Although no definite conclusions were provided by the computers, the questions raised by Wolfe were worth asking (Wolfe 1969).

Elizabeth Tooker (1968) has explored a related problem, the relationship between masking and matrilineality. While Wolfe's paper concerns African societies, Tooker's deals with North American Indian tribes. In a sample of 64 tribes, she found that, although masks are often found in societies lacking matrilineal moieties, no society that has matrilineal moieties is without masks. Early in the 20th century, the German anthropologist Fritz Graebner noted that matrilineal moieties and secret societies with masks tended to be associated in Melanesia and certain other areas. Tooker also found matrilineal descent in general, rather than just matrilineal moieties, to be associated with masking. She hypothesized that the more important matrilineal institutions are in a society, the more important masking will be in religious ritual. Tooker found some confirmation for this hypothesis in the Pueblo societies of the American Southwest. Masking is more important in the western Pueblos than in the eastern ones, and so are matrilineal institutions.

If Tooker is right, the hypothesis that originally suggested itself to Wolfe—that there is a relationship between matrilineality and productivity in art—seems to receive some support; for, if men make masks, they are apt to make other art objects as well in connection with the masked men's cult. But, of course, much productivity in art may also be found in societies that are not matrilineal and do not have masks.

A good, brief introduction is provided by Erna Gunther, "Art in the Life of Primitive Peoples," in *Introduction to Cultural Anthropology: Essays in the Scope and Methods of the Science of Man,* ed. James A. Clifton (Boston: Houghton Mifflin Co., 1968), pp. 76–114. Another is Ruth Bunzel, "Art," in *General Anthropology,* ed. Franz Boas (New York: D. C. Heath & Co., 1938), pp. 535–88.

A classic work is Franz Boas, *Primitive Art* (New York: Dover Publications, 1955). (First published in 1927.) See also Paul S. Wingert, *Primitive Art: Its Traditions and Styles* (New York: Oxford University Press, 1962); Gene Weltfish, *The Origins of Art* (Indianapolis: Bobbs-Merrill Co., 1953).

A beautifully published work, especially interesting for its discussion of trans-Pacific diffusion, is Miguel Covarrubias, *The Eagle, the Jaguar, and the Serpent: Indian Art of the Americas; North America: Alaska, Canada, the United States* (New York: Alfred A. Knopf, 1954). There is a companion volume by Covarrubias: *Indian Art of Mexico and Central America* (New York: Alfred A. Knopf, 1957).

The various arts have not been dealt with separately in this chapter; a few references may be suggested for a beginning.

For the dance: Gertrude Prokosch Kurath, "Panorama of Dance Ethnology," *Current Anthropology,* vol. 1 (May 1960), pp. 233–54.

For ethnomusicology: Alan P. Merriam, *The Anthropology of Music* (Evanston, Ill.: Northwestern University Press, 1964).

For architecture: Charles Harris Whitaker, *Rameses to Rockefeller: The Story of Architecture* (New York: Random House, 1934).

The making of gardens is an art that has been highly developed in some societies, notably China and Japan. For two beautiful books with good commentaries, see Osvald Siren, *Gardens of China* (New York: Ronald Press Co., 1949); David H. Engel, *Japanese Gardens for Today* (Rutland, Vt.: Charles E. Tuttle Co., 1967).

Suggestions for further reading

part nine

Culture and personality

20

Growing up in different societies

This chapter deals with the issues of growing up in different cultural contexts. It concerns problems such as these: How important is early childhood experience for personality formation? What happens under conditions of maternal deprivation? How divergent are child-rearing practices and how do they relate to personality formation?

In previous chapters we have seen that human sociocultural systems may differ greatly from one another in subsistence basis, forms of marriage, postmarital residence, social and political organization, and other respects. Children born into these different systems must adjust to them and learn the rules and values of the culture, whatever they may be. The adults of each society teach their own conceptions of reality to the young. Since they generally have no alternative models to follow, the young accept these teachings, identify with their parents, and strive, with varying degrees of effort and success, to approximate the ideal type of their society.

Psychological schools as different as those of behaviorism and psychoanalysis place a central emphasis on the childhood years. From their points of view, the adult personality is formed mainly in childhood. The behaviorists believe that so-called instincts and emotions are largely learned reactions. Freud, on the other hand, believed that humans, even as children, have to cope with strong instincts or drives. The ways in which these instincts are thwarted or find expression in the childhood years determine what kind of personality will develop. Behaviorism and psychoanalysis, then, have different assumptions about human nature, but they both agree

Significance of early childhood

301

on the great importance of the early years, an emphasis shared by still other psychological schools. This consideration underlies the work that has been done in the cross-cultural study of child development.

Maternal deprivation

Normal human development depends upon an adequate amount of maternal care. Among human beings the absence of such a relationship, without adequate substitutes, may have very severe effects upon the development of the individual. It has been argued by several writers that children suffering from maternal deprivation fail to develop normally in later years. The evidence for this, however, is conflicting, and there are differences of opinion as to what constitutes the essential deprivation from which the children suffer.

Soon after birth all primates, except for humans, cling to their mothers; they remain in close contact with them throughout infancy. Harry Harlow (1962) showed that when rhesus monkeys were deprived of their mothers, they did not develop normal patterns of heterosexual behavior in later years. When deprived female rhesus monkeys were impregnated by normal male monkeys, they failed to develop maternal feelings toward their offspring and treated them with indifference or hostility. However, Harlow also found that infant monkeys who had been deprived of their mothers but allowed to play with other young members of their species for 20 minutes a day seemed to develop normally with regard to social and sexual interaction.

Such experiments in deprivation, fortunately, are not made with human beings, but a roughly analogous trauma may be seen in cases of children who have been separated from their mothers and placed in institutions. If such a child is between 15 and 20 months old and has had an adequate relationship with the mother before separation, it will react in a predictable manner, which John Bowlby (1969:27) has broken down into the successive, overlapping stages of protest, despair, and detachment. If the separation is sufficiently prolonged, the child will show no relief or satisfaction when the mother returns but will seem apathetic and disinterested, a condition that may persist into later years. In cases of briefer separation, a period of detachment may be succeeded by ambivalent phases of alternate rejection and demands for parental attention.

René Spitz (1945) contrasted the development of infants living in a foundling home with those reared in a prison nursery. Although physical care was good in the foundling home, the infants had no opportunity to have close contacts with adults. The infants in the prison nursery, however, had daily sessions with their mothers.

Maternally deprived, young rhesus monkeys huddle together for compensatory close contact.

The foundling-home infants showed various emotional disturbances, states of depression, and actual physical deterioration, sometimes even leading to death. However, institutionalization does not always have such negative results. No doubt the age of the child at the time of institutionalization, the nature of the institution, and the number and character of the caretakers all make a difference.

As was mentioned earlier, there is a difference of opinion as to what constitutes the basic deprivation from which institutionalized children suffer. Spitz believed that it is lack of mother love. Other writers, however, have argued that the basic problem is lack of stimulation. When there are many children and few caretakers, the latter do not have the time to give much personal attention or stimulation to their charges. Wayne Dennis (1960) studied the behavioral development of children in three institutions in Iran. In two of these institutions, the children were greatly retarded in many respects, including the ability to sit alone, to stand, and to walk. In the third institution, the children were not retarded in these respects. Dennis believes that the differences were due to the fact that, in the first two institutions, there was not enough handling of the children by their attendants, who did not place them in the sitting and prone positions. The children were thus not able to learn to sit up and look around but spent most of their time lying on their backs. Lack of experience in the prone position led to failure to learn to creep and to a general retardation of locomotion.

When retardation has developed among institutionalized children, is the condition reversible? Can the experiences of later years overcome the setbacks the children have suffered? An indication that retardation is reversible is provided by a study made by A. I. Rabin of children raised in an Israeli *kibbutz*. A *kibbutz* is a quite different kind of institution from a foundling home or orphanage. Although a child lives with members of his age set in a separate building with nurse supervisors, he continues to see his parents daily for evening visits. This system, which was briefly described in Chapter 7, would not seem to bring about either maternal deprivation or lack of stimulation. Nevertheless, according to Rabin, *kibbutz* children at one year of age were less mature in general development than a control group of children with which they were compared.

Kibbutz children

In the *kibbutz* a mother breast-feeds her baby on demand for the first six weeks, after which the feedings are reduced and the mother resumes work on a part-time basis. There are nurses in charge of the Infant's House, usually one for every five or six children. At six to nine months old, a group of four to six children is assigned a permanent nurse, who stays with the group for the next four or five years, until or after they enter kindergarten. She is thus a kind of surrogate mother. Meanwhile, the real mother continues to visit the child in the evenings, and the child also visits his parents' quarters. Children in such a *kibbutz* are thus reared in an institutional setting but do maintain a continuing, though limited, relationship with the parents.

Rabin (1965) gave various psychological tests to children of the *kibbutz* in four age groups: 1-year-old infants, 10-year-old children, 17-year-old adolescents, and army men of 19 and 20. The same tests were given to a control group from a *Moshav*, a cooperative, but not communal, Israeli settlement, in which the family structure had not been altered. Both communities were primarily agricultural, with the members coming from similar countries of origin. They shared many of the same values and political attitudes and had about the same levels of education. The tests given both groups included a Mental Development Scale, Social Maturity Scale (these two for infants); Draw-a-Person test, Sentence Completions, the Rorschach Test (see p. 309), Blacky pictures for the 4-to-10-year-olds, and the Thematic Apperception Test.

When *kibbutz* and non-*kibbutz* children were tested on general development and social maturity, the non-*kibbutz* children proved to be superior to the *kibbutz* children in both. This might be due to frustration or anxiety among the *kibbutz* children concerning the multiple mothering, reduced identification with adults, and limited contacts with adults and older siblings, which would involve diminished stimulation. In any case, the disparity between the *kibbutz* and non-*kibbutz* children was overcome by the age of 10. The *kibbutz* children tested at 10 years of age proved to be at least as well developed intellectually as the non-*kibbutz* children, and to some extent better, thus reversing the former trend. They were better in ego strength and overall maturity, as measured by the tests, but had less superego development. They showed less intense sibling rivalry and less emotional ambivalence.

Rabin's findings suggest that the early institutional experience in the *kibbutz* does have some depriving features but that there are enough positive aspects in the life of the *kibbutz*, as the child develops, to counteract them.

Loss of contact with a parental figure or emotional rejection of a child by its parents seems to have negative effects on the child in any cultural setting, although these effects may be reversed. Ronald P. Rohner (1975) has argued that parental rejection universally brings in train a complex of personality traits that include hostility, dependency, and low self-esteem.

Freudian theory

Erik Homburger Erikson, a modified Freudian, believes that experiences in the first year of life, especially in relation to the mother, establish a sense of basic trust or else basic mistrust. This period corresponds to Freud's oral stage, when much of the child's contact with the outside world, including its mother, is channeled through the mouth and lips. If sufficient trust is acquired during the first year of life, the child moves on to a succeeding stage when, according to Erikson (1963:chap. 7), there is a conflict between the sense of autonomy and feelings of shame and doubt. This period (the second year) corresponds to Freud's anal stage, when toilet training is initiated in many societies. During this period the child develops a sense of control over himself and his environment and learns both literally and figuratively to stand on his own two feet, although he is still dependent on his parents. The years from three to five are a period of rapid physical development and locomotion, awareness of genital sensations, and the appearance of the Freudian Oedipus complex, in which attachment to the mother is combined with jealous hostility toward the father. Freud calls this period the phallic stage, which is followed by a latency period of sexual quiescence until the coming of puberty and the attainment of genital primacy. From Freud's point of view, traumas and disappointments during this developmental sequence may lead to fixation at a particular stage or regression to an earlier one, if the trauma is sufficiently severe, thus forming neurotic or psychotic personality patterns. The child's ego is vulnerable to traumatic experiences because it is still in the process of development, not yet ready to cope with crises which it could handle easily at a later stage of maturity. Freudian interpretations of childhood psychosexual development are not accepted by everyone, but they have influenced many anthropologists in the field of culture-and-personality.

Maturation and development

Stages of motor development in childhood may vary somewhat because of cultural factors. Thus, Balinese children do not go through a crawling phase, as American children do, because they are habitually carried about by the mother and other persons during the first year of life. Creeping on all fours is disapproved of as animal-like. Hence, Balinese children are less active than American children of that age (Mead and MacGregor 1951:42 ff).

The tempo of maturation in some respects may be affected by cultural patterns. The development of infants in Uganda is a case in point. When compared with the stage of development of European infants of the same age, all aspects of development among Uganda children during their first two years have been reported to be "precocious," including prehension, manipulation, adaptivity, and language development. It has been stated that Uganda children can sit alone a couple of months before English children, and the same is reported of crawling, standing, and walking. There may be a problem here as to whether observers of children in different countries have used the same definitions or criteria of such acts as "sitting," "crawling," and "standing." However, Marcelle Géber, who examined 252 Uganda infants and young children in or near Kampala, believes they manifest precocity in these respects, and she attributes it to close mother-child relationship, demand feeding, and intimate physical contact. Géber suggests that the way the child is carried on the mother's back may strengthen its ability to hold

Uganda baby with mother.

the head steady and may help the child to sit alone earlier. If so, this shows the importance of stimulating experience and close maternal contact in the child's first year of life, just as the studies of institutionalized children reveal the consequences of their absence or scarcity.

The precocity of Uganda children is less marked in their second year of life, and, after three years of age, Uganda children are less advanced than European children. This decline is thought to be due to the traumatic abruptness of the weaning process in Uganda and to a subsequent diminution of mother-child interaction. When another baby is born, the mother gives her full attention to the new infant and pays little attention to older children, who have few toys and playthings and engage in few organized activities. There is reported to be relatively little stimulation for them after the first year (Ainsworth 1967). Claims of precocity have been made for the children of other sub-Saharan nations besides Uganda.[1]

---

[1] For a critical review of this literature, see Warren 1972.

Child-rearing practices in different societies

In some societies the amount of mother-child contact and interaction is greater than in our own. This is true, for example, in Japan, where there is more continuous sleeping together of mother and child and more closeness in back-carrying and bathing patterns (Barnouw 1973:223–27). Comparable patterns occur in some other societies. There are societies that have a postpartum sex taboo for a year or more after the child is born; the parents then have no sexual relations, and throughout this period the child sleeps with its mother. Some writers have argued that this must establish strong dependent ties on the mother or an identification with her on the part of the child. A long suckling period is believed to have the same result, although that may be countered by later experiences. Societies differ greatly in the length of the suckling period. In the United States it is generally very brief, in comparison to most other societies. In one of the earliest studies to make use of the Human Relations Area Files, John W. M. Whiting and Irvin L. Child found that in 75 societies the median age of weaning was two and a half years old.

Like the satisfaction of oral needs, the manner of toilet training is also held to influence personality, whether it is instituted early or late in life and the extent to which lapses are punished. In the study just mentioned, Whiting and Child (1953) drew attention to the fact that anal training is stricter in the United States than in most other societies studied. Slightly over half of the primitive societies begin toilet training somewhere between the ages of one and a half and two and a half years old.

It is understandable that nomadic people would be less fussy about toilet training than middle-class Americans who have wall-to-wall carpeting. The nomadic Sirionó of Bolivia, for example, make little effort to teach sphincter control to their children and do not punish them for soiling. These differences in child-training patterns in different societies must have consequences for personality formation, although this has not been well documented by anthropologists. Severe toilet training in early childhood is believed to generate compulsive tendencies involving such personality traits as fussiness, pedantry, obstinacy, self-righteousness, and suspicion of others. Belief that severe toilet training leads to such traits rests on clinical evidence, which some writers have rejected (Orlansky 1949) and others have supported (Axelrad 1962).

Sexual disciplines vary considerably in different societies, as was noted in Chapter 17, and this too must have different consequences in personality formation. The latency period, which Freud distinguished as a phase of childhood in which there is a loss of interest in sex, was declared by Malinowski (1953) to be missing among the

Trobriand Islanders, who are very permissive in their acceptance of sex play among children. Adolescence is traditionally a time of "storm and stress" in the Western world, but Margaret Mead (1928) found this was not the case among Samoan girls, where, again, there are permissive attitudes toward premarital lovemaking. Although culture impinges at every phase in the developmental cycle, this is not, of course, to deny the importance of biological or biochemical factors. The cultural context may, however, place them in a different configuration in one society than in another.

An outstanding work in culture-and-personality is *The People of Alor* (1944) by Cora DuBois. This study not only relied upon the observation of behavior and interviews with informants but also made use of some psychological tests, particularly the Rorschach (ink blot) Test, which was given to 37 subjects. This test consists of ten bilaterally symmetrical inkblots which are always shown to test subjects in the same order. The subject is required to tell what he or she sees in the blots. Although the blots are objectively the same for all subjects, the responses given to them vary enormously. This shows that the persons taking the test project something into the blots, which is why the Rorschach is called a *projective* test. Analysis of the nature of the subject's responses provides clues to his personality organization. DuBois also collected children's drawings from 33 boys and 22 girls and recorded eight rather long life histories. **The Alor study**

One innovation of this project was the procedure of "blind analysis," submitting the projective materials to different specialists who were given no information about the culture. The Rorschachs were analyzed by a Rorschach analyst, the drawings by a drawing analyst, and the life histories were analyzed by Abram Kardiner. Each specialist was required to give a general personality description of the Alorese on the basis of the material submitted. If these descriptions had turned out to differ quite a bit from one another, one would have been inclined to doubt the validity of the methods employed. As it turned out, however, there was a good deal of congruence among the reports and agreement with the impressions of the ethnographer. This method minimized the possibility of bias and subjectivity in the personality description of the Alorese.

Emil Oberholzer, the Rorschach analyst, remarked that the Alorese were suspicious and mistrustful of one another. He concluded that they were passive and uncreative, lacking in goals that involved sustained effort. He assumed that the Alorese readily gave way to emotional outbursts, rage, and temper and that they did not have close friendships.

The drawing analyst remarked that the children had a feeling of aloneness and lacked creativity.

Kardiner observed that parental figures were not idealized and that superego formation was weak.

What aspects of life are responsible for this depressing picture? Kardiner and DuBois believe that it is largely due to maternal neglect in infancy. This is a society in which the women play the main role in subsistence; they are the agriculturalists, while the men busy themselves with the financial exchanges of pigs, gongs, and kettledrums. Between ten days and two weeks after the birth of a child, the mother returns to the fields to resume regular agricultural work. She does not take the baby with her to the fields, as is done in some societies, but leaves it in the care of its father, brother, sister, or grandparents. She is gone most of the day. A child may sometimes be nursed by another woman, but, since such substitutes are not consistently available, the child suffers from oral deprivation. When the mother comes home in late afternoon, she offers her child the breast. According to DuBois, frustrations become worse after the walking stage is reached. The child is no longer carried about and thus loses the constant skin contact and support previously experienced. He is fed irregularly by older siblings and others. Teasing of the child and provoking jealousy is practiced by mothers. Youngsters are playfully menaced by adults with knives and threats of cutting off their hands or ears.

Temper tantrums are a common aspect of Alorese childhood. They occur when the mother sets off for the fields in the morning. A child may then go into a rage and beat his head on the ground. These tantrums begin to cease around the age of five or six.

Kardiner and DuBois find the explanation for Alorese personality traits in these childhood frustrations. Relations between men and women in adult life are strained; they average two divorces apiece. It is interpreted that male-female tensions develop from the child's original ambivalence toward the mother and the male's continuing search for a nurturing mother. Since the wife cannot adequately fill this nurturant role, the frustrations persist.

Although criticisms have been made of some aspects of this study, *The People of Alor* remains an impressive accomplishment. If the reader is skeptical of some of the analytic interpretations, he can examine the data on which they are based. The life histories make up about half the book. Many of the children's drawings are reproduced. Some of the Rorschach records are presented, together with Oberholzer's detailed analysis of the records.

Abram Kardiner has made some broad generalizations about the basic personality structure of the Western world, which he believes has remained essentially the same for the past 3,000 years (Kardiner et al. 1945:432). Kardiner says this because characters like Job and others in the Old Testament, and the characters in plays of Sophocles and Shakespeare are much like ourselves. The Western basic personality structure is based on good maternal care, which makes possible a strong attachment to parents, a capacity to idealize the parent and to form a strong superego. Belief in a loving father God is associated with this. The religious concepts of Judaism and Christianity are seen as being projections of this childhood experience, which is not very different, according to Kardiner (1945:365), in different economic or social classes.

Personality in the Western world

The good parental care gives scope to investigative, constructive, and artistic capacities (Kardiner et al. 1945:451). Thus we have a syndrome antithetical to that of Alor, which is described as having a lack of interest in the outer world, in artistic creation, and in the making of shrines and effigies of the gods. Kardiner sees childhood experience and adult projection systems as having remained much the same in the Western world for 3,000 years.

There are other views of the history of childhood which present quite a different picture. According to Philippe Ariès (1965), childhood was a relatively happy time in the Middle Ages in Europe, when there were no divisions of rank or ages. Children were treated as adults, wore the same kinds of clothes, and played the same games. People had more leisure and spent more time with children and in sociable entertainment and play. The facts of life and death were not hidden from children. But this changed in the 17th century, when boys were dressed like girls and wore lace collars, although girls went on dressing like grown women. Boys were the first specialized children. They began to go to school in large numbers in the late 16th and early 17th century, while girls' education developed much more slowly. Ariès thus sees a decline of freedom and spontaneity in childhood in Europe.

A different picture is given by Lloyd de Mause (1974:28, 32–33), another historian of childhood, who believes that the lot of children has greatly improved in the course of time. Infanticide was a regular practice in antiquity, and killing children was not considered murder in Rome until A.D. 374. Children were very tightly swaddled in medieval Europe. Wealthy parents turned infants over to wet nurses, and later they were cared for by other servants, so they spent little time with their parents. Fosterage was a common European practice; infants were dispatched to be reared in another family, and well-to-do children were sent out to apprenticeship, monastery, or school by the age of seven. Punishments for misbehavior were severe; not until the 19th century did whipping go out of style.

James Bruce Ross (1974) presents a similar picture for urban Italy from the 14th to early 16th centuries. Whereas a Kardinerian interpretation would see the popularity of the madonna-and-infant motif in the Italian painting of that time as representing a projection of good maternal care, the data presented by de Mause and Ross suggest a contrasting view: perhaps it was a compensation for earlier deprivation and a fantasy of the enjoyment of motherly love. The following four stages characterized the lives of middle-class urban boys in Renaissance Italy: (1) removal from mother to wet nurse, (2) return to the family after two years' absence, (3) school education at seven, and (4) apprenticeship at a bank or shop at ten to twelve. Ross (1974:216) asks the intriguing question: "How could the deprived and neglected infants of the middle classes develop into the architects of a vigorous and creative era which we call 'the Renaissance'?" However, a review of the early childhood of unusual men and women (Illingsworth and Illingsworth 1966) shows that many outstanding, creative persons had most unhappy childhoods.

The Six Cultures project

The fullest and most ambitious investigation in the cross-cultural study of childhood was undertaken by a group of scholars from Cornell, Harvard, and Yale under the direction of William W. Lambert, Irvin L. Child, and John W. M. Whiting (Whiting 1963; Minturn and Lambert 1964; Whiting and Whiting 1975). An effort was made to bring about comparability in the ethnographic reports of the six teams of investigators involved in this project. Each team spent from 6 to 14 months in the field. The six communities studied were: a Gusii community in Kenya, East Africa; a Rājpūt community in northern India; a village on Okinawa; a town in Mexico; a barrio in the Philippines; and a New England town in the United States. Each field team, usually consisting of a husband and wife, worked in a community of between 50 and 100 families and with a sample of 24 mothers, each of whom had at least one child aged three to ten years. The mothers were interviewed on a standard schedule, and the children were systematically observed and interviewed. Each team was provided with a guide, John W. M. Whiting et al., *Field Guide for a Study of Socialization in Five Societies* (1954).

The last production of the Six Cultures project was a review by Whiting and Whiting (1975), in which the authors found some consistent differences between the three culturally more complex groups (in India, Okinawa, and the United States) and the three simpler ones (in Africa, Mexico, and the Philippines). Cultural complexity was determined by such factors as the degree of occupational and religious specialization, differentiation of settlement patterns, social stratification and political centralization. In the simpler group, children were on the whole more nurturant and responsible, in keeping with demands for cooperation and performance of chores within the family and community. In the more complex societies there was more schooling and also evidence of more egoism and competitiveness among the children. The simpler societies assigned more chores to children and assigned them at an earlier age. This is a general feature in many tribal and peasant societies. Bringing firewood and water, taking care of animals, farm work, running errands, and looking after junior siblings are common experiences in many parts of the world. Since this work represents a real contribution, the regular performance of such tasks must give many of these children feelings of worth, responsibility, and competence, although they must also often resent these obligations.

In societies with formal education, children cannot be saddled with so many chores, since they must attend school for part of the day. The more complex societies are hierarchically organized, which may encourage competitiveness and orientation toward achievement. Whiting and Whiting (1975:128) found that "Children brought up in complex cultures tended to be more dependent-dominant and less nurturant-responsible than children brought up in simpler cultures."

The Six Cultures project has provided detailed information about how children are brought up in six different sociocultural worlds and should be amenable to analysis from various theoretical points of view. Whiting's *Field Guide* has been used by other ethnologists in the organization of their fieldwork and will undoubtedly be so used in the future, which will provide more comparable accounts of different cultures.

Culture, cognition, and perception

Not only is personality directed along somewhat different lines in different cultural settings, but the same is true of cognition and perception. Consider, for example, the Müller-Lyer illusion (see Figure A). The Müller-Lyer illusion is that the horizontal line to the left in Figure A looks longer than the one on the right but is the same length. Non-Western subjects in parts of Melanesia, South India, and Africa are less susceptible to this illusion than are Europeans and Americans. Segall, Campbell, and Herskovits (1966), who tested 1,878 persons in 14 non-European areas and in the United States, suggest that people who live in a "carpentered world" and have an "experience with two-dimensional representation of reality," as

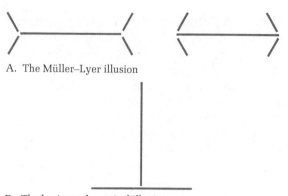

A. The Müller–Lyer illusion

B. The horizontal–vertical illusion

Western peoples do, are more susceptible to the Müller-Lyer illusion than are non-Western peoples. They also suggest that people who inhabit areas with broad horizontal vistas are more likely to be subject to the horizontal-vertical illusion (Figure B) than are persons who live in restricted environments such as forests. The illusion in the latter figure is that the vertical line is longer, although both lines are equal. While the data amassed by Segall, Campbell, and Herskovits fit their hypotheses, there are other studies which do not confirm or only partially confirm their findings (Price-Williams 1975: 11–14). Still, it does seem to have been shown that the nature of one's culture and environment influences some aspects of visual perception.

To consider another aspect of perception, individuals differ in the speed with which they can find a hidden figure embedded in a picture. Herman A. Witkin and his associates (1962) use the term "field independent" for those who are quick to do so, while "field dependent" persons have difficulty in separating the figure from the organized ground. Persons respond consistently in three different kinds of tests for these differences in cognitive style (Witkin 1967). Field independence is seen to represent a tendency toward psychological differentiation; it increases with age, although a child who is more "field dependent" than his age mates tends to have a similar position as a young adult. Field-dependent persons are said to have a less differentiated body image than field-independent persons and tend to repress their feelings. The tests for field dependence have been given in some different cultures, and contrasting results have been found in some cases. For example, the Temne of Sierra Leone rated high on field dependence, while the Eskimo of Baffin Island proved to be much more field independent (J. W. Berry 1966). Much work has been done recently in the cross-cultural study of perception and cognition, including attempts to test the degree of uniformity in different cultures of the sequence of stages in cognitive development during childhood, which have been distinguished by Jean Piaget (see Dasen 1972). The article by Dasen just cited appears in a new journal devoted to such issues: *Journal of Cross-Cultural Psychology.*

Some of the material in this chapter has been drawn from Victor Barnouw, *Culture and Personality,* rev. ed. (Homewood, Ill.: Dorsey Press, 1973).

Suggestions for further reading

Several good readers are available: Clyde Kluckhohn and Henry A. Murray, eds., *Personality in Nature, Society, and Culture* (New York: Alfred A. Knopf, 1948); Douglas G. Haring, ed., *Personal Character and Cultural Milieu,* 3d ed. (Syracuse, N.Y.: Syracuse University Press, 1956); Bert Kaplan, ed., *Studying Personality Cross-Culturally* (Evanston, Ill.: Row, Peterson & Co., 1961); Francis L. K. Hsu, ed., *Psychological Anthropology* (Cambridge, Mass.: Schenkman, 1972); Robert Hunt, ed., *Personalities and Cultures: Readings in Psychological Anthropology* (New York: Natural History Press, 1967).

Three studies which can be recommended are: Erich Fromm and Michael Maccoby, *Social Character in a Mexican Village: A Sociopsychoanalytic Study* (Englewood Cliffs, N.J.: Prentice-Hall, Inc., 1970); Robert B. Edgerton, *The Individual in Cultural Adaptation. A Study of Four East African Peoples* (Berkeley: University of California Press, 1971); and George A. De Vos, with contributions by Hiroshi Wagatsuma, William Caudill, and Keichi Mizhuma, *Socialization for Achievement: Essays on the Cultural Psychology of the Japanese* (Berkeley: University of California Press, 1973).

For a recent reader on cognition and perception, see J. W. Berry and P. R. Dasen, eds., *Culture and Cognition: Readings in Cross-Cultural Psychology* (London: Methuen and Co., 1974). See also Robert L. Munroe and Ruth H. Munroe, *Cross-Cultural Human Development* (Monterey, Calif.: Brooks/ Cole Publishing Co., 1975).

part ten

Culture change

21

Some aspects of culture change

Our present age is a time of rapid culture change. The cultures of the world have always undergone alterations, but the tempo of such change has varied in different times and places. When Europeans first landed in Australia, they found people who had no agriculture, weaving, or pottery, no clothing, no bow and arrows. This does not mean that the Australian aborigines had experienced no culture change before the coming of Europeans, but, at least in the realm of technology, their hunting-gathering way of life had changed relatively little for thousands of years. An advanced civilization may also have long periods of stability, as was true of Egypt between around 2700 and 1700 B.C. However, change is more likely to take place in a complex society than in a simple one. The more complex a culture is, the more likely it will be to produce innovations, which depend upon combinations of previously existent patterns. Invention of the lost-wax process of casting, for example, was made possible by the prior existence of several inventions (knowledge of the properties of wax, fired clay, and molten metal), just as the development of the atomic bomb depended upon a particular level of knowledge about physics, chemistry, mathematics, and industrial technology. Cultural evolution is cumulative; it has involved an advance through progressively higher plateaus of cultural complexity. The more material there is to work with in the shape of tools, patterns, and ideas, the more possible combinations may be made.

Culture change within a society may be brought about either by internal invention and development or through contact with other societies. New ideas may spread through diffusion, not only between two societies, A and B, which are in contact, but also between socie-

319

ties A and E through intervening societies B, C, and D, which may have trade or other relations with one another. A new item, such as the practice of smoking tobacco, may be passed on directly from one society to another, or else there may be stimulus diffusion, in which a foreign notion stimulates the development of a local innovation, as in the case of the invention of a successful Cherokee syllabary by an Indian who was illiterate but who grasped the basic *principle* of writing (not the system itself) by watching white men read and write.

The term *acculturation* has been given to phenomena involving culture changes that occur when two formerly distinct cultures come into contact with one another. Relations between societies that have different cultural traditions vary in many respects. One variable concerns the extent to which such societies may be said to be "permeable," "flexible," and "open," rather than "rigid" and "closed." Using such terminology, Homer Barnett and his associates (1954) have suggested that "hard-shelled vertebrate" cultural systems, which have many boundary-maintaining mechanisms and rigid internal structures, may be less susceptible to change in acculturation than "soft-shelled invertebrate" cultural systems, which are more "open" and "flexible."

Societies are apt to be selective in what innovations they accept from others. Ruth Benedict (1934) showed that, although the Hopi,

Zuñi, and other Pueblo Indians of the Southwest had long been in contact with non-Pueblo tribes, such as the Apache and Navaho, they did not accept from other tribes various cultural patterns that ran counter to their own values, such as the use of drugs, self-torture, or ecstatic religious practices.

Even when an alien culture pattern is accepted by members of a receiving society, they may consciously or unconsciously change the innovation so that it will fit into their own cultural framework.

The Hopi and Zuñi had highly integrated cultures. If a sufficiently isolated society like that of the Hopi has time to develop an internally consistent way of life, lacking in conflicts and contradictions, we speak of its culture as being *integrated*. This is a relative term, since there are always some internal conflicts in any sociocultural system, but some cultures appear to be more highly integrated than others. This tendency should foster stability; the members of such a society have a similar outlook and a shared set of values.

Integration versus change

Contact with another society may serve to jolt a highly integrated society, however, leading either to a change of values or to reaffirmation of traditional ones. Around 1900 the U.S. government ordered the Hopi of Oraibi to send their children to a government boarding school away from the reservation. This led to a split between the "Friendlies," who favored cooperation with the whites, and the "Hostiles," who opposed it. Since unity of sentiment within a community was important to the Hopi, it was decided that one of the two factions should leave the pueblo. The issue was decided in 1906 by a tug-of-war in the plaza. The Hostiles lost and left Oraibi to found a new settlement. This episode expresses both continuity and change. There was internal conflict, in opposition to Hopi ideals, but it was peacefully resolved by the tug-of-war and the departure of the losing faction. Hopi children did go away to the government school, but this did not dissolve the integration of Hopi culture, as may be seen in the strong affirmation of Hopi values by one of the school graduates from Oraibi who wrote the best autobiography we have by an American Indian (Simmons 1942).

In some cases, an integrated culture may break up quickly under the impact of outside forces. This seems to have happened on the small island of Tikopia in western Polynesia, whose population was 1,281 in 1929. There were four clans, each associated with the magical control of aspects of nature. One clan had control over yams, another over taro, a third over breadfruit, and a fourth over coconuts. Each clan was also associated with one of the wind points or directions from which rains and storms came. Elaborate religious rituals involving mutual reciprocal behavior between the clans, headed by their chiefs, who acted as priests, served to promote the growth of crops and success of fishing expeditions.

Despite all this reciprocity and interdependence, there was also rivalry between the clans and districts of the island, which may have contributed to the breakup of the system. In 1923 the chief of one of the four clans became converted to Christianity and ordered the people of his district to do the same. Before this time there had been a drought and poor crops for about eight months. Since the weather got better after the conversion, it was taken as a sign that the new religion was effective. The defecting clan chief no longer took part in the traditional crop-promoting rituals, leaving a gap in the religious fabric. By 1929 half of the island had become Christian. A final blow to the old system came in 1955, when 200 people died in an epidemic, including two of the clan chiefs. One of these was succeeded by a Christian, which left only two non-Christian chiefs. These men then decided to convert to the new religion, and most of their clan members followed suit. A highly elaborate, integrated religious system thus dissolved within a generation, to be replaced by a foreign one imported by missionaries.[1]

Early learning versus change

It has been argued that culture patterns learned early in life are more resistant to change than those acquired at later age levels. Edward M. Bruner (1956) has made a case for this hypothesis in explaining why the Mandan-Hidatsa Indians have preserved some aspects of their traditional culture (such as the kinship system, role conceptions and values), while others, such as the age-grade-society system and the religious complex, have disappeared. The former patterns were learned early in life from members of Ego's lineage, while the latter patterns were learned late from persons who were not members of Ego's lineage. It would be interesting to see how well this hypothesis is supported in studies of other cultures in contact situations.

Efforts to resist change

In some integrated cultures, innovations are resisted because of ideological traditions. On religious grounds, the more conservative members of the Old Order Amish of Pennsylvania will not use such modern contraptions as automobiles, telephones, and radios; they will not even use buttons on their clothes but have hooks and eyes instead.

---

[1] This process has been traced in detail in a series of books by Raymond Firth, beginning with *We, The Tikopia* (1936).

In some cases an ideology favoring conservatism affects outsiders. The anthropologist Verrier Elwin (1943) strongly opposed contacts between aboriginal hill tribes in India and the outside world. It was his belief that the hill tribes had a vigorous, creative way of life that would be spoiled by the growing influence of village India. Elwin's campaign to isolate the hill tribes was attacked by Indian nationalists who wanted to develop a unified, modern nation.

Vested interests may oppose culture change, such as a doctor's opposition to Medicare or socialized medicine, or the rejection by 17th-century theologians of Galileo's assertion that the earth revolved around the sun. Factory workers may oppose automation, which deprives them of jobs.

Efforts to induce change

For ideological reasons, certain agents seek to induce culture change, such as the missionaries of proselytizing sects or the members of revolutionary movements. An agriculture extension agent tries to persuade farmers to plant a new type of corn or use a new farming technique.

Culture change in regard to industrialization and modernization is deliberately planned by modern governments, such as in the five-year plans of the Soviet Union, India, and other nations. The space program and moon explorations of the United States provide another example. Deliberate planning for change in some aspects is carried out by modern industrial corporations as well.

Reform movements are also agents of change. Abolition of slavery, women's suffrage, the black-power movement, and antiwar protests are all attempts to bring about changes in public opinion and the laws of the land.

Different segments of the population respond differently to such campaigns and to culture change in general. Being more flexible and less committed to tradition, young people are often more receptive to new alternatives than are members of older age brackets. According to Everett E. Hagen (1962), members of groups that have lost status are more eager for culture change than are members of the establishment in an agrarian or developing society.

As the world becomes smaller, the technologically advanced societies come into ever closer contact with less advanced ones. When new gadgets such as electric ranges and refrigerators first appear in a new setting, as in New Guinea, it is usually only a small minority of well-to-do, non-native people who can afford to get them. Feelings of "relative deprivation" consequently develop among the natives, who did not have such feelings before. They may resent and envy the possessors of such goods, the higher standard of living they enjoy, and the attitude of superiority they may express. The sense of relative deprivation may in time lead to the development of nationalistic or revolutionary political movements, or else to nativistic religious cults, such as the Cargo cults of Melanesia (see p. 246). In either case, changes in culture follow, involving changes in attitudes, values, and feelings of group solidarity and political cohesion among the rebels or the cultists.

Internal causes of change

A distinction may be made between internal and external causes of culture change. The former have to do with human motivation, while the latter concern environmental or situational factors.

Great man theory

To emphasize the role of the inventor or innovator is to invoke the internal principle. A man of inventive mind or genius makes a new discovery, which is transmitted to others and thus becomes part of the now-modified culture. This is sometimes called the great man theory. A. L. Kroeber and Leslie A. White both criticized this notion by pointing to simultaneous discoveries of the same invention by different men. Their point is that, when culture has reached a certain level, some particular inventions are inevitable and will be made sooner or later by somebody. Moreover, to become part of culture, a new invention must be shared with others. A genius may make a discovery that is ahead of his time; if he cannot convey his meaning, it will not be incorporated into the culture. Leonardo da Vinci made sketches of airplanes in his notebooks, but the technology of his age was not ready for further advances in this field; his sketches remained confined to his notes. It may be that other brilliant men of Leonardo's period made similar sketches and speculations, but nothing could come of them then.

Isaac Newton and G. W. Leibniz both invented the infinitesimal calculus. Anticipating the views of Kroeber and White, Thomas Babington Macaulay wrote in 1828: ". . . mathematical science, indeed, had then reached such a point that, if neither of them had ever existed, the principle must inevitably have occurred to some person within a few years" (Macaulay 1877:324).

Gregor Mendel gave two reports on his discoveries in genetics before the Brünn Society for the Study of Natural Science in 1865, and he published a paper on his findings in that society's proceedings in 1866. But Mendel apparently spoke to deaf ears; no attention was given to his work until the simultaneous rediscovery of his principles by three men in 1900: W. O. Focke, Hugo de Vries, and

Gregor Mendel.

Karl Correns. These cases seem to illustrate the "inevitability" argument.

However, some support for the great man theory has come from Tertius Chandler, who claims that in these cases the men did not work independently. Newton and Leibniz corresponded with each other, and Mendel's work was not altogether forgotten, for Correns knew of it by 1897. Chandler reviews a series of alleged parallel discoveries and in most cases is able to single out an originator who preceded the others. His conclusion (1960:497) is: "Where originality is needed, one man of keen mind is required. If he fail, the job may well stay undone forever." However, it is necessary to remember the point made earlier: a certain level of cultural evolution may be necessary before a new invention or pattern can be assimilated in a society.

It may be noted that the argument about parallel discoveries concerns inventions but could not be applied so well to the arts. Could we say that if Beethoven had not lived, someone else would have written his Fifth Symphony?

Protestant ethic and achievement motivation

Apart from the great man theory, there have been other "internal" explanations for culture change that emphasize the role of motivation. Some related examples are Max Weber's notion of the Protestant ethic, David Riesman's theory of inner direction, and David C. McClelland's concept of achievement motivation.

The sociologist Max Weber noted that the great economic advance in Europe after the Industrial Revolution was associated with Protestant rather than Catholic countries, and he concluded that this was due to the greater Protestant stress on independence, asceticism, and hard work.

David Riesman coined the phrase "inner direction" for a means of ensuring conformity in a society undergoing population growth and economic expansion. This is a time of opening frontiers, economic opportunities, and greater individualism than in a traditional society with a stable population. Wealth, fame, and achievement are goals toward which people strive through hard work and determination. At a later period, when a modern, industralized state has developed and population growth has slackened off, a new mode of conformity develops, which Riesman calls "other direction." The production system now demands harmonious working within an established organization and a personality that is adaptable to the moods and feelings of others (Riesman 1950).

David C. McClelland's work (1961) is related to the ideas of Weber and Riesman. For McClelland, the Protestant ethic is only a special case of a more general phenomenon, since there are non-Protestant countries, such as modern Japan and the Soviet Union, that have a similar stress on hard work. McClelland sees the key psychological factor as being a high need for achievement, which he believes precedes economic growth, and he has found some ingenious ways to demonstrate this point. He cites some studies which indicate that parental attitudes in childhood may stimulate a need for achievement by setting high standards while granting autonomy to the children, so that they can work things out for themselves.

Studies in Japan have indicated that personality tendencies analogous to the Protestant ethic, with a high need for achievement, help to account for the remarkable economic development of that nation (Bellah 1957; De Vos 1973).

External causes of change

There are various external sources of culture change, such as population increase, wars, and economic dislocation, among others. Only a few examples will be cited here.

Population increase

Population increase as a "prime mover" forms the basis for various theories about cultural evolution. According to Lewis R. Binford (1968) and Kent V. Flannery (1969), population increase in sedentary Mesolithic communities in the Old World led to a budding off of daughter groups which impinged on surrounding marginal populations. Groups in the marginal zone were forced to adopt a broad-spectrum pattern of food exploitation, including wild grains and cereals, from which the domestication of plants ultimately developed.

According to Ester Boserup (1965), population increase in horticultural societies leads to a shortening of the fallow period and the adoption of more intensive advanced forms of agriculture. As we saw in Chapter 14, population increase in a circumscribed setting provides the basis for Robert L. Carneiro's explanation for the origin of the state.

Economic dislocation

The Industrial Revolution and its accompanying commercial revolution not only shook up the European nations, where they originated, but also were exported abroad, introducing the standards of a money economy into societies that had not formerly known them. In colonial countries, peasants were under pressure to switch from subsistence farming to cash crops. Toward the end of the 18th century in India, the British East India company demanded that revenue be paid in cash instead of in crops, as formerly, which forced peasants to turn to cash crops, such as cotton, indigo, and opium, in order to pay their taxes. The rise in rural indebtedness led to a rise of moneylenders and the spread of Marwaris, who specialized in this field, to all parts of India. The hand of the moneylender was strengthened by new laws introduced in the courts, under which land could be attached and sold for nonpayment of revenue, a new state of affairs for the peasant. At the same time, many artisans like weavers were losing their markets, since England imported cheap factory-made goods into India.

In all colonial areas the world of the peasant was thrown into upheaval. In *Peasant Wars of the Twentieth Century* (1969), Eric R. Wolf documented the similar dislocations, problems, and responses of the peasants in six countries: Mexico, Russia, China, Vietnam, Algeria, and Cuba.

The colonial system also introduced new inventions into these countries, the products of Europe's Industrial Revolution, which, of course, brought many more changes. To use India again in illustration: In 1817 a line of telegraphs was installed between Calcutta and Nagpur. Steam navigation on the Ganges River began in 1828, and the first railway started in 1853.

**Rampur
revisited**

In January 1973 the author paid a brief visit to the village of Rampur, whose *jajmani* system was described in Chapter 12. This village has changed remarkably since 1952–53, when Oscar Lewis did his research there. To mention some of these changes will give an idea of how the lives of many peasants are being transformed today.

The first big change is that a surfaced road now goes directly to the village, and there is regular bus service (about every two hours) between Delhi and Rampur. In 1953, villagers had to walk two miles to catch a bus to Delhi, and most transportation to and from the village was by bullock cart. Moreover, the city can be said to be closer to Rampur than it was in 1953, since Delhi has been steadily expanding, and the highway that passes near Rampur is lined with factories that were not there a few years ago. These provide some of the new job opportunities for men in Rampur.

The second big change is that electricity was brought to the village around 1963. Almost all houses now have electric lights. There are two television sets and about 50 radios in the village.

At the time of Lewis' study the members of lower castes tended to live in one-room mud houses, while the upper castes lived in homes made of fired brick. Now, all of the houses in the village are made of fired brick, including the homes of the Chamars, the untouchable leatherworkers.

There has been a great increase in education, particularly for girls. In 1953 only 40 girls from Rampur attended school, and their education was limited to the ages between 5 and 14. Now, there is a secondary school for girls in Rampur (grades 6 through 11), with an enrollment of 270, some coming from neighboring villages. This school has one of the two TV sets in the village. (The other one, provided by the government, is in one of the men's clubhouses.) The girls (most of whom are married) watch TV programs that are broadcast to schools throughout Delhi state, dealing with science and instruction in English.

One villager estimated that about 70 percent of the men in Rampur now have jobs in Delhi. Twenty tractors used in the village have taken the place of farmhands. Thus, Rampur is being more intricately incorporated into the fabric of an expanding industrial city.

Summary

To summarize some of the points made in this chapter: We have seen that societies vary in rates of culture change. Cultural complexity favors culture change, since there is more material to work with and more possible combinations to be made. Change may come about either through internal invention or else through contact with other societies. Such contacts need not be direct but may be mediated through intervening societies.

Societies are apt to be selective in what new culture patterns they accept from others. They also often bring about changes in the innovations that are accepted, so that they will be in keeping with the society's particular cultural configuration. A highly integrated culture may resist change. On the other hand, once new patterns are accepted in such a society, culture change may rapidly take place, with factional splits developing in the process. Vested interests and ideological traditions may either resist or encourage such changes.

A distinction may be made between internal causes (involving human motivation) and external (environmental) causes of culture change. The great man theory emphasizes the role of the inventor or innovator, while cultural evolutionists of the Leslie White school play down this role by pointing to the frequency of independent parallel inventions. The role of individual motivation is emphasized in such concepts as Weber's Protestant ethic, Riesman's inner direction, and McClelland's need for achievement. Among the external causes of culture change to which analysts have drawn attention are such factors as population increase and the economic dislocations brought about by the great transformations of the industrial and commercial revolutions and by colonialism.

Suggestions for further reading

Still a good source for the discussion of culture change is A. L. Kroeber, *Anthropology* (New York: Harcourt, Brace & Co., 1948), especially Chapters 9–12. A work often cited is Homer G. Barnett, *Innovation: The Basis of Cultural Change* (New York: McGraw-Hill Book Co., 1953). See also Homer G. Barnett et al., "Acculturation: An Exploratory Formulation," *American Anthropologist*, vol. 56 (1954), pp. 973–1002; Godfrey Wilson and Monica Wilson, *The Analysis of Social Change* (Cambridge, England: Cambridge University Press, 1945).

On cultural evolution, see Leslie A. White, *The Evolution of Culture* (New York: McGraw-Hill Book Co., 1959); Julian H. Steward, *Theory of Culture Change: The Methodology of Multilinear Evolution* (Urbana: University of Illinois Press, 1955).

22

Applied anthropology

The world's population of about 3 billion is expected to double within the next 35 years. The doubling will occur sooner in the so-called developing nations than in the industrially more advanced ones. Before World War II, developing nations such as those of Latin America were exporters of grain, but now they must import grain to feed their people. The world's food resources are not increasing sufficiently to keep up with the rise in population; hence, many demographers and agronomists warn that widespread famines will strike the world before long. Famines were already reported during 1974 for parts of North Africa, India, and Bangladesh. A so-called green revolution, involving the use of new seeds, has improved matters in parts of Southeast Asia and India, but population increase still poses a threat in those regions.

To cope with these problems, many countries have instituted village development programs. For example, in its first Five-Year Plan, in 1951 India launched a Community Development Movement that had multiple aims, including the following: land reclamation and increased irrigation; development of rural electrification; provision of fertilizers and improved seeds; spreading of agricultural information; introduction of better agricultural implements and practices; provision of marketing and credit facilities; improvement of roads and transportation; increase of education; public health work in sanitation, drainage, waste disposal, control of malaria, and other diseases; provision of medical care and midwife services; and many other programs.

The U.S. government has given aid in such enterprises in Point Four agricultural programs and through the Agency for International

Development. Private foundations, such as the Ford Foundation, and churches, missions, and other agencies have all tried in various ways to help increase the agricultural productivity of less-developed nations and improve their conditions of health.

Much good work has, of course, been accomplished along these lines. But observers have often been surprised that agricultural improvements are sometimes not welcomed by the farmers; improved seeds are rejected and health facilities not used. There are many reasons for such failures. Sometimes it is necessary to study the culture of the community in question to understand why a particular project failed. This is one of the roles of the applied anthropologist, or action anthropologist. Sometimes he may also be able to suggest ways of overcoming the difficulty, whatever it is, although this is not always possible. Let us consider some examples of resistance to or rejection of innovations.

Resistance to innovations

Improved seeds

If an agricultural extension worker tries to persuade a group of farmers to use a new type of seed, one might expect that they would be willing to try it, since he is, after all, a man of authority. But farmers are often reluctant to do so. This is true not only of peasants in India or Latin America but also of farmers in Texas, who, in the 1930s, were very disinclined to try the new hybrid corn then being introduced. One farmer jokingly offered to plant some of the new seed if the extension man would promise to pay the difference in profit if the new seed produced less than the old. The extension worker decided to take the chance; so half of a field was planted with the old seed and half with the new. The hybrid variety was drought-resistant, and during that summer there was little rain. The old seeds thus fared poorly, while the hybrid corn grew up bright green. All the farmers round about came to look at the field and became convinced, but it required this demonstration to turn the tide of public opinion (Arensberg and Niehoff 1964:84–85).

Although new seeds may be introduced in this way, farmers sometimes reject them after a trial. Hybrid corn was introduced into a Spanish-American community in New Mexico in 1946. A demonstration plot yielded a harvest three times the normal one. By 1947 about three fourths of the farmers were using the hybrid seed, but two years later almost all of them had reverted to the former variety. The reason was that the women of the community did not like the hybrid corn; it did not hang together well in the making of tortillas, and they did not care for the taste (Apadaca 1952). A similar response has been reported for some villages in India where new seeds have been introduced. In one community the villagers acknowledged the superiority of the new seed with regard to yield, disease resistance, and other qualities, but they preferred their old variety on grounds of taste and amenability in food preparation (Dube 1958:133). In another Indian village it was found that the cows and bullocks did not like the straw of the new wheat, and it did not make good thatching for roofs. The old wheat was not used just for food but served multiple purposes (Marriott 1952).

It may sound strange, but taste preferences have had a conservative effect in Indian villages with regard to the use of cow dung for fuel. The villagers realize that manure would be more valuable as fertilizer than as fuel, but they find that burning cow dung is the best way to slowly heat milk in preparing ghee, or clarified butter, an essential part of their diet. It is also the most satisfactory fuel to use in smoking water pipes; the use of other fuels reduces the pleasure (Dube 1958:134).

Consumption of milk among Zulus

The Zulus of southwestern Natal had bad health conditions in 1940; their infant mortality rate was very high, and more than 80 percent of the people showed signs of malnutrition. Pellagra and kwashiorkor, a disease afflicting severely malnourished infants and children, were common; there was much tuberculosis, venereal disease, and dysentery. One of the efforts made by members of a health center was to urge the Zulus to consume more eggs and milk. For various reasons, eggs were not commonly eaten; it was thought uneconomical to eat an egg that might later hatch, and eating eggs was considered a sign of greed and a source of licentiousness among girls. However, these ideas were not strongly held, and the members of the health center, through an educational campaign, were able to increase egg consumption considerably.

Milk proved to be more of a problem. The Zulus raise cattle and are much attached to them. Milk was thus available and was consumed by the men, but a complex of beliefs restricted milk consumption by women. The milk produced by a man's cattle can only be consumed by members of his kin group. One cannot get milk from another family. Moreover, once women have started to menstruate, they must not pass near cattle or drink milk. A married woman who lives with her husband's people is under a double restriction, being in a different kin group. Hence, married women were the persons least likely to drink milk. Members of the health center could not challenge this deep-seated belief system. At the same time, they wanted to provide better nutrition, including milk, for expectant and lactating mothers. This problem seemed insuperable, but there turned out to be a surprisingly easy partial solution: introduction of powdered milk. The Zulus knew that this was milk, but it was different, not subject to the taboos and restrictions of "real" milk, and milk consumption rapidly rose.

The workers at the health center were also able to increase the growing and consumption of green vegetables. Through their efforts, there was a marked decrease in malnutrition within a ten-year period. The incidence of kwashiorkor fell from 12 to more cases a week to less than 12 cases a year (Cassell 1955).

Compost pits in an Indian village

In the villages of northern India, women pile cow dung in a corner of the courtyard or in an open space near the house. Village-level workers engaged in India's community development program

Indian village with dung pile.

tried to persuade the villagers to place refuse and dung in compost pits outside the village. This could be more sanitary; it would help clean up the village and preserve manure more effectively. However, in some villages, although compost pits were dug, they remained unused.

Although women of high caste may handle cow dung and stack it up near their homes, they do not want to be seen carrying dung to the edge of the village. Very few families have servants to do such work, and men cannot do it because it is considered to be women's work. So the traditional practices continued (Dube 1958:68, 71, 135).

Introducing latrines

In community development programs in different parts of the world, efforts have often been made to introduce latrines, for obvious hygienic reasons. Such efforts have been resisted for various reasons. In Uganda, people believe that one should never let enemies know where one defecates, since feces are used in sorcery. Under such circumstances latrines would hardly be popular.

A different consideration underlay opposition to latrines in an Indian village where women were accustomed to going out into the fields to defecate. This gave them an opportunity to meet and talk with women friends, an occasion particularly valued by high-caste women who were generally confined to their homes (Foster 1969:11).

Maintenance of innovations

New appliances may be introduced into a community and become accepted by the people, but they may later be abandoned, not because the people resist them or fail to appreciate their benefits but simply because they lack the technical knowledge to repair the new gadgets and keep them in good working order. An example is provided by the wells that were installed in Laos by an American drilling company. The local people were glad to have some good sources of water available, but, within two years, almost three fourths of the wells were out of commission because the people did not know how to repair the pumps. It happened that some of the wells had been drilled in Buddhist temple grounds, and these were kept in good repair by the monks. If the drilling company had given the Laotian villagers some instructions about maintenance, and if they had drilled more wells in temple grounds, there might have been better success with this innovation (Arensberg and Niehoff 1964: 4–5).

Innovations and the social order

Some innovations brought about by a community development project may differentially affect segments of the community; some people may benefit by the innovations, while others may resent them. For example, communal road building was encouraged by village-level workers in India. The idea was to get a whole village to cooperate in an undertaking which was conceived to benefit everyone. At the same time, such activity dramatized the dignity of labor. The more well-to-do men of higher caste welcomed these work drives, for the new roads made it possible for them to transport more grain and sugarcane to markets outside the village. The poorer men of lower caste did not have large crops of sugarcane or wheat, nor did they own bullock carts to transport such goods; hence, they did not feel the same enthusiasm for the roads. To add insult to injury, the higher-caste men assumed supervisory roles in the communal work drives, and it was the lower-caste men who had to do most of the manual work, for which they received no wages (Dube 1958:80–82).

Sometimes it is the well-to-do members of a community who resist innovations, regarding them as a threat to the status quo. This was the case in the Vicos Project supported by Cornell University and directed by anthropologist Allan Holmberg (1960) in Peru. The purpose was to modernize and democratize a large hacienda. The project was successful enough to arouse fears of revolution among the landowning classes, not only in the Vicos Valley but throughout Peru.

A medical clinic established in the Mexican town of Tepoztlán was seen as a threat by an influential local *curandero,* or healer, who campaigned against it by spreading various false charges and rumors. Some local political officials joined in the criticism, and the clinic was ultimately abandoned (Lewis 1955). Thus, considerations of class and politics may affect the fate of innovations designed to help the community at large.

This chapter has perhaps given an unduly negative impression of efforts in directed culture change. It is true that much of the literature of applied anthropology has to do with failures, such as the inadequacy of a program to persuade Peruvians to boil their drinking water, the failure of the Tepoztlán clinic, and the lack of success of many village development projects in India. But much can be learned from these failures, and later efforts along similar lines can thus be better prepared. Anthropologists may learn to anticipate some of the side effects of culture patterns undergoing change.

Formerly, ethnologists did not try to change the culture of the society in which they did their fieldwork. Sometimes they even hoped it would be preserved as it was, as much as possible. The anthropologists took field notes and described what they saw. On their return to civilization, they hoped to publish their findings. These publications might or might not have some influence on the community where they had worked. In this respect the applied anthropologists differ, for they no longer simply describe the culture and go home; they try to bring about deliberate changes in the society they study.

There are dangers in this, and the anthropologist may make mistakes. But culture change is inevitable in the less-developed countries of the world today, and, if the anthropologist is hesitant about becoming involved in such activities, there are plenty of people — often with less knowledge and goodwill — who are ready enough to influence the course of events in one way or another. The goals discussed in this chapter are purposes of which no one need be ashamed: increased food production, sanitation, and public health.

Criticisms of applied anthropology

Nevertheless, serious criticisms have been made of the work of applied anthropologists. Guillermo B. Batalla has made the following charges (1966:89–92):

1. There has been too much emphasis on psychological factors, such as native concepts of disease and health, and not enough examination of the basic causes of sickness and malnutrition.

2. The applied anthropologists are anxious to avoid rapid changes that may lead to social and cultural disorganization; hence, they are essentially conservative.

3. The anthropological tradition of cultural relativism makes anthropologists hesitate to pronounce value judgments about cultures and institutions. But, if one cannot say that one culture or institution is better than another, there is no point in doing work in applied anthropology.

4. Anthropologists tend to believe in multiple causation and hold that it is impossible to know all the causes of a given phenomenon. General social laws are hard to formulate, since no two groups have the same needs or problems. In each case, therefore, a detailed study of the local community is required. This often results in a monograph about a particular community without consideration of its ties with the larger world. There is an implicit conservative bias in this approach.

5. Most social problems in developing countries are related to low income levels and an unequal distribution of wealth. Most anthropologists, however, seem to believe that income levels can change only very slowly. They do not wish to challenge the social system that causes and perpetuates poverty.

6. Anthropologists seem to think that diffusion is the most important process in bringing about change. They rarely establish goals to accelerate change in internal institutions. Applied anthropologists

change what is necessary so that things can stay as they are, and so they have allied themselves with the conservative elements of the society.

Glynn Cochrane (1971) has also criticized applied anthropologists for concerning themselves with only small community studies. He claims that anthropologists do not know the contributions of other disciplines and professions in development work and cannot collaborate well with them. According to Cochrane, applied anthropologists should become familiar with the practical aspects of bureaucratic administration and should specialize in economic or legal anthropology in order to be more effective in their work.

For someone who wishes to read more about applied anthropology, it might be best to begin with two readers. Each presents a series of cases; both are well written. The first is Edward H. Spicer, ed., *Human Problems in Technological Change: A Casebook* (New York: Russell Sage Foundation, 1952). The second is Benjamin D. Paul, ed., *Health, Culture, and Community: Case Studies of Public Reactions to Health Programs* (New York: Russell Sage Foundation, 1955). **Suggestions for further reading**

Four general works may be recommended: George M. Foster, *Applied Anthropology* (Boston: Little, Brown & Co., 1969); Conrad M. Arensberg and Arthur H. Niehoff, *Introducing Social Change: A Manual for Americans Overseas* (Chicago: Aldine Publishing Co., 1964); Ward Hunt Goodenough, *Cooperation in Change* (New York: Russell Sage Foundation, 1963); Charles J. Erasmus, *Man Takes Control: Cultural Development and American Aid* (Minneapolis: University of Minnesota Press, 1961).

The Vicos Project supported by Cornell University is described in Allan R. Holmberg, "Changing Community Attitudes and Values in Peru: A Case Study in Guided Change," in *Social Change in Latin America Today: Its Implications for United States Policy*, ed. Richard N. Adams et al. (New York: Harper & Brothers, 1960), pp. 63–107.

Batalla's criticisms and other articles on applied anthropology may be found in James A. Clifton, ed., *Applied Anthropology: Readings in the Uses of the Science of Man* (Boston: Houghton Mifflin Co., 1970).

23

Man's urban environment

Our man-made urban environment progressively covers more of the earth. In 1800 there were only 50 cities in the world with a population of over 100,000; today there are more than 1,400 such cities. By 1969 there were over 140 cities that had 1 million or more inhabitants and contained 11 percent of the world's population (Ferkiss 1969:114). In 1790, 95 percent of Americans lived in rural areas; by 1960, 70 percent lived in urban areas.

In the early development of the world's big cities, the population increase was largely due to migration from the countryside, where birth rates were higher than in the cities. The cities also had higher death rates related to their overcrowding and poor sanitary conditions. But with better medical facilities now available and more public health funds going to cities, the people in the world's cities are now multiplying more rapidly, and rural-urban migration is a less significant factor in urban population increase.

Preindustrial cities

The first cities came into being in Bronze Age times. Harappa and Mohenjo-daro, which flourished around 2000 B.C. in the Indus Valley region of Pakistan, show evidence of city planning, having housefronts lined up in straight lines and streets intersecting at right angles. Sewers ran along beneath the street level, with pipes emptying into them from the houses. The *Arthashastra*, composed around 300 B.C., describes how an Indian royal city should be laid out, with the four *varna*—Brahman, Kshatriya, Vaishya, and Shudra (see p. 177)—being assigned to different quarters of the city, as were followers of different occupations. A similar segregation existed in some Arab cities, such as Fez in Morocco and Aleppo in Syria. Occupational and ethnic groups occupied different wards closed in by walls, the gates to which were locked at night. In both Near Eastern and Indian cities it was customary to have special streets occupied by members of a particular trade, such as goldsmiths.

There was planning in the organization of cities of the Roman Empire. The forum, where public affairs were transacted, was surrounded by law courts, offices, temples, and baths. Aqueducts brought water into the city; sewers and roads also give evidence of city planning. Yet these large urban centers disintegrated in Europe in the 8th century A.D., and western Europe reverted to an agrarian economy with very little trade or urban settlement.

As Basil Davidson has shown (1959), there were preindustrial cities in Africa, south of the Sahara, before the European colonial period began. Yoruba cities in West Africa were inhabited by many farmers who, in contrast with modern suburban commuters, left the city every morning for their farms on the outskirts. William Bascom (1963) has pointed out how these preindustrial cities differed from the modern African cities that developed as a result of European contact. Most inhabitants spent their lives in the city from birth, whereas in modern African cities there are many recent migrants who live in the city only temporarily and hope to return to their villages before they die. In the traditional Yoruba city, husbands lived with their wives and children, and family and lineage ties remained intact. There was little social disorganization or crime, in comparison with modern cities. This suggests that city life need not of itself lead to rootlessness, anomie, and crime, as some writers have asserted; the circumstances of urbanization must be taken into account.

Two special types of preindustrial cities include political centers (Delhi in India, Peking in China) and religious centers of pilgrimage (Banaras in India, Karbala in Iraq).

Colonial cities

A particular type of political center developed in colonial regions dominated by European powers. The Spaniards in Mexico and Peru established capital cities on the sites of former native centers of power (Tenochtitlán, Cuzco). Hugo G. Nuttini (1972) has noted that the Spaniards and Portuguese, who aimed to Catholicize as well as dominate the native peoples, located their cities in inland regions, in contrast to the British, French, and Dutch in North America who established coastal towns linked to Europe by trade across the sea.

Spanish colonial cities have an imposing square in the center where the government buildings and cathedral are located. This is the case, for example, in Mexico City, where the conqueror Cortés forced the Indians to move out of the central area. The finest homes, including that of Cortés, were located near the center. Mexico City today has a residence pattern which differs from that of many North American cities, where it is common to find deteriorating slum areas near the central business district. In Mexico City the worst slums are on the outer edge of the metropolitan area, a condition that has persisted for more than 440 years (Hayner 1966). Mexico City may be called a *primate* city, i.e., a city that dominates a surrounding area and is much larger than the other urban centers. It is the center of transportation, manufactures, and political and intellectual life for the nation. A difference between most Latin-American cities and the cities of North America is that industralization developed slowly in Latin America. At the same time, the population of large cities in Latin America is now doubling every 14 years (L. R. Brown 1972:78).

British colonial cities in India have a character somewhat similar to the Spanish colonial ones. In cities where troops were stationed, there is a modern section known as the *cantonment,* which has straight, broad streets, in contrast to the narrow, jumbled alleys of the old preindustrial city. The cantonment contains offices of government, law courts, churches, clubs, banks, and stores with European goods. As in Mexico City and many other Latin-American cities, the poor tend to be located in slums on the city's outskirts, rather than near the central business district, while the well-to-do tend to live fairly close to the center. The lowest castes are often grouped on the outskirts of India's cities, as they are in many Indian villages. There are caste neighborhoods in some Indian cities, where one may find, for example, a high percentage of Brahmans.

A striking feature of Indian cities is the number of homeless persons who sleep on the streets. Estimates of their number in Calcutta have ranged between 100,000 and 300,000. In an article in the *New York Times* of September 8, 1967, Joseph Lelyveld described a young Calcutta couple with two children who share the same patch of sidewalk every night; they have never lived indoors. They do, however, rent a stall about five-feet square in a shanty across the street, where they eat and where the woman gave birth to the two children. But the stall is less comfortable to sleep in than the pavement outside. Most of Calcutta's sidewalk dwellers, says Lelyveld, have such a stall, which gives them a legal existence, an address to qualify for a ration card or a place in school for their children. The homeless inhabitants of Calcutta illustrate the problems faced by industrializing countries in which urbanization is developing rapidly, while job opportunities remain insufficient for the growing population. India's urban growth had a slow start but

Slum area on the outskirts of Madras, south India. In the background is a laundry-drying area used by people of Dhobi (laundryman) caste.

is now increasing rapidly. In 1951 there were only two cities in India with a population of over 1 million, but now there are seven such cities.

Industrial cities

Industrial cities differ from preindustrial ones by the presence of industries that rely on inanimate sources of power, such as steam and electricity. This system, which originated in Europe, is now in operation to a greater or lesser degree in all nations. Development of the railroad accompanied industrialization. In the United States there are key railroad and port centers, like Chicago and Buffalo, that are centers of both industry and transportation.

Studies made by sociologists Robert E. Park, Ernest W. Burgess, and others in the 1920s and 1930s showed that there was a concentric zonal pattern in Chicago. Zone I was the central business district, containing the department stores, office buildings, and centers of economic, political, and social life. Zone II was a transitional zone, including the factory district and a rundown roominghouse area. Zone III was a zone of workingmen's homes; Zone IV, a better residential area; and Zone V, a commuters' zone. Thus there was seen to be a series of concentric circles, with better residential areas toward the periphery (Burgess 1961). A similar pattern has been described for other U.S. cities, although not all fit the scheme so well. We have noted that Latin-American and Indian cities do not have this particular zonal plan and their slums are located on the peripheries rather than near the central business district.

Early urban studies by sociologists such as Louis Wirth emphasized the anonymity and impersonality of life in a modern city. Anthropologist Robert Redfield echoed this view in his concept of the folk-urban continuum, in which homogeneous folk society was contrasted with heterogeneous city life. In the small, face-to-face folk society, according to Redfield, kin relationships are important, and religion is incorporated into other aspects of the culture; but, in the more secular city, kin ties lose their importance and the individual is more isolated from others. Redfield (1941) tried to document these generalizations by comparing four communities in Yucatán, from the modern city of Merida to a small, unacculturated tribal village, with two intermediate communities in between.

The central slum areas of modern cities were thought to be particularly disorganized and conducive to anomie and schizophrenia (Faris and Dunham 1939). The absence of close personal relationships and rarity of voluntary associations were cited as causative

factors. Such views were commonly expressed in the 1930s and 1940s, particularly by writers dealing with the city of Chicago.

More recently it has been realized that city dwellers are not deprived of close friendships and associations, even in rundown slum areas. William F. Whyte (1943) wrote a detailed study of Italian-American street corner life in Boston, in which he showed that close personal ties often extend beyond adolescence. Herbert J. Gans (1962) and Marc Fried (1963) have also written about the sense of community experienced in an Italian Boston slum. Voluntary associations do exist in such slum areas, and informal opportunities for social contact are also present (e.g., C. E. Richards 1963–64).

Cities are heterogeneous centers with immigrants from many countries and regions. This is less true of a more racially and culturally homogeneous nation like Japan, although Japan has Chinese and Korean minority groups and localized diversities in culture. But the cities of Africa contain persons from many tribes, and the cities of India have migrants from different parts of the subcontinent who speak various languages. Adjustment to city life forces some degree of "melting pot" accommodation to the dominant urban culture. On the other hand, strangers to a city tend to seek out relatives and friends from their own region, and thus one often finds ethnic clustering—a Chinatown, a German Yorkville in New York, a Polish or Italian neighborhood. When Italian immigrants poured into New York in the 19th and early 20th centuries, they clustered in specific neighborhoods: those from Naples settling in the Mulberry Bend area, those from Genoa on Baxter Street, those from Sicily on Elizabeth Street, and those from North Italy in the Eighth and Fifteenth wards west of Broadway (Jones 1960). Such centers of common origin formed the basis for voluntary associations and provided an in-group with some sense of social solidarity, mutual aid, and a center for learning about sources of employment and other useful information. Similar developments took place in other American cities. Particular national groups sometimes specialized in certain occupations. In Chicago in the late 19th century sailors in Great Lakes shipping tended to be Scandinavians, apartment janitors were often Flemish, while eastern European Jews went into the garment industry (Pelling 1960).

Ethnic grouping

Since newly arriving immigrants were often poor, they tended to accept low-paid unskilled work and to live in slum areas. These circumstances fostered the development of stereotyped attitudes toward these minorities by higher-status, longer-established Americans. Many of the opinions which are now held by well-to-do whites about American urban blacks were also held about the Irish in the 19th century. A book entitled *The Dangerous Classes of New York*, published in 1872, dealt mainly with the Irish (Kristol 1970).

The experience of prejudice may lead to some closing of ranks and attempts toward solidarity within the disadvantaged group. Thus, blacks are urged in the black press and churches to patronize black business firms when there is competition with white-owned firms. Most of the basis for black capitalism is within the black community itself (Hannerz 1974:55).

While ethnicity may provide a basis for support within the in-group, it may also create obstacles to economic and social advance-ment for individuals. Hence immigrants with higher status often look down upon later arrivals with whom they do not wish to be identified.

Despite the "melting pot" tendencies of American life, ethnic groups are still identifiable and are often a source of pride and self-identity. Thus efforts are made to retain or re-establish old ethnic patterns. The Irish march on St. Patrick's day. German and Polish groups in Milwaukee practice traditional folk dances from the old country. Urban American Indians from different tribes try to find a new or old identity in the Pan-Indian movement. Blacks speak about soul and wear their hair in Afro style. These varied activities, whether traditional or synthetic, provide some heterogeneity and color in American life, as do the various kinds of ethnic foods— Jewish delicatessen, Italian pasta, and Chinese chop suey, to men-tion only a few.

Suggestions for further reading

A reader on urbanism with a cross-cultural emphasis is Sylvia Fleis Fava, ed., *Urbanization in World Perspective: A Reader* (New York: Thomas Y. Crowell Co., 1968). A good reader on U.S. urban life is Joe R. Feagan, *The Urban Scene: Myths and Realities* (New York: Random House, 1973).

Works by anthropologists about non-Western cities include the follow-ing: John Gulick, *Tripoli: A Modern Arab City* (Cambridge, Mass.: Harvard University Press, 1967); Hortense Powdermaker, *Copper Town: Changing Africa: The Human Situation on the Rhodesian Copperbelt* (New York: Harper & Row, 1962); Andrew H. Whiteford, *Two Cities of Latin America: A Comparative Description of Social Classes* (New York: Doubleday Anchor Books, 1964).

On ethnic groups, see Abner Cohen, ed., *Urban Ethnicity* (London: Tavistock Publications, 1974), particularly the chapter by Ulf Hannerz, "Ethnicity and Opportunity in Urban America," pp. 37–76. See also Nathan Glazer and Daniel Patrick Moynihan, *Beyond the Melting Pot* (Cambridge, Mass.: MIT Press, 1963).

Two studies of American urban life are recommended: William F. Whyte, *Street Corner Society: The Social Structure of an Italian Slum* (Chicago:

University of Chicago Press, 1943); Elliot Liebow, *Tally's Corner: A Study of Negro Streetcorner Men* (Boston: Little, Brown & Co., 1967). See also William Mangin, ed., *Peasants in Cities: Readings in the Anthropology of Urbanization* (Boston: Houghton Mifflin Co., 1970); Joseph G. Jorgensen and Marcello Truzzi, eds., *Anthropology and American Life* (Englewood Cliffs, N.J.: Prentice-Hall, Inc., 1974).

24

Anthropological theory:
A historical review

One of the first problems dealt with by late 19th-century writers on anthropology was how to explain similarities of culture in widely separated societies. Edward B. Tylor argued that cultural evolution had often progressed along similar lines in different parts of the world.

Parallel inventions versus diffusion

Tylor believed that cultural similarities in different regions are due to the "like working of men's minds under like conditions." There is, in other words, a psychic unity of mankind, independent of race or language, so that people in different societies, when faced with similar problems, have come up with similar solutions to them.

Tylor was aware that there is another explanation for similarities of culture in different parts of the world, namely *diffusion*, the spread of a culture trait from one society to another. Indeed, he wrote that civilization is a plant much more often propagated than independently developed. Both parallel invention and diffusion contribute to the content of a culture, and it is not always easy to be sure which process has been responsible for the presence of a particular culture pattern.

A problem that intrigued Tylor (1896) was whether the Aztec game of patolli was related to the game of pachisi, which originated in India and later spread to Europe and America; some readers of this book will recognize it as the game of Parcheesi. Both patolli and pachisi involve the movement of counters along spaces on a cruciform board according to the throw of "dice" (although the Aztec "dice" were flat, not cubical, and more than just two were thrown). In both games there were penalty or safety stations and the rule

346

that a person can "kill" an opponent's counter if he lands on the same space, forcing that counter to go back to the starting point. Since there were so many rules common to both games, Tylor concluded that the games must be related; so perhaps pachisi diffused from Asia to Mexico. He was, thus, perfectly aware of the importance of diffusion, but he was more interested in parallel cultural evolution in different parts of the world.

In Chapter 15, Tylor's theory of animism was set forth. Tylor saw religious concepts as being based on ideas about spiritual beings which understandably developed from human speculations about dreams, trance states, and death. Here, again, was another illustration of the psychic unity of mankind, resulting in the development of similar ideas and practices in different parts of the world.

The first large-scale study of kinship was carried out by Lewis Henry Morgan. In this area, too, Morgan found many widespread similarities in different cultures which demanded some explanation. From his study of Iroquois culture Morgan learned that the Iroquois had different ways of reckoning kin than did Europeans and Americans. They had what Morgan terms a *classificatory* kinship system in contrast to the Euro-American *descriptive* system. In our descriptive system, terms applied to lineal kinsmen are not applied to collateral relatives, but in the classificatory system, such terms as *father, mother, brother, sister, son,* and *daughter* are extended to many persons who are not lineal kinsmen.

Morgan and the study of kinship

In connection with a financial interest in railway construction, Morgan made some trips to Wisconsin in the 1850s. While there, he visited a Chippewa Indian reservation and inquired into their kinship system. Chippewa kinship is quite different from Iroquois; the Chippewa have clans with patrilineal rather than matrilineal descent. But Morgan was more struck by the similarities than the differences. He wondered whether clans and classificatory systems were characteristic of American Indian societies in general. To find out, Morgan sent a questionnaire to missions and federal agencies west of the Mississippi. Morgan had the idea that if all American Indian tribes turned out to have classificatory kinship systems, and if such systems were also found in Asia, that would prove the Asiatic origin of the Indians. Morgan himself traveled to Kansas and Nebraska to collect information at Indian reservations. One of the persons to whom Morgan sent a questionnaire was an American missionary in southern India. Upon receipt of the missionary's Tamil kinship chart, Morgan burst excitedly into a friend's office to show him its close similarities to the Iroquois system. Morgan decided that the next problem was to find out in which areas of the world descriptive systems existed—how widespread classificatory systems were. He now sent out questionnaires on a worldwide scale in the hope of covering other parts of India, Mongolia, Siberia, China, Japan, Australia, the islands of the Pacific, Africa, and South America. These questionnaires were sent to consular and diplomatic representatives of the United States under the auspices of the Smithsonian Institution. The resulting tables, together with Morgan's analysis, were published as *Systems of Consanguinity and Affinity of the Human Family* by the Smithsonian Institution in 1870.

Morgan assumed that the widespread classificatory system was the earlier form, from which a descriptive system developed among the Aryans and Semites. But why did that change take place? Morgan thought that such a transition could develop only through "great reformatory movements"; but another catalytic influence was the idea of property. Morgan began to speculate about the relationships between kinship and economic and political institutions, and this resulted in the publication of *Ancient Society* (1877), his best-known work. *Ancient Society* presented a scheme of cultural evolution, showing that technology, government, and family organization had passed through different stages of Savagery, Barbarism, and Civilization. These stages were the same as Tylor's, but Morgan subdivided the first two stages into Lower, Middle, and Upper. During Lower Savagery, men lived on fruits and nuts, without the use of fire. They had fire and added fish to their diet in the Middle phase and acquired bows and arrows in the Upper. Pottery was made in Lower Barbarism. In the Middle phase, men domesticated animals in the Old World and cultivated maize in the New. Iron tools came in with Upper Barbarism, alphabet and writing with Civilization.

The comparative method

How did 19th-century writers like Morgan draw up their stages of cultural evolution? What sort of information was at their disposal? In those days archaeological evidence was still limited, although it did suggest that there had been a general development from simpler to more complex cultures. Written history provided fuller documentation but was also quite limited, dealing mainly with relatively late civilizations of the Western world. This left one important source of information: reports about non-Western societies at different levels of subsistence: hunting-gathering, horticulture, and agriculture. Such societies could be seen as having remained arrested at a level of cultural evolution that others had transcended. So one could get an idea of what the Paleolithic was like by studying the Australian aborigines and learn about the Neolithic from the Pueblo Indians. There are many different societies at a hunting-gathering level and their cultures are not all alike, but one can get a general idea of this stage of cultural evolution from the elements that they have in common. In this way Morgan reconstructed stages of cultural evolution from ethnographic accounts, supplemented by some guesswork. There were many weaknesses in Morgan's scheme. Men have been hunters for millions of years; neither a nuts-and-fruit stage nor a subsequent fishing stage seems plausible. If we were to follow Morgan's scheme, the Polynesians would appear at the same cultural evolutionary level as the Australian aborigines, while the Inca and Maya would rank below African tribes that have acquired iron. These and many other criticisms have been made of Morgan's outline, but at least it had the advantage of setting forth a provisional plan of evolutionary development.

Different stages were characterized, according to Morgan, by **Cultural** different forms of family and kinship organization. Morgan's ideas on **evolution** this subject were influenced by (and contributed to) the thinking of other 19th-century writers. There were strong differences of opinion among some of these men. Tylor, John F. McLennan (1827–81), and John Lubbock (1834–1913) severely criticized Morgan's work. But there were also some widespread ideas shared by many of the late 19th-century writers, including, for example, Johann Jacob Bachofen (1815–87). It was generally believed that the first human beings lived in a state of sexual promiscuity and later in a somewhat more controlled form of group marriage. Since a child would never know who its father was under such a system, the term *father* would be extended to all males of the first ascending generation. The term *mother* would also be extended to all women of the first ascending generation who were potential stepmothers. In this way Morgan accounted for the development of a "Hawaiian" system of kinship terminology (see p. 125).

When unilineal kinship systems came into being, they were first matrilineal, since at least a child would know who its mother was; but, in the course of time, it was held, matrilineal clans gave way to patrilineal ones as the married pair became a more stable unit and as a sense of private property developed. For Morgan and most other 19th-century writers, the monogamous family of the Western world was the supreme development in the evolution of a family.

The concept of *survivals* was used in reconstructing aspects of cultural evolution. Tylor used this term to refer to culture patterns that have been carried from an earlier into a later stage of culture through force of habit, with the result that their original significance has been forgotten. The presence of such a pattern provides a clue to past practices. Tylor made use of this concept in a statistical exercise in which he tried to show that matrilineal descent and matrilocal residence must have preceded patrilineal descent and patrilocal residence. This study is important as a pioneer cross-cultural survey like those used later with the resources of the Human Relations Area Files. Tylor (1889) collected data about 350 peoples "ranging from insignificant savage hordes to great cultured nations." Unfortunately, he did not list them, and there is no way of knowing now who his 350 peoples were or where they were located. Tylor presented a series of tables showing correlations among certain institutions. When he found a greater than chance coexistence of two or more institutions, he concluded that there was some inherent connection between them. He found, for example, that there was a relationship between matrilocal residence and mother-in-law avoidance by a man. Tylor concluded that in such households marrying-in men are formally treated as strangers. There was also a relationship between matrilocal residence and *teknonymy*, the practice of naming the parents, usually the father, from the child, so that a man is called "Father of So-and-So." In a matrilocal household, reasoned Tylor, the husband would acquire status as a father; hence the correlation. Tylor also considered correlations with the customs of levirate, couvade, and bride-capture and concluded from all this that matrilineal descent generally preceded patrilineal. The presence of survivals from an earlier period indicated to him that a particular stage was later than one in which such survivals were absent. Patrilineal cultures would retain some matrilineal survivals but not the other way around.

In the discussion that followed Tylor's presentation of this paper at the Royal Anthropological Institute in 1889, Francis Galton pointed out that some of the tribes in question might have borrowed their practices from neighboring peoples and that Tylor had not taken diffusion into account. If the different societies could not be counted as separate units, the chance-probability statistics would then become rather meaningless.

Cultural evolution was a lively field of speculation in the late 19th century, stimulated by the Darwinian concepts about biological evolution which were then being debated. Although their views challenged traditional ones, men like Tylor and Morgan were not radicals. Indeed, Morgan asserted that the dominance of the concept of property over the other passions marked the commencement of civilization.

Under the circumstances, it seems odd that Morgan was taken up by the Marxists and eventually became a hero in the Soviet Union. Karl Marx claimed that Morgan had independently discovered the materialist conception of history. Friedrich Engels, who collaborated with Marx in writing the *Communist Manifesto*, wrote *The Origin of the Family, Private Property and the State* (1884) as a leftwing *Reader's Digest* version of Morgan's *Ancient Society*.

The Marxists gave a new twist to Morgan's ideas. Just as capitalism and private property, from their point of view, do not represent the final stage of economic development, in the same way monogamy will be superseded with a change in social conditions. Primitive bands were communistic; their cohesion gave way with the development of the idea of private property. But the society of the future will once again become communist, and the isolation of the bourgeois family will then disappear. This view conjured up visions of a "return" to conditions of sexual promiscuity. In practice, the Soviet Union has supported the integrity of the individual family; if Engels predicted its withering away under communism, it has not yet done so there.

The Marxist canonization of Morgan has led to many of his doctrines being accepted as virtual laws, including the universal priority of matriliny before patriliny. Much of Soviet archaeology has been dominated by Morgan's conceptions. As we shall see, Morgan's ideas met with a different, more fluctuating, reception in the United States.

Diffusionism

In addition to cultural evolutionist schemes, the later 19th and early 20th centuries also produced schools that emphasized the role of diffusion. There were two main schools, one British, the other German and Austrian. The leading spokesmen of the British school were G. Elliot Smith, William J. Perry, and W. H. R. Rivers. It was their belief that most aspects of higher civilization first developed in Egypt and then diffused to other parts of the world. If agriculture, pottery making, weaving, pyramid building, and various other features were to be found in the Americas and elsewhere, it was due to the explorations of Egyptians or of people who had been in contact with Egyptian civilization. These notions were based upon the assumptions that most people are uninventive and that parallel cultural evolution is rare. American anthropologists were hostile to this school of thought, which seems by now to have become extinct.

The German and Austrian *Kulturkreis* (culture circle) school was represented by Fritz Graebner and Father Wilhelm Schmidt, among others. Their reconstructions represent an amalgam of cultural evolution and diffusion, sharing with the pan-Egyptian school some skepticism about alleged cases of parallel evolution, since they too believed that human beings are generally uninventive. Members of this school held that diffusion of culture traits may take place over great distances and that they may diffuse in great complexes of traits. For example, Graebner related the "Melanesian bow culture" to the Neolithic culture of central Europe, since both had pile dwellings with rectangular ground plans, coiled pottery, a special way of hafting adzes, and spoons.

Father Schmidt isolated a group of what he considered to be the "ethnologically oldest" peoples. These consisted of hunting-gathering bands which were remnants of societies that had diverged from the world's oldest culture without having since added many new cultural trappings, since they had made their ways into marginal areas of the world—in the Arctic, Tierra del Fuego, deep jungles, deserts, and other isolated regions. This early horizon is represented by the Pygmies, Semang, Andamanese, Australian aborigines, Tasmanians, Eskimos, Algonkian Indians, Indians of central California, and some of the tribes of Tierra del Fuego. By studying the common characteristics of these cultures, Father Schmidt suggested, we may be able to reconstruct characteristics of the oldest culture of the world.

One of the later cultural strata (of which there are several) was a matrilineal horticultural type of society in which women gained prestige through their association with tillage and hence developed matrilocality, matrilineal descent, female puberty ceremonies, and worship of female deities. Men reacted against this domination by developing masked secret societies which aimed to replace the worship of goddesses with that of male ancestors.

While the posited functional relationships may be plausible, not much documentation was provided for the existence of these *Kulturkreise* and their influences upon one another. As Robert Lowie remarked (1937:190), "Until these events are actually documented somewhere on the globe we must reject the scheme as not a whit more empirical than Morgan's." The *Kulturkreis* doctrine is more complex and hydra-headed than that of the pan-Egyptian school and hence harder to refute. While no American anthropologists seem to have supported the pan-Egyptian dogma, there was some support for the *Kulturkreis* school (e.g., Kluckhohn 1936).

Anthropology as an academic discipline came into being in an age of imperialism. Racist beliefs and ideas about the uninventiveness of nonwhite peoples were part of the ideology of imperialism and colonialism. The concept of the white man's burden, with its theme of *noblesse oblige,* was a more benevolent aspect of the same outlook, assuming the superior ability and motivation of the white man.

A reaction against 19th-century cultural evolutionism and diffu- **Franz Boas**
sionism came from the work of Franz Boas and his students. Born
in 1858, Boas was reared and educated in Germany.

Boas' first fieldwork was among the Central Eskimos from 1883 to
1884. He had been influenced by the concept of geographical
determinism and wanted to see to what extent the culture of the
Eskimos was shaped by their environment. His experience in Baffin-
land led Boas to conclude that geography plays a mainly limiting
rather than creative role. The Eskimos did things in spite of their
environment, not just because of it; they had a particular history and
set of traditions behind them that were different from those of other
northerly peoples, such as the Siberian Chukchee, who lived in a
similar environment. A culture is shaped by many historical forces,
including contacts with other societies.

This awareness of the complexity of determinants led Boas to be
skeptical of universal laws such as those set forth by the cultural
evolutionists. He thought that broad generalizations might perhaps
be arrived at; but, if so, these might turn out to be only common-
place truisms. Rather than announcing any new doctrine, Boas attacked the works of previous writers, and his students followed this
critical bent. For example, John Swanton showed that the tribes of
North America did not show the progression of kinship organization
postulated by Morgan and others. Hunting bands with bilateral or
patrilineal descent lived at a simpler level of culture than the more
advanced Hopi, Zuñi, Creek, and Natchez Indians who had matrilineal descent.

Boas thought that the global generalizations about cultural evolution made by 19th-century writers were premature, based on inadequate information about primitive cultures collected from the
writings of traders, sea captains, and missionaries, who often had
only a biased, superficial understanding of the people whom they
observed. Boas declared for a moratorium on theorizing. He recommended that we first get the facts and build up a body of ethnographic
data from which more reliable generalizations can later be made.
Meanwhile, he warned, primitive cultures all over the world are
disappearing under the impact of Western civilization. He pointed
out that time is short and that we must go out and record the facts of
native life before these cultures vanish.

Boas followed his own prescription. From 1886 to 1931, he made
13 field trips to the Northwest Coast of North America. He trained
himself to learn the languages of Indians of the area, as he had earlier
learned Eskimo. Boas was a leader in the development of American
linguistics. One reason for this emphasis was that he believed a
culture should be understood in terms of the categories of the natives

Franz Boas

themselves, not in those imposed by an outside observer. The purpose should be to see how the world looks to a member of that culture. Folktales were recorded by Boas in the native language and later translated. The recording of texts was one of his main activities in the field. Some understanding of the language was necessary, he believed, when dealing with complex sets of ideas, such as those concerning religion, which may be distorted when translated by an interpreter.

Boas' students worked in this tradition. Hence, we have today an impressive body of field reports on American Indian cultures, on the Winnebago, Crow, Arapaho, and the tribes of the Pueblo area and California. Boas' students were often interested in different topics and problems; hence it is often asserted that there was no "Boas school." Marian Smith has suggested that Boas wanted the data collected to be as free of bias as possible; interpretations should be made only after the ethnography has been recorded. Smith (1959:53) noted, "It therefore followed that information gathered for a particular purpose became suspect, for selection in itself suggested distortion."

Boas trained his students to be camera eyes, recording everything and anything. Smith (1959:54) has characterized this as a "natural history" approach and describes it as follows:

Interest lies not mainly in systems per se, but in "the surrounding world." There is a fascination in following the details of a subject just for its intrinsic interest, and there is also the knowledge that, once accumulated, such systematic data will have value — sometimes in wholly unexpected directions.

This fascination for details may lead to a lack of focus. For example, Boas recorded page after page of blueberry-pie recipes in the Kwakiutl language, with the English translation on facing pages. We still do not know to what use they may ultimately be put.

Boas' effort to learn as much as possible about a particular culture in all of its minutiae is an *idiographic* approach to culture, as opposed to a *nomothetic* approach, which involves a search for general laws or regularities. As has been mentioned, he was skeptical about the possibility of finding cultural laws and suggested that it would be better to reconstruct the historical development of particular cultures. If this were done on a sufficiently large scale, it might become possible to compare histories of cultural development and see if regularities were discernible.

By 1930, however, Boas was skeptical of such an outcome:

An error of modern anthropology, as I see it, lies in the overemphasis on historical reconstruction, the importance of which should not be minimized, as against a penetrating study of the individual under the stress of the culture in which he lives (quoted in Harris 1968:281).

Boas thus advocated a turn to the field of culture-and-personality, in which his students Ruth Benedict and Margaret Mead distinguished themselves.

The idiographic approach of Boas and many of his followers, with its mistrust of laws and generalities, led finally to critical attacks by Leslie White and others who wanted to make anthropology more of a generalizing science.

Bronislaw Malinowski

After studying anthropology in England for four years, just before World War I, Malinowski set out to do fieldwork in Melanesia and Australia, where he was interned as an enemy alien but allowed to continue his work from 1915 to 1918. Malinowski's prolonged stay in the Trobriand Islands formed the basis for a series of ethnographic works that have become classics in anthropology. He was attracted to the social life of Europeans in the islands, but he determined to cut himself off from these contacts and to live among the Trobriand people, whose language he learned. Like Boas, Malinowksi took down texts in the native tongue and tried to find the natives' own terms of classification for their institutions and practices in an effort to "get inside the native's skin." Also like Boas, he was interested in the many interrelated aspects of the total culture and in what he called "the imponderabilia of actual life." He was not, however, concerned with trying to reconstruct the antecedents of Trobriand culture, about which he thought little could be learned. Malinowski promoted an approach he called "functionalism," seeing the culture of a society as providing various means for satisfying the needs of its members. He wrote (1926b:132):

The functional view of culture insists upon the principle that every type of civilization, every custom, material object, idea, and belief fulfills some vital function, has some task to accomplish, represents an indispensable part within a working whole.

This view was partly in reaction to the attitude that the customs of non-Western societies are often bizarre, irrational, or represent "survivals" from earlier stages of cultural development; earlier in the same passage Malinowski wrote:

The field worker who lives among savages soon discards the antiquarian outlook. He sees every implement constantly used; every custom backed up by strong feeling and cogent ideas; every detail of social organization active and effective.

There is a danger, however, in characterizing certain institutions or culture patterns as "indispensable" in meeting human needs, for these needs may be met by other means. Malinowski's view implies a somewhat rigid and static concept of culture (see Merton 1949:28–79). At the same time, however, Malinowski did not see individuals as being dominated by their culture. He suggested that perhaps "the

Bronislaw
Malinowski.

heathen can be as self-seeking and self-interested as any Christian"
(Malinowski 1926a:ix). Whenever a Trobriand native can escape his
obligations without losing prestige, he is likely to do so.

In his work Malinowski's focus was on a particular society at a
given moment in time. He was interested in seeing how food is
acquired from the environment and distributed within the society,
how social conflicts are handled and adjusted, and how social cohesion and cooperation are insured. This involves a study of the inter-
relations between economics, social organization, religion, and other
institutions, for Malinowski saw all aspects of culture as being
closely interwoven. This integration was exemplified in Malinowski's discussion of the kula trade ring, presented in Chapter 6.

Malinowski's interest in the functions of magic and religion in
meeting human psychological needs was touched on in Chapter 15.
Magic, said Malinowski, comes into play when normal, rational
means to an end meet with failure. People may then resort to magic,
which has the effect of giving them confidence to persevere toward
their goal.

As his interpretation of magic indicates, Malinowski was always
interested in the individual member of society. Although he referred
to Trobriand natives as "savages" in the 19th-century fashion, and
although he sometimes wrote of them contemptuously in the day-
by-day journal which he kept, Malinowski described the Trobrianders in his books and articles as reasonable, pragmatic persons,
whose behavior is altogether understandable when one knows their
cultural premises.

A. R. Radcliffe-Brown

Alfred Reginald Radcliffe-Brown was born and educated in
England and studied anthropology under W. H. R. Rivers and A. C.
Haddon. He did ethnological fieldwork in the Andaman Islands
from 1906 to 1908, providing the material for his book *The Andaman
Islanders*. From 1910 to 1912 he did fieldwork in Australia, and in
subsequent years taught anthropology in universities in many parts
of the world, including Capetown, Sydney, Chicago, and Oxford.

Like Malinowski, Radcliffe-Brown was interested in the synchronic study of a particular society at one period of time and was
not concerned with historical reconstruction. He sometimes called
himself a functionalist and wrote about the concept of function,
stating that the function of an institution is the contribution it makes
to the maintenance of structural continuity in the society. Radcliffe-
Brown's view of functionalism was not allied to Malinowski's notion
about cultural institutions satisfying human needs. Rather, he placed
the emphasis on the maintenance of social structures. Hence, his

A. R. Radcliffe-
Brown.

approach has sometimes been called "structural-functional." It is
largely through his influence that British social anthropologists, and
many Americans as well, have focused their attention on the kinship
systems of different societies.

The proper focus for investigation, for Radcliffe-Brown, was not
the culture of a society – too vague and broad a concept for him – but
its social structure, the network of social relations. Kinship ties are
always important in the tribal societies studied by Radcliffe-Brown
and his students. The emphasis on social structure made Radcliffe-
Brown a kind of sociologist, as he himself declared. Radcliffe-Brown
saw himself as a social scientist seeking nomothetic social laws, but
the laws he claimed to have discovered are usually rather vague and
do not seem to add a great deal to our understanding of social issues.
Nevertheless, he was an extremely influential teacher, commanding
great loyalty among his students.

**Culture-and-
personality**

We have seen that by 1930 Franz Boas was advocating "a penetrating study of the individual under the stress of the culture in
which he lives." *Patterns of Culture* (1934) written by Boas' student
Ruth Benedict, was an effort in that direction; in this popular work
Benedict contrasted three cultures, Pueblo, Dobu, and Kwakiutl.
She emphasized the differences in values and world view characterizing these three cultural worlds. A child born into the Kwakiutl

Margaret Mead.

society is destined to have very different experiences and to be driven toward different goals and underlying assumptions about life from those of a child born among the Hopi or Zuñi.

Margaret Mead's early studies (1939) also drew attention to the importance of cultural milieu in shaping personality. She contrasted the easygoing adolescence of Samoan girls with the tenser coming-of-age of American youngsters. Mead also observed and recorded the typical childhood experiences of the Manus of New Guinea and pointed out ways in which these experiences resembled and differed from those of American children.

The cross-cultural study of childhood has been a relatively recent development in anthropology, which was originally concerned with adult culture. If any attention was paid to child training in the earlier ethnography, it was usually a secondary matter, a side issue. An interest in child training among anthropologists was brought about partly by the influence of Freudian theory and also by the influence of John Dewey in education. Both of these currents may be seen in the work of Margaret Mead. Bronislaw Malinowski (1953) was also one of the first to concern himself with childhood experience and the relevance of psychoanalytic theory in a non-Western society.

In the late 1930s and 1940s, a seminar in culture-and-personality was given at Columbia University by Ralph Linton, an anthropologist, and Abram Kardiner, a psychoanalyst. In this seminar a series of nonliterate cultures was analyzed with regard to the relationship between childhood training practices and other aspects of the culture. Kardiner developed the concept of "basic personality structure," referring to the common aspects of personality shared by the members of a particular society. He noted that child-training methods, such as those involving suckling and toilet training, tend to be fairly standardized within a particular society, so that women tend to suckle their children for about the same length of time as their neighbors do, feed them the same foods, and apply the same kinds of toilet training and other disciplines. Therefore, the children who grow up within a particular society pass through the same general gamut of childhood experiences. They are apt to react to such experiences in much the same ways and therefore develop many personality traits in common. As Linton has put it: "The *basic personality type* for any society is that personality configuration which is shared by the bulk of the society's members as a result of the early experiences which they have in common" (Kardiner et al. 1945:viii).

This school emphasized the need for getting more data on child-training practices in different societies. Two outstanding field studies influenced by this school of thought are *The People of Alor* by Cora DuBois (1944) and *Truk: Man in Paradise* by Thomas Gladwin and Seymour B. Sarason (1953). DuBois' work was discussed in Chapter 20.

Cross-cultural surveys

Another kind of research was made possible in the 1940s with the development of the Yale Cross-Cultural Survey, which later became known as the Human Relations Area Files (HRAF). These files contain ethnographic data about a few hundred societies from the various culture areas of the world. A simple coding system makes it possible for someone to quickly find the information he seeks about cultural practices in different societies, whether they be fishing techniques or toilet-training practices. The leading figure in organizing the Yale files was George P. Murdock.

One advantage of this method of data organization is that it facilitates the discovery of correlations of culture patterns. For example, we may ask, as Tylor did: With which forms of postmarital residence is the custom of mother-in-law avoidance most often found? With which forms is it negatively correlated? The files readily provide answers to such questions. The files also permit the testing of hypotheses. One may predict that certain correlations will appear under particular conditions. On the other hand, correlations do not speak for themselves; when they do appear there may be conflicting explanations for them, with inconclusive results.

A common criticism of studies based on the HRAF files is that the method involves pulling items out of context for comparative, quantitative purposes. But perhaps that is necessary if comparisons are to be made. Indeed, if they are not made, how can anthropology claim to be a scientific discipline?

Broad cross-cultural surveys, like those making use of the HRAF files, are quite different in nature from the intensive description of a single culture, like that of Malinowski. The former studies tend to be nomothetic, the latter idiographic and relativistic. Malinowski's desire to "get inside the native's skin" and see the world as a Trobriander sees it has been called an *emic* approach to the study of culture, in contrast to an *etic* approach which relies upon classifications and judgments agreed upon by outside "scientific" observers. These terms, emic and etic, were coined by the linguist Kenneth Pike on the analogy of the terms *phonemic* and *phonetic*. An etic analysis may consist of observation of behavior that does not involve learning the viewpoints of those involved. The categories of the Human Relations Area Files provide an etic grid which may be applied to the cultures of the world.

Many problems are involved in the use of the cross-cultural survey method. One is Galton's problem, referred to in relation to Tylor's pioneer statistical study, concerning the role of diffusion as a "contaminating" factor. However, various attempts have been made to control for the factor of diffusion (Naroll 1961, 1964; Naroll and D'Andrade 1963). Despite the many difficulties, an extensive collection of books and articles has appeared, making use of the HRAF files.

One of Murdock's chief colleagues in developing the files was John W. M. Whiting, who has made use of HRAF cross-cultural data in many articles on child-training practices. In coauthorship with Irvin L. Child, Whiting produced an influential book, *Child Training and Personality: A Cross-Cultural Study* (1953). One weakness of this work, and of other early HRAF cross-cultural studies of childhood, was that the information about childhood was very uneven in the Human Relations Area Files. For some societies there were abundant data, for others almost none. It was clear that more complete descriptions were needed of childhood experience in different societies. Whiting and his associates extended their cross-cultural investigations of childhood experience in the Six Cultures project, which is discussed in Chapter 20.

We have seen that Boas and his followers were often critical of the works of 19th-century cultural evolutionists, including Morgan and Tylor, and that they were skeptical of the value of making broad cross-cultural generalizations. Beginning in the 1930s, the Boasian

The return to cultural evolution

emphasis on historical particularism came in for a series of polemic attacks by Leslie A. White. White became an ardent champion of Morgan and Tylor and a proponent for the study of cultural evolution. In time, he acquired a band of enthusiastic disciples, while another constellation of disciples (some of whom were also followers of White) formed about another prominent student of cultural evolution, Julian H. Steward. White and Steward have sometimes been referred to as "neoevolutionists," a term rejected by White, who claimed that he was simply carrying on the 19th-century traditions of Tylor and had added nothing new.

White did, however, add something new; for one thing, he propounded a "Basic Law of Evolution," which read as follows: "Other factors remaining constant, culture evolves as the amount of energy harnessed per capita per year is increased or as the efficiency of the means of putting the energy to work is increased" (White 1959:368–69). What distinguishes a stage of evolution from a preceding stage is the increase in available energy. For White, adaptation and culture change are not synonymous with evolution; history is not evolution. Cultural evolution occurs when more energy is made available to humans; this tends to be associated with increased complexity of social organization and social differentiation.

White claims that Steward has sometimes failed to make a proper distinction between mere culture change and evolution. A case in point is a comparison Steward made between two groups adapting to European contact—the horticultural Mundurucú of Brazil and the hunting-gathering Algonquin Indians of North America. Although the two ecological and cultural settings were very different, both groups became similarly dependent upon European trading posts. Steward saw this as a convergent evolutionary development, but to White these adaptations had nothing to do with evolution. It is evident that different interpretations may be made as to what constitutes cultural evolution.

Steward (1955:14–15) has made a distinction between three schools of evolutionary thought:

First, *unilinear evolution,* the classical nineteenth-century formulation, dealt with particular cultures, placing them in stages of a universal sequence. Second, *universal evolution*—a rather arbitrary label to designate the modern revamping of unilinear evolution—is concerned with culture rather than with cultures. Third, *multilinear evolution,* a somewhat less ambitious approach than the other two, is like unilinear evolution in dealing with developmental sequences, but is distinctive in searching for parallels of limited occurrence instead of universals.

Morgan and Tylor, then, would be unilinear evolutionists, White a universal evolutionist, and Steward a multilinear evolutionist.

An example of parallel cultural evolution: (above) Pyramid in Egypt near Cairo, (below) pyramid in Mexico at Chichén Itźa. Presumably some parallel features of social organization made such structures possible.

Steward has been concerned with discovering cross-cultural regularities, similar patterns in cultural development such as occurred in the Bronze Age Old World civilizations, on the one hand, and the New World civilizations of Mexico and Peru, on the other. Analysis of such regularities may reveal underlying processes that have led to the appearance of similar institutions. For this reason, Steward was attracted to Wittfogel's theory about the role of irrigation in the formation of despotic societies.

**Human
ecology**

Ecology is the study of the interrelationship of organisms and their environment, including both the physical environment and other living organisms. Human adaptation to the environment involves culture; hence, Steward used the term *cultural ecology* for the study of human adjustment to particular geographical settings. He followed three basic procedures, involving analyses of: (1) the relationship between technology and environment, (2) behavior patterns involved in exploiting a particular area with a particular technology, and (3) the extent to which these behavior patterns affect other aspects of culture.

Steward noted that hunting-gathering bands varied in size and composition, depending on local resources and circumstances. Some had large, composite bands, while others had small family units, like the Shoshone Indians. Steward's interests were not limited to the hunting-gathering level of sociocultural integration but extended to large hydraulic civilizations and modern nations as well. Thus there is a close relationship between Steward's work in cultural ecology and his outline of cultural evolution.

There have been other approaches besides Steward's to the study of human ecology. Andrew P. Vayda and Roy A. Rappaport (1968) have a more biological and functional orientation, hoping to bring ecological studies in anthropology within the theoretical framework of general ecology. This is evidenced in Rappaport's study (1967) of the Tsembaga of New Guinea, who periodically slaughter large numbers of pigs. He argues that these ritual slaughters keep the land from being overrun with pigs and maintain balances between the people and their sweet-potato crops and fauna. This is a form of functionalist analysis, with an ecological emphasis.

**Cognitive
anthropology**

During the past 20 years a small but influential group of anthropologists, consisting mainly of anthropological linguists, has advocated and applied an ethnographic approach which involves eliciting from native speakers of a society under investigation the taxonomic features of their language. The aim is to see how the speakers of this language categorize the phenomena of their world, what distinctions are important to them, what organizing principles determine their conceptions of reality. It is believed that this method of ethnographic research avoids the imposition of the fieldworker's own categories upon the culture. Charles Frake, one spokesman for this group, states that "... an ethnography should be a theory of cultural behavior in a particular society, the adequacy of which is to be evaluated by the ability of a stranger to the culture ... to use the ethnography's statements as instructions for appropriately anticipating the scenes of the society" (Frake 1964:112).

The aim is to be able to look through the eyes of a "native speaker" and see the world as he does. This aim is not new, for both Boas and Malinowski, among others, expressed it in one way or another; but cognitive anthropologists believe that their linguistic approach is a more rigorous means to that end than were earlier approaches. One criticism of this school has been that learning the rules of a culture does not necessarily help one to understand the actual behavior of members of that society.

Claude Lévi-Strauss

Claude Lévi-Strauss, who seems to be presently the leading figure in anthropology in continental Europe, is the exponent of what he calls *structural anthropology*, the title of a collection of his papers published in 1963. One might think that structural anthropology has to do with the analysis of social structure in the manner of Radcliffe-Brown and his followers. Indeed, Lévi-Strauss is the author of an influential paper on "Social Structure" (1953), and his book *The Elementary Structures of Kinship*, first published in 1949, has to do with kinship organization. Nevertheless, despite his close familiar-

Claude
Lévi-Strauss.

ity with this field, Lévi-Strauss's interests are more psychological than sociological. He has stated that "ethnology is first of all psychology," and it is significant that the comment appears in a work entitled *La Pensée Sauvage,* which has been translated into English as *The Savage Mind* (1966a:131).

This interest in psychology does not concern the emotional aspects of personality that have been investigated by some workers in the field of culture-and-personality; rather, Lévi-Strauss's concern is with cognitive processes very much along the lines of the school of cognitive anthropology just discussed. Early in *The Elementary Structures of Kinship* the author devotes a chapter to studies of child psychology in order to clarify the psychological basis for the idea of reciprocity. Ways in which people classify things and make order of the world around them is a matter of particular fascination to Lévi-Strauss and forms the main theme of *The Savage Mind.*

An important point made by the author is that the mental abilities of "primitive" peoples have long been greatly underrated. He presents a good deal of evidence that peoples with a relatively simple technological culture often have highly elaborate systems for classifying plants and animals, involving much accurate knowledge. This close observation is not limited to species that are edible or useful in other ways. The classifications seem to be generated by sheer intellectual curiosity and by a desire to impose order on the world. This concern is also devoted to making distinctions between moieties, clans, and other social units.

Structuralism is an approach that is not limited to anthropology. Persons who call themselves structuralists are also found in the fields of mathematics, psychology, and philosophy (Lane 1970). But the main source of structuralism has been linguistics. Lévi-Strauss has compared his approach to ethnological data with the methods of structural linguistics which stress the study of the unconscious infrastructure that underlies linguistic phenomena. Similarly, Lévi-Strauss tries to reveal the "mental structures" that underlie human behavior. According to him, these usually take the form of binary contrasts or oppositions. Hence the frequency with which moieties or other forms of dual organization are associated with contrasting qualities, such as left and right, low and high, cold and warm, earth and sky, north and south, white and black, and so forth.

Lévi-Strauss's effort to understand the inner logic of primitive thought has led him to take a special interest in mythology. In Chapter 18 a sample of his South American Indian myths was examined. Lévi-Strauss's work in both kinship and mythology has won both acclaim and severe criticism. It must be admitted that some of his theories seem bizarre. For example, in an article entitled "The Culinary Triangle" (1966b), Lévi-Strauss states that the cooking practices of a society may be analyzed in the same way as a language; like a language, they contain certain structural oppositions. He finds a significant contrast between roasting and boiling. The former is more primitive, involving direct exposure of food to the fire, whereas boiling makes use of a container. The author hypothesizes that boiling is associated with in-group solidarity, while roasted food is served to guests. He then extends this discussion to cannibalism, with the suggestion that boiling may be used when eating either relatives or enemies, but roasting would more frequently be used with enemies.

Not many of Lévi-Strauss's theories are open to testing, but this one is, and it has fared poorly under investigation (Shankman 1969).

On the other hand, Lévi-Strauss has written much that is thoughtful and stimulating, particularly in *The Savage Mind*.

In this chapter, some current schools of thought in ethnology have been briefly presented, but this survey is by no means complete. Many anthropologists cannot be fitted into particular pigeonholes, such as "functionalism," "structural anthropology," or whatnot. Present-day anthropology is characterized by remarkable diversity; it is like Stephen Leacock's knight who jumped on his horse and rode off in all directions. Perhaps the best way to get an idea of the variety of interests, aims, and methods in anthropology is to look through a list of the titles of papers given at one of the recent annual meetings of the American Anthropological Association. This diversity gives reason to believe that the younger generation of anthropologists is not likely to become brainwashed by any one ethnological doctrine or school of thought.

Suggestions for further reading

The best approach to the authors cited in this chapter would be to read some of their original writings. For example, the articles by A. R. Radcliffe-Brown, collected in *Structure and Function in Primitive Society: Essays and Addresses* (Glencoe, Ill.: The Free Press, 1952), are written with economy and elegance. Also worth reading is Malinowski's "Introduction" to his *Argonauts of the Western Pacific* (New York: E. P. Dutton, 1961), pp. 1–26; it gives a good account of his fieldwork methods. Margaret Mead's early books are very readable, especially *Coming of Age in Samoa* (1928) and *Growing Up in New Guinea* (1930). Together with *Sex and Temperament in Three Primitive Societies* (1935), these books are collected in one volume in Margaret Mead, *From the South Seas: Studies of Adolescence and Sex in Primitive Societies* (New York: William Morrow & Co., 1939). The most readable of Lévi-Strauss's books is *The Savage Mind* (Chicago: University of Chicago Press, 1966).

For a stimulating review of anthropological theory, though one rather biased in favor of "cultural materialism," see Marvin Harris, *The Rise of Anthropological Theory: A History of Theories of Culture* (New York: Thomas Y. Crowell Co., 1968). Brief biographies and commentaries on such figures as Edward Tylor, Franz Boas, Bronislaw Malinowski, Ruth Benedict, and others are available in Abram Kardiner and Edward Preble, *They Studied Man* (Cleveland: World Publishing Co., 1961). Nineteenth-century cultural evolutionism is discussed in Robert L. Carneiro, "Classical Evolution," in Raoul Naroll and Frada Naroll, eds., *Main Currents in Cultural Anthropology* (New York: Appleton-Century-Crofts, 1973), pp. 57–121.

The career and ideas of Lewis Henry Morgan are presented in Carl Resek, *Lewis Henry Morgan: American Scholar* (Chicago: University of Chicago Press, 1960).

A series of articles about Franz Boas and his work is available in *The Anthropology of Franz Boas: Essays on the Centennial of His Birth*, ed. Walter Goldschmidt, American Anthropological Association Memoir no. 89, 1959. For a critical assessment of both Boas and Radcliffe-Brown, see Leslie A. White, *The Social Organization of Ethnological Theory* (Houston, Texas: Rice University Studies, vol. 52, 1966), pp. 1–66.

Adam Kuper's *Anthropologists and Anthropology: The British School: 1922–1972* (New York: Pica Press, 1973) deals with the works of Malinowski, Radcliffe-Brown, Lévi-Strauss, and their followers in England. On Lévi-Strauss, see Edmund Leach, *Claude Lévi-Strauss* (New York: Viking press, 1970). For two critical assessments, see Francis Korn, *Elementary Structures Reconsidered: Lévi-Strauss on Kinship* (Berkeley: University of California Press, 1973), and Philip Pettit, *The Concept of Structuralism: A Critical Analysis* (Berkeley: University of California Press, 1975).

25

The futures of mankind

Mankind has many futures, not only in the sense that the future of India, let us say, will be somewhat different from that of the United States, but also in the sense that the cultures of the world will, no doubt, be quite different at different points in time, from century to century, assuming that we still have some centuries ahead of us. Some prophets, like Jacques Ellul in *The Technological Society* (1964), disapprove of the future and do not want to go there. (Ellul's counterparts in fiction are the grim anti-Utopias of Aldous Huxley's *Brave New World* and George Orwell's *1984*.) On the other hand, there are also enthusiasts of the future, writers like Arthur C. Clarke and Richard Landers, who are fascinated by the marvels of 21st-century technology. It is possible that both the pessimists and optimists are right. Many futurists are agreed that the next two decades or so will bring hard times for the human species. If we can navigate and survive the near future, the distant shores of the technological society may indeed be bright. Our problem is how to get there from here, if that is where we want to go.

We cannot know the future, although remarkable prophecies have sometimes been made. Ten years before the event, Arthur C. Clarke made a bet that the first man to land on the moon would do so by June 1969. He was only a month off (Bernstein 1969:40). Clarke, who invented the idea of a communications satellite and coauthored the film *2001: A Space Odyssey*, has a good record for such forecasts, but some of his predictions may prove to be quite wrong.

If we had a battery of reliable cultural or social laws, predictions might perhaps be made with more confidence. Charles Issawi has offered some tongue-in-cheek "laws of social motion," which seem

369

to be just about as acceptable as more solemnly proposed social laws. His "Law of Conservation of Evil" runs: "The total amount of evil in any system remains constant. Hence any diminution in one direction—for instance a reduction in poverty or unemployment —is accompanied by an increase in another, e.g., crime or air pollution." Issawi's second law is, "Most things get steadily worse." He points out that this does not contradict his first law, for a few things have become much better, such as surgery, economic theory, and long-playing records (Issawi 1970:42).

Since we cannot know the future, it is surprising, at first glance, that the literature about it is so enormous. Man has always been interested in speculating about the future and planning for it, but this interest has greatly increased in recent years. There are committees and "think tanks" dedicated to this cause. The World Futures Society, founded in 1965 in Washington, publishes a journal called *The Futurist*. The first International Congress of Futures Research was held in Oslo in 1968.

Much of the planning and forecasting in the United States has to do with the needs of the military-industrial complex. The RAND Corporation, the Hudson Institute, and the Institute of Defense Analysis are examples. In 1965 the American Academy of Arts and Sciences created the Commission on the Year 2000. Its leader, sociologist Daniel Bell (1967:xxvi), has explained that the commission's effort is not ". . . to 'predict' the future, as if this were some far-flung rug of time unrolled to some distant point, but the effort to sketch 'alternative futures'—in other words, the likely results of different choices, so that the polity can understand the costs and consequences of different desires." Organizations similar to the Commission on the Year 2000 exist in England, France, and other countries. In the Soviet Union (where science fiction is as popular as in the United States), futures planning has long been related to government five- and ten-year plans. In this chapter, we shall briefly review some of the topics that are prominent in publications about the future. Needless to say, there are often differences of opinion among the authorities.

Population increase

Except for warfare, the most immediate problem facing the world is the population explosion. One authority states: "The present rate of world population increase—20 per 1,000—is almost certainly without precedent, and it is hundreds of times greater than the rate that has been the norm for most of man's history" (Coale 1974:51). Our species reached its first billion mark in 1850, its second in 1930, its third in 1960, and its fourth in 1976. This population boom may bring in its train a host of calamities, including widespread famine. The world's population is now doubling within a period of 35 years, but the rate is faster in the less-developed nations. The population of India may double within 28 years. In 1971 India's population was about 548 million; it adds 13 million a year, and may reach 1 billion by A.D. 2000. There have been predictions that 75 percent of the world's population by then will be living in Africa, Asia, and Latin America. China should have over 1 billion people by A.D. 2000.

In former periods, population increased most in the more successful, expanding economies, but now it is the poor, less-developed nations that are seeing the greatest increase. This boom is not due to higher birth rates but, rather, to lower death rates resulting from the introduction of better sanitary and medical practices. Even the introduction and greater use of soap have made a difference, and there has been a drop in malaria and other diseases due to DDT spraying campaigns. Vaccination, inoculation, use of penicillin, and improved medical facilities have led to a reduction in smallpox, typhoid, plague, cholera, tuberculosis, and other ailments, in spite of the low number of doctors in relation to the population in the less-developed nations.

Another reason for further population growth in such countries is that nearly half the people in them are under 15 years of age, and they will soon have families of their own. In India almost everyone gets married, marries early, and brides have many reproductive years ahead of them. Nowadays, they live longer; in India the expectation of life at birth rose from 23 years in 1931 to 46 years in 1961. But while, in the last six decades of British rule, the population of India increased over 50 percent, the increase of cultivable land in that time was only 1.5 percent. Similarly, between 1960 and 1965, the production of food went up by 6 percent in Latin America, but the population increased by 11 percent.

In 1965 the Director General of the Food and Agriculture Organization (FAO) announced that there had been no appreciable increase in food production per head of the world's population in the past seven years. In the following year, the FAO stated there had been no increase in agricultural production in 1966, although the world's population had grown that year by 70 million (Paddock and Paddock 1967:45).

It has been estimated that the countries of eastern and southern Asia, Africa, and Latin America must increase their food production within 10 years by 26 percent just to maintain their present inadequate dietary levels. It seems unlikely they will be able to do so (Ibid:55). Consequently, some demographers and agronomists have warned that famines will occur before long. In 1966 the then Secre-

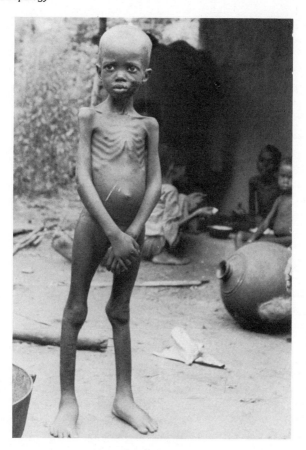

Famine victim.

tary of Agriculture Orville L. Freeman estimated that the United States could continue to export wheat to the hungry nations of the world until 1984; but, after that year, the total agricultural productivity of the United States will no longer be enough to avert famines.

To be sure, other estimates are more optimistic. Donald Bogue (1968) believes that the population explosion has been exaggerated and that the gloomy prophecies are based on the premise, "If recent trends continue . . . ," whereas recent trends are not continuing. In their generally optimistic forecast of the future, Kahn, Brown, and Martel (1976:34, 212) predict that 200 years from now the earth's population will be about 15 billion, give or take a factor of two, and that this population will be rather stable. The authors claim that the rate of population growth is now declining in almost all developed countries. Hence there may be no need for alarm about world population growth in the long run.

The problem, however, is that meanwhile population is still in- **Food** creasing, while food resources are uncertain. In recent years there **resources** have been widespread famines in the Sahel area south of the Sahara and in parts of South Asia. A World Food Conference study esti- mates that half of all child deaths are "in some way attributable to malnutrition" and that 200 million living children are undernour- ished (Rothschild 1974:30–31).

One problem, not always remembered, is that there must also be enough food resources for our domesticated animals, as well as for humans. John McHale (1969:79) writes:

Recent calculations . . . suggest that the present maintenance of three bil- lion humans in the biosphere requires a plant yield sufficient to accommo- date 14.5 billion other consumers. These others, the animal populations, are an essential element in maintaining the humans by acting as inter- mediate processors for many plant products indigestible by man. Pigs, for example, consume as much food as 1,600 million people, when measured on a global scale; the world horse population has a protein intake corre- sponding to that of 650 million humans—almost the population of China.

In 1968 and 1969, there were reports of a "green revolution" in India, with such improved agricultural productivity that India ex- pected to achieve self-sufficiency in food production within four years. This hope was based upon the introduction of new high-yield strains of rice and wheat, chemical fertilizers, and advanced irriga- tion techniques. It was reported that the 1968 wheat crop had topped India's previous record harvest by 35 percent, or by 4.3 million tons. Between 1967 and 1970 Pakistan increased its wheat harvest by over 70 percent. But the green revolution is vulnerable. It depends upon the free use of fertilizers, including petroleum-based chemical ferti- lizers, the prices of which went up sharply in 1974 at the time of the fuel crisis. Moreover, the new grains planted on a wide scale are susceptible to pests and rust and may require the development of pesticides which do not, at the same time, otherwise damage the environment. Water scarcity is another problem. So it remains to be seen whether this agricultural boom can be sustained and whether it will keep pace with the population increase. Similar booms have been reported for Pakistan, Sri Lanka, the Philippines, China, Turkey, and Mexico, but all these countries are also experiencing population explosions.

India and some of the other less-developed countries have em- **Birth control** barked on birth-control programs. By 1968, 4.2 million persons in India had been sterilized. Ninety percent of these sterilizations were vasectomies; the rest were tubectomies. By 1968, 2.4 million IUD "loops" (intrauterine devices) were in use, and about 100,000 women were taking contraceptive pills under medical supervision. Other methods of contraception were also being advanced by offices of family planning. It has been estimated that through these methods India has prevented the arrival of some 10 million to 15 million babies (Chandrasekhar 1968). The sterilization campaign was intensified in the year preceding Indira Gandhi's ouster in the elections of 1977; between April 1976 and January 1977, 7.8 million persons were sterilized. But it remains to be seen how this program will affect India's population increase in the long run. Most men in India who submit to sterilization already have a few children, at least one or two sons, and many of them have large families.

In any case, it seems likely that many other nations will have to engage in programs like India's if they hope to curb the population boom. Attitudes and values concerning optimum family size will undergo change. Conservative religious opposition to birth control, whether it be Hindu, Islamic, Christian, or whatever, will be challenged in different parts of the world as the numbers of people increase and reserves of food diminish.

Poor and rich nations

Related to the problems of food resources and population increase is the fact that the world seems to be dividing into two unequal blocs: a poor, largely southern area (Latin America, Africa, Asia) and a better-off northern area (North America, Europe, the Soviet Union, and Japan). The disparity may be seen in the fact that in the 1970s, income per person in the United States was more than $4,000, and in India, less than $100. The rich-poor gap is widening, rather than narrowing, largely because of the poorer countries' population increase, which is double that of the richer group. The enormous energy consumption of the United States underlines the present gap in wealth: with 6 percent of the world's population, the United States uses one third of the world's energy and consumes between one fourth and one half of most minerals.

The poorer countries are also the nations with the lowest rates of literacy. Adult illiteracy occurs mainly in Asia, Africa, and Latin America. Despite a worldwide increase in education, there are more illiterate persons today than there were 20 years ago because of the growth in population. About two fifths of the world's adults cannot read and write. The countries with the least to spend on education are those with the highest birth rates (L. R. Brown 1972:116, 127).

The poorer countries are dependent on the richer ones for capital and technology, but the rich ones are dependent on the poor countries for essential minerals. The United States must import aluminum, manganese, nickel, tin, zinc, and chromium. Unfortunately, however, the rich countries tend to trade more with one another than with the poorer countries.

Something to watch in the future will be the effect of multinational corporations on international relations. The 1960s and 1970s have seen a great growth in companies whose plants are located in different nations. Most U.S. products delivered to foreign markets are now produced abroad, not made in factories in the United States.

Multinational corporations

Some of the large multinational corporations are comparable to modern states in wealth and power. The gross annual sales of General Motors are larger than the gross national product of East Germany. GM has 127 plants in the United States and 45 in other nations. When companies have many stockholders and employees in different parts of the world, it becomes more difficult to associate such a company with a particular nation. Companies of this sort no longer manufacture goods in one country and export them from there but produce goods in different countries and supply customers from those sources.

Some of the large corporations have resulted from mergers, which occur at the rate of about 5,000 a year. These are not usually combinations of former rivals; instead, more than 80 percent of the mergers in mining and manufacturing are conglomerates that bring unrelated activities together under one management. Barber (1970: 264) sees this as a worldwide trend. "A good guess is that by 1980 three hundred large corporations will control 75 percent of all the world's manufacturing assets." Barber may be wrong in this prediction, but he is right to draw attention to the growth of the multinational corporations and their potential bearing on the future.

It has been estimated that by 1980 there may be between 55 million and 60 million *more* persons in metropolitan areas than there were in 1960. Population increase is apt to affect all the world's city populations.

Megalopolis

Kahn and Wiener (1967:61–62) predict that the United States will have three giant megalopolitan areas in A.D. 2000, to which they give the picturesque names of Boswash, Chipitts, and Sansan. Boswash will extend from Boston to Washington and may contain almost one fourth of the U.S. population. Chipitts, concentrated around the Great Lakes, will stretch from Chicago to Pittsburgh and may extend north to Detroit, Toledo, Cleveland, Akron, Buffalo, and Rochester. Sansan would stretch initially from San Diego to Santa Barbara and ultimately from Santa Barbara to San Francisco. The three megalopolitan areas are expected to include about half the U.S. population in the year 2000. It is predicted that similar megalopolitan areas will develop in other parts of the world—in southeastern England, in the Tokyo-Osaka strip in Japan, and elsewhere.

The potentialities for further air and water pollution in such massed agglomerations are obviously immense, particularly if the present form of automobile continues to be used.

Energy sources

The world now depends on energy from fossil fuels, supplies of which are finite, but within the next 50 years it will have to rely increasingly on alternate sources such as solar, wind, geothermal energy, and nuclear power. During the transition period there will probably be heavy dependence on coal and shale to supplement resources of oil and natural gas. The Energy Research and Development Administration projects that by the end of the century the percentage of our country's energy needs supplied by oil and gas will be down to 45–50 percent, although it is now about 75 percent.

Solar energy has been used to provide heat and hot water (with backup systems of electricity or gas for sunless periods) and could also be used to generate electricity, although the methods now devised would be expensive and require large tracts of land. In 1977 the federal government was spending just less than $300 million on solar energy; it might supply as much as one fourth of our energy needs in the next century.

Large modern windmills, strategically located, could be in operation by the 1980s, and ocean tides could be tapped for power. Geothermal energy, heat within the earth, may also be tapped through deep-drilling operations. Some pilot projects are underway to develop energy systems along new lines. A team from Oklahoma State University, under contract from the United Nations, will design an energy center for a village in Sri Lanka (Ceylon) which will make use of solar energy, wind power, and energy from agricultural wastes.

In the last edition of this book optimistic expectations were expressed about the future uses of nuclear power. Similar optimism was then being voiced by government spokespersons. In a fact sheet issued by the Federal Energy Administration in 1975 it was estimated that atomic power would account for about 15 percent of demand by 1985 and between 30 and 40 percent by the year 2000. But since then more attention has been paid to the drawbacks, expenses, and dangers of radioactivity and the possibility of explosions, leakage, and sabotage in nuclear fission plants. Some hope, however, has been placed in the future development of nuclear fusion, in which these dangers would be much reduced.

Fuels require engines built of iron, copper, zinc, and other metals. Although copper is now abundant, it may be in short supply 200 years from now, and there may also be shortages of mercury, gold, silver, lead, and other metals (Skinner 1976). Even if recycling methods improve in the future, the rate of use of recycled metals will decline, requiring an increased dependence on iron and other abundant metals.

Social unrest

Much social unrest is expected to occur all over the world between now and the year 2000. One of the reasons for this will be unemployment. In the developing countries of the world, industrialization provides many new jobs, but, at the same time, the population, as we have seen, is increasing. There were three times as many unemployed in India in 1961 (9 million) as in 1951 (3 million). In 1965 there were 15 million totally unemployed. If the "underemployed" were counted, the figure would be much higher. College graduates in India are often unable to find jobs. It is not surprising that many turn to extremist left-wing or right-wing movements and sometimes engage in rioting. Political unrest and clashes between different linguistic and religious groups, such as Hindu and Muslim, may be expected to continue in the future.

Similar conditions exist in some of the more industrially advanced nations, where automation (to be discussed further below) adds to the ranks of the unemployed. In the United States mechanical farm equipment and factory automation have reduced opportunities for unskilled labor, leading to a cityward migration of southern blacks. During the last 60 years the rundown central areas of many American cities have become increasingly populated by Negroes from the south, while whites have been moving out to the suburbs, an exodus that has been more difficult for nonwhites. Between 1940 and 1950 the white population in America's largest cities increased 3.7 percent, while the Negro population rose 67.8 percent. (Grodzins 1970:293). Since much of this population is concentrated in the central areas, a kind of racial segregation has in effect come about, which raises problems concerning educational facilities and related issues. This is a potentially dangerous situation, especially since inflation and widespread unemployment have made the problems of urban blacks worse than ever.

Social unrest is widespread throughout the world: tribalism and nationalism in Africa, racial tensions in South Africa and Rhodesia, conflicts between regional and linguistic groups and between high and low castes in India, between political factions in China, between social classes in Latin America, and so forth. Moreover, judging from past experience, it seems likely that wars will continue to break out in different parts of the world during the next two decades.

Such hazards, of course, are not new, but relatively new are the enhanced potentialities of terrorism. The high level of the world's technology and the complex interdependence of our institutions make for great vulnerability to terrorist activity, including bombing, kidnapping, hijacking, and seizure of hostages. A small number of terrorists can wreak a great deal of damage in a short time, and since it is difficult to adequately forestall such assaults, we may expect to see more of them in the coming decades.

Expansion of knowledge

So far, our survey of possible future developments has drawn a bleak and depressing picture. When it comes to the advance of human knowledge and technology, the outlook seems more encouraging, although it is just this aspect of the future that alarms Jacques Ellul, as he has indicated in his *The Technological Society*. The problem, of course, is: How will people use the new knowledge at their disposal? Will a totalitarian superstate emerge to manipulate vast subservient populations, as in the nightmare worlds of Aldous Huxley and George Orwell? That is a possibility, but we need not assume it will happen.

Some scientists are quite confident about the future. Here is a statement by Emmanuel Mesthene, director of the Harvard Program in Science and Technology:

We have now, or know how to acquire, the technical capacity to do very nearly everything we want. Can we transplant human hearts, control personality, order the weather that suits us, travel to Mars or Venus? Of course we can, if not now or in five or ten years, then certainly in 25 or in 50 or 100 (quoted in Sullivan 1967).

The idea that anything is possible for science is expressed in what Arthur C. Clarke has called Clarke's Law:

If a distinguished but elderly scientist says that something is possible he is almost certainly correct. If he says that something is impossible he is very probably wrong.

Clarke adds, "By elderly scientist I mean anyone over thirty" (Clarke 1968:247).

Twice in 1969 men were sent to the moon, landed safely, and returned to earth. These dramatic events made it seem that, indeed, scientists can accomplish anything they put their minds to. However, scientific projects like the moon landing require funding, and this has been made difficult recently by economic problems, the energy crisis, and inflation.

Astronaut James B.
Irwin on the moon.

While astronauts have been exploring outer space, aquanauts have been probing the "inner space" of the world's oceans. Not only are the oceans rich in untapped plant and animal food resources but they are also rich in minerals, including manganese, cobalt, nickel, and copper. Special underwater vehicles, living quarters, and laboratories have been designed. The first manned undersea work station was established off Marseilles in 1962 by Jacques-Yves Cousteau; two men stayed underwater for a week at a depth of 33 feet, daily exploring outside to a depth of 85 feet. A later undersea work station was inhabited by six men for 30 days (McHale 1969: 203). Four American scientists spent 60 days on the ocean floor in February–April of 1969.

Another remarkable scientific development has been the orbiting of a series of communications satellites, one over the Pacific Ocean, one over the Indian Ocean, and two over the Atlantic. These form a global communications link, making it possible to communicate between any two parts on earth through a single electronic system. The space shuttle is another new device, scheduled to start operations in 1979.

With these accomplishments on record, it is understandable that we are now trying to chart new pathways in space. The moon is seen by some as a prospective site for colonies equipped with strategic telescopes, a source for valuable minerals, and a sanitarium for earthly patients who will benefit from the weak lunar gravity. Adrian Berry (1974), who discusses these possibilities, goes on to visualize some more ambitious probes into the universe, such as to Venus, whose impossible "hellish" climate will, he believes (following a suggestion by Carl Sagan), undergo far-reaching man-made changes. Berry shrugs off cutbacks in space budgets as mere temporary deterrents in the exploration of space, for he is thinking in terms of thousands of years, not just decades or centuries.

Automation and computers

Although the word *automation* has come to refer to laborsaving machinery in general, it also has a more precise meaning, referring to machines with a feedback system, so they can control their own operations. If something goes wrong, the machine corrects itself, thus obviating the human attendant. A thermostat governing an oil burner provides an example of feedback; when temperature in the room reaches a predetermined level, the thermostat turns off the burner, but turns it back on again if the temperature drops below this level.

A computer is a self-regulating machine, which has been characterized as a complex, fast-operating sort of abacus. Computers regulate the sequences in automated machinery. They can provide an integrated data-processing system for businesses, replacing older, slower manual methods. Computers have enabled banks to dispense with manual operations and provide their customers with improved services. Information about patients in hospitals, tax data, and crime records may all be made available very quickly by computers. They are widely employed in scientific work and research. We could not have landed men on the moon without computers.

The computer industry is expected to multiply in the near future. According to a House of Commons Select Committee in 1971, it will be the world's third largest industry in the 1980s, after automobiles and oil (A. Berry 1974:144).

Computerlike machines, along with other advances in medicine, should help to prolong the human life-span. We already have heart-lung machines, artificial kidneys, electronic pacemakers, organ and tissue banks, and organ transplants.

A combination of inventions involving computers, satellites, and other devices has made possible new systems of telecommunication which will make it as simple to communicate with Peking as to complete a local call. Scientists visualize two-way communication instead of the one-way television reception we have now, allowing for conversations and conferences among widely separated persons who will appear on one another's screens.

If automation makes more leisure possible, more time could be given to education by young people. In 1971 half of the U.S. population was under 15 years of age, and 40 percent of those of college age were in college. Since then there has been some falling off in college enrollments, partly because of inflation, high tuition costs, and the end of the post-World War II "baby boom." The number of college-educated people in the United States remains impressive, however, especially when compared with conditions only 50 years ago. According to U.S. Bureau of the Census statistics, 50,000 students were enrolled in colleges and universities in 1871, or 0.3 percent of the American population. By 1930 the figure had climbed to 1,100,000, or 4.4 percent, and by 1971 to 8,090,000, or 10.1 percent (Lenski and Lenski 1974:405).

Education

Education of the present generation prepares the groundwork for education of the next generation. Well-educated parents want their children to be well educated too. A child grows up with a better start for learning in such a setting. By itself, education is no panacea, but it does develop critical skills and judgment to some degree. The steady and rather remarkable increase in higher education is therefore a promising sign. We may hope for a more open-minded and better educated generation, able to cope with the strange transformations of the world today. We depend upon these young men and women to help bring our world humanely and adventuresomely into the 21st century.

Herman Kahn and his associates have been the most persistent American futurologists, responsible for the following books: Herman Kahn and Anthony J. Wiener, eds., *The Year 2000: A Framework for Speculation on the Next Thirty-Three Years* (New York: Macmillan Co., 1967); Herman Kahn and B. Bruce-Briggs, *Things to Come: Thinking About the Seventies and Eighties* (New York: Macmillan Co., 1972); Herman Kahn, William Brown, and Leon Martel, *The Next Two Hundred Years: A Scenario for America and the World* (New York: William Morrow and Co., 1976). Kahn has been concerned with relatively short-range projections of the future. Stimulating for its more long-range forecasts is Adrian Berry, *The Next Ten Thousand Years: A Vision of Man's Future in the Universe* (New York: E. P. Dutton and Co., 1974). For a variety of viewpoints, see Alvin Toffler, ed., *The Futurists* (New York: Random House, 1972). On computers, robots, and cyborgs, see David M. Rorvik, *As Man Becomes Machine: The Evolution of the Cyborg* (New York: Doubleday & Co., 1971). See also: Stuart

Suggestions for further reading

Chase, *The Most Probable World* (New York: Harper & Row, 1968); John McHale, *The Future of the Future* (New York: George Braziller, 1969); Victor C. Ferkiss, *Technological Man: The Myth and the Reality* (New York: George Braziller, 1969); Lester R. Brown, *World Without Borders* (New York: Random House, 1972).

Many of the foregoing works have an optimistic bias. For a less hopeful view, see Gordon Rattray Taylor, *How to Avoid the Future* (London: Secker and Warburg, 1975).

peoples and tribes, glossary, references cited, illustrations

Peoples and tribes: Identification and geographical locations

A

Alorese. Agricultural people on the island of Alor in Indonesia, about halfway between Java and New Guinea.

Anang. Bantoid-speaking horticultural people of southern Nigeria.

Andaman Islanders. Negrito hunting-gathering people in islands in the Bay of Bengal south of Burma.

Apa Tani. Advanced sedentary horticultural tribe inhabiting the Subansiri Valley in Arunachal Pradesh (formerly the Northeast Frontier Agency) in northeastern India.

Apache. Athapaskan-speaking hunting-gathering tribes of the American Southwest.

Arunta. Hunting-gathering tribe in central Australia.

Aymara. Large group of Indians, mostly peasants, in Bolivia and Peru.

Aztecs. Dominant ruling tribe in the Valley of Mexico at the time of the Spanish conquest.

B

Balinese. Inhabitants of the island of Bali in Indonesia east of Java.

Berbers. Hamitic-speaking Caucasoid peoples of North Africa, most of whom are agriculturalists.

Blackfoot. Algonkian-speaking Indians of Montana who were Plains Indian mounted hunters during the early 19th century.

Bondo. Highland people of Orissa in central east India who practice horticulture and agriculture.

Bororo. A sedentary horticultural tribe in Central Brazil.

Bushman. Short-statured hunting-gathering people of the Kalahari Desert region of South Africa.

C

Chaga, or Chagga. Bantu-speaking agriculturalists who occupy the slopes of Mt. Kilimanjaro and Mt. Meru in Kenya, East Africa.

Cheyenne. An Algonkian-speaking tribe of the western Plains of North America.

Chippewa. See **Ojibwa Indians.**

Creek. A confederacy of mostly Muskoghean-speaking Indians formerly inhabiting Alabama, Georgia, and Florida.

Crow. A Siouan-speaking Plains tribe inhabiting the region between the Platte and Yellowstone Rivers.

D

Dafla. Seminomadic pastoral and horticultural tribe in the Subansiri Valley of Arunachal Pradesh (formerly the Northeast Frontier Agency) in northeastern India.

Dahomey. West African kingdom on the Gulf of Guinea during the 19th century.

Dinka. Tribe in the Nilotic Sudan which combines pastoralism and horticulture.

Dobu. Melanesian tribe on an island near the Trobriand Islands.

Dogrib. Scattered Athapaskan-speaking people in northwestern Canada.

E

Eskimo. Hunting people scattered mainly along the coastal regions of Arctic North America from Alaska to Greenland.

F

Flathead Indians. Tribe in Montana formerly having a Plains Indian culture.

G

Gusii. A pastoral and agricultural Bantu-speaking tribe in Kenya, East Africa.

H

Hopi. A sedentary Shoshonean-speaking agricultural Pueblo tribe in northeastern Arizona.

I

Iatmul. A formerly head-hunting Melanesian tribe in the Sepik River region of New Guinea.

Ifugao. A hill people in northern Luzon in the Philippines who cultivate rice on terraced hillsides.

Inca. Ruling tribe in Peru and adjacent regions of South America at the time of the Spanish conquest.

Iroquois. Confederacy of tribes in the region of present-day New York state who combined maize-growing with hunting and gathering in pre-Columbian and early contact times.

J

Jats. Farming people in the region of Delhi in North India.

K

Karimojong. Pastoral tribe in northwest Kenya and adjacent parts of Uganda in North Africa.

Kutchin. Athapaskan-speaking tribe in the Yukon territory of Alaska.

Kwakiutl. Northwest Coast American Indian hunting-gathering tribe on Vancouver Island and British Columbia which had permanent settlements due to relative abundance of food resources.

L

Lepcha. Mongoloid people in Sikkim, between India and Tibet, mostly Buddhist by religion.

M

Mandan-Hidatsa. The lumping together of two Siouan-speaking sedentary tribes located on the upper Missouri River.

Manus. Trading and fishing people of the Admiralty Islands north of New Guinea, who before World War II lived in houses raised on stilts above the waters of a lagoon. They now live on the mainland.

Marquesans. Polynesians of the Marquesas Islands.

Marri Baluch. Pastoral tribe in Baluchistan in western Pakistan.

Maya. Advanced horticultural people of Mexico, Guatemala, and Honduras, who had one of the highest civilizations of the pre-Columbian New World.

Minangkabau. Matrilineal agricultural people in the high valleys in interior Sumatra in Indonesia, having both wet-rice and swidden cultivation.

Mundurucú. A horticultural tribe located east of the upper Tapajós River in Brazil.

Muria. An agricultural hill tribe in Orissa in central eastern India.

Murngin. A hunting-gathering tribe in northeastern Arnhem Land in northern Australia.

N

Navaho. Athapaskan-speaking tribe in Arizona, New Mexico, and Utah, formerly hunting-gathering but now with a farming and pastoral basis of subsistence.

Nayar. A formerly martial caste located in Kerala on the Malabar coast of South India.

Ngombe. Bantu-speaking farming people of the Congo basin.

Nyakyusa. An agricultural Bantu-speaking tribe in Tanzania, East Africa.

O

Ojibwa Indians. Algonkian-speaking, formerly mainly hunting-gathering peoples located in the Great Lakes region of North America.

Omaha. A Siouan-speaking tribe now located in northeastern Nebraska.

Ona. Hunting-gathering tribe of Tierra del Fuego near the southernmost tip of South America.

P

Pilagá. A hunting-gathering, fishing, and horticultural tribe living near the Pilcomayo River in the Argentine Gran Chaco.

R

Rājpūts. A tribal group in North India which prides itself on its martial traditions.

S

Samoans. Polynesians of the Samoan Islands.

Shilluk. Pastoral-horticultural tribe of the Nilotic Sudan.

Sirionó. Nomadic hunting-gathering tribe of Bolivia.

Siwai. Melanesian horticultural tribe.

Swazi. Bantu-speaking sedentary agricultural and pastoral tribe in South Africa.

T

Tikopia. Small island in western Polynesia whose inhabitants are dependent on horticulture and fishing.

Tiv. Mainly horticultural tribe of the Nigerian plateau in West Africa, having many domesticated animals.

Tlingit. Northwest Coast American Indian hunting-gathering tribe, whose northernmost representatives live on the coast of Alaska and who had permanent settlements due to relative abundance of food resources.

Toda. Pastoral tribe in the Nilgiri Hills of South India.

Trobriand Islanders. Horticultural and fishing Melanesian people of the Trobriand Islands off the southeast end of New Guinea, located mainly on the island of Kiriwina.

Trukese. Inhabitants of the island of Truk in Micronesia.

Tsembaga. A Maring-speaking horticultural tribe in the Australian-administered Territory of New Guinea.

Tswana. A Bantu-speaking tribe in Botswana, formerly Bechuanaland, South Africa.

U

Uganda. East African nation north of Lake Victoria, formerly a kingdom during the 19th century.

V

Vedda. Hunting-gathering tribe in Śri Lanka or Ceylon.

Y

Yako. Bantoid-speaking horticultural tribe in southern Nigeria.

Yokuts. Hunting-gathering tribe in the San Joaquin Valley and adjacent regions of California in pre-Columbian times.

Z

Zulu. Bantu-speaking people in South Africa who developed a centralized political system under a king in the late 18th and early 19th centuries.

Zuñi. A sedentary agricultural Pueblo tribe in New Mexico.

Glossary

Acculturation. Phenomena involving culture change when two formerly distinct cultures come into contact with one another.

Adolescence. Period between puberty and adulthood.

Aerophone. Air or wind instrument.

Affinal. Related by marriage.

Age grade. Members of a society who belong to a particular age bracket for which there is usually a separate term.

Age set. A group of persons of the same sex and about the same age who advance from one age grade to another.

Agribusiness. The organization along business lines of advanced, modern, large-scale agriculture.

Agriculture. A system of food production that makes use of plow and draft animals (Old World) or fertilizing, terracing, irrigation, or use of *chinampas* (pre-Columbian New World).

Animatism. Belief in impersonal supernatural power such as *mana.* '

Animism. Belief in spiritual beings.

Anthropoidea. The suborder of Primates containing the higher primates, such as monkeys, apes, and human beings.

Anticipatory levirate. Allowance of sexual relations between a man and his older brother's wife.

Ape. Member of the family Pongidae within the superfamily Hominoidea, including chimpanzees, gorillas, orangutans, gibbons, and siamangs.

Apparatchiki. Full-time Communist Party functionaries in the Soviet Union.

Applied anthropology. A branch of anthropology concerned with directed culture change.

Archaeology. A main division of cultural anthropology that deals with past cultures through excavation and analysis of their remains.

Australopithecines. Hominids of the late Pliocene and early Pleistocene epochs with small cranial capacity and upright posture.

Avunculocal residence. Residence of a married couple with or near the husband's male matrilineal kinsmen, particularly his mother's brother.

B

Basic personality structure. The common aspects of personality shared by the members of a particular society.

Bifurcate merging. A form of kinship system that merges father and father's brother, while distinguishing them from mother's brother, and that merges mother and mother's sister, while distinguishing them from father's sister. Related to this is a distinction between cross and parallel cousins, with the latter being equated with Ego's siblings.

Bilateral descent. Reckoning of kinship equally through both parents.

Bilocal residence. Either patrilocal or matrilocal residence for a married couple, with about equal frequency of each.

Bipedalism. Upright locomotion on two feet.

Blind analysis. The submission of materials such as the Rorschach Test, Thematic Apperception Test, or drawings to analysts who know nothing about the culture from which the materials were collected and who must make an analysis without access to other information.

Broad-spectrum food exploitation. The practice of exploiting a great range of different plant and animal food resources within a particular environment.

C

Calendrical rite. A ritual performed at a regular point in the yearly cycle.

Cargo cult of Melanesia. Magico-religious movement in which predictions are made about the future advent of ships or planes bearing cargo for the Melanesians.

Caste. An endogamous, hierarchically ranked social group that is sometimes associated with a particular occupation.

Chinampa. A man-made islet, anchored by willow trees, constructed by pre-Columbian Aztecs of Mexico to support topsoil for growing crops.

Churinga. Wooden or stone slab carved with totemic designs by male Australian aborigines, regarded as a sacred object not to be seen by women or children.

Civilization. Advanced form of culture associated with agriculture, metallurgy, division of labor, class stratification, formation of a state, and city life.

Clan. A unilineal descent group whose members believe they are related to one another through descent from a common ancestor or ancestress.

Class. A division of social stratification determined by economic factors and relationship to strategic resources.

Classificatory system. A form of kinship system in which merging is often employed, so that terms such as father, mother, brother, sister, son, and daughter are extended to persons who are not lineal kinsmen.

Cognate words. Words that have both semantic and phonemic correspondence in two or more related languages.

Cognition. The process of knowing.

Cognitive anthropology. A branch of anthropology, more particularly of anthropological linguistics, that is concerned with the ways in which the speakers of particular languages classify and conceptualize phenomena. Sometimes known as ethnoscience.

Collateral relative. A relative related indirectly through a linking relative.

Communal cult. A religious performance carried out by laymen, not requiring a magico-religious specialist.

Comparative method. The method used by 19th-century cultural evolutionists to reconstruct stages of cultural evolution on the basis of ethnographic descriptions of different cultures ranging from those of hunting-gathering societies to advanced civilizations.

Competence. In linguistics, refers to an individual's grasp of the principles underlying his language, knowledge of the rules needed to speak it.

Composite tool. A tool consisting of different parts and made with different materials.

Conflict resolution. The process of finding a settlement between parties in a dispute.

Consanguine. Related through descent.

Cordophone. Stringed musical instrument.

Corporate community. A relatively isolated, integrated social group, with common ownership of land and a tendency toward endogamy.

Corvée labor. Forced unpaid labor exacted by the state.

Court. An assembly for the transaction of judicial business.

Couvade. The practice of a husband resting up and observing taboos after his wife has given birth.

Cross cousins. Children of siblings of opposite sex.

Cross-cultural survey. A comparison of data from a group of societies, such as those described in the Human Relations Area Files, for the purpose of finding correlations between particular institutions and practices.

Cultural anthropology. With physical anthropology, one of the two main divisions of anthropology; it includes the fields of linguistics, ethnology, and archaeology, all of which have to do with the study of human cultures.

Cultural diffusion. The spreading of a culture trait from one society to another.

Cultural ecology. The study of human sociocultural adaptation to our environments.

Cultural evolution. The development of culture through progressively more complex stages, with increases in the energy available to humans.

Cultural integration. The tendency of a culture to reconcile or overcome internal conflicts or inconsistencies.

Cultural relativism. The idea that a practice or institution must be understood in the context of its culture, thus tending to an abstention from critical value judgments.

Culture. The shared behavior learned by members of a society, the way of life of a group of people. (For other definitions, see pages 4–5.)

D

Deep structure. In linguistics, the underlying meaning of an utterance.

Descriptive linguistics. A branch of linguistics concerned with the analysis of a language as a synchronic system, its phonemes, morphemes, and rules of syntax. Also called structural linguistics.

Descriptive system. As opposed to classificatory system, a kinship system in which merging is not employed and in which terms such as father, mother, brother, sister, son, and daughter are not extended to other relatives.

Diachronic study. A study (of a culture or language) involving the time dimension.

Diffusion. See **Cultural diffusion.**

Double descent. A kinship system in which a person belongs to both his father's patrilineal group and his mother's matrilineal group.

E

Ecclesiastical cult institution. A religious organization involving a priesthood.

Ecological niche. The particular environment to which a population adjusts itself.

Ecology. The study of the interrelationship of organisms and their environment, including both the physical environment and other living organisms.

Ego. In kinship diagrams, the person from whom relationships are reckoned.

Emic. Referring to interpretations in terms of distinctions made by the members of a particular society under investigation.

Endogamy. The requirement to marry within a particular group.

Ethnocentrism. Value judgment in terms of the standards of one's own culture.

Ethnography. *a.* A detailed written description of a particular culture.
b. The general body of such literature.

Ethnology. A main division of cultural anthropology which deals with the study of living cultures.

Ethnoscience. See **Cognitive anthropology.**

Etic. Referring to interpretations in terms of distinctions made by a community of outside observers, not in terms of distinctions made by members of the society under investigation.

Exogamy. The requirement to marry outside of a particular group.

F

Fetish. In religion, an object considered sacred because it is believed to be inhabited by, or associated with, a spirit. To be contrasted with an amulet, an object considered sacred because it is believed to contain some inherent power.

Feudalism. A method of government involving relationships between a lord and his vassals, which usually includes military service.

Fictive kinship. The incorporation of an outsider into a kin network.

Folklore. Defined in narrow terms: oral literature, consisting of stories, myths, folktales, legends, riddles, and proverbs. Defined in broader terms, it also includes costume, dance, games, and other aspects of culture.

Folk society. A term used by Robert Redfield for homogeneous tribal and peasant societies having close face-to-face relations, with kinship and religious practices playing important roles.

Folktale. An oral narrative dealing with the adventures of a hero or trickster.

Folk taxonomy. The ways in which plants, animals, and other phenomena are classified in particular societies.

Folk-urban continuum. Robert Redfield's bipolar contrast of large, heterogeneous modern city and small, face-to-face homogeneous folk society, with intermediate communities ranged in between.

Forced observation. In linguistics, a phenomenal distinction determined by the characteristics of a particular language.

Formalism. In anthropological economics, a view that economic theory, using such concepts as "maximizing" and "economizing," can be applied to the study of primitive or non-Western economic systems.

Fraternal polyandry. A form of marriage in which a woman is married to two or more men who are brothers.

Functionalism. A school of thought or approach in anthropology that attempts to determine the functions fulfilled by different institutions in a society under investigation.

G

Generative grammar. *See* **Transformational grammar.**

Geographical determinism. The notion that geographical environment is a prime determinant of the characteristics of a culture.

Geology. The study of the earth and its changes over time through the analysis of its different layers and their fossil contents.

Ghotul. A dormitory among the Muria of Orissa, where boys and girls live together before they marry.

Glottochronology. *See* **Lexicostatistics.**

Go-between. An intermediary in a dispute.

Grammar. The body of rules that governs the arrangement of words and morphemes in a language.

Great man theory. The idea that changes in culture are due to the inventions and new ideas of exceptional men.

Group marriage. A form of marriage in which more than one man is married to more than one woman.

H

Hand axe. A pear-shaped, unhafted stone tool widely used in the Lower Paleolithic period.

Historic site archaeology. Archaeology concerned with relatively recent times when written records are available.

Historical linguistics. The diachronic study of languages as they change over time.

Hominid. Member of the family Hominidae, which includes present-day human beings and their precursors, such as *Homo erectus* and the australopithecines.

Hominoidea. The primate superfamily that includes both apes and human beings.

Homo erectus. A form of hominid that lived between 1 million and 300,000 years ago, represented by such examples as Java man and Peking man.

***Homo sapiens* (*sapiens*).** Modern humans.

Horticulture. A system of food production lacking the use of plow and draft animals and utilizing a simple technology, principally a digging stick.

Human ecology. The study of human adaptation to environment.

Human Relations Area Files (HRAF). An extensive file of ethnographic data.

Hunting-gathering. A means of subsistence without horticulture or agriculture, dependent upon the collecting of plants, nuts, and fruits, and the hunting of animals.

Hydraulic society. An advanced agricultural society making use of irrigation and tending to have a high degree of political centralization.

I

Idiographic approach. An ethnographic approach that aims at a thorough and objective documentation of a culture in all its unique features without involving a search for general principles or laws.

Idiophone. A musical instrument that produces sounds through vibrations, such as rattles, gongs, and bells.

Immediate constituent (IC). In linguistics, a subdivision of an utterance.

Incest taboos. Taboos on sexual relations between members of a designated kin group, such as a nuclear family.

Independent invention. The discovery of the same invention by two or more different persons or in two or more different cultures.

Individualistic cult institution. A solitary ritual performed by someone who is not a religious specialist.

Indo-European languages. A family of languages found in most of Europe and parts of the Middle East and South Asia.

Industrial Revolution. The development of the factory system and associated phenomena that began in England in the 18th century.

Industrial society. A society making use of a factory system and a money economy.

Initiation ceremony. A rite of passage to signal a change of status in the initiated person, such as the transition from childhood to a more adult status in puberty ceremonies.

Inner direction. David Riesman's term for a mode of conformity associated with a period of population growth, opening frontiers, and expanding economic opportunities, involving an emphasis on hard work, discipline, and achievement.

J

Jajmani system. A system by which members of different castes in rural villages in India exchange goods and services with little exchange of money.

K

Kamin. A person who performs services for a client in the jajmani system.

Katcina, or **kachina.** Among the Hopi and Zuñi, ancestors and rain gods enacted by masked men in rituals.

Kibbutz. An Israeli collective community.

Kindred. A person's bilateral relatives on both the maternal and paternal sides.

Kinship. The classification of persons on the basis of relationship through descent or marriage.

Kiva. An underground chamber where rituals are performed among the Hopi and Zuñi.

Kula ring. An intertribal cycle of ceremonial exchanges among the Trobriand Islanders and their neighbors in Melanesia.

L

Law. A body of social norms in a society, which its members must abide by and which may be enforced by an agency recognized as having political authority in that society.

Leveling mechanism. A means of preventing too much accumulation of wealth by particular groups or persons.

Levirate. A custom whereby, when a man dies, his widow is expected to marry a brother of the deceased.

Lexicostatistics. A method involving the attempt to assign an approximate age for the time of the splitting of a parent language into two offshoots.

Lineage. A unilineal descent group whose members believe they are related to one another through descent from a common ancestor or ancestress and who are able to trace their descent to known forebears.

Lineal kin. Persons related in a single line, as grandfather-father-son.

Linguistics. The study of languages.

M

Magic. The use of rituals to direct and control supernatural forces.

Mammals. The class of warm-blooded vertebrates to which human beings belong.

Mana. Melanesian and Polynesian concept of impersonal supernatural power.

Market. A place where goods are regularly bought and sold.

Marriage. A socially recognized union of man and wife.

Matrilineal descent. The tracing of descent in the female line, from mother through daughter.

Matrilocal residence. Residence of a married couple with or near the wife's female matrilineal kinsmen.

Medicine man. See **Shaman.**

Membranophone. Skin musical instrument, such as a drum.

Merging. The practice of using the same kinship terms for lineal and collateral relatives.

Mesolithic. A period between the Paleolithic and Neolithic, dated in Europe between 11,000 and 5000 B.C.

Moiety. One half of a dual division of a society divided into two exogamous groups.

Monkey. A member of the suborder Anthropoidea, or higher primates, distinguished from the apes and humans and divided into two subfamilies, one of Old World and one of New World monkeys.

Monogamy. A form of marriage in which one man is married to one woman.

Monotheism. Belief in a single God or supreme being.

Morpheme. A unit of meaning in a language, the smallest unit that is grammatically significant.

Multilinear evolution. A school of ethnology associated with Julian H. Steward, which is concerned with the analysis of cross-cultural regularities in culture change.

Myth. A sacred story that is believed to be true in the society in which it is told.

N

Neanderthal. A late Pleistocene type of *Homo sapiens* that preceded modern humans.

Neo-evolutionism. A school of ethnology that, while admitting the weaknesses in the works of Tylor and Morgan, reaffirms the importance of studying the evolution of human culture.

Neolithic. The New Stone Age period in which plants and animals were domesticated in the Old World.

Neolocal residence. The practice of a married couple to set up a separate residence, living with neither the husband's nor the wife's parents.

Nomothetic approach. An approach in ethnology that seeks to establish general laws or regularities.

Numaym. A named landholding kinship group among the Kwakiutl Indians.

O

Olympian ecclesiastical cult. A religious cult involving a priesthood that worships a pantheon of gods.

Oral literature. See **Folklore.**

Other direction. David Riesman's term for a mode of ensuring conformity in a modern industrial society in which there is an emphasis on sensitivity to the needs and feelings of others.

P

Paleolithic. The Old Stone Age, dating from the first use of tools to around 11,000 B.C.

Paleontology. The study of the forms of life of past geological periods from their fossil remains.

Paradigmatic approach. In folklore, an analytic approach involving a search for significant patterns.

Parallel cousins.   Children of siblings of the same sex.

Participant observation.   A method of ethnological fieldwork that involves participation in community activities and informal conversations with its members.

Pastoralism.   A means of subsistence relying heavily on domesticated herding animals.

Patrilineal descent.   A form of unilineal descent in which descent is reckoned through males, from father through son.

Patrilocal residence.   Residence of a married couple with or near the husband's patrilineal kinsmen.

Peasants.   Agriculturalists who are connected with a state or city life but who mainly engage in subsistence farming on a family basis and do not hire labor or specialize in cash crops.

Performance.   In linguistics, actual speech.

Phoneme.   A minimal significant sound unit in a language which serves to distinguish one word or syllable from another for the speakers of that language.

Phonetics.   The study and classification by linguists of the different sounds made in speech utterances.

Phratry.   A group of two or more closely associated clans which may become an exogamous unit.

Physical anthropology.   With cultural anthropology, one of the two main divisions of anthropology, a field that deals with humans as physical organisms.

Pleistocene epoch.   A geological period between around 1.8 million and 10,000 years ago.

Pliocene epoch.   A geological period between around 5 million and 1.8 million years ago.

Political organization.   The aspects of social organization related to the management of public policy.

Polyandry.   A form of marriage in which one woman is married to more than one man.

Polygamy.   A general term for plural marriage, including both polyandry and polygyny.

Polygyny.   A form of marriage in which one man is married to more than one woman.

Polytheism.   A belief in many gods.

Possession.   A belief that a spirit may temporarily occupy a person's body.

Postpartum sex taboo.   Abstention from sexual relations by a husband and wife for a year or two after childbirth.

Potlatch.   A feast among the Indians of the Northwest Coast of North America at which gifts were distributed.

Prehistory.   The period before the advent of writing systems.

Priest.   A religious specialist who performs rituals and who is elected or appointed to office within a cult organization, in contrast to the more individualistic shaman, who is believed to communicate directly with the supernatural world through his own abilities.

Primate city.   A city that dominates its surrounding area and is much larger than the other urban centers in the nation.

Primates.   The order of mammals that includes lemurs, tarsiers, monkeys, apes, and human beings.

Primogeniture.   Rule of the inheritance of property by the oldest son.

Projection.   Apperceptive distortion in which inner concepts are attributed to the outer world.

Prosimian.   Member of the Prosimii, the suborder of Primates containing the lower primates, such as lemurs and tarsiers.

Protestant ethic. A set of attitudes and values that emphasizes the virtues of asceticism, hard work, and responsibility, advocated in the teachings of the Protestant Reformation.

Psychic unity of mankind. The assumption that all human beings, regardless of race or level of cultural development, share the same mental attributes and capacities.

Pueblo Indians. American Indians of the southwestern United States, including the Hopi and Zuñi among others, who raise crops and live in communities with houses made of adobe mud, wood, and stone.

R

Racism. The explanation of a people's behavior in terms of genetic endowment, usually associated with a belief in the innate superiority and inferiority of particular groups.

Reciprocity. The giving of goods or services with an expectation of a roughly equivalent return.

Redistribution. A system of economic exchange in which goods are funneled to a central place of storage and then distributed by some central administrative authority.

Religion. Beliefs and practices related to the supernatural world.

Rorschach Test. A projective personality test in which the subjects are asked to give responses about what they see in a series of ten standardized ink blots.

S

Sanction. A reaction by members of a society to show approval or disapproval of certain behavior as a way of bringing about conformity to social norms.

Secret society. A voluntary association whose membership is secret.

Semantic. Related to meaning in a language.

Semantic domain. A class of objects that share some characteristic feature or features which differentiate them from other domains.

Sexual dimorphism. Contrasts in size and strength between males and females.

Shaman, or **medicine man.** A magico-religious specialist who acts as an intermediary between the members of his society and the supernatural world on the basis of self-acquired powers, in contrast to a priest, who is an appointed member of a cult organization.

Sibling. General term for brother or sister without specifying sex.

Slash-and-burn horticulture. See **Swidden cultivation.**

Social anthropology. A branch of anthropology concerned with analyzing networks of social relations.

Social stratification. Social organization involving hierarchical distinctions of caste or class.

Society. A more or less organized group of people of both sexes who share a common culture.

Sororal polygyny. A form of marriage in which a man is married to two or more women who are sisters.

Sororate. The custom whereby, when a woman dies, her husband is expected to marry one of her sisters.

Stereoscopic vision. Depth perception made possible by having both eyes on the frontal plane with an overlapping field of vision.

Structural anthropology. A school of ethnology, of which Claude Lévi-Strauss is the leading exponent, that seeks to uncover the "mental structures" which are believed to underlie human behavior.

Structural-functionalism. A functional approach in social anthropology that is concerned with how social structures are maintained.

Structural linguistics. See **Descriptive linguistics.**

Substantivism. In anthropological economics, the view that economic theory, using such concepts as "maximization" and "economizing," cannot be meaningfully applied to the study of primitive or non-Western economic systems.

Surface structure. In linguistics, the organization of spoken utterances, which may be analyzed through the method of immediate constituents, in contrast to the underlying deep structure.

Swidden cultivation, or **slash-and-burn horticulture.** A method of food production that involves clearing a patch of land by burning, planting crops, and tending them until the fertility of the soil begins to be exhausted; the land is then allowed to lie fallow.

Synchronic study. The study (of a language or culture) at one time period.

Syncretism. A blending of two or more different forms, as in religion or musical styles.

Syntagmatic approach. A structural approach in folklore that analyzes the linear sequence of episodes.

Syntax. The branch of grammar concerned with the order in which morphemes are arranged and sentences constructed.

T

Teknonymy. The custom of naming a parent after his or her child, e.g., "Father (or Mother) of So-and-so."

Thematic Apperception Test. A projective personality test in which the subject is asked to tell stories in response to a series of standardized pictures.

Totemism. A set of beliefs concerning the relationship of clan members to the totemic animal from which the clan gets its name and from which the members are often believed to be descended. In some cases this may involve a taboo on eating the flesh of the totem animal.

Transformational grammar. A way of analyzing grammar developed by Noam Chomsky and his followers that makes a distinction between deep structures and surface structures.

Trans-Pacific diffusion. The notion that some American Indian culture patterns, including some art motifs, reached the New World by diffusion across the Pacific in pre-Columbian times.

U

Unilineal descent. The tracing of descent in a single line, either through males or through females.

Unilinear evolution. The conception of cultural evolution held by 19th-century writers involving human progression through the stages of savagery, barbarism, and civilization.

Universal aspects of culture. Aspects of culture found in all known societies but not necessarily among all individuals.

Universal evolution. The view of the general evolution of culture held by Leslie A. White.

Universal grammar. Features of grammar that Noam Chomsky believes to be characteristic of all languages.

Untouchability. The belief that it is polluting for persons of higher caste to be touched by low-caste persons.

Uxorilocal residence. Residence of a married couple at the wife's residence; the wife is not necessarily living matrilocally.

V

Virilocal residence.   Residence of a married couple at the husband's residence; the husband is not necessarily living patrilocally.

Voluntary association.   A group open to members of different age sets and kin groups, entrance to which is voluntary.

References cited

Aberle, David F., et al.
  1963 The Incest Taboo and the Mating Patterns of Animals. American Anthropologist 65:253–65.

Adams, Richard N.
  1960 An Inquiry Into the Nature of the Family. In Essays in the Science of Culture. Gertrude E. Dole and Robert Carneiro, eds. Pp. 30–49. New York: Thomas Y. Crowell.

Adams, Robert McCormick
  1966 The Evolution of Urban Society: Early Mesopotamia and Prehistoric Mexico. Chicago: Aldine Publishing Co.

Ainsworth, Mary D. Salter
  1967 Infancy in Uganda: Infant Care and the Growth of Love. Baltimore: Johns Hopkins Press.

Ammar, Hamed
  1966 Growing up in an Egyptian Village. New York: Octagon Books.

Apadaca, Anacleto
  1952 Corn and Custom: Introduction of Hybrid Corn to Spanish American Farmers in New Mexico. In Human Problems in Technological Change: A Casebook. Edward H. Spicer, ed. Pp. 35–39. New York: Russell Sage Foundation.

Ardrey, Robert
  1966 The Territorial Imperative. New York: Atheneum.
  1970 The Social Contract. New York: Atheneum.
  1976 The Hunting Hypothesis. New York: Atheneum.

Arensberg, Conrad M., and Arthur H. Niehoff
  1964 Introducing Social Change: A Manual for Americans Overseas. Chicago: Aldine Publishing Co.

Ariès, Philippe
  1965 Centuries of Childhood: A Social History of Family Life. Robert Baldick, trans. New York: Random House, Vintage Books.

Axelrad, Sidney
  1962 Infant Care and Personality Reconsidered: A Rejoinder to Orlansky. In The Psychoanalytic Study of Society. Warner Muensterberger and Sidney Axelrad, eds. Vol. 2, pp. 75–132. New York: International Universities Press.

401

Banfield, Edward C.
    1958   The Moral Basis of a Backward Society. Glencoe, Ill.: The Free Press.

Barber, Richard J.
    1970   The American Corporation: Its Power, Its Money, Its Politics. New York: E. P.
    Dutton & Co.

Barnett, Homer G., et al.
    1954   Acculturation: An Exploratory Formulation. American Anthropologist, 56:975–79.

Barnouw, Victor
    1973   Culture and Personality. Rev. ed. Homewood, Ill.: Dorsey Press.

Barry, Herbert, III, Margaret K. Bacon, and Irvin L. Child
    1957   A Cross-Cultural Survey of Some Sex Differences in Socialization. Journal of Ab-
    normal and Social Psychology 55:327–32.

Barth, Fredrik
    1956   Ecological Relationships of Ethnic Groups in Swat, North Pakistan. American An-
    thropologist 58:1079–89.
    1961   Nomads of South Persia: The Basseri Tribe of the Khamsheh Confederacy. Boston:
    Little, Brown & Co.

Barton, R. F.
    1946   The Religion of the Ifugao. American Anthropological Association Memoir no. 65.

Bascom, William
    1963   The Urban African and His World. Cahiers D'Etudes Africaines 164–83.
    1965   The Forms of Folklore. Journal of American Folklore 78:3–20.

Basham, A. L.
    1954   The Wonder That Was India. New York: Grove Press.

Batalla, Guillermo Bonfil
    1966   Conservative Thought in Applied Anthropology: A Critique. Human Organization
    25:89–92.

Beattie, John
    1964   Other Cultures: Aims, Methods, and Achievements in Social Anthropology. New
    York: Free Press.

Bell, Daniel
    1967   Introduction. *In* Kahn and Wiener 1967.

Bellah, Robert N.
    1957   Tokugawa Religion: The Values of Pre-Industrial Japan. Glencoe, Ill.: The Free
    Press.
    1964   Religious Evolution. American Sociological Review 29:358–74.

Belo, Jane
    1935   The Balinese Temper. Character and Personality 4:120–46.

Benedict, Ruth
    1934   Patterns of Culture. Boston: Houghton Mifflin Co.
    1938a   Religion. *In* General Anthropology. Franz Boas, ed. Pp. 627–64. New York:
    D. C. Heath & Co.
    1938b   Continuities and Discontinuities in Cultural Conditioning. Psychiatry 1:161–67.

Bernstein, Jeremy
    1969   Out of the Ego Chamber. The New Yorker. August 9, pp. 40–65.

Berry, Adrian
    1974   The Next Ten Thousand Years: A Vision of Man's Future in the Universe. New York:
    Saturday Review Press/E. P. Dutton & Co., Inc.

Berry, J. W.
1966   Temne and Eskimo Perceptual Skills. International Journal of Psychology 1: 207–29.

Binford, Lewis R.
1968   Post-Pleistocene Adaptations. *In* New Perspectives in Archaeology. Sally R. Binford and Lewis R. Binford, eds. Pp. 313–41. Chicago: Aldine Publishing Co.

Birdsell, Joseph B.
1953   Some Environmental and Cultural Factors Influencing the Structuring of Australian Aboriginal Populations. American Naturalist 87:171–207.

Birket-Smith, Kaj
1959   The Eskimos. London: Methuen & Co.

Black, Donald
1976   The Behavior of Law. New York: Academic Press.

Blakeney, E. H., ed.
1936   The History of Herodotus. George Rawlinson, trans. Vol. 1. London: J. M. Dent & Sons.

Bloomfield, Leonard
1933   Language. New York: Henry Holt & Co.

Boas, Franz
1884   The Central Eskimo. Bureau of American Ethnology Annual Report no. 6. Pp. 399–664. Washington, D.C.: Smithsonian Institution.
1930   The Religion of the Kwakiutl Indians. Vol. 10, part 2. New York: Columbia University Contributions to Anthropology.
1955   Primitive Art. New York: Dover Publications. (First published in 1927.)

Bock, Philip K.
1969   Modern Cultural Anthropology: An Introduction. New York: Alfred A. Knopf.

Bogue, Donald
1968   End of the Population Explosion? U.S. News and World Report 64 (March 11):59–61.

Borhegyi, Stephan de, and Suzanne de Borhegyi
1963   The Rubber Ball Game of Ancient America. Lore 13:44–53.

Boserup, Ester
1965   The Conditions of Agricultural Growth: The Economics of Agrarian Change Under Population Pressure. Chicago: Aldine Publishing Co.

Bowen, Elenore Smith
1964   Return to Laughter. New York: Doubleday & Co.

Bowlby, John
1969   Attachment and Loss. Volume I, Attachment. New York: Basic Books, Inc.

Bridges, E. Lucas
1950   Uttermost Part of the Earth. London: Hodder and Stoughton. (Published in the United States by E. P. Dutton.)

Briggs, Jean L.
1974   Eskimo Women: Makers of Men. *In* Many Sisters: Women in Cross-Cultural Perspective. Carolyn J. Matthieson, ed. Pp. 261–304. New York: The Free Press.

Bronfenbrenner, Urie
1970   Two Worlds of Childhood: U.S. and U.S.S.R. New York: Russell Sage Foundation.

Brown, Judith K.
1963   A Cross-Cultural Study of Female Initiation Rites. American Anthropologist 65: 837–53.
1970   Economic Organization Among the Iroquois. Ethnohistory 17:151–67.

Brown, Lester R.
1972   World Without Borders. New York: Random House.

Brown, Roger, and Ursula Bellugi
1966   Three Processes in the Child's Acquisition of Syntax. *In* New Directions in the Study of Language. Eric H. Lenneberg, ed. Pp. 131–61. Cambridge, Mass.: MIT Press.

Bruner, Edward M.
1956   Cultural Transmission and Cultural Change. Southwestern Journal of Anthropology 12:191–99.

Burgess, Ernest W.
1961   The Growth of the City: An Introduction to a Research Project. *In* Studies in Human Ecology. George A. Theodorson, ed. Pp. 37–44. New York: Harper & Row.

Burton, Roger V., and John W. M. Whiting
1961   The Absent Father and Cross-Sex Identity. Merrill-Palmer Quarterly of Behavior and Development 7:85–95.

Bygott, J. D.
1972   Cannibalism Among Wild Chimpanzees. Nature 238:410–11.

Campbell, Joseph
1949   The Hero With a Thousand Faces. Bollingen Series no. 17. Princeton, N.J.: Princeton University Press.

Carneiro, Robert L.
1970   A Theory of the Origin of the State. Science 169:733–38.

Carrasco, Pedro
1959   Land and Polity in Tibet. Seattle: University of Washington Press.

Carrigher, Sally
1968   War is Not in Our Genes. *In* Man and Aggression. M. F. Ashley Montagu, ed. Pp. 37–50. London: Oxford University Press.

Cassell, John
1955   A Comprehensive Health Program Among South African Zulus. *In* Health, Culture, and Community: Case Studies of Public Reactions to Health Programs. Benjamin D. Paul, ed. Pp. 15–41. New York: Russell Sage Foundation.

Chagnon, Napoleon
1968   Yanomamö Social Organization and Warfare. *In* Fried, Harris, and Murphy 1968: 109–59.

Chandler, Tertius
1960   Duplicate Inventions? American Anthropologist 62:495–98.

Chandrasekhar, S.
1968   How India is Tackling Her Population Problem. Foreign Affairs 7:138–50.

Chase, Stuart
1968   The Most Probable World. New York: Harper & Row.

Chayanov, A. V.
1966   The Theory of Peasant Economy. Daniel Thorner, Basile Kerblay, and R. E. F. Smith, eds. Homewood, Ill.: Richard D. Irwin, Inc.

Child, Irvin L., Thomas Storm, and Joseph Veroff
1958   Achievement Themes in Folk Tales Related to Socialization Practice. *In* Motives in Fantasy, Action, and Society. John W. Atkinson, ed. Pp. 479–92. Princeton, N.J.: D. Van Nostrand Co.

Clarke, Arthur C.
1968   Explorations in Tomorrow. *In* Man and the Future. James E. Gunn, ed. Pp. 246–77. Lawrence: University Press of Kansas.

Clignet, Remi
1970 Many Wives, Many Powers: Authority and Power in Polygynous Families. Evanston, Ill.: Northwestern University Press.

Coale, Ansley J.
1974 The History of the Human Population. Scientific American 231:41–51.

Cochrane, Glynn
1971 Developmental Anthropology. New York: Oxford University Press.

Cohen, Yehudi A.
1964 The Transition from Childhood to Adolescence: Cross-Cultural Studies of Initiation Ceremonies, Legal Systems, and Incest Taboos. Chicago: Aldine Publishing Co.

Coser, Lewis A.
1956 The Functions of Social Conflict. Glencoe, Ill.: Free Press.

Coulborn, Rushton, ed.
1965 Feudalism in History. Hamden, Conn.: Archon Books.

Coult, Allan D.
1963 Causality and Cross-Sex Prohibitions. American Anthropologist 65:266–77.

Covarrubias, Miguel
1937 The Island of Bali. New York: Alfred A. Knopf.
1954 The Eagle, the Jaguar, and the Serpent: Indian Art of the Americas: North America, Alaska, Canada, the United States. New York: Alfred A. Knopf.

Cunningham, Clark E.
1964 Order in the Atoni House. Bijdragen tot de Taal-Land-en Volkenkunde. Deel 120, le Aflevering, pp. 34–68. *Reprinted in* Reader in Comparative Religion; An Anthropological Approach. Third ed. William A. Lessa and Evon Z. Vogt, eds. Pp. 116–35. New York: Harper & Row, 1972.

Cushing, Frank Hamilton
1896 Outlines of Zuñi Creation Myths. Bureau of American Ethnology Annual Report no. 16. Washington D.C.: Smithsonian Institution.
1965 The Cock and the Mouse. *In* Dundes 1965:269–76.

Dalton, George
1969 Theoretical Issues in Economic Anthropology. Current Anthropology 10:63–102.

Dasen, Pierre R.
1972 Cross-Cultural Piagetian Research: A Summary. Journal of Cross-Cultural Psychology 1:23–39.

Davenport, William
1959 Nonunilinear Descent and Descent Groups. American Anthropologist 61:557–72.

Davidson, Basil
1959 The Lost Cities of Africa. Boston: Little, Brown & Co.

Davis, Allison, Burleigh B. Gardner, and Mary R. Gardner
1941 Deep South: A Social Anthropological Study of Caste and Class. Chicago: University of Chicago Press.

Degler, Carl N.
1964 Revolution Without Ideology: The Changing Place of Women in America. Daedalus: Journal of the American Academy of Arts and Sciences 93:653–70.

De la Vega, Garcilaso
1962 The Incas. The Royal Commentaries of the Inca, Garcilaso de la Vega, 1539–1616. Maria Jolas, trans. New York: Orion Press.

De Mause, Lloyd
1974 The History of Childhood. Psychohistory Press.

Denig, Edwin T.
1928–29   Indian Tribes of the Upper Missouri. Bureau of American Ethnology Annual Report no. 46. Washington D.C.: Smithsonian Institution.

Dennis, Wayne
1960   Causes of Retardation Among Institutionalized Children: Iran. Journal of Genetic Psychology 90:47–59.

De Vore, Irven, ed.
1965   Primate Behavior: Field Studies of Monkeys and Apes. New York: Holt, Rinehart & Winston.

De Vos, George A., ed.
1973   Socialization for Achievement: Essays on the Cultural Psychology of the Japanese. Berkeley: University of California Press.

De Vos, George A., and Hiroshi Wagatsuma, eds.
1966   Japan's Invisible Race: Caste in Culture and Personality. Berkeley: University of California Press.

Dole, Gertrude E.
1966   Anarchy Without Chaos: Alternatives to Political Authority Among the Kuikuru. *In* Political Anthropology. Marc J. Swartz, Victor W. Turner, and Arthur Tuden, eds. Pp. 73–87. Chicago: Aldine Publishing Co.

Dollard, John
1949   Class and Caste in a Southern Town. Second ed. New York: Harper & Row.

Domhoff, William
1967   Who Rules America? Englewood Cliffs, N.J.: Prentice-Hall, Inc.

Dore, R. P.
1965   City Life in Japan: A Study of a Tokyo Ward. Berkeley: University of California Press.

Dube, S. C.
1958   India's Changing Villages: Human Factors in Community Development. Ithaca, N.Y.: Cornell University Press.

Du Bois, Cora
1960   The People of Alor: A Socio-Psychological Study of an East Indian Island. Cambridge, Mass.: Harvard University Press. (First published in 1944.)

Dumond, D. E.
1965   Population Growth and Cultural Change. Southwestern Journal of Anthropology 21:302–24.

Dundes, Alan
1964   The Morphology of North American Indian Folktales. Folklore Fellows Communication no. 195. Helsinki.
1965   The Study of Folklore. Englewood Cliffs, N.J.: Prentice-Hall.

Durkheim, Émile
1965   The Elementary Forms of the Religious Life. Joseph Ward Swain, trans. New York: Free Press. (First published in 1915.)

Dyson-Hudson, Neville
1966   Karimojong Politics. Oxford, England: Clarendon Press.

Eastman, Max
1936   Enjoyment of Laughter. New York: Simon & Schuster.

Eberhard, Wolfram
1958   Review of Oriental Despotism by Karl A. Wittfogel. American Sociological Review 23:446–48.
1965   Conquerors and Rulers: Social Forces in Medieval China. Leiden, Netherlands: E. J. Brill.

Ekholm, Gordon F.
1953 A Possible Focus of Asiatic Influence in the Late Classic Cultures of Mesoamerica. *In* Asia and North America: Transpacific Contacts. Marian W. Smith, ed. Pp. 72–89. Memoirs of the Society for American Archaeology No. 9.

Eliade, Mircea
1950 Shamanism. *In* Ancient Religions. Vergilius Ferm, ed. Pp. 297–308. New York: Philosophical Library.

Elkin, A. P.
1954 The Australian Aborigines: How to Understand Them. Sydney: Angus & Robertson.

Elwin, Verrier
1943 The Aboriginals. Oxford University Pamphlets on Indian Affairs.
1947 The Muria and Their Ghotul. Bombay: Oxford University Press.
1950 Bondo Highlander. Bombay: Oxford University Press.

Ember, Carol R.
1973 Feminine Task Assignment and the Social Behavior of Boys. Ethos 1:424–39.

Erasmus, Charles J.
1956 Culture Structure and Process: The Occurrence and Disappearance of Reciprocal Farm Labor. Southwestern Journal of Anthropology 12:444–69.

Erikson, Erik Homburger
1963 Childhood and Society. Second ed. New York: W. W. Norton and Co.

Faris, Robert E. L., and H. Warren Dunham
1939 Mental Disorders in Urban Areas. Chicago: University of Chicago Press.

Fei, Hsiao-Tung
1953 China's Gentry: Essays in Rural-Urban Relations. Chicago: University of Chicago Press.

Ferkiss, Victor C.
1969 Technological Man: The Myth and the Reality. New York: George Braziller.

Firth, Raymond
1936 We, the Tikopia. London: George Allen and Unwin.
1968: Oral Traditions in Relation to Social Status. *In* Georges 1968:168–83.

Flannery, Kent V.
1969 Origins and Ecological Effects of Early Domestication in Iran and the Near East. *In* The Domestication and Exploitation of Plants and Animals. Peter J. Ucko and G. W. Dimbleby, eds. Pp. 73–100. Chicago: Aldine Publishing Co.

Ford, Clellan S., and Frank A. Beach
1951 Patterns of Sexual Behavior. New York: Ace Books.

Fortes, Meyer, and E. E. Evans-Pritchard, eds.
1940 African Political Systems. London: Oxford University Press.

Foster, George M.
1967 Introduction: What is a Peasant? *In* Peasant Society: A Reader, Jack M. Potter, May N. Diaz, and George M. Foster, eds. Boston: Little, Brown and Co.
1969 Applied Anthropology. Boston: Little, Brown & Co.

Fox, Robin
1967 Kinship and Marriage; An Anthropological Perspective. Baltimore: Penguin Books.

Frake, Charles O.
1964 A Structural Description of Subanun "Religious Behavior." *In* Goodenough 1964: 111–29.

Frazer, James George
1943 The Golden Bough: A Study in Magic and Religion. 1 vol. Abridged ed. New York: Macmillan Co. (First published in 1890. Revised 12-vol. edition published in 1911–15.)

Freud, Sigmund
  1938 Totem and Taboo. *In* The Basic Writings of Sigmund Freud. New York: Modern
    Library.
  1957 The Future of an Illusion. New York: Doubleday & Co. (First published in 1927.)
Fried, Marc
  1963 Grieving for a Lost Home. *In* The Urban Condition. Leonard J. Duhl, ed. Pp. 151–
    70. New York: Basic Books.
Fried, Morton H.
  1967 The Evolution of Political Society: An Essay in Political Anthropology. New York:
    Random House.
Fried, Morton H., Marvin Harris, and Robert Murphy, eds.
  1968 War: The Anthropology of Armed Conflict and Aggression. New York: Natural
    History Press.
Friedl, Ernestine
  1975 Women and Men: An Anthropologist's View. New York: Holt, Rinehart & Winston.
Gans, Herbert J.
  1962 The Urban Villagers. New York: The Free Press of Glencoe.
Gardner, R. Allen, and Beatrice T. Gardner
  1969 Teaching Sign Language to a Chimpanzee. Science 165:644–72.
Geertz, Clifford
  1968 Agricultural Involution: The Process of Ecological Change in Indonesia. Berkeley:
    University of California Press.
Georges, Robert A., ed.
  1968 Studies on Mythology. Homewood, Ill.: Dorsey Press.
Gladwin, Thomas, and Seymour B. Sarason
  1953 Truk: Man in Paradise. New York: Viking Fund Publications in Anthropology.
Gleason, H. A., Jr.
  1955 An Introduction to Descriptive Linguistics. New York: Henry Holt & Co.
Gluckman, Max
  1950 Kinship and Marriage among the Lozi of Northern Rhodesia and the Zulu of Natal.
    In Radcliffe-Brown and Forde 1950:166–206.
Goldschmidt, Walter
  1959 Man's Way: A Preface to the Understanding of Human Society. New York: Henry
    Holt & Co.
Goodenough, Ward. H.
  1949 Premarital Freedom on Truk: Theory and Practice. American Anthropologist 51:
    615–20.
  1957 Cultural Anthropology and Linguistics. *In* Report of the 7th Annual Round Table
    Meeting on Linguistics and Language Study. Paul L. Garvin, ed. Monograph Series on
    Languages and Linguistics no. 9. Pp. 167–73. Washington D.C.: Institute of Languages
    and Linguistics, Georgetown University.
  1964 Explorations in Cultural Anthropology: Essays in Honor of George Peter Murdock.
    New York: McGraw-Hill Book Co.
Gorer, Geoffrey
  1948 Justification by Numbers. The American Scholar 17:280–86.
  1955 Exploring English Character. New York: Criterion Books.
Gough, E. Kathleen
  1959 The Nayars and the Definition of Marriage. Journal of the Royal Anthropological
    Institute of Great Britain and Ireland 89:23–34.
  1961 Variation in Residence. *In* Schneider and Gough 1961:545–76.

Gouldner, Alvin W.
1960   The Norm of Reciprocity: A Preliminary Statement. American Sociological Review 25:161–78.

Grodzins, Martin
1970   The Metropolitan Area as a Racial Problem. *In* Urban Man and Society: A Reader in Urban Sociology. Albert N. Cousins and Hans Nagpaul, eds. Pp. 293–99. New York: Alfred A. Knopf.

Hagen, Everett E.
1962   On the Theory of Social Change: How Economic Growth Begins. Homewood, Ill.: Dorsey Press.

Hall, John W.
1968   Feudalism in Japan – A Reassessment. *In* Studies in the Institutional History of Early Modern Japan. John W. Hall and Marius B. Jansen, eds. Princeton, N.J.: Princeton University Press.

Hallowell, A. Irving
1942   The Role of Conjuring in Saulteaux Society. Philadelphia: University of Pennsylvania Press.
1949   Psychosexual Adjustment, Personality, and the Good Life in a Nonliterate Culture. *In* Psychosexual Development in Health and Disease. Paul H. Hoch and Joseph Zubin, eds. Pp. 102–23. New York: Grune & Stratton.
1955   Culture and Experience. Philadelphia: University of Pennsylvania Press.

Hannerz, Ulf
1974   Ethnicity and Opportunity in Urban America. *In* Urban Ethnicity. Abner Cohen, ed. Pp. 37–76. London: Tavistock Publications.

Harlow, Harry
1962   The Heterosexual Affectional System in Monkeys. American Psychologist 17:1–9.

Harris, Marvin
1968   The Rise of Anthropological Theory: A History of Theories of Culture. New York: Thomas Y. Crowell Co.

Hawthorn, Harry B.
1961   The Artist in Tribal Society: The Northwest Coast. *In* The Artist in Tribal Society. Marian W. Smith, ed. Pp. 59–70. New York: The Free Press of Glencoe.

Hayes, Cathy
1951   The Ape in Our House. New York: Harper & Row.

Hayner, Norman S., in collaboration with Una Middleton Hayner
1966   New Patterns in Old Mexico. New Haven, Conn.: College and University Press.

Hays, H. R.
1958   From Ape to Angel. New York: Alfred A. Knopf.

Helm, June
1968   The Nature of Dogrib Socioterritorial Groups. *In* Lee and DeVore 1968:118–25.

Henry, Jules
1944   Jungle People. New York: J. J. Augustin.

Herskovits, Melville J.
1962   The Human Factor in Changing Africa. New York: Alfred A. Knopf.

Higbee, Edward
1963   Farms and Farmers in an Urban Age. New York: The Twentieth Century Fund.

Hinde, R. A.
1974   Biological Bases of Human Social Behavior. New York: McGraw-Hill Book Co.

Hockett, Charles F.
  1958   A Course in Modern Linguistics. New York: Macmillan Co.
  1964   The Proto-Central Algonquian Kinship System. *In* Goodenough 1964:239–58.

Hollingshead, August B.
  1949   Elmtown's Youth. New York: John Wiley & Sons.

Hollingshead, August B., and Fredrick C. Redlich
  1958   Social Class and Mental Illness: A Community Study. New York: John Wiley & Sons.

Holmberg, Allan R.
  1950   Nomads of the Long Bow: The Siriono of Eastern Bolivia. Institute of Social Anthropology Publication no. 10. Washington D.C.: Smithsonian Institution.
  1960   Changing Community Attitudes and Values in Peru: A Case Study in Guided Change. *In* Social Change in Latin America Today: Its Implications for United States Policy. Richard N. Adams et al., Pp. 63–107. New York: Harper & Brothers.

Homans, George C., and David M. Schneider
  1955   Marriage, Authority, and Final Causes: A Study of Unilateral Cross-Cousin Marriage. Glencoe, Ill.: Free Press.

Horsley, J. Stephen
  1943   Narco-Analysis. Oxford: Oxford University Press.

Howard, James H., and Gertrude P. Kurath
  1959   Ponca Dances, Ceremonies, and Music. Ethnomusicology 3:1–14.

Howell, F. Clark and the Editors of Life
  1964   Early Man. New York: Life Nature Series.

Hsu, Francis L. K.
  1952   Religion, Science, and Human Crises. London: Routledge and Kegan Paul.

Huizinga, Johan
  1955   Homo Ludens: A Study of the Play-Element in Culture. Boston: Beacon Press.

Hymes, Dell H.
  1960   Lexicostatistics So Far. Current Anthropology 1:3–44.

Ibn-Khaldun
  1967   An Introduction to History: The Muqaddimah. N. J. Dawood, ed. Franz Rosenthal, trans. London: Routledge and Kegan Paul.

Illingsworth, R. S., and C. M. Illingsworth
  1966   Lessons From Childhood: Some Aspects of the Early Life of Unusual Men and Women. Baltimore: William and Wilkins Co.

Inkeles, Alex
  1950   Stratification and Mobility in the Soviet Union. American Sociological Review 15:465–79.

Issawi, Charles
  1970   Issawi's Laws of Social Motion. Columbia Forum 13:42–43.

Jacobs, Melville
  1959   The Content and Style of an Oral Literature: Clackamas Chinook Myths and Tales. New York: Viking Fund Publications in Anthropology no. 26. New York:

James, Preston E., with the collaboration of Hibberd V. B. Kline, Jr.
  1959   A Geography of Man. Boston: Ginn & Co.

Jones, Maldwyn Allen
  1960   American Immigration. Chicago: University of Chicago Press.

Kahn, Herman, William Brown, and Leon Martel
  1976   The Next Two Hundred Years: A Scenario for America and the World. New York: William Morrow and Co.

Kahn, Herman, and Anthony J. Wiener, eds.
  1967 The Year 2000: A Framework for Speculation on the Next Thirty-Three Years. New York: Macmillan Co.

Kardiner, Abram, et al.
  1945 The Psychological Frontiers of Society. New York: Columbia University Press.

Kardiner, Abram, and Ralph Linton
  1939 The Individual and His Society: The Psychodynamics of Primitive Social Organization. New York: Columbia University Press.

Kinsey, Alfred C., Wardell B. Pomeroy, and Clyde E. Martin
  1948 Sexual Behavior in the Human Male. Philadelphia: W. B. Saunders Co.

Kinsey, Alfred C., Wardell B. Pomeroy, Clyde E. Martin, and Paul H. Gebhard
  1953 Sexual Behavior in the Human Female. Philadelphia: W. B. Saunders Co.

Kluckhohn, Clyde
  1936 Some Reflections on the Method and Theory of the Kulturkreis Lehre. American Anthropologist 38:157–96.
  1965 Recurrent Themes in Myths and Mythmaking. In Dundes 1965:158–68.

Köhler, Wolfgang
  1927 The Mentality of Apes. Second ed. New York: Humanities Press.

Krader, Lawrence
  1965 Ecology of Central Asian Pastoralism. Southwestern Journal of Anthropology 11:301–26.

Kristol, Irving
  1970 The Negro Today is Like the Immigrant Yesterday. In Cities in Trouble. Nathan Glazer, ed. Pp. 139–57. Chicago: Quadrangle Books.

Kroeber, A. L.
  1909 Classificatory Systems of Relationship. Journal of the Royal Anthropological Institute 39:77–84.
  1939 Cultural and Natural Areas of Native North America. University of California Publications in American Archaeology and Ethnology Vol. 38.
  1948 Anthropology. New York: Harcourt, Brace & Co.

Kuper, Hilda
  1950 Kinship Among the Swazi. In Radcliffe-Brown and Forde 1950:86–110.

La Barre, Weston
  1966 The Aymara: History and Worldview. In The Anthropologist Looks at Myth. Melville Jacobs and John Greenway, eds. Pp. 130–44. Austin: University of Texas Press.

Lambert, Berndt
  1966 The Economic Activities of a Gilbertese Chief. In Swartz, Turner, and Tuden 1966: 155–72.

Lambert, William W., Leigh Minturn Triandis, and Margery Wolf
  1959 Some Correlates of Beliefs in the Malevolence and Benevolence of Supernatural Beings: A Cross-Societal Study. Journal of Abnormal and Social Psychology 58:162–69.

Landes, Ruth
  1968 Ojibwa Religion and the Midéwiwin. Madison: University of Wisconsin Press.

Lane, Michael, ed.
  1970 Introduction to Structuralism. New York: Basic Books.

Lang, Andrew
  1909 The Making of Religion. London: Longmans, Green & Co.

Lantis, Margaret
  1953 Nunivak Eskimo Personality as Revealed in the Mythology. Anthropological Papers of the University of Alaska. Vol. 2. No. 1.

Leach, Edmund R.
1967   Genesis as Myth. *In* Myth and Cosmos: Readings in Mythology and Symbolism. John Middleton, ed. Pp. 1–13. New York: Natural History Press.
1968   Myth as a Justification for Faction and Social Change. *In* Georges 1968:184–98.

Leacock, Stephen
1935   Humor: Its Theory and Technique. New York: Dodd, Mead & Co.

Lee, Richard B.
1966   !Kung Bushman Subsistence: An Input-Output Analysis. *In* Ecological Essays. David Damas, ed. Proceedings of the Conference on Cultural Ecology. Ottawa: National Museum of Canada Bulletin no. 230. Reprinted with minor revisions in Environment and Cultural Behavior. Andrew P. Vayda, ed. Pp. 47–79. New York: Natural History Press, 1969.
1972   Work Effort, Group Structure, and Land-Use in Contemporary Hunter-Gatherers. *In* Man, Settlement, and Urbanism. Peter J. Ucko, Ruth Tringham, and G. W. Dimbleby, eds. Pp. 177–85. Cambridge, Mass.: Schenkman Publishing Co.

Lee, Richard B., and Irven DeVore, eds.
1968   Man the Hunter. Chicago: Aldine Publishing Co.

Lenneberg, Eric H.
1966   A Biological Perspective of Language. *In* New Directions in the Study of Language. Eric H. Lenneberg, ed. Pp. 65–88. Cambridge, Mass.: MIT Press.
1967   Biological Foundations of Language. New York: John Wiley & Sons.

Lenski, Gerhard E.
1966   Power and Privilege: A Theory of Social Stratification. New York: McGraw-Hill Book Co.

Lenski, Gerhard, and Jean Lenski
1974   Human Societies: An Introduction to Macrosociology. Second ed. New York: McGraw-Hill Book Co.

Leopold, A. Carl, and Robert Ardrey
1972   Toxic Substances in Plants and the Food Habits of Early Man. Science 176:512–14.

LeVine, Robert A.
1961   Africa. *In* Psychological Anthropology: Approaches to Culture and Personality. Francis L. K. Hsu, ed. Homewood, Ill.: Dorsey Press.

LeVine, Robert A., and Barbara B. LeVine
1963   Nyansongo: A Gusii Community in Kenya. *In* Whiting 1963:15–202.

Lévi-Strauss, Claude
1953   Social Structure. *In* Anthropology Today: An Encyclopedic Inventory. A. L. Kroeber, ed. Pp. 524–53. Chicago: University of Chicago Press.
1960   The Family. *In* Man, Culture, and Society. Harry L. Shapiro, ed. Pp. 261–85. New York: Oxford University Press.
1966a   The Savage Mind. Chicago: University of Chicago Press.
1966b   The Culinary Triangle. Partisan Review 33:586–95.
1967   The Structural Study of Myth. *In* Claude Lévi-Strauss. Structural Anthropology. Claire Jacobson and Brooke Grundfest Schoepf, trans, Pp. 202–28. New York: Doubleday Anchor Books.
1969a   The Elementary Structures of Kinship. James H. Bell, John R. von Sturmer, and Rodney Needham, trans. Boston: Beacon Press.
1969b   The Raw and the Cooked: Introduction to a Science of Mythology. John and Doreen Weightman, trans. Vol. I. New York: Harper & Row.

Lewis, Oscar
1951   Life in a Mexican Village: Tepoztlán Restudied. Urbana: University of Illinois Press.
1955   Medicine and Politics in a Mexican Village. *In* Health, Culture, and Community:

Case Studies of Public Reactions to Health Programs. Benjamin D. Paul, ed. Pp. 403–34. New York: Russell Sage Foundation.

1968 La Vida: A Puerto Rican Family in the Culture of Poverty — San Juan and New York. New York: Random House.

Lewis, Oscar, with the assistance of Victor Barnouw
1958 Village Life in Northern India: Studies in a Delhi Village. Urbana: University of Illinois Press.

Liebow, Elliot
1967 Tally's Corner: A Study of Negro Streetcorner Men. Boston: Little, Brown & Co.

Lilley, Samuel
1966 Men, Machines, and History: The Story of Tools and Machines in Relation to Social Progress. Rev. ed. New York: International Publishers.

Linton, Ralph
1936 The Study of Man. New York: D. Appleton-Century Co.
1945 The Cultural Background of Personality. New York: Appleton Century Co.
1955 The Tree of Culture. New York: Alfred A. Knopf.

Little, Kenneth L.
1949 The Role of the Secret Society in Cultural Specialization. American Anthropologist 51:199–212.

Livingstone, Frank B.
1968 The Effects of War on the Biology of the Human Species. In Fried, Harris, and Murphy 1968:3–15.

Llewellyn, Karl N., and E. Adamson Hoebel
1941 The Cheyenne Way: Conflict and Case Law in Primitive Jurisprudence. Norman: The University of Oklahoma Press.

Loeb, Edwin M.
1929 Shaman and Seer. American Anthropologist 31:60–84.
1935 Sumatra: Its History and People. Vienna.

Lorenz, Konrad
1967 On Aggression. New York: Bantam Books.

Lowie, Robert H.
1929 Culture and Ethnology. New York: Peter Smith.
1937 The History of Ethnological Theory. New York: Farrar and Rinehart.
1940 An Introduction to Cultural Anthropology. New York: Rinehart & Co.
1967 Some Aspects of Political Organization Among the American Indians. In Comparative Political Systems: Studies in the Politics of Pre-Industrial Societies. Ronald Cohen and John Middleton, eds. Pp. 63–87. New York: Natural History Press.

Lynd, Robert S., and Helen Merrell Lynd
1929 Middletown: A Study in American Culture. New York: Harcourt, Brace & Co.
1937 Middletown in Transition: A Study in Cultural Conflicts. New York: Harcourt, Brace & Co.

Macaulay, Thomas Babington
1877 Critical, Historical and Miscellaneous Essays. Vol. 1. New York: Hurd and Houghton.

Malinowski, Bronislaw
1922 Argonauts of the Western Pacific: An Account of Native Enterprise and Adventure in the Archipelagoes of Melanesian New Guinea. London: George Routledge and Sons.
1926a Crime and Custom in Savage Society. New York: Harcourt, Brace & Co.
1926b Anthropology. Encyclopaedia Britannica. First supplementary volume; 132.
1929 The Sexual Life of Savages in North-Western Melanesia. New York: Harcourt, Brace & Co.

1953   Sex and Repression in Savage Society. London: Routledge & Kegan Paul. (First published in 1927.)

1954   Magic, Science and Religion and Other Essays. New York: Doubleday-Anchor Books.

Mantoux, Paul
1961   The Industrial Revolution in the Eighteenth Century. London: Jonathan Cape.

Maquet, J. J.
1960   The Problem of Tutsi Domination. *In* Cultures and Societies of Africa. Simon Ottenberg and Phoebe Ottenberg, eds. New York: Random House.

Marett, R. R.
1914   The Threshold of Religion. London: Methuen & Co.

Marriott, McKim
1952   Technological Change in Overdeveloped Rural Areas. Economic Development and Cultural Change 1:261–72.

Marshall, Lorna
1967   !Kung Bushman Bands. *In* Comparative Political Systems: Studies in the Politics of Pre-Industrial Societies. Ronald Cohen and John Middleton, eds. Pp. 15–43. New York: Natural History Press.

Martin, M. Kay, and Barbara Voorhies
1975   Female of the Species. New York: Columbia University Press.

McClelland, David C.
1961   The Achieving Society. Princeton, N.J.: D. Van Nostrand Co.

McClelland, David C., and G. A. Friedman
1952   A Cross-Cultural Study of the Relationship Between Child Training Practices and Achievement Motivation Appearing in Folk Tales. *In* Readings in Social Psychology. Rev. ed. Guy E. Swanson, Theodore M. Newcomb, and Eugene L. Hartley, eds. Pp. 243–49. New York: Henry Holt & Co.

McHale, John
1969   The Future of the Future. New York: George Braziller.

Mead, Margaret
1928   Coming of Age in Samoa. New York: William Morrow & Co.

1930   Growing Up in New Guinea: A Comparative Study of Primitive Education. New York: William Morrow & Co.

1939   From the South Seas: Studies of Adolescence and Sex in Primitive Societies. New York: William Morrow & Co.

Mead, Margaret, and Frances Cooke MacGregor
1951   Growth and Culture: A Photographic Analysis. New York: G. P. Putnam's Sons.

Merriam, Alan P.
1964   The Anthropology of Music. Evanston, Ill.: Northwestern University Press.

Merton, Robert K.
1949   Social Theory and Social Structure. Glencoe, Ill.: Free Press.

Messenger, John C.
1958   Reflections on Aesthetic Talent. Basic College Quarterly. Vol. 4. East Lansing: Michigan State University.

Michaelson, Evalyn J., and Walter Goldschmidt
1971   Female Roles and Male Dominance Among Peasants. Southwestern Journal of Anthropology 27:330–53.

Milgram, Stanley
1974   Obedience to Authority: An Experimental View. New York: Harper & Row.

Miller, Herman P.
1964 Rich Man, Poor Man. New York: Thomas Y. Crowell Co.

Miller, Walter B.
1955 Two Concepts of Authority. American Anthropologist 57:271–89.

Minturn, Leigh, and John T. Hitchcock
1963 The Rājpūts of Khalapur, India. *In* Whiting 1963:203–361.

Minturn, Leigh, and William W. Lambert
1964 Mothers of Six Cultures: Antecedents of Child Rearing. New York: John Wiley & Sons.

Montaigne, Michel de
1947 Essays of Michel de Montaigne. Charles Cotton, trans. New York: Doubleday & Co.

Morey, Robert
1940 Upset in Emotions. Journal of Social Psychology 12:333–56.

Morris, Desmond
1962 The Biology of Art: A Study in the Picture-Making Behavior of the Great Apes and Its Relationship to Human Art. New York: Alfred A. Knopf.
1969 The Naked Ape. New York: Dell Publishing Co.

Mumford, Lewis
1934 Technics and Civilization. New York: Harcourt, Brace & Co.

Murdock, George Peter
1945 The Common Denominator of Cultures. *In* The Science of Man in the World Crisis. Ralph Linton, ed. New York: Columbia University Press.
1949 Social Structure. New York: Free Press.
1957 World Ethnographic Sample. American Anthropologist 59:664–87.
1959 Africa: Its Peoples and Their Culture History. New York: McGraw-Hill Book Co.

Murphy, Jane M.
1964 Psychotherapeutic Aspects of Shamanism on St. Lawrence Island. *In* Magic, Faith and Healing: Studies in Primitive Psychiatry Today. Ari Kiev, ed. Pp. 53–83. London: Free Press of Glencoe.

Murphy, Yolanda, and Robert F. Murphy
1974 Women of the Forest. New York: Columbia University Press.

Myrdal, Gunnar, with the assistance of Richard Sterne and Arnold Rose
1944 An American Dilemma: The Negro Problem and Modern Democracy. New York: Harper & Brothers.

Naroll, Raoul
1961 Two Solutions to Galton's Problem. Philosophy of Science 28:15–39.
1964 A Fifth Solution to Galton's Problem. American Anthropologist 66:863–67.

Naroll, Raoul, and Roy G. D'Andrade
1963 Two Further Solutions to Galton's Problem. American Anthropologist 65:1053–67.

Nash, Manning
1966 Primitive and Peasant Economic Systems. San Francisco: Chandler Publishing Co.

Needham, Rodney
1962 Structure and Sentiment: A Test Case in Social Anthropology. Chicago: University of Chicago Press.
1974 Remarks and Inventions: Skeptical Essays About Kinship. London: Tavistock Publications.

Nuttini, Hugo G.
1972 A Latin American City: A Cultural-Historical Approach. *In* The Anthropology of Urban Environments. Thomas Weaver and Douglas White, eds. Society for Applied Anthropology Monograph no. 11.

Oberg, Kalervo
1940   The Kingdom of Ankole in Uganda. *In* Fortes and Evans-Pritchard 1940:121–62.
1955   Types of Social Structure Among the Lowland Tribes of South and Central America. American Anthropologist 57:472–87.

Oesterreich, T. K.
1930   Possession, Demoniacal and Other. D. Ibberson, trans. New York: Richard R. Smith. *(First published in German in 1922.)*

Opler, Morris E.
1936   An Interpretation of Ambivalence in Two American Indian Tribes. Journal of Social Psychology 7:82–115.

Orlansky, Harold
1949   Infant Care and Personality. Psychological Bulletin 46:1–48.

Paddock, William, and Paul Paddock
1967   Famine – 1975! America's Decision: Who Will Survive? Boston: Little, Brown & Co.

Parker, Seymour
1976   The Precultural Basis of the Incest Taboo: Toward a Biosocial Theory. American Anthropologist 78:285–305.

Pehrson, Robert N.
1966   The Social Organization of the Marri Baluch. New York: Viking Fund Publications in Anthropology no. 43.

Pelling, Henry
1960   American Labor. Chicago: University of Chicago Press.

Perrot, Nicolas
1911   Memoir on the Manners, Customs and Religion of the Savages of North America. *In* The Indian Tribes of the Upper Mississippi Valley and Region of the Great Lakes. Emma Helen Blair, ed. I:31–372. Cleveland: Clark.

Peter, Prince of Greece and Denmark
1963   A Study of Polyandry. The Hague: Mouton & Co.

Piggott, Stuart
1950   Prehistoric India to 1000 B.C. Harmondsworth: Penguin Books.

Polanyi, Karl
1957a   The Great Transformation. Boston: Beacon Press.
1957b   The Economy as Instituted Process. *In* Trade and Market in the Early Empires; Economies in History and Theory. Karl Polanyi, Conrad M. Arensberg, and Harry W. Pearson, eds. Pp. 243–70. New York: Free Press.

Premack, Ann James, and David Premack
1972   Teaching Language to an Ape. Scientific American 227:92–99.

Price-Williams, Douglass R.
1975   Explorations in Cross-Cultural Psychology. San Francisco: Chandler & Sharp.

Propp, Vladimir
1968   The Morphology of the Folktale. Second ed. Publications of the American Folklore Society, Bibliographical and Special Series. Rev. ed. Vol. 9. *(First published in Russian in 1928.)*

Rabin, A. I.
1965   Growing Up in the Kibbutz. New York: Springer Publishing Co.

Radcliffe-Brown, A. R.
1924   The Mother's Brother in South Africa. South African Journal of Science 21:542–55. Reprinted in Radcliffe-Brown 1952:15–31.

1950 Introduction. *In* Radcliffe-Brown and Forde 1950:1–85.

1952 Structure and Function in Primitive Society: Essays and Addresses. Glencoe, Ill.: Free Press.

Radcliffe-Brown, A. R., and Daryll Forde, eds.

1950 African Systems of Kinship and Marriage. London: Oxford University Press.

Radin, Paul

1957 Primitive Religion: Its Nature and Origin. New York: Dover Publications. *(First published in 1937.)*

Raglan, Lord

1937 The Hero: A Study in Tradition, Myth and Drama. New York: Oxford University Press.

Randall, Betty Uchitelle

1949 The Cinderella Theme in Northwest Coast Folklore. *In* Indians of the Urban Northwest. Marian W. Smith, ed. Pp. 243–85. New York: Columbia University Press.

Rank, Otto

1956 The Myth of the Birth of the Hero. New York: Random House.

Rappaport, Roy A.

1967 Pigs for the Ancestors: Ritual in the Ecology of a New Guinea People. New Haven, Conn.: Yale University Press.

1971 The Flow of Energy in an Agricultural Society. Scientific American 225:116–22.

Rasmussen, Knud

1921 Eskimo Folk Tales. W. Worster, trans. Copenhagen: Gyldendal.

1929 Intellectual Culture of the Iglulik Eskimos: Report of the Fifth Thule Expedition, 1921–24. Vol. 7, no. 1. Copenhagen: Gyldendalske Boghandel, Nordisk Forlag.

1930 Observations on the Intellectual Culture of the Caribou Eskimos: Report of the Fifth Thule Expedition, 1921–24. Vol. 7, no. 2. Copenhagen: Gyldendalske Boghandel, Nordisk Forlag.

Redfield, Robert

1941 The Folk Culture of Yucatan. Chicago: University of Chicago Press.

Richards, A. I.

1950 Some Types of Family Structure Among the Central Bantu. *In* Radcliffe-Brown and Forde 1950:207–51.

Richards, Cara E.

1963–64 City Taverns. Human Organization 22:260–68.

Riesman, David

1950 The Lonely Crowd: A Study of the Changing American Character. New Haven, Conn.: Yale University Press.

Ritzenthaler, Pat

1966 The Fon of Bafut. New York: Thomas Y. Crowell.

Rivers, W. H. R.

1968 The Sociological Significance of Myth. *In* Georges 1968:27–45.

Roberts, John M., Malcolm J. Arth, and Robert R. Bush

1959 Games in Culture. American Anthropologist 61:597–605.

Roberts, John M., and Brian Sutton-Smith

1962 Child Training and Game Involvement. Ethnology 1:166–85.

Rohner, Ronald P.

1975 They Love Me, They Love Me Not. HRAF Press.

1976 Sex Differences in Aggression: Phylogenetic and Enculturation Perspectives. Ethos 4:57–72.

Rose, Ronald
   1956 Living Magic: The Realities Underlying the Psychical Practices and Beliefs of Australian Aborigines. Skokie, Ill.: Rand McNally & Co.

Ross, James Bruce
   1974 The Middle-Class Child in Urban Italy, Fourteenth to Early Sixteenth Century. *In* De Mause 1974: 183–228.

Rothschild, Emma
   1974 Running out of Food. The New York Review. September 19, pp. 30–32.

Rowe, John Howland
   1965 The Renaissance Foundations of Anthropology. American Anthropologist 67:1–20.

Roy, Paul Ewell
   1967 Exploring Agribusiness. Danville, Ill.: Interstate Printers and Publishers.

Sahlins, Marshall
   1972 Stone Age Economics. Chicago: Aldine-Atherton, Inc.

Saksena, R. N.
   1962 Social Economy of a Polyandrous People. Bombay: Asia Publishing House.

Sanders, William, and Barbara J. Price
   1968 Mesoamerica: The Evolution of a Civilization. New York: Random House.

Schapera, I.
   1950 Kinship and Marriage Among the Tswana. *In* Radcliffe-Brown and Forde 1950: 140–65.

Scheinfeld, Amram
   1947 Women and Men. London: Chatto and Windus.

Schneider, David M.
   1961 Introduction: The Distinctive Features of Matrilineal Descent Groups. *In* Matrilineal Kinship. David M. Schneider and Kathleen Gough, eds. Berkeley and Los Angeles: University of California Press.

Segall, Marshall H., Donald T. Campbell, and Melville J. Herskovits
   1966 The Influence of Culture on Visual Perception. Indianapolis: Bobbs-Merrill Co.

Service, Elman R.
   1962 Primitive Social Organization: An Evolutionary Perspective. New York: Random House.
   1968 War and Our Contemporary Ancestors. *In* Fried, Harris, and Murphy 1968:160-67.

Shankman, Paul
   1969 Le Rôti et le Bouilli: Lévi-Strauss' Theory of Cannibalism. American Anthropologist 71:54–69.

Simmons, Leo, ed.
   1942 Sun Chief: The Autobiography of a Hopi Indian. New Haven, Conn.: Yale University Press.

Skilling, H. Gordon, and Franklyn Griffiths, eds.
   1971 Interest Groups in Soviet Politics. Princeton, N.J.: Princeton University Press.

Skinner, Brian J.
   1976 A Second Iron Age Ahead? American Scientist 64:258–69.

Slater, Mariam Kreiselman
   1959 Ecological Factors in the Origin of Incest. American Anthropologist 61:1042–59.

Slotkin, J. S., ed.
   1965 Readings in Early Anthropology. Viking Fund Publications in Anthropology no. 40. Chicago: Aldine Publishing Co.

Smith, Marian W.
1959   Boas' "Natural History" Approach to Field Material. *In* The Anthropology of Franz Boas: Essays on the Centennial of his Birth. Walter Goldschmidt, ed. American Anthropological Association Memoir no. 89.

Spencer, Baldwin, and F. J. Gillen
1927   The Arunta: A Study of a Stone Age People. 2 vols. London: Macmillan & Co., Ltd.

Spiro, Melford E.
1954   Is the Family Universal? American Anthropologist 56:839–46.
1956   Kibbutz: Venture in Utopia. Cambridge, Mass.: Harvard University Press.
1958   Children of the Kibbutz. Cambridge, Mass.: Harvard University Press.

Spitz, Rene A.
1945   Hospitalism: An Inquiry into the Genesis of Psychiatric Conditions in Early Childhood. *In* The Psychoanalytic Study of the Child. Vol. 1. Pp. 53–74. New York: International Universities Press.

Stephens, William N.
1963   The Family in Cross-Cultural Perspective. New York: Holt, Rinehart & Winston.

Stern, Claudio, and Joseph A. Kahl
1968   Stratification Since the Revolution. *In* Comparative Perspectives on Stratification: Mexico, Great Britain, Japan. Joseph A. Kahl, ed. Boston: Little, Brown & Co.

Stern, Theodore
1948   The Rubber Ball Games of the Americas. Monographs of the American Ethnological Society no. 17. New York: J. J. Augustin.

Steward, Julian H.
1955   Theory of Culture Change: The Methodology of Multilinear Evolution. Urbana: University of Illinois Press.

Steward, Julian, and Louis C. Faron
1959   Native Peoples of South America. New York: McGraw-Hill Book Co.

Stewart, Omer C.
1956   Fire as the First Great Force Employed by Man. *In* Man's Role in Changing the Face of the Earth. William I. Thomas, ed. Pp. 115–33. Chicago: University of Chicago Press.

Sullivan, Walter
1967   Our Future is Incomputable. New York Times. March 26.

Swanson, Guy E.
1969   The Birth of the Gods. Ann Arbor: University of Michigan Press.

Swartz, Marc J., Victor W. Turner, and Arthur Tuden, eds.
1966   Political Anthropology. Chicago: Aldine Publishing Co.

Thalbitzer, W.
1931   Shamans of the East Greenland Eskimo. *In* Sourcebook in Anthropology. A. L. Kroeber and T. T. Waterman, eds. Pp. 430–36. New York: Harcourt, Brace and Co.

Thieme, Paul
1964   The Comparative Method of Reconstruction in Linguistics. *In* Language in Culture and Society: A Reader in Linguistics and Anthropology. Dell Hymes, ed. Pp. 585–97. New York: Harper & Row.

Thomas, Elizabeth Marshall
1959   The Harmless People. New York: Alfred A. Knopf.

Tiger, Lionel, and Robin Fox
1971   The Imperial Animal. New York: Holt, Rinehart & Winston.

Tocqueville, Alexis de
1954   Democracy in America. 2 vols. New York: Alfred A. Knopf, Vintage Books.

Tooker, Elizabeth
  1968 Masking and Matrilineality in North America. American Anthropologist 70:1170–76.
Tschopik, Harry, Jr.
  1951 The Aymara of Chucuito, Peru; I, Magic. New York: American Museum of Natural History Anthropological Papers no. 44.
Tumin, Melvin M.
  1952 Caste in a Peasant Society: A Case Study in the Dynamics of Caste. Princeton, N.J.: Princeton University Press.
Turner, Victor W.
  1957 Schism and Continuity in an African Society: A Study of Ndembu Village Life. Manchester, England: Manchester University Press.
Tyler, Stephen A.
  1969 Introduction. *In* Cognitive Anthropology. Stephen A. Tyler, ed. Pp. 1–23. New York: Holt, Rinehart & Winston.
Tylor, Edward B.
  1877 Primitive Culture: Researches Into the Development of Mythology, Philosophy, Religion, Language, Art, and Customs. 2 vols. New York: Henry Holt & Co.
  1889 On a Method of Investigating the Development of Institutions Applied to Laws of Marriage and Descent. Journal of the Royal Anthropological Institute of Great Britain and Ireland 18:245–69.
  1896 On American Lot-Games as Evidence of Asiatic Intercourse Before the Time of Columbus. Ethnographische Beitrage. Supplement to Internationales Archiv für Ethnographie 9:55–67.
Van der Kroef, Justus
  1954 Dualism and Symbolic Antithesis in Indonesian Societies. American Anthropologist 56:847–62.
Vayda, Andrew P.
  1961 Expansion and Warfare Among Swidden Agriculturists. American Anthropologist 63:346–58.
Vayda, Andrew P., and Roy A. Rappaport
  1968 Ecology: Cultural and Non-cultural. *In* Introduction to Cultural Anthropology: Essays in the Scope and Methods of the Science of Man. James A. Clifton, ed. Pp. 476–97. Boston: Houghton Mifflin Co.
von Fürer-Haimendorf, Christoph
  1943 The Chenchus: Jungle Folk of the Deccan: The Aboriginal Tribes of Hyderabad. Vol. 1. London: Macmillan.
  1956 Himalayan Barbary. New York: Abelard-Schuman.
  1962 The Apa Tanis and Their Neighbours: A Primitive Civilization of the Eastern Himalayas. London: Routledge and Kegan Paul.
Wallace, Anthony F. C.
  1966 Religion: An Anthropological View. New York: Random House.
Warner, W. Lloyd
  1958 A Black Civilization: A Social Study of an Australian Tribe. Rev. ed. New York: Harper & Row.
Warner, W. Lloyd, et al.
  1949 Democracy in Jonesville. New York: Harper & Brothers.
Warner, W. Lloyd, and Paul S. Lunt
  1941 The Social Life of a Modern Community. New Haven, Conn.: Yale University Press.
Warren, N.
  1972 African Infant Precocity. Psychological Bulletin 78:353–67.

Waterman, Richard A.
1952   African Influence on the Music of the Americas. *In* Acculturation in the Americas. Sol Tax, ed. Vol. 2. Pp. 207–18. Chicago: Proceedings of the 29th International Congress of Americanists.

Weltfish, Gene
1953   The Origins of Art. Indianapolis: Bobbs-Merrill Co.

Weyer, Edward
1932   The Eskimos. New Haven, Conn.: Yale University Press.

White, Leslie A.
1959   The Evolution of Culture. New York: McGraw-Hill Book Co.

Whiting, Beatrice B., ed.
1963   Six Cultures: Studies of Child Rearing. New York: John Wiley & Sons.

Whiting, Beatrice, and Carolyn Pope Edwards
1973   A Cross-Cultural Analysis of Sex Differences in the Behavior of Children Aged Three Through Eleven. Journal of Social Psychology 91:171–88.

Whiting, Beatrice B., and John W. M. Whiting
1975   Children of Six Cultures: A Psycho-Cultural Analysis. Cambridge: Harvard University Press.

Whiting, John W. M., and Irvin L. Child
1953   Child Training and Personality: A Cross-Cultural Study. New Haven, Conn.: Yale University Press.

Whiting, John W. M., Richard Kluckhohn, and Albert Anthony
1958   The Function of Male Initiation Ceremonies at Puberty. *In* Readings in Social Psychology. Third ed. Eleanor E. Maccoby, Theodore M. Newcomb, and Eugene L. Hartley, eds. Pp. 359–70. New York: Henry Holt & Co.

Whyte, William F.
1943   Street Corner Society: The Social Structure of an Italian Slum. Chicago: University of Chicago Press.

Wilson, Monica
1950   Nyakyusa Kinship. *In* Radcliffe-Brown and Forde 1950:111–39.
1951   Good Company: A Study of Nyakyusa Age-Villages. London: Oxford University Press.

Wissler, Clark
1926   The Relation of Man to Nature in Aboriginal North America. New York: D. Appleton.

Witkin, Herman A.
1967   A Cognitive-Style Approach to Cross-Cultural Research. International Journal of Psychology 2:233–50.

Witkin, Herman A., R. B. Dyk, H. F. Faterson, D. R. Goodenough, and S. A. Karp
1962   Psychological Differentiation: Studies of Development. New York: John Wiley & Sons.

Wittfogel, Karl A.
1956   The Hydraulic Civilizations. *In* Man's Role in Changing the Face of the Earth. William I. Thomas, Jr., ed. Pp. 152–64. Chicago: University of Chicago Press.
1957   Oriental Despotism: A Comparative Study of Total Power. New Haven, Conn.: Yale University Press.

Wolf, Arthur P.
1966   Childhood Association, Sexual Attraction, and the Incest Taboo: A Chinese Case. American Anthropologist 68:883–98.

Wolf, Eric R.
  1955 Types of Latin American Peasantry: A Preliminary Discussion. American Anthropologist 57:452–71.
  1957 Closed Corporate Peasant Communities in Mesoamerica and Central Java. Southwestern Journal of Anthropology 13:7–12.
  1966 Peasants. Englewood Cliffs, N.J.: Prentice-Hall, Inc.

Wolf, Margery
  1972 Women and the Family in Rural Taiwan. Stanford, Calif.: Stanford University Press.

Wolfe, Alvin
  1969 Social-Structural Bases of Art. Current Anthropology 10:3–44.

Wood, Clement
  1931 Dreams: Their Meaning and Practical Application. New York: Greenberg Publisher.

Woods, Ralph L.
  1947 The World of Dreams: An Anthology. New York: Random House.

Wright, Harry B.
  1957 Witness to Witchcraft. New York: Funk & Wagnalls.

Young, Frank W.
  1962 The Function of Male Initiation Ceremonies: A Cross-Cultural Test of an Alternative Hypothesis. American Journal of Sociology 67:379–91.

Young, William C., Robert W. Goy, and Charles H. Phoenix
  1964 Hormones and Sexual Behavior. Science 143:212–18.

Yutang, Lin
  1937 The Importance of Living. New York: Reynal & Hitchcock.

Illustrations

index

Index

*This book has been set in 10 and 9 point
Caledonia, leaded 2 points. Part numbers are
36 point Souvenir Bold and part titles are
24 point Souvenir Medium italic. Chapter
numbers are 48 point Souvenir Bold and
chapter titles are 18 point Souvenir Medium.
The overall type area is 33¹/₂ by 46¹/₂ picas.*